I AM (JESUS)

ray d. brown

Printed in the United States of America

ISBN 979-821807-25-68 (paperback)

Inspirational

Vox Dei Books / rdb publishing

Cover design by selfpubbookcovers.mailer@bestcoverdesign.com

Interior layout and typesetting by waynekehoe.com

Contents

*This book is dedicated to the glory of GOD and
the express deity of the LORD Jesus Christ – and
in remembrance of Aaron William Brown*

*

*A special thanks goes out to Pastor Mitchell Tolle, Sr.
of Man O' War Church of GOD in Lexington, KY
for his inexhaustible grace and earnest prayer.*

*

*Also, thank you Wayne Kehoe of Reedsy for the
interior layout. Thank you everyone at Ingram
Spark for your professionalism and assistance
with my technological inexperience.*

1

I AM the Bread of Life

"And Jesus said unto them, I AM the Bread of Life:
he that cometh to me shall never hunger; and
he that believeth on me shall never thirst."

–John 6:35

By way of introduction, this is GOD speaking here, the eternal Word. This is Grace and Truth personified declaring GOD from the bosom of GOD. This is emphatically GOD speaking for himself. This is the express image of the invisible GOD uttering the thoughts and feelings and manifest identity of GOD.

This is *Jesus the Christ* speaking, the fullness of the Godhead bodily (re. Col. 2:9). The word *fullness* here is best interpreted as the repletion of divine perfections. It pleased (and pleases) the Father to be represented in the Son, and this is accomplished by the Holy Spirit.

Moreover, by a dynamic faith, working by love unto obedience and sanctification, it pleases GOD to dwell within his children. *"Jesus answered and said unto him, If a man love me, he will keep my words: and my Father will love him, and WE will come unto him, and make OUR abode with him"* (John 14:23).

The Holy Spirit is establishing early in this manuscript that Jesus Christ is LORD, that he is *the Almighty GOD*, and nothing lacking. When we receive Jesus Christ by faith as our LORD and Savior, we receive *BOTH* the Father *and* the Son by the Holy Spirit, the *WE* and the *OUR* of John 14:23. Jesus Christ said so.

We receive the Spirit of this living Word of GOD, and he is Holy. Concisely, *"GOD is a Spirit"* (re. John 4:24), and he is a *Holy* Spirit. This is what I call one of the absolutes of GOD, so-called to assist me into a perpetual abiding consciousness of the nature of him with whom I have to do.

In the dispensation of the Son of man here in John 6:35, GOD is speaking by the Spirit through his only begotten

Son Jesus Christ, the Word of GOD made flesh. And he has just said something so infinitely profound that it defies finite expression.

Naturally, this discourse is as limitless and inexhaustible as him who uttered it. For this reason, I humbly submit to the same Spirit for an exposition heretofore unheard. That's right, I entreaty the Almighty GOD for an uncommon grace; for a new thing, for fresh breath.

By contrition and penury, I endeavor to qualify my seeking. By importunity and poverty, but by the violence of my faith, I come. My eye is single for the Father's glory in the Son, and I accede to his searching to establish that it is so.

This is my only accreditation, that GOD will speak for me as I speak for him. (As you can receive it), out of the mind of Christ, I write in the auspices of greater grace, and beneath the mantle of an immeasurable mercy.

It is the Word of GOD whom we have come to hear. I am but a guide, a life hidden within the agonies of greater grace and suffering associations of Christ. Let us launch out into the deep and let down our nets for a draught (see Luke 5:4). Children, beyond the complacency and compromise common to contemporary Christianity, beyond the teaching and the traditions of our elders, past the perfunctory presentation and the posturing piety and past all the pretty, unchartered waters await the intrepid and the disenfranchised of fragmented, sectarian, conventional religion. It is time to get real or stay home.

If I really want to know who GOD is, I will have to step into the full light of him, and into the unmitigated truth and absolute exposure of myself. I cannot remain in the shadows and peek at God, presuming upon his grace. However, there is nothing so liberating as being completely known. Ah, and in the full light of GOD's love there is greater grace for the truth of it. (It) being the unqualified (raw and bleeding) excruciating revelation of me.

The Word of GOD is as rich and bountiful as it is a fire, and a hammer, and a sword. The truth of GOD's Word streamlines me for a strait gate and a narrow way. It gives life and healing as definitively as it excises necrotic flesh, cauterizes open wounds, and thins a crowd.

The dynamic of a genuine faith is the reality of Jesus Christ and him crucified. The body of sin, self-will and world-worship must die. The panacea for the pride of life is the offering up of that life in complete surrender, pleading and trusting the life and the blood of Jesus for its arbitration and conciliation. A sincere and absolute repentance of sin is the effectual catalyst unto the remission of sins.

To put our exposition in its proper context, I have sought to know the heart and mind of its audience. That is, the motivation of the peoples, whom seeking the LORD Jesus at the shores of Lake Tiberias (the Sea of Galilee), but not finding him, were obviously inspired enough to procure shipping and pursue him across the lake, which is, incidentally, approximately 8 miles wide and 13 miles in length. Frankly, when I see their following in the context of Jesus saying, "*he that cometh to me*," I am initially encouraged by their efforts.

This discourse on the bread of life encompasses a lengthy and enigmatic conversation. These words are *Spirit*, and they are

Life (re. John 6:63). The dialogue continues after the Jews have found and encountered Jesus on the other side of the sea and extends to his teaching in the synagogue at Capernaum on the northern shore of the Sea of Galilee.

It is important to note that much of this crowd has come directly from the occasion of Jesus feeding five thousand men with a young boy's lunch of five barley loaves and two small fishes (see John 6:9). In fact, chapter 6 begins with a great multitude following Jesus after they had seen the miracles of him healing various folk that were diseased (re. John 6:1-2).

To know these men, and to better know their motivation, I look for evidence in their favor. Everything at first points to their following with enthusiasm. When they witness the miracle of the multiplication of the loaves and fishes, they were so moved that Jesus perceived that they would come and take him by force to make him a king, and he was compelled to depart into a mountain alone (see John 6:14-15).

Everything initially indicates that these people were sincere, excited, even zealous. They were following Jesus and expending an inordinate amount of energy doing so. To me, this effort (at first) indicates that they have a demonstrative, viable, and qualifiable faith.

In prayer and meditation, I go among these people to know the rationale of their heart and mind. During this discourse with the LORD they are progressively revealed. By their questions of the LORD the desires of their heart are made known, *"for out of the abundance of the heart, the mouth speaks"* (re. Matt. 12:34).

Initially (to me) their seeking Jesus out on the other side of the Sea of Galilee, and the effort it took in following him, lends credence to the genuineness and sincerity of their heart. That is, until Jesus' response to their following him stops them in their tracks, as it were, and gives me pause, as well.

※

Jesus answered them and said, Verily, verily, I say unto you, Ye seek me, not because ye saw the miracles, but because ye did eat of the loaves, and were filled.
JOHN 6:26

※

This is one of those portions of scripture that for decades I did not understand. It didn't make sense to me. Intimidated by its depth, and by the investment and commitment (and the loss of life) that it would take to delve into its hidden wisdom and mysteries, I would repeatedly skim its surface (if you will) and quickly move on to something less challenging. Ah, now this is getting honest. My reading was as superficial as these people's seeking of Jesus was found to be.

These people had partaken of the loaves and the fishes that Jesus had miraculously multiplied. They witnessed it as a supernatural phenomenon and were moved and intrigued to be a participant in such a revolutionary and momentous event. It must have been exhilarating to have been there.

Jesus says they were not following because they saw the underlying divine truth (the real miracle) which was shrouded within the miracle, but that the thrill of eating the loaves and fishes that had been supernaturally multiplied appealed to and satisfied their temporary lust for excitement. They liked being a part of something new, experiencing something fresh, revolutionary. It was fulfilling to be part of the show, being moved by the elation of the crowd. Jesus says (if I may), But you do not want to be miraculously and radically changed, you want to be temporarily touched.

By all appearances (I had preliminarily concluded) this crowd was sincere, that they were seeking the substance and the essence and the transforming power of "*the person*" of GOD who had perpetrated this miracle, to work a miracle in their life, too. Jesus said they just wanted to be filled again, to experience that temporary exhilaration again, just another transient touch, another temporary fix. He would (no doubt solemnly) tell them, "*Labour not for the meat which perisheth, but for that meat which endureth unto everlasting life, which the Son of man shall give unto you: for him hath GOD the Father sealed*" (John 6:27).

This is enlightening. It is not a physical hunger that the LORD Jesus Christ is addressing here. These people were not seeking more loaves and fishes just to have another meal, or to meet some physiological or biological need for sustenance. This was not what drove them. Personally, I don't think they were looking for a free lunch, as we say.

With much effort (and at some expense) they had just crossed the Sea of Galilee. This is not to be deliberately glib or crass, but surely, embarking from one shore and touching down upon another, someone must have been selling fish and chips along the way. This was a fishing community.

Jesus plainly told them that they did not come for a substantive (everlasting) miracle, they came for a transitory touch. They came for the revival, or the camp meeting: to put the experience in their repertoire of fun and exciting (and religious) things to have done. In the natural, it would have been like going to Disneyland or visiting the Smithsonian, or the Grand Canyon.

The experience had ministered to their ego and gave them a momentary and transitory boost in their self-esteem and self-importance. Not everyone has witnessed the multiplication of loaves and fishes. They were part of the show and of the ceremony, and fleetingly a part of something bigger than themselves. They now had something new to talk (and pontificate) about back at the men's breakfast at church, or in the parking lot; you know, fuel for their one-up-man-ship, to promote their religious persona back at Pharisee Sunday school.

But this experience was external, superficial, temporary. It didn't last. That is, the high did not last. Their faith was not in Jesus Christ as LORD, but in the experience. Had they tapped into the power of the LORD Jesus Christ by a genuine faith, the kingdom of GOD would have begun to be established internally by the radical transformation of their heart and soul and mind, the spontaneous repentance of sin and cessation of evil behavior, the inexplicable miraculous eradication of bad attitudes, the conversion of soul and the metamorphosis of character.

We come for grace and gravy, but not for the responsibilities and accountability of living for GOD. We come for a temporal touch, but not to submit to the strictures and austerity of the truth, and that strait gate and narrow way unto eternal life. We delight to be one of the many but being one of the few casts too much light upon our superficial Christianity.

We come to be near the light, but not to live in it. Uh, that level of exposure doesn't leave much left of my life.

Children, I have prayed earnestly for this interpretation, and for its relative prophetic portend for contemporary Christianity. Hear me. The best of us go to Church for the loaves and fishes, for the transitory touch, and not for the miracle of the radical transformation of raw redemption. We just want to get our feet wet. We're not looking for waters in which to swim. (Thank you, Pastor Tolle).

Jesus (in effect) tells this multitude: You did not seek me for the miracle of conversion and the metamorphosis of your character, you sought me as an experience to cite in your religious resume. What you are pursuing is more of yourself in the pride of your life beneath a religious cloak. You want to be a Bigger Christian. Ah, you seek a religious experience to make you feel pious, to add to your formula, a star in your self-promotion, something to refer to as evidence that you are righteous.

Jesus Christ will not aid and abet a feel-good Christianity at the expense of my conversion. He wants the radical transformation of my character. He wants me to seek the miracle. *"Marvel not that I said unto thee, Ye must be born again"* (John 3:7).

Let's not mistake a temporary touch for a genuine transformation. Uh, just because I got full (as it were) on the loaves and fishes. It is a good thing to experience invigorating and even intoxicating religious (spiritual) church services and worship events. It is good to be filled, but it is better to have your own source.

We can go to church for decades, be inspired afresh every Sunday, and then miss the miracle of the internal transformation, or as the LORD puts it, *"that meat which endureth unto everlasting life"* (re. John 6:27).

Sadly, I speak from personal experience, subsisting from one church service to another, or meal after meal. During revivals (at least 8 days in a row back then, Sunday to Sunday), I never missed a day. I sought out hymn-sings and gospel concerts and attended preaching and worship events at other churches. I couldn't get enough loaves and fishes, plainly because I was seeking my sustenance outside myself by temporary touch.

Duh. I lived from touch to touch, I reveled in the Holy Spirit's transient touch, but vigorously resisted the transformation. On the surface, I was an exemplary Christian. But deep inside I had secrets. Not that I was a monumental hypocrite or prodigious sinner during this time, but I had hurts and hang-ups and personality horrors that Satan had convinced me could not be fixed. No one was allowed to look at that stuff; I couldn't bear to look at that stuff. That emotional (and spiritual) baggage could not be opened under any circumstances.

(Honestly and forthrightly), I labored more strenuously and industriously than most of the Christians I associated with, but I was laboring for the meat that perishes. I was trying to prove to myself (and others) that I was a Christian by virtue of outward religious ceremony. Jesus said, *"The kingdom of*

GOD cometh not with observation. Neither shall they say, Lo here or, lo there! for, behold, the kingdom of God is within you" (Luke 17:20-21).

That is, the miracle of redemption occurs in the heart and soul of my spirit-man, and from where the renewing of my mind ensues. The life and soul transaction of my radical conversion occurs within me by faith. The revolutionary communion which comprehensively conforms my character to that of Jesus Christ's is an internal one. Here is its exemplification: *"Behold, I stand at the door, and knock: if any man hear my voice, and open the door, I will come in to him, and will sup with him, and he with me"* (Rev. 3:20).

There was a time that I facilitated a food pantry for a church in southern West Virginia, and I assure you that we fed a lot of poor people. And there are sundry other altruistic activities that I participated in, that I would sometimes (arrogantly and ignorantly) cite as my Christian credentials, if you follow. While these activities are necessary and honorable, they are not substantive evidence that the kingdom of GOD is being realized within me.

If my participation in religious services and activities does not originate and emanate from an intimate identification and burgeoning personal relationship with the LORD Jesus Christ, then (I am afraid) that they are works of the flesh. Uh, too often works of self-righteousness.

My service may be a necessary one, and others may well benefit from the activity (such as feeding the poor), but the anointing and power of the LORD's presence will not be upon the work. It will just be food for the physical body (if you follow), loaves and fishes without the miracle of redemption, religious form without the abiding fellowship of a genuine faith.

(Still using myself as an example), if my philanthropy and compassion does not arise out of my being made one with the love of GOD in Jesus Christ for the poor, my service may well be only a self-promoting religious chore designed to inflate my Christianity. Hopefully, this is an unconscious (ignorant) motivation on my part.

The poor and the homeless may be getting fed while (the Christian) worker feeds their religious persona, and thereby maintains some perceived, inferred righteousness by the works of the flesh. This is, concisely, laboring for the meat which perishes. Moreover, it is a shameful ministering to my own self-image and covetousness to appear a Bigger (more benevolent) Christian.

Conversely, to labor for the meat which endures unto everlasting life is to be conscientious and solicitous (even possessive) (fanatical, as needed) toward my relationship with GOD in Christ Jesus. This means that I cultivate an ear to recognize his voice, and his knocking; that I keep the door to my heart and soul unimpeded and easily accessible, that I am circumspect in my housekeeping skills (as it were), and that my spirit-man is amenable and conducive to holy conversation.

"*GOD is a Spirit*" (John 4:24). His abiding presence is my priority. I structure and rule my environment to encourage and proliferate our relationship. I am vigilant and faithful to do my part, and to facilitate his promise. The LORD Jesus Christ has said he will come in unto me, and sup with me, and me with him (see Rev. 3:20). This, children, is the meat that endures unto everlasting life. It is the *Bread of Life*, and it is broken by faith in the inner sanctum of the soul of the believer.

GOD wants us to aspire to more than the outward observation of religious service or ceremony. The external show will never satisfy without the internal transformation. This is the miracle of the abiding Christ, and the multiplication of loaves and fishes all the time. The indwelling Christ of GOD by the Holy Ghost is the effectual catalyst of all evangelical outreach, the reality of what makes me a Christian: the love of GOD living inside of me. Here is its consummation: *"If a man love me, he will keep my words: and my Father will love him, and WE will come unto him, and make OUR abode with him"* (John 14:23).

Jesus (essentially) says, seek the miracle within, not the external show, (not just another meal). Religious ceremony, no matter how solemn or celestial (or ostentatious), cannot sustain a vibrant Christianity without the power of the resident Christ.

The catalyst and sustaining impetus of my Christianity, and the precipitate of my miraculous transformation is the indwelling of Almighty GOD, both the Father and the Son by the Holy Ghost, (the *WE* and the *OUR* of GOD) as delineated in John 14:23. Moreover, this is *the doctrine of Christ* (see 2 John, verse 9), and the heart of the fellowship of Christianity.

He is the same abiding Word of GOD that spoke light into the darkness and order into the universe. Here is its exemplification, *"For ye are the temple of the living GOD; as GOD has said, I will dwell in them, and walk in them; and I will be their GOD, and they shall be my people"* (see 2 Cor. 6:14-16).

Children, a temple is specifically and definitively a holy place where prayer and communion are wont to be made. The magnificence and the exceeding excellency of the grace of it is inexpressible: that GOD would choose to make his abode within the spirit-man and spirit-woman of his sanctified children. This is (as I have said), the catalyst and sustaining impetus (and power) of the Christ of our Christianity, GOD from the inside-out.

This will be a developing (and abiding) theme of all these notebooks (or chapters): that Jesus Christ is LORD, that he is the I AM THAT I AM, and the express image of the invisible GOD. Or, as he said it himself, *"I and my Father are One"* (John 10:30). But for now, I must stay on task (and on text) to ensure that we have ample room for this entire (extensive) discourse on Jesus Christ as the Bread of Life.

Before moving on, the Holy Spirit (for now) adds the following imperative and binding codicil of the Promise, if you follow. This is a stipulation of the last will and testament of Jesus Christ as the Son of man. Before I quote this scripture, it behooves me to say that the liberties (I seemingly) take with the Word and character of GOD are given me by the greater grace and intimacy of suffering association, and that I take nothing upon myself (or unto myself), but that I scribe in the sanction and substantiation of the Holy Ghost. He that hath an ear, let him hear what the Spirit is saying unto the Church of GOD.

(As you can receive it) it is by conscription that I include the following discourse into our primary text. I will try to be brief. The LORD Jesus wants us to get our eyes (and expectation) off the outward religious observation which we cite as evidence of our Christianity. He wants us to get our eyes (and expectation) off the loaves and fishes, in other words, and rather look to the miracle of redemption, and the realization of the kingdom of GOD within us.

Children, the multiplication of loaves and fishes to feed a hungry world first emanates in the heart and soul of the individual Christian where, as we quoted, the LORD Jesus Christ says he will enter in to sup (see Rev. 3:20). First, *"God is a Spirit"* (re. John 4:24). And this is how he comes. *"Even the Spirit of Truth; whom the world cannot receive, because it seeth him not, neither knoweth him: but ye know him; for he dwelleth with you, and shall be in you"* (John 14:17).

Please bear with me. The Holy Spirit has some things to say about himself (his character and essence) before we return to our primary text. He wants us to functionally realize the import and power of his Promise, his comprehensive presence in all its breathtaking implications. Hence, he also (of a necessity) has some concise (and real) things to say about our character and essence.

Please keep in mind that the chapters of this manuscript will naturally overlap and converge, and hopefully coalesce into One harmonious exposition of the essence and identity and continuing revelation of Jesus Christ as the Almighty GOD. I want to prepare you for some redundancy, but I think the urgency and imperative of the Word of GOD can bear the burden of its own repetition. There will be a good bit of this specific subject matter that I have addressed in other volumes, as well.

It is Jesus Christ who calls the Holy Spirit *"the Spirit of Truth"* (please see John 14:17, 15:26, 16:13). It is the LORD Jesus Christ who specifically says of himself that he *is* the Truth (see John 14:6). Moreover, it is Jesus who says the Word of GOD *is* Truth, and that this is what definitively separates the children of GOD from the tyranny and subjugation of this evil world system, (see John 17:14-17).

Concisely, GOD is love and peace and joy, (and manifest innumerable inexhaustible grace and boundless blessing). And Jesus could have referred to the Holy Spirit as any of these. However, in John 14:17, which I listed in its entirety a few paragraphs ago, Jesus pointedly refers to the coming Holy Spirit explicitly as *the Spirit of Truth*, and then goes on to categorically and unapologetically say that he is *WHOM THE WORLD CANNOT RECEIVE.*

In the past, I have written that our attachment to (and love for) the world, and our allegiance to (and love for) the LORD Jesus Christ, are two extremes on a continuum (or scale) that it behooves us to examine in the light and truth of the comprehensive Word of GOD. The Holy Spirit obliges me to cite the decisive parameters of GOD's perspective of sanctification.

✻

"Love not the world, neither the things that are in the world. If any man love the world, the love of the Father is not in him."
1 JOHN 2:15

✻

Children, we live in a society governed by the same world system which collaborated with the chief priests (spiritual wickedness in high places) that coerced the Romans into crucifying Jesus Christ. It should not surprise us that *"friendship with the world is enmity with GOD"* (re. James 4:4). Concisely, we will have to come out of the world to receive the Spirit of Truth, because Jesus unequivocally says that the world cannot receive him, *"because it seeth him not, neither knoweth him"* *(re John 14:17).*

Jesus is saying that the world system does not value or honor or respect the Spirit of Truth (whom GOD is) primarily because they have chosen to live in a state of insurrection and volitional delusion. Pharaoh succinctly expressed the world's arrogant philosophy and willful ignorance when confronted with the man of GOD, Moses, who had cautioned him to let the LORD's people go. *"And Pharaoh said: Who is the LORD, that I should obey his voice to let Israel go? I know not the LORD, neither will I let Israel go"* (Exodus 5:2).

With wanton disregard and premeditated animus, the truth must be suppressed (and with much effort) so that the illusion can be received. This world system's moral standard is broadly based upon what I call *The Big Lie* from which all other lies are spawned: *"Ye shall not surely die"* (see Genesis 3:4).

(And, here, I must try to more clearly establish something.) Now, GOD is a Spirit (re. John 4:24), and as many as receive him, to them gives he the power to become the sons and daughters of GOD (see John 1:11). He is the *WE* and the *OUR* of John 14:23. He is whom I call the Christ of GOD, and he is *BOTH* the Father and the Son by the Holy Ghost.

This teaching is the Word (the essence and character) of GOD. This is both the *Oneness* and the *plurality* (or the Trinity) of GOD: *"For there are three that bear record in heaven, the Father, the Word, and the Holy Ghost: and these three are One"* (1 John 5:7).

John the Beloved was circumspect to emphasize that this teaching was (is) not singly or independently his, but that it is pointedly the doctrine (teaching) of the LORD Jesus Christ. It is also delivered to us all with a dire prophetic portend by the Holy Ghost.

※

"Whosoever transgresseth, and abideth not in the Doctrine of Christ, hath not GOD. He that abideth in the Doctrine of Christ, he hath BOTH the Father and the Son."
2 John, verse 9

※

The LORD Jesus Christ himself, of course, gives this doctrine its singular unambiguous emphasis when he says, *"I and my Father are One"* (John 10:30). This, I call, one of the absolutes of GOD.

This short dissertation on the plurality and oneness of GOD, is brought to you by GOD. That is, the Holy Spirit wants to cast a singular significance upon just who it is that we receive into our spirit-man or spirit-woman when we make a declaration of faith in the blood and body of Jesus Christ. We receive both the Father and the Son by the Holy Spirit, the *WE* and the *OUR* of John 14:23.

This brief critique on the identity of the Spirit of GOD who we receive is that we might solemnly esteem the magnificence and preeminence and excellency of the power which we house (host, quarter, shelter) within our earthen vessel. We no longer are just eating loaves and fishes, that is, attending religious events or church services or hearing sermons, we are housing him with the authority and power to multiply loaves and fishes. That is, the power to perpetuate the kingdom of GOD.

We are no longer just partaking of the end-product of the miracle, as it were, but we are being made an integral part of the miracle. We are being radically transformed from a consumer into a producer. We are no longer being exclusively ministered unto, but we are being empowered and authorized to minister.

This transcends seeking Jesus to be fed, or for our own transitory touch, or to be temporarily filled. Ah, this is seeking Jesus aright, accurately esteeming the glory of the miracle. This is seeking the LORD for someone else's hunger than my own.

Children, the Spirit of GOD transforms you into the temple of GOD, a holy place of prayer and worship – where kings and priests and prophets are made. Jesus says that we should not only seek for ourselves to be filled, but that our neighbors be filled, also. Ah, as we consider it, we will realize that we have friends and family (and church folk) within our immediate orbit of influence, whom in the midnight of their soul, need a miracle.

We are not to labor exclusively to be temporarily filled, but to be eternally a part of the miracle, a disseminator of loaves and fishes; indeed, and even greater works than these.

This is the meat that endures unto everlasting life – to labor in the love of GOD for the soul of the world: not just to partake of the miracle, but to be made One with the miracle in Jesus Christ.

From GOD's perspective, my hunger is incorporated into that of my neighbor's hunger. This is the meaning (and the commandment) of love. How to be filled, and the whole world hungry? Ah, behold the incongruity of our greed in the light of GOD's amazing grace, our disaffection, our patent unapologetic indifference to anyone' hunger other than our own.

Christian, we ought to be whom the hungry in our neighborhood resort to and rely upon in their hunger. We ought to be the definitive source of the abiding Christ Jesus who still multiplies loaves and fishes.

"And lo a voice from heaven, saying, This is my beloved Son, in whom I am well pleased" (Matt. 3:17). Ah, this is him whom the Father has sealed, the Son of man, the giver of Life, and the Baptizer with the Holy Ghost and with fire. Hear ye him. Become One with the miracle.

At this point, I still hope for this crowd pursuing Jesus. Until the Holy Spirit illuminated my understanding with light and truth and the breath of GOD upon his own Word, I thought perhaps these people's seeking was genuine and in depth. Their question seems to, at least initially, substantiate this. *"Then said they unto him, What shall we do, that we might work the works of God"* (John 6:28)?

By all appearances, or by their approach, and with their preliminary question, it seems that they are earnest in seeking to do that which is pleasing in GOD's sight. From their own mouths they indicate that they are willing to work for it. (At least, to me) they allude to establishing a working relationship with GOD, which can only mean reconciliation. Without referring to my Matthew Henry, it is plain to me that they are seeking how they might qualify for eternal life, although they appear to be seeking it by the works of the flesh.

Jesus immediately intuits (and circumvents) our covetousness to misappropriate some little (oblique) credit in respect to the saving of our soul. The pride of our life compels us to wrest control of every circumstance, uh, so that we may take credit for its resolution.

The Word of GOD gets us out of the way (of ourselves) you might say. The LORD Jesus Christ comes by an irrepressible grace and truth, invalidating and countermanding our self-seeking. *"Jesus answered and said unto them, this is the work of GOD, that ye believe on him whom he hath sent"* (John 6:29).

Now, this is definitive. The LORD Jesus unambiguously establishes that there will, indeed, be work involved, just as he had previously exhorted us to *labor* for that meat which endures unto everlasting life. Ah, while grace is free, the dynamics of faith command some effort on our part. This is the truth about grace, that the goodness of GOD resolutely leads me into the godly works of a vibrant faith.

This is the work of GOD, Jesus says, that you believe on him whom he has sent. GOD says, trust me, and in it you shall find work enough.

Trust your portion, says GOD; believe that what I send you is more than enough. *"Have faith in GOD,"* says Jesus (re. Mark 11:22).

What Word of GOD has reached you recently, Christian, and you did not care for the vehicle or the circumstances of its arrival? Be careful not to hold GOD's courier within the rigid constraints of your self-righteous presumption and contempt. GOD appoints whom he will in the particulars of trust and private counsel. You can be assured, that them which he sends before his face, he follows after. *"He that heareth you heareth me; and he that despiseth you despiseth me; and he that despiseth me despiseth him that sent me"* (Luke 10:16).

GOD draws no distinction between the emissary and his Master who sent him. Ah, but it is not the man who bears the momentum, but his message. The Word of GOD bears its own sanctity, and solemnity. The sin is in not believing what GOD has said.

These Jews following Jesus were comprised of, or constituents of, that great multitude which was initially following him at the very beginning of John, chapter 6, *"because they saw his miracles which he did on them that were diseased"* (re. John 6:2). Its impossible to imagine all the miracles they have already seen. They had also witnessed five thousand men fed with a young boy's lunch, and an astounding twelve baskets filled with the fragments gathered up after they had eaten and were filled.

Among this multitude were undoubtedly some of the same crowd which had declared Jesus to be *"that prophet that should come into the world"* (re. John 6:14). Moreover, the Word of GOD goes on to say that they were prepared to take him by force and make him a king. Up to this point, it is these things that have been my difficulty: that appearances suggest that this group of followers are sincere believers in the LORD Jesus

Christ. That is, until the very next verse. *"They said therefore unto him, What sign shewest thou then, that we may see, and believe thee? what* dost *thou work?"* (John 6:30)?

(Walking by sight always demands to see more). We must petition the LORD for his thoughts and feelings, and by the Word of GOD form the mind of Christ. The sin of unbelief is always revealed to be a lack of trust, or an impure motivation.

Sometimes my seeking is skewed (I often call it shady). You know, when one's self interests are not aligned with GOD's interests. When my seeking is not to know Jesus Christ better (per se) but to realize myself. Uh, show me another miracle. My lust for the supernatural does not automatically presuppose that I want to know GOD so that I may live for GOD.

I was trying to follow the dialogue (in order) so that we did not miss anything, and I really do not want to get ahead of myself (or ahead of the LORD), as it were, but Jesus knows that these people have seen him, and still do not believe (see John 6:36). Sometimes the miracle isn't enough, that is, if it is not coupled with a pure heart and a singular, genuine GOD-honoring motivation. If my seeking is just to appease my appetite then I will never be full, I am essentially ministering to myself. If my eye is not single for the LORD, my vision will be cloudy.

These people were demanding a sign, and they had already seen many miraculous signs. When I am not definitively seeking a miraculous internal transformation, when I am not seeking to be born again, so that I can live anew for GOD, then signs and wonders (and loaves and fishes) will never satisfy or be enough to sate my appetite for self-realization.

Remember the LORD's teaching on the rich man and Lazarus in Luke 16:19-31? The rich man had died and went to hell, and Lazarus died, and was carried by the angels into Abraham's bosom. The rich man and Abraham were conversing, and the rich man was imploring Abraham to send Lazarus to his father's house and testify to his five brothers so that they would not also end up in that place of great torment. Abraham said let them hear Moses and the prophets, or concisely, let them hear the Word of GOD they already have. The rich man's reasoning was that if one appeared unto them risen from the dead, then they would repent. Uh, that is, show us a greater miracle other than the innumerable ones we have already seen, and we will believe the Word of GOD and repent. Abraham said, *"If they hear not Moses and the prophets, neither will they be persuaded though one rose from the dead"* (see Luke 16:31).

For them who are not willing to change (repent), there is no miracle momentous enough to sate their demand for greater evidence. As phenomenal as the multiplication of loaves and fishes certainly is, if I do not have a genuine desire for a radical transformation (of repentance and conversion), then I am afraid they are just another meal. Albeit a delightful meal, a refreshing change of diet and a welcome break from religious monotony, ah, perhaps even a novelty and a milestone in my self-righteous, self-promoting Christian biography, and something else to brag about in the company of the saints.

Show me another miracle and I will be the front man in your entourage. You know, keep the loaves and fishes fresh. Give me something innovative and engaging for my religious braggadocio and one-up-man-ship among the righteous assembly.

You know how we do it. Raise somebody from the dead and give us something to really talk about. *"What sign showest thou then, that we may see, and believe thee? What does thou work?"* (re. John 6:30).

Let's just get honest. For some of us, Jesus just can't multiply the loaves and fishes fast enough. In fact, show us more. Uh, meaning give us more. Greater grace and no accountability. But don't ask me to get involved. That is, don't ask me to become one with the miracle, to enter into the transformation, to become a minister. Just let me eat. Just let me sit here and look holy. Just let me sit here and have the saints and angels (and the preacher) wait on me hand and foot.

If I will not believe Moses and the prophets (and Jesus), duh, if I will not believe the Word of GOD already given, no miracle will be spectacular enough to sate my one-dimensional, gluttonous, proprietary, exclusive self-seeking appetite.

This group following Jesus (whom we are following) have transitioned from what seemed to be genuine, aspiring disciples to a mob of impudent, presumptuous, challenging antagonists. They appear to be capricious, ambivalent; oppositional, adversarial. (Thank you, dear reader, as I run my fingers through this Word of GOD soliciting revelation). They sound like a bunch of mercurial church-folk.

This group seems to be asking Jesus for a miracle or sign, some work, that would outclass or surpass the miracle of the children of Israel receiving manna in the wilderness. You know, eclipse or upstage the miracle of manna (with some new and improved miracle, a new model, the latest upgrade) (uh, give us something that they don't have over there) and we may condescend to believe. Oops. This is revelatory. Uh, exposing. Give us more than what they had. *"Our fathers did eat manna in the desert; as it is written, He gave them bread from heaven to eat"* (John 6:31).

Dear reader, as briefly as possible (so as to stay on text), I share with you what the Holy Spirit is showing me. By their own words, this group of Jews (GOD's chosen) precisely identify themselves as the progeny of another generation that incited GOD's wrath through unbelief. As we have already noted, these Jews in our current text who witnessed the multiplication of the loaves and fishes, had also seen the miracles of divine healing that Jesus had performed on those who were diseased (re. John 6:2). Their demanding another sign undeniably reveals their pronounced unbelief. (Uh, what does this say about me seeking signs above, or outside, my portion)?

The comprehensive Word of GOD declares such gross mistrust of GOD an evil heart of unbelief, and a provocation to his holy person. The essence of GOD's character (expressed finitely) is his Word. It is who GOD is. Behind our mistrust of GOD lurks the exceeding sinfulness of sin.

Dear reader, to keep this short, I presume upon your knowledge and familiarity with the particulars of the children of Israel in the wilderness, and that generation who could not enter into the promised land because of unbelief. GOD says of them, *"So I sware in my wrath, They shall not enter into my rest"* (Heb. 3:11).

These Jews who reference their fathers in the desert are of the same distinct genre of blatant unbelief. The apple didn't fall too far from the tree, the old-timers would say. As my friends in A. A. used to say (back in the day), if nothing changes, nothing changes.

We may presume ourselves to have advanced far beyond our fathers. We may consider ourselves the new and improved religious metamorphosis upon the denominational market. We have a revolutionary band, the prettiest choir, and the coolest preacher. But the percipient omniscient eye of the Holy One sees our unbelief hiding beneath our religious rags, just another hypocrite upon the hierarchy, another form, or the flavor of the week.

Jesus knows that not many of us are seeking the miracle, just give us fish and loaves and let us keep our life. Ah, and as I have written, the Omniscient One knows the true ratio upon the religious continuum is the *many* and the *few*. Its urgency and tragedy demand the assessment of our souls in the light of its truth without excuse.

＊

"Enter ye in at the strait gate: for wide is the gate, and broad is the way, that leadeth to destruction, and many there be which go in thereat. Because strait is the gate, and narrow is the way, which leadeth unto life, and few there be that find it"
Matt. 7:13-14

＊

For some time, these Jews following Jesus in the sixth chapter of John (to me) appeared to be, uh, well, real Christians. We all want a miracle. Christian folk certainly want a miracle. We are supposed to demonstrate a modicum of religious zeal, don't you know? Why, even sinners want a miracle. But not many of us want to *BE* the miracle, if you follow. Jesus said we would be few.

Few that are seeking beyond our own appetite and own agenda, that is. Few that see themselves integral in GOD's plan to meet the hunger of the whole world, extending to (what we now call) the margins of society. Children, the heart of the Holy One hungers for the very worst of humanity. We don't need bigger churches, mega-churches of the compromised and worldly capitulated glutting themselves on loaves and fishes for a meticulously defined hour on Sunday morning celebrating, uh, well, essentially and exclusively ourselves. We need the miracle of bigger hearts.

Wide is the gate of worldly infiltration into our worship, broad is the way of infidels and the forms of faith which afford us the saving of the sacrifice for ourselves. Strait is the gate of sanctification, of suffering association in the intercessions of the next sinner's soul. Narrow is the way of genuine love, the adjuvant and impetus of faith, the mover of mountains.

Wide is the gate of an all-permissive grace; the attraction of mega-congregations, the salve for my guilty conscience, the illusion of forgiveness for the sin I continue to allow. Broad is the way of an abbreviated, attenuated Word of GOD so that mainstream Christianity may preserve their love for the world. Pandemic is the worldly compromise in the pew where contemporary Christianity sits.

Jesus wasn't impressed with the numbers, He intuitively, instinctively, divinely knew the many, as well as he knew the few.

Jesus wasn't impressed with their misinterpretation of their father's experience in the wilderness. Uh, he was there, and not only with GOD, but as GOD. Whether ignorantly, or with a deliberately calculated misleading, these Jews attributed the miracle of manna in the wilderness to Moses. (To me) this smells suspiciously of the innate (inbred) one-up-man-ship of the righteous congregation, the covetousness of wanting to be a Bigger Christian in the shameless posturing of the pride of life. We ingratiate ourselves to the glory of the good ole days (and the hard work of other men), to pump up the illusion of our own self-righteousness.

The LORD Jesus Christ knew this crowd wanted to see a bigger miracle for the novelty, and for the notoriety of it when it was retold at camp-meeting or Christian retreat. You know exactly how we do it. Let me tell you what I saw. When our own Christian experience and vain religious routine is nothing more than a superficial form, we are forced to cite the next fellow's hard work of real faith.

Dear reader, I have petitioned the Holy Spirit for the raw expression of the heart and mind of the HOLY. We must have the thoughts and Spirit of the Word of GOD to have the power and life of GOD. Later in this same chapter from which we study, the LORD Jesus says it best. "*It is the Spirit that quickeneth (gives life), the flesh profiteth nothing: the Words that I speak unto you, they are Spirit, and they are Life*" (John 6:63).

There is a sword upon the horizon of mainstream contemporary Christianity, set in the mind of GOD to sever his children from the charlatans and chameleons and front men of religious affectation and mass fraud. We have no time for delicate spiritual sensibilities here.

Children, we must be so intimately identified with the LORD Jesus Christ that there is no misunderstanding to whom we belong. An eternal sanctification is being irrepressibly and irrevocably set today, even in this moment. The salvation of GOD is in this moment. The sanctification being set now will exactly parallel that final sanctification when the Son of man sits upon the throne of his glory.

✳

> *"And before him shall be gathered all nations: and*
> *he shall separate them one from another, as a*
> *shepherd divideth his sheep from the goats"*
> MATT. 25:32

✳

We must not be found subsisting on a religious ceremony that is progressively and systematically being amalgamated and corrupted with worldly elements, playing church – unchanged.

We must not be found living on memories of miracles past, ruminations of revivals in retrospect, adding to the miracle in the telling of its memory. We must be found in Christ Jesus, and Christ Jesus be found in us. *"For the Bread of GOD is he which cometh down from heaven, and giveth Life unto the world"* (John 6:33).

This crowd immediately asks for this bread, and this (once more) encourages me in their behalf. Uh, you know, that these was good Christian folk following the LORD Jesus. *"Then said they unto him, Lord, evermore give us this bread"* (John 6:34).

First, the Holy Spirit shows me that these folks want this bread once and done, as it were, or as they phrased it, *evermore.* Ah, but this is a daily bread. In contemporary vernacular this might be interpreted as *once saved, always saved.* Uh, just saying. You know, kind of like, let me get this ordeal of salvation concluded as quickly and painlessly as possible, so that I can get back to living my life.

Second, they are still seeking loaves and fishes and temporal, superficial sustenance. They are still wanting the loaves and fishes (the bread) which is a by-product of the miracle, if you will, but they are not seeing Jesus *as the miracle*, as the gift of GOD for the life and soul of the world.

They are still laboring for the meat which perishes. Getting ahead of our text once more, Jesus says in verse 36 that they have also seen him, and still believe not. (If I may) Jesus is saying, *"You see me, but you don't see me."*

This gives me pause. These scriptures eluded my casual perusal for literal decades, as much as I regret admitting it. These people are following Jesus, doing what they are supposed to be doing. (In my mind, I defended them). According to appearances, I concluded, these are good Christian folk.

Every Sunday in America, an innumerable amount of loaves and fishes are consumed, and our appetites are temporarily sated. Perhaps a few of us are refreshed. Many will not even eat what they are served, but they continue to go through the motions of coming to the table, if you will allow the allegory. Uh, we presume to have already received this bread *evermore* when we first got saved, and as I suggested a moment ago, (Boy) are we glad that ordeal is over.

The best of us (the many) perdure unchanged Sunday to Sunday, going no deeper into Christ, delving no deeper into the miracle. It can be said that we (relatively) occlude the portal to the kingdom of GOD. Many of us relegate a daily bread to a weekly ration. And then on Sunday we eat religious ceremony (if you follow).

Does this offend you? Not half as much as it offends the LORD Jesus Christ. The mysteries and wisdom of GOD, and the salvation of GOD in Jesus Christ, is found in the faithful daily consumption and fellowship of a *daily* bread.

Jesus Christ is the miracle of GOD that transforms me into the image of Christ from the inside-out. I cannot be a Christian without an abiding Christ.

The manna in the wilderness was a *type* of Christ, it had to be gathered and consumed every day. I cannot be sustained all week on what the preacher said Sunday, or by a touchy-feely superficial loaves and fishes Christianity. In the recesses and hiding places of my soul this daily bread must be broken, and this Word of GOD rightly divided. I must gather this Christ of GOD for myself by faith, and by the Word of GOD. My pantry, and my appetite, is ultimately my responsibility. By the violence of my faith, I gather my portion of grace. If I will not work, I will not eat.

Jesus Christ is the miracle whom GOD has sent, his only begotten Son. It is my responsibility to look into it; to eat, and then eat some more. In a glorious moment of greater grace, in personal prayer and fasting, in perpetual awe and wonder one glorious morning, I heard that still small voice of the Spirit of GOD say: *"Reach hither thy hand."* Startled, I knew the LORD had been talking to Thomas, whom they called Didymus. This is what Jesus told him: *"Reach hither thy finger, and behold my hands; and reach hither thy hand, and thrust it into my side: and be not faithless, but believing"* (re. John 20:27).

Reaching into Christ is a great deep, and more than a finite allegory. It is the divine reality of GOD, and a glimpse by grace through faith into the face of Jesus Christ, even into infinity.

⁂

Son of man, I AM an inexhaustible pantry and a bottomless well, saith the LORD. I AM as immeasurable as the stars in the heavens on a cloudless night, as incalculable and unfathomable as the depths of the deepest seas. Yet, unto babes and suckling I open the secrets of my storehouse, and by gradients of grace and truth to the believing, I irrepressibly come.

I AM the wild daisy in the hand of your toddler, and the unbridled laughter upon his lips. I AM the summer's breeze through your open bedroom window, and the deep stillness upon a fresh, snow laden winter's morn. My witness is the quiet within the peace.

I AM the staff of life and a daily measure. He that gathers much has nothing over, and he that gathers little has no lack. Son of man, I AM best a portion possessed while it is called today, and without a thought for tomorrow. Selah.

⁂

Continuing with our odyssey, the multitude that is soliciting the LORD Jesus Christ to give them this bread *evermore,* are still missing the implications and the prerequisites, as it were, of the miracle, the variables and parameters and the processing of the infinite phenomenon of being born again. Succinctly, they are not coming to him with the recognition and apprehension of the revelation of Jesus as the I AM THAT I AM, the creator of the heavens and the earth, and the source of all life. *"For if ye believe not that I AM (HE), ye shall die in your sins"* (re. John 8:24. Uh, you see me, but you don't see me.

✳

"And Jesus said unto them, I AM the Bread of Life:
he that cometh to me shall never hunger; and
he that believeth on me shall never thirst"
JOHN 6:35

✳

The LORD Jesus Christ is effectually saying (and teaching us) that he is not pie-in-the-sky or a free lunch upon demand for the mercurial and the frivolous, or a quick fix for the temperamental: for them who are hungry one day, but too petulant and self-absorbed, too conditional (and complaining) to eat the next day.

We want loaves and fishes *evermore* without being (or becoming) invested. We do not want to lose our life (or give our life) for the kingdom of GOD; we want GOD to supplement the life we already have. I want your loaves and fishes, and then I do not want you to trouble me (or expect of me) concerning anything else. I will consult you when I am hungry again, or when I am hurting again, or when my life is off the rails again.

We see through Christ or past Christ without reaching into Christ. "*But I say unto you, That ye also have seen me, and believe not*" (John 6:36). You do not see past what I can do for you right now, says the LORD. You cannot see beyond your own hunger to that of your neighbor, and to that of the whole world.

But for the gluttony and the clutching, we cannot see beyond the loaves and the fishes. To get something for nothing, to ensure that we get as much or more than the next guy, has occluded our vision, and the next revelation of GOD. We stuff our face with the temporal and miss the miracle of the eternal. GOD wants to give us a world vision, but we cannot see beyond our own dinner plate. The Spirit weeps for all we cannot have, for the little we will not give.

GOD wants to alleviate my temporal hunger and thirst by making me One with the miracle, and the reconciliation of mankind. Jesus Christ wants to give me a concept and working revelation of my neighbor's hunger, but my own greed has rendered me one-dimensional and close-minded.

Beyond the grace of the loaves and fishes is the startling reality of the truth, and the revelation of my neighbor's hunger amalgamated to mine. It is Jesus Christ who incorporated my love for GOD into my love for my neighbor, to make them One commandment. And as I follow on to know the LORD, I find them absolutely indivisible. Alas, I eat my bread in the sweat of my brow, and in the astute inescapable knowledge of the next man's hunger.

The Word of GOD comes with an irrepressible living Spirit and searches me to the uttermost. My hunger and thirst are meticulously and assiduously assessed in the unsparing light and truth of the Word of GOD. The revelation is for me: of me. Children, the intrepid and the fearless come this way.

When I allow Jesus Christ to incorporate my hunger and thirst into the hunger and thirst of all humanity, they are truly satiated and satisfied. The miracle is, indeed, the love of the Father in Jesus Christ the Son by the Holy Spirit for the whole world of whomsoever will. My motivation for following Jesus Christ, my driving reason for coming to him, is assessed in the light and truth of this miracle. My hunger and thirst are proved (and then my life lost), in the realization of the miracle of Jesus Christ. *"All that the Father giveth me shall come to me; and him that cometh to me I will in no wise cast out"* (John 6:37).

In the wisdom and foreknowledge of GOD, my hunger and thirst and the motive for my coming to Jesus Christ was evaluated and altogether known unto GOD before (what we know as time) began. GOD knows who is looking for a miracle, and who is just looking for another meal. Children, GOD knows when our own hunger and thirst transcends our seeking.

There is a distinct difference between a superficial hunger and thirst, and a true seeker of GOD. Jesus Christ unapologetically and unsparingly separates the children of GOD from the pretenders.

Contemporary Christianity has become quite proficient at producing transient methodical repetitive ceremonial loaves and fishes without an eternal substance. (Please, no punctuation). Form without a genuine faith, in other words. We circumvent the cross of Jesus Christ and the loss of our own hunger and thirst, and the surrendering up of our life as part of the living sacrifice, as part of the miracle – so GOD can feed the world.

The preponderance of us (the many) have *Church*, and then we return to our lives as seamlessly as possible. But for them called according to GOD's purposes, how to eat and enjoy a sandwich in the knowledge of your neighbor's hunger, you cannot find.

(Broadly) we are meticulous (ah, even persnickety) about procuring our own loaves and fishes, and (frankly) our neighbor can get his own. And I wish him Godspeed, but also gravely caution him, please, do not get in the way of me getting mine. (Broadly) we are content with religious ceremony and the meager loaves and fishes that the man of GOD serves up, you know, just enough to alleviate our conscience.

(Ah, but not enough to awaken our conscience). We wouldn't want to look too closely into the blackened abyss of our perfunctory Christian heart: uh, to see our real hunger and thirst, if you follow. We don't want the revelation to ruin our appetite. Children, the LORD Jesus Christ sees and knows and distinguishes the fair-weather seeker from the one with a genuine faith.

It is the sincere penitent upon whom rests the Spirit and power and metamorphosis of the new birth. Them whose eyes are opened to behold the light of the glory of GOD and the dynamic of the LORD's salvation in the face of Jesus Christ have forever forgotten their own hunger. They have come to do the will of the Father. The loaves and fishes are (by far) no longer the primary attraction.

(Let's try another perspective for what I have no adequate finite expression of). That the poor are fed is the work of GOD. But, children, the Spirit (upon the man) and behind the breaking and dissemination of the loaves and fishes is the Gift of GOD. He is whom GOD sent. Uh, let's not let works or religious ritual and ceremony obscure the revelation of just whom has come. This is Emmanuel, GOD with us.

The preponderance of us have also seen, and still believe not. We play church, pursue religious works and copious *churchly* activities and present pious for having done so. Jesus Christ has come to give us the power to become the sons and daughters of GOD, to radically make all things new, and we concern ourselves with the next meal.

Children, Jesus is trying to tell us something here. GOD wants us to look past the superficial and the external, past the religious trappings to receive the miracle of whom he has sent into our midst, not to play church or to even feed the poor, (that, will naturally manifest), but to first embrace the eternal transforming power of the Holy Spirit whom GOD is.

GOD did not send the man-made spirit of religious fervor and activities into our midst for us to preen and pontificate and present (before one another as pious), he sent the Spirit of his Son that we might receive the power to become the sons and daughters of GOD. We labor for the meat that perishes, and for the spurious honor of the duplicitous, the doctrinally and denominationally-divided approval of them that despise us. We labor to be seen of men more corrupt than ourselves. We labor in the self-righteous shadow one of another (to see who can be the bigger hypocrite), and the light passes us by.

Them that come to the Father as children have seen the miracle behind the loaves and fishes. To have Jesus Christ, I relinquish all temporal hunger and thirst, and all religious posturing, too. These Jews following Jesus were seeking a temporal satisfaction in the loaves and fishes (and just like many of us) could not see past their own hunger. They were blind to the miracle of the Word of GOD made flesh.

The unbelieving, the faithless, do not see GOD Incarnate. Like these Jews, they see Jesus whose father and mother they knew, and they murmured because he said, *"I AM the Bread which came down from heaven"* (see John 6:41-42).

We must see Jesus as the Christ, the Son of the living GOD, and believe on him to have everlasting life (re. John 6:40). Moreover, I must believe what the LORD Jesus Christ says about himself and the Father – what I call the absolute utterance of God. *"I and my Father are One"* (John 10:30). Children, none but GOD could utter such a thing. I must have this faith to receive the Spirit of the Glorified Christ, (whom is Both the Spirit of the Father and the Spirit of the Son); and should the LORD tarry, this Spirit whom raises me to life now, shall also raise me up in the last day.

He is more than loaves and fishes; he is the miracle of GOD with me, and the Promise of God within me. He is more than religious observation, or the flurry of mindless activity, superficial ceremony. He is the Christ of GOD from the inside-out, uh, transforming me into a Christian. The metamorphosis of a sinner like me into a saint is the explicit, indefensible, inexcusable miracle of Grace.

GOD calls, deep unto deep, and a man answers him. Great is the mystery of grace and mercy, the handmaiden of the HOLY, and the heart of GOD set upon a man. Behold, I sit among the saints in the grace and auspices of the Holy One, the edge upon his sword; *that the purpose of GOD according to election might stand, not of works, but of him that calleth* (re. Rom. 9:11).

When once we see the Son, the loaves and fishes are put into proper perspective. Duh, I'm not even hungry anymore. I must have an encounter. Marvel not that it takes GOD to give me GOD. *"All things are delivered to me of my Father: and no man knoweth who the Son is, but the Father; and who the Father is, but the Son, and he to whom the Son will reveal him"* (Luke 10:29).

Children, the conundrum and dilemma of unregenerate man must be addressed. As it is written in the prophets, I must be taught of GOD, and the eyes of my enlightenment must be opened by grace, and unto grace. It is given unto me to hear, and to exercise my will.

We speak of the Jews in our text as seeing in the natural. They see Jesus, the son of Joseph and Mary, but they do not see the Christ, the Son of the living God. Neither the unprecedented miracle of the multiplication of the loaves and fishes, or the copious miracles of healing they have witnessed, have opened their eyes to the true identity of Jesus Christ. We must conclude that the grace of GOD which brings salvation abounds, but they have not exercised their wills to receive its revelation. We must conclude that they are content with the hunger and thirst they already have, and its temporal satiation. Not unlike much of contemporary Christianity, Sunday after

Sunday, satisfied with the ritual, but resisting and denying the miracle of an internal transformation.

Here is the quandary and seeming paradox of unregenerate mankind, but it must be cast in its correlation and perspective to the phenomenon of the foreknowledge and sovereignty of Almighty GOD. Let us run our fingers through the progressive revelation of the prophetic (perpetually fulfilling) Word of GOD.

By grace and mercy, in the counsel of GOD's own pleasure and sovereign permission, we press into the Word of GOD. *"No man can come to me, except the Father which hath sent me DRAW him: and I will raise him up at the last day"* (John 6:44).

Interesting, and revelatory, is the word *draw* in this context. Concisely, it means to *drag.* Specifically, by example, for Paul and Silas (see Acts 16:19), it means to *force before magistrates.* It means to *induce* or *prevail upon.* Of this, I personally bear witness, that in my insurrectionist, recalcitrant state, I was more taken prisoner than that I voluntarily capitulated. Succinctly, I was overtaken and subdued by Grace.

Uh, I ask you, therefore: What merit is one's unconditional surrender (after that) you have already been (unapologetically and completely) vanquished and unceremoniously imprisoned? Duh. *"Ye have not chosen me, but I have chosen you"* (re. John 15:16).

Uh, kind of exposes and invalidates all my religious posturing and one-up-man-ship. Unsparing is the revelation of all the ceremonial loaves and fishes as the vanity and empty labor for temporal meat. Duh. Just another garden-variety sinner saved by grace after all, and all my righteousness as filthy rags.

This is what I have learned, and it is the revelation of my abject penury. This is what I have heard, "*All flesh is grass, and the goodliness thereof is as the flower of the field*" (re. Isaiah 40:6).

Children, this is where Grace found me. "*Every man therefore that hath heard, and hath learned of the Father, cometh unto me*" (re. John 6:45).

Dear children, unless the Father shows me the Son, I shall not see him or know him; and unless the Son reveals the Father unto me, I will neither see him, nor realize him (re. Luke 10:29).

"*GOD is a Spirit*" (re. John 4:24). This is what I refer to as absolute of GOD. This is my hiding place, my respite from the storm. And I come here to *reboot*, as it were.

It is by faith that I see down the inscrutable corridor of the good pleasure and foreknowledge of GOD to draw grace and mercy unto myself.

(Some of you follow). GOD must find me there seeking. By the violence of my faith nigh unto trespass he shall find me there. In my irrepressible and indefatigable pursuit, by faith, I wrap the election of GOD around myself.

I will not sit here anesthetized and stupefied and allow adverse and oppressive circumstance to immobilize me. I delve into the deep of Christ indomitable and defiant of predator or opponent to apprehend him whom first apprehended me, deep unto deep. Uh, it takes GOD to show me GOD and give me GOD. I go to the source.

As I often quote, Oswald Chambers said few prove themselves chosen. I liken it to the gold seeking the refiner's fire, commanding revelation. If you have been there, you know it is so. The Father draws what he first put it, or in some cases, he drags it out of us. Faith meets him in foreknowledge, and in the mystery and hidden wisdom of GOD's good pleasure, amazing Grace sweeps us under. It is GOD who expresses mercy. My best is to serve the LORD with fear and rejoice with trembling (re. Psalm 2:11).

Great is the mystery, and the unsearchable wisdom of GOD in the sovereign election of grace and mercy, the enigmatic working of foreknowledge with faith, the treasures of the HOLY. Children, GOD will show me, or I shall not know it.

The more I glean of the righteousness of GOD in his Christ, the more I gather grace unto myself, and worship in the awe and wonder of a little child. My greatest aspiration is to present empty, my hope to be still. To wait in the quiet expectation of perfect trust is the highest grace, the spiritual poise of the perpetually impoverished – to give it all away, and to feel the rush of being filled once again.

Jesus says them that have heard, and have learned of the Father, come unto him (re. John 6:45). Dear children, it was grace I heard in the footfalls and echoes of the love of GOD in Jesus Christ: calling me, shadowing me, overwhelming me. I was not so much surrendered (as I have said) as taken. Frankly, the ardor of GOD's love in the crucible of his election and foreknowledge is frightening (if you follow).

Faith and hearing are inseparable, this is one of the fundamentals of the kingdom of GOD, and an indispensable key to the gospel of Jesus Christ and him crucified. "*So then faith cometh by hearing, and hearing by the Word of GOD"* (Rom. 10:17).

Let me establish that I speak and write of my own experience and learning first. The further I reach into Christ the more grace I find. My righteousness is the exclusive purview of the LORD Jesus Christ, and grace is my portion. How shall I say it? All that is given me, eventually, I must fight for, and fight to sustain; this is the way of grace through faith that I have found. *"For by grace are ye saved through faith; and that not of yourselves: it is the gift of God"* (Eph. 2:8). Nevertheless, only the stalwart and the intrepid come this way.

Lest I come invested and assiduous, my inquiry will be unproductive and unrewarding. Grace is a gift that must be cultivated, as love commands requital (or so I have found it). Rather than come dispassionate, I am better served staying home.

How shall I say it? but that *"he (opens) awakens mine ear to hear as the learned"* (re. Is. 50:4). Favor and inspiration must be nourished with action, grace without a practical application is a gift unopened. I rise to GOD's benevolence and by faith make it perform. My gold is on the other side of the fire.

I must come to the table (as it were). *"O taste and see that the LORD is good: blessed is the man that trusteth in him"* (Ps. 34:8). Ah, even my appetite (I have found) is of grace; but GOD will not force me to eat. As a young, aspiring (struggling) Christian, GOD led me to the following Word which I have found perpetually and dynamically invaluable.

✸

*"Take heed what you hear: with what measure
ye mete, it shall be measured to you: and unto
you that hear shall more be given."*
MARK 4:24

✳

It is Father GOD who drew me to Jesus Christ, his Son, by the effectual working of the Holy Spirit. He showed me my abject poverty: my absolute need, my unequivocal helplessness. These are lessons taught of Father GOD (uh) as part and parcel of the comprehensive gift, pointing to the universal panacea of Jesus Christ. And Jesus says, them that have *heard* and have *learned* of the Father, come unto him (that is, unto Jesus Christ, the Son) (see John 6:45).

Take heed what you hear. Be careful (and conscious of) whom you are listening to. There is One Truth, and he is the Word of GOD, the LORD Jesus Christ.

With what measure ye mete, it shall be measured to you. My return is correlative to my investment. Except that GOD answers exponentially more that I can ever imagine, even *"exceeding abundantly above all that we ask or think, according to the power that worketh in us"* (see Eph. 3:20).

My enthusiasm is met with the incalculable earnestness of GOD, faith to faith into infinity, I press unto trespass (as I have called it). Children, the degree of my seeking is assessed by the omniscient eye of the HOLY. My desire is minutely evaluated. It shall be seen if I am seeking GOD, or if I am seeking more of myself. My aspiration and my ambition, and my appetite, are naked in the light and truth of GOD's Word.

Dispassionate and uninvested, the preponderance of us come seeking miracles, and go away sorrowful and disgruntled that GOD was not impressed with out apathetic appearance and perfunctory Christian presentation. Indeed, that our luke-warm religious ritual and self-celebratory ceremony does not disconcert, us confirms us in patent unbelief.

Frankly, we are uninvested and aloof, going through the motions, prisoners of a form of faith to emulate forward momentum. Going nowhere. We are captive to the religious ceremony which we presume upon to call ourselves Christian. Someone has to say so.

We like to sing and dance, pontificate and signify. Well, some of us just want to set here. The best of us are on the broad way of an hour of suspect entertainment and religious side-shows and secular amusement, you know, hybrid ceremony: the world let into our worship, the spurious wise-men and witch doctors and worldly counsel that allows us to save our lives for ourselves. Many of us have church, but few of us look into the Word of GOD with calculated intent.

The measure I mete is intended to turn inward, and the Word of GOD transform me from the inside-out. This is where the miracle of the Word of GOD manifests, and the kingdom of GOD being formed within me. It is not in the church building, or in the white face of the self-serving religious ceremony. It is in the offering up of my life unto GOD.

Many of us want to subsist as Christians unchanged, and a few of us are crucified with Christ. Well? A few of us are dead to the ceremony and unaffected by the ritualistic ostentatious religious pageantry, and the many of us are prisoners to it.

The many cannot be Christian outside of Church, that is, we have no real identity with Jesus Christ, uh, because we have no effectual cross: no life-transforming suffering association with the LORD (no fellowship with his sufferings), and no conformity to his death – and certainly no resurrection power.

We have not first died to have an actual new-birth experience. We get out of it what we put into it, the show without substance. There is no spiritual (or heavenly) caloric value, if you will, in the finest loaves and fishes (uh, religious ceremony) that is not also replete with the Word of GOD.

"It is written, Man shall not live by bread alone, but by every Word that proceedeth out of the mouth of God" (re. Matt. 4:4). This is so fundamental and so critical to Christian life and vitality that the evidence (or the lack thereof) suggests that the question must still be asked, But are we listening? Or, to whose voice are we listening, to whose counsel? Uh, when (and if) we read the Word of GOD, with what measure do we mete?

That is, dear Christian, how invested are we in eternity? Or, conversely, to what degree do the cares and pleasures of this life, and let's not forget the deceitfulness of riches, choke the Word of GOD? This could get graphic (so I will try to adhere to first-person narrative). Uh, is my fruit thirty, sixty, or one-hundred-fold? What state of suppression and repression has the god of this world imposed upon my witness for my LORD and Savior, Jesus Christ? Uh, how blighted and riddled with worldly influence am I? How choked and occluded and sullied is my conduit?

(I am intentionally inverting verses 47 and 48 of John chapter 6 to make a point). *"I AM the Bread of life. Verily, verily, I say unto you, He that believeth on me hath everlasting life."* We know, of course, that our believing on Jesus Christ is our faith in him. And faith comes by the Word of GOD. Now, GOD uses, or attempts to use, everyday circumstance to increase (my) faith, but (as for me), those circumstances have no positive influence upon my faith outside the scope of the Word of GOD.

To live by every Word that proceeds out of the mouth of GOD is to implement that Word into my every circumstance. I see my world in the light and truth of GOD's Holy Word, this is to live for GOD. Everything in my world submits to the authority of the Word of GOD, the LORD Jesus Christ.

Every circumstance, and every person within my orbit of influence is impacted and transformed by the Word of GOD which directs and empowers my steps. (If) I maintain an astute enough awareness of GOD's presence with me and in me, (ideally) I speak the Word of GOD into every single life (or person) with whom I come into contact. No person or circumstance can gainsay or prevent the present and effectual power of the Word of GOD in my life. It will not return to GOD empty.

During the course of this teaching the LORD Jesus Christ distinctly and repetitively emphasized that he was (and is) the Bread of Life. Children, there is none other source of life and sustenance but he, none other staple or staff of life. But there are counterfeits and cosmetic substitutes, kind of like that bowl of artificial fruit upon Mama's dining room table.

"Your fathers did eat manna in the wilderness, and are *dead"* (John 6:49). Let us establish something, or rather, state something

that is already established. Succinctly, the Word of GOD is that sword of Jehovah (if you will) which severs the pretenders and the posers from the genuine children of GOD. The apostle Paul phrases it like this, "*Not as though the Word of GOD hath taken none effect. For they are not all Israel, which are of Israel*" (Rom. 9:6).

The Word of GOD is living and breathing and irrepressibly prophetic. That is, it is perpetually fulfilling, and it will not be bound nor hindered, cannot be effectively (or realistically) attenuated or circumvented. That is correct, I cannot escape its exacting and excruciating revelation of me. Believe it or not, sometimes we Christians (and even preachers) attempt to water it down to give our flesh a pass, but in vain.

The prophetic nature of GOD's Word is timeless. It is eternal. And it is Now. Although many of us read it, or peruse it casually as a historical document, it emphatically and inescapably is not. Uh, it has found us right where we live, and I refer specifically to mainstream contemporary Christianity.

The Word of GOD will indubitably and unmistakably identify whom is a child of GOD and whom is not. And what applied to GOD's chosen people then (Israel), applies to GOD's chosen people now, whom I invariably call mainstream contemporary Christianity.

That is, they are not all Israel which are of Israel, just like not all who call themselves Christian have an abiding Christ ruling their lives from the throne room and inner sanctum of their soul.

There was an entire generation of the children of Israel in the wilderness who considered themselves GOD's chosen, but who did not get to enter into the promised land. Because of unbelief they did not get to enter into GOD's rest (re. Heb. 3:19), either in this life, or in the next one. These Jews whom Jesus is talking to, cited the experience of their forefathers with GOD in the wilderness. Jesus concisely reminds them that they are dead; and not only dead, but twice dead, if you will, both physically and spiritually.

The manna they ate can be likened to the sermons much of contemporary Christianity is served every Sunday morning. If I do not ingest the Word of GOD, that is, if I do not effectually hear the Word of GOD and implement it into my life circumstance by faith, it will not benefit me. It can figuratively be said of me that I ate manna this past Sunday (or loaves and fishes), or for multiple decades of Sundays, but if I do not willingly receive it and allow it to transform my character, then I am just as dead to GOD as I ever was.

"Your fathers did eat manna in the wilderness, and are dead" (John 6:49). Those men not only were favored with manna from heaven, but also from water out of the Rock. They saw GOD's glory and the various miracles he did both in Egypt and in the wilderness. Much like them, I can experience GOD's miraculous blessings of healing, financial breakthrough, and great deliverance from my enemies, and still remain fundamentally unchanged in my heart and attitudes.

The sun rises as well upon the evil as upon the good, and the rain falls upon both as well (re. Matt. 5:45). This is as grace not mixed with faith; grace not acknowledged and honored by gratitude and worship. I can be inundated with grace, showered with external blessings and surrounded with religious experiences and ostentatious ceremonies, but it takes faith to honor GOD as my source. In this sense, (I want to say, I dare to say) that grace is sanctified through faith.

Faith is the catalyst and the dynamic by which GOD's grace imbues me with its eternal benefit. Without faith, it is just rain. By faith, in faith, and through faith, I sing and dance and worship in the rain.

I can be very religious, and still be dead as doornail. (The term *dead as a doornail* was used in the 1500's by William Shakespeare, and by Charles Dickens in 1843). In fact, I can gather manna for 40 years and be physically sustained by its nutrients, but still be eternally lost, eternally exempt (cut off) from rest, eternally barred from the promised land by unbelief. Sadly, innumerable multitudes of people are blessed with the sun and the rain, but never honor GOD as their source. "*For the grace of God that bringeth salvation hath appeared to all men. Teaching us that, denying ungodliness and worldly lusts, we should live soberly, righteously, and godly, in this present world*" (Titus 2:11-12).

Duh (as it were). To rightly acknowledge and esteem the grace of GOD spontaneously incites my soul unto faith. Not to receive the innate teaching of grace is the egregious and willful insurrection of original sin.

The truth of GOD is intrinsic to his grace. That is, Jesus Christ came by *grace AND truth* (re. John 1:17). In fact, he is full of grace and truth (re. John 1:14), and we cannot have one without the other.

This leaves many of us in a complex predicament. In order to effectively save our lives for ourselves, and to retain the erroneous notion and illusion that we are lord (*little "l"*) of our own life, we must obdurately and perversely suppress the truth which inherently accompanies the grace we enjoy. Otherwise, we would have to live for GOD instead of living for ourselves. Ouch. Really, we use GOD's grace to aid and abet our treason. This is sin.

Children, there is no sense (meaning, no benefit) in my putting a different, or mitigating, spin on my abuse of the LORD's grace, you know, to appease some contrary appetite and give my flesh a pass.

Grace is a teacher. The goodness of GOD speaks volumes. Sadly, we take the money and run (as it were). With an inflated sense of entitlement and privilege, we grab the goodness of GOD on the reckless (thoughtless) broad way of self-realization and self-indulgence. An unthankful child is the heartbreak of GOD, but gratitude keeps the window of grace open wide. It is GOD's nature to give, but, alas, it is man's nature to take.

The grace of GOD speaks for GOD. The revelation of his goodness would have me recognize and realize its source. The ultimate gift of GOD is his only begotten Son, Jesus Christ. *"This is the bread which cometh down from heaven, that a man may eat thereof, and not die"* (John 6:50). During this lengthy discourse, the LORD Jesus Christ repeatedly emphasizes, *"I AM that Bread of Life"* (John 6:48).

Jesus knows, as only our Creator and GOD can know, that in our unbridled pursuit of self-realization we have indiscriminate appetites, and that we are mercilessly driven by the lust of our flesh in the pride of our life. Many of us have tried (seemingly) everything under the sun to satisfy the aching abyss of our aimless, eclectic promiscuity and covetousness. We eat (as it were) when we are not even hungry. Not to be deliberately gross, but to keep it real, I share an astute unsparing observation from the hills and hollows of West Virginia: Some hound dogs will eat and eat until they get sick.

Children, the grace of GOD points to what is nutritious and uncontaminated, teaches us what is healthy and spiritually edifying, right-minded, ethical, honorable, clean. Grace educates and enlightens, reveals the character of GOD, instructs and illuminates us in the love of the truth.

Here, this is bold. Jesus Christ is the manifest grace and truth by which GOD came to reconcile mankind unto himself. Yes, GOD came. That is, the Word was made flesh, and that Word was not only with GOD in the beginning, but that Word was and is GOD now (re. John 1:1).

So elusive is the revelation of Jesus Christ as GOD, and so wonderfully exhilarating and edifying that I find myself running my metaphorical fingers through its infinite truth and wisdom at every opportunity.

So complex and insidious, so subtle, yet so convoluted and evil is this world system's clandestine determination to diminish the deity of Jesus Christ that about six years ago now, I began to spell the word *LORD* with all capital letters. This is to remind myself (first) that Jesus Christ is the Almighty GOD, the Alpha and Omega of creation, and the Author and Finisher of our faith.

Jesus Christ is what I call the absolute of GOD. He is every Word that proceeds out of the mouth of GOD that mankind is commanded to live by. He came to tell us and show us who

GOD is. *"No man hath seen GOD at any time; the only begotten Son, which is in the bosom of the Father, he hath declared him"* (John 1:18).

Here are what I call two more absolutes of GOD, out of the mouth of GOD. *"I and my Father are One"* (John 10:30). Second, it never fails to astound me that the LORD Jesus Christ concisely tells a sinner woman at Jacob's well, and her a Samaritan, that *"God is a Spirit"* (re. John 4:24). He is much more forthcoming with her in the fourth chapter of John than he was with one of religion's finest, Nicodemus, in chapter three. Also, I believe he is speaking indirectly to mankind's propensity (in every era) toward ethnic bigotry.

Of course, the entire Bible is a comprehensive revelation of GOD, but these scriptures above are my *"go to"* scriptures when I need to reboot and regroup and reestablish the greatest conceptualization of GOD (the Biggest GOD) that I can lay my hands (and my heart) upon.

You might say that John 10:30 is the epicenter of the earthquake, uh, from which a tsunami (John 4:24) then emanates and radiates outward, or vice versa. All communication and fellowship between the Father and the Son transpire (occur) (and are realized) by (or within) the One Spirit whom GOD is.

Jesus Christ is the image of the invisible GOD (see Col. 1:15). Before I share another (couple of) astute observations that the apostle Paul conveyed to the saints at Colosse, let us remember that he saw the LORD up close and personal, as it were, one magnificent (and dreadful) day on the Road to Damascus.

Saul of Tarsus saw a light from heaven above the brightness of the sun which would subsequently blind him for three days.

Uh, his formal (unorthodox) introduction is as follows. Lying prostrate in the dust he asked, *"Who art thou Lord?"* (And the LORD answered) *"I AM Jesus of Nazareth, whom thou persecutest"* (see Acts 22:8).

Duh. The Jesus whom Saul of Tarsus met was decidedly different from the impression I had formed from the religious teaching and traditions of my forefathers. Uh, he saw the glory of the resurrected Christ, and did not see another thing (physically) for three days. There are those who will say I am reaching (and I am) but the LORD's appearing above the brightness of the sun (re. Acts 26:13) may be likened to the Word of GOD in the beginning, in the Genesis of creation when GOD said, *"Let there be light: and there was light"* (re. Gen. 1:3). Moreover, Saul of Tarsus was probably favored with just a glimpse.

Children, this is the very same Word of GOD that was made flesh and dwelt among us (re. John 1:14). We might say it is all a matter of perspective. But by the Holy Ghost, I say that it is faith which forms an accurate, and even incendiary conceptualization of GOD. By the violence of our faith we may dwell upon the precipice and cutting edge of the perpetually fulfilling prophetic revelation of GOD, (uh, to have fresh bread all the time).

The apostle Paul shares his apprehension and realization of GOD by suffering association and acute intimacy, and by writing much of the New Testament. He would go on to write the following scripture to the Colossian saints. *"For by him were all things created, that are in heaven, and that are in earth, visible and invisible, whether they be thrones, or dominions, or principalities, or powers: all things were created by him, and for him"* (Col. 1:16).

We might say that the apostle Paul knew the LORD Jesus Christ by a singular (and frightening) familiarity. (If I may) he knew that the LORD Jesus Christ was the whole loaf of that living bread which came down from heaven. *"For it pleased the Father that in him (Jesus Christ) should all fulness dwell"* (Col. 1:19). In the next chapter he rephrases the comprehensive (incisive) conceptualization of the LORD Jesus Christ he has formed. *"For in him dwelleth all the fulness of the Godhead bodily"* (Col. 2:9). Concisely, *ALL* of GOD in bodily form.

The perpetual (living) revelation of the deity and magnificence of the LORD Jesus Christ astounds. Ideally, the identity of GOD unfolds as the Christian evolves into the image and likeness of Jesus Christ. My conceptualization of GOD corresponds with my own radical metamorphosis and militant transformation from sinner into saint: from servant to steward to son.

The phenomenon of my being born again is my awakening and assimilation of my *God-likeness*: my reconciliation with GOD by the Holy Spirit, and my faith in the shed blood and sacrifice of Jesus Christ. GOD is restoring his chosen from humanity to the place from where Adam fell, as kings and priests in the earth. My intercessions for my neighbor are a reflection of this. I am being restored to the place of authority I was intended to have within the sphere of my influence, to rule the orbit (and the circumstances) I occupy.

The Christian is one in whom (ideally) the identity of GOD is being realized by Jesus Christ. The power of a Christian's influence to impact and transform their environment is cor-relative to the revelation of GOD that they have apprehended by the Word of GOD: by faith, by fight and by favor and by force. By fire. To know who you are in GOD is to have pre-vailed as a prince to have power with men and with GOD (see Gen. 32:28).

It is by faith that I make the Word of GOD manifest, and pro-gressively realize the kingdom of GOD within me. Periodically, all I know must be shaken, so that what is capable of being shaken may be removed, and so only that which cannot be shaken may remain (re. Heb. 12:27).

This is he: the comprehensive Christ, the Almighty GOD. *"This is the bread which cometh down from heaven, that a man may eat thereof, and not die"* (John 6:50).

This is not dead works; this is the Living GOD. This is not religious ceremony or self-righteousness; this is every Word that proceeds out of the mouth of GOD. This is the Grace and Truth by which GOD came to fulfill and satisfy the Law. His name is Jesus. He is *all* GOD, and I celebrate his deity and majesty as KING OF KINGS and LORD OF LORDS as record-ed in Revelation 19:16. Because this is how he is coming back.

But here in the dispensation of the Son of man, and of the Lamb of GOD, presenting himself unto his own people, it may be accurately said that *"He was in the world, and the world was made by him, and the world knew him not"* (John 1:10).

This must be addressed. So pernicious and invasive, so en-grained the prevailing unbelief, and so profoundly and effec-tively has the god of this world system blinded the minds of them that believe not, that on Sunday mornings at Harbor

House when I quote this scripture attesting to the deity of the LORD Jesus Christ, the unbelief of the men gathered there is markedly apparent on their faces. A fortress.

(I dare say) that the unbelief of the ordinary congregation is so pronounced and so pervasive, and such a seemingly insurmountable obstacle, that the deity of the LORD Jesus Christ is seldom or reluctantly preached. We preach Christian conduct and things easy to understand, uh, genteel teachings, and dishes of all permissive grace and copious carnal accommodations, things more palatable. Instead of the deity of the LORD Jesus Christ and the austerity of the utter (raw) and bleeding Gospel of Jesus Christ and him crucified, we teach sweet meats and delicacies.

Intellectually, we know that the Word of GOD was made flesh and dwelt among us, but our understanding is finite, linear, or one-dimensional, earthly. Some of you know that I am fond of saying that it takes GOD to show me GOD. Unless I solicit GOD by prayer and fasting, and by the unspeakable intercessions and groanings of his own Holy Spirit which he gave me, I shall not apprehend the deeper mysteries of the Almighty GOD revealed in his Christ. Church of GOD, we need the Baptism of the Holy Ghost.

The bloodline of the Spirit-filled in America has been attenuated, and often (both cause and effect) is watered-down preaching. Someone has to say it. America, *"Therefore say I unto you, The kingdom of GOD shall be taken from you, and given to a nation bringing forth the fruits there of"* (Matt. 21:43).

We, as contemporary Christianity, have not realistically apprehended the prophetic implications of this Word of GOD.

This surely does not apply to us, after all, we are the Church, GOD's chosen. Children, the solemnity and the gravity and the perpetual prophetic revelatory nature of the Word of GOD applies to all of humanity, every era, every generation.

The Word of GOD finds us right where we live and play and hide, if we will hear it. It finds us where we have settled into complacency, where we try the dimensions and strain the boundaries of grace, where we hide within the ritual and the religion and the same old church ceremony: where we presume our elitist denominational appellation entitles us to a pass.

The revelation of GOD is on the dynamic continuum of a living faith. While I have breath there is more of GOD to realize, that is, internally, personally. I cannot imagine that the irascible personality GOD is compelled to sometimes show me (meaning mine) has arrived at some blessed Christian nirvana where I can afford to stop growing in grace.

Great is the mystery of GOD manifest in the flesh (re. 1 Tim. 3:16). Children, we must have the progressive (irrepressible) revelation of it realized and apprehended within our own heart and mind and soul to be saved. This is the effectual realization of the kingdom of GOD within me, within my own flesh, that is. I want and need the Word of GOD to be made flesh in me, if you follow. I need the Christ-child to come alive in me, and then faith to faith resolutely grow into maturity: to speak the Word of GOD out of me, to witness and to speak healing and blessing and deliverance – to cast Satan out.

To be a son of GOD in good standing, I must first (and concurrently) be a faithful servant and a steadfast, conscientious steward of the LORD's resources. I must wield the grace and power of the LORD Jesus Christ in the full knowledge and apprehension of his indisputable deity. Uh, I must be fully informed and comprehensively illuminated. Ah, but I must have the unction, the anointing and the effectual utterance of the Holy Ghost upon this knowledge and enlightenment. This is to be empowered.

❋

"If ye abide in me, and my Words abide in you, ye shall ask what ye will, and it shall be done unto you"
John 15:7

❋

I must know my need of the indwelling Word of GOD. I must acknowledge and apprehend its deity – that it is the defining essence and character of Almighty GOD. I must adequately understand and internally assimilate that this Word was with GOD in the beginning, and that this Word was and is GOD *"Now,"* within my bosom, abiding within the temple of my spirit man, living and reigning within the throne room and sanctuary of my very soul.

This is the same Word which proceeds out of the mouth of GOD that I am to live by: the true manna from heaven. Sin has rendered fallen mankind so obtuse and insensate that the LORD Jesus Christ is compelled to utter this truth multiple times. *"I AM the Living Bread which came down from heaven: if any man eat of this Bread, he shall live forever: and the Bread that I will give is my flesh, which I will give for the life of the world"* (John 6:51).

My faith in the living Word of GOD is the dynamic of my salvation and the sustaining impetus of my progressive (and perpetual) transformation: my believing that Jesus Christ is the express image of the invisible GOD, come to declare the comprehensive Grace and Truth of all that GOD has to say and to (perform) fulfill his own Law. Jesus Christ is the all-sufficient sacrifice of GOD for the total reconciliation of mankind, made freely available to whosoever will.

In simplistic, finite terms, Jesus Christ as the Word of GOD is the substance of what Father GOD has to say, and the Holy Spirit gives it illumination. My comprehension of what GOD has said is accomplished by the Spirit of GOD quickening (or giving life to) my understanding. This is an integral component of the Father drawing me to the LORD Jesus Christ.

In further finite terms, I must submit my will to the Spirit's illumination of the Word of GOD to accept what he has said as absolutely true. Otherwise, the Word of GOD remains linear, flat, lifeless. Surrendering to GOD's will, and the leading of his Holy Spirit, can be likened to having ears to hear.

I am sure that the experience of many of you in this regard is comparable to mine before I totally submitted to the leading of GOD's will by the Spirit. There was many a church service when the Word of GOD went forth and the Holy Spirit was illuminating the truth of that Word, tugging on my heart and my mind and my will, attempting to lead me into surrendering my insurrection to GOD and urging me to kneel before Jesus Christ as Savior and LORD.

It occurs to me that one of the fundamental reasons that Jesus Christ repeatedly and emphatically declares that he is the *Bread of Life* is because it is one of the finite terms or expressions which best represents and describes his infinite nature. We know that bread is referred to as the *staff of life*. [Unfortunately, the origins and particulars of this expression cannot be given without a lengthy exposition.]

It is GOD who said that "*Man shall not live by bread alone, but by every Word that proceedeth out of the mouth of GOD*" (re. Matt. 4:4). The word *bread* in the Word of GOD often alludes to our all-inclusive need for food so that our physical body can be sustained. GOD says we are not to live by this "alone," or being concerned only with the physical and the temporal. Moreover, GOD has promised that if we would seek his kingdom and his righteousness first, that everything else would be added unto us (Matt. 6:33, paraphrase mine).

Prayer and fasting is often called for: to re-establish the priorities in my life, and so that the Word of GOD may have the preeminence in my (sometimes seemingly) ordinary business and conversation of the day. I often call this vigilance of the Spirit to procure the first place in my life *Christ-consciousness*. The patriarch, Job, put it like this, "*I have esteemed the Words of his mouth more than my necessary food*" (re. Job 23:12).

Uh, (if I may), by the astute percipience and omniscience of the Holy Ghost, I have intuitively discerned the way that I should take (in this moment) and what is the perfect will of GOD in my day-to-day. This is to rightly esteem the Words of his mouth. To minutely evaluate and honor their immediate significance unto me, and to wholly submit myself unto GOD, this is the offering up of spiritual sacrifices: a sweet-smelling savor unto God, and my acceptance in the beloved.

The Word of GOD is a *Living Bread*, an eternal sustenance, an infinite concept. To live by the Word of GOD is infinitely more than reading my Bible or listening to preaching: this is the very flesh of the Son of GOD for the life of the world (re. John 6:51).

✳

Having therefore, brethren, boldness to enter into the holiest by the blood of Jesus. By a new and living way, which he hath consecrated for us, through the veil, that is to say, his flesh.
HEBREWS 10:19-20

✳

Children of GOD, this is infinite and incomprehensible analogy of which none of us is worthy. I call these glimpses of GOD's inexpressible glory *"greater grace."*

The intrepid and the steadfast, the faithful, are favored to peer over the precipice of the finite into infinity, into the mysteries of the deep and dark, hard sayings and shadows of the unspeakable mind of GOD in Christ, ah, and as by a Spirit whose first name is *Holy*.

Can I just get blatantly (butt-naked) honest for a moment, and not just for myself, but for all of us? All we do not know about GOD is a black hole, and it totally eclipses all we think we know. If once we could see how vain our denominational and doctrinal differences are, how asinine and empty our religious posturing, how shallow our self-seeking, we would see them as a device of the enemy.

In truth, none of us are worthy to lay hands upon such great mysteries and wisdom of GOD hidden (or shrouded) within his Christ. When we first believe in Jesus Christ, it is our very childlike, unfeigned, earnest approach of faith which sanctifies (consecrates) us along with the host we receive.

Without becoming too technical, the body and the blood is the Eucharist of Christ we receive by faith unto salvation. When we first get saved, it might be said that we partake in an unseen Holy Communion, or LORD's Supper by faith in the torn flesh and the shed blood of the LORD Jesus Christ, the bread and wine of the New Testament, or New Covenant.

It is our faith when partaking of the LORD's Supper that consecrates the change of the whole substance of the bread and the wine into the substance of the body and the blood of Jesus Christ, the Passover Lamb of GOD. This process is called (technically) *transubstantiation*. As often as we do this, we are doing it in remembrance of the LORD. Notably, this transubstantiation is ideally intended to elicit a substantial transformation within each of us Christians.

Now, the reality of the figure is a macabre and dreadful comprehension. The raw and harrowing truth about the cross of Jesus Christ and the grace we so casually enjoy and wantonly take for granted is that the veil we pass through on our way to the mercy seat is the torn and bleeding flesh of Jesus Christ, the Son of GOD.

Our way through the veil has been consecrated (hallowed) or made holy by the blood of Jesus. Relatively, to a Holy GOD, the veil suffers (or allows) our passing through the torn body of the Lamb of GOD to make our way to the mercy seat where the blood is applied.

The twenty-second Psalm is one of the most horrific and prophetically accurate (descriptive) utterances of the crucifixion of Jesus Christ recorded in the Word of GOD. David prophetically foretold the crucifixion of Jesus Christ about 1,000 years before he was born. Moreover, most historians agree that he wrote Psalm 22 about 800 years before crucifixion was even introduced into Hebrew culture.

I believe, that throughout much of this Psalm, David is prophetically quoting Jesus Christ by the unction (or anointing) of the Holy Spirit. I will cite three parallels with the New Testament before making a point relative to our (present) primary text of Hebrews 10:19-20 delineating the flesh of Jesus Christ as the (torn or rent) veil into the Most Holy place.

The first is Psalm 22:1 as a direct quote from Matthew 27:46. *"My GOD, my GOD, why hast thou forsaken me?"*

The second is taken from Psalm 22:16, and we are all acquainted with its prophetic fulfilling in the four gospel narratives of Matthew, Mark, Luke and John. *"For dogs have compassed me: the assembly of the wicked have inclosed me: they pierced my hands and my feet."*

The third is Psalm 22:18. *"They part my garments among them, and cast lots upon my vesture."* This verse is an unmistakable and accurate prophetic portrayal of what occurs in John 19:23-24, and I will allow you to prayerfully compare them.

The point I make relative to our text concerns the flesh of Jesus Christ. (Please regard our discussion in remembrance of the title of our chapter, *I AM the Bread of Life*). His body was so emaciated through torture, and his frame and stature so elongated by the crucifixion process, that as a result his bones were so pronounced and extended that they could be counted. In fact, I propose that at least the first half of Psalm 22:17 is another utterance of Jesus Christ himself, prophetically spoken and written by David. *"I may tell (number, or count) all my bones: they look and stare upon me."*

Dear reader, from what we know of the cruel ability of the whips the Roman soldiers used, it is not improbable or far-fetched to conclude that they removed a significant portion of the mass (of the flesh) from the frame of Jesus Christ's body. In fact, one expositor of the Cambridge Bible says he was reduced to *a living skeleton.*

The patriarch, Job, describes the manifest suffering of such a man. *"His flesh is consumed away, that it cannot be seen; and his bones that were not seen stick out"* (Job 33:21). Church, to pass this way means to look upon him there, to esteem the weight of our sin laid upon the Son of GOD.

Children, this is not the *"feel good about me"* mainstream Christianity of America. This is the Reality of GOD, the anguish of the Son of man, the manifest evidence of the horror of sin upon the Son of GOD.

Christian, this is the narrow way, and the death of sin in the flesh. This is what it took, the enormity of the price that was paid for the redemption of mankind. It took the rending of the flesh of the Son of GOD, and the heartbreak of the Father.

This is the way we must come, but we think to come without looking. We presume to come without an astute reckoning of the reality of sin in the flesh. We submit (subliminally and superficially) to the death of the Son of GOD, and then silently give ourselves a pass.

We mostly have religion so that we do not have to die. Well? I speak broadly but no less concisely. Uh, fundamentally we must first die before we can be born again. And according to the comprehensive teaching of the LORD Jesus Christ, he is not referring to my stopping a couple of bad behaviors, but about the crucifixion and death of sin in the flesh.

The gospel of Jesus Christ reaches to the heart and the marrow, and to the roots of the tree, to the eradication of bad attitudes and childhood prejudices and bigotry, to the total (unabbreviated, unsparing) radical transformation of character. (Marvel not that you must be born again).

Church of GOD, to come this way the veil must be rent from the top to the bottom to facilitate our access to the mercy seat. "*And, behold, the veil of the temple was rent in twain from the top to the bottom; and the earth did quake, and the rocks rent*" (Matt. 27:51).

The Word of GOD is often figurative, but type and shadow never mitigate the commands and austerity of the reality (if you follow). Sin in the flesh cannot be spared or excused, the veil must be rent from the top to the bottom. Yes, Christian, GOD is talking to you, (but me first). The voice of the Word of GOD reaches me right where I live, and GOD intends that my transformation be total, from the top to the bottom.

The Jews also attempted to refute the teaching of Jesus, the Word of GOD, by citing their seemingly insurmountable misunderstanding of the figurative. "*The Jews therefore strove among themselves, saying, How can this man give us his flesh to eat?*" (John 6:52)

To strive with other men concerning the Word of GOD never benefited anyone. It is the individual wrestling with the Word of GOD by faith in the midnight of the soul that prevails to have power with GOD and with men. By the violence of my faith, l press into the Word of GOD, and if l am purposed, and pure in heart, faith can make that Word of GOD manifest.

There was a time that l looked for loopholes in the Word of GOD, escape clauses, technicalities, if you will. Some of you are feigning as if you didn't know what I was talking about. There was a protracted season in my Christian (uh) procrastination and dissimulation that I earnestly (urgently and minutely) endeavored to put the Word of GOD in its proper context and perspective, you know, succinctly meaning one that did not apply to me. I was painstaking in my research. The more austere the Word of GOD, the more fastidious I was to escape it. Indeed. Ah, it was as l yielded that the Holy Spirit led me into the simplicity (and liberty) that is in Christ, to consider all of the Word of GOD as written distinctly and directly to me personally.

The Word of GOD, even when figurative, is precisely and explicitly and inescapably the Reality of God. *"Then said Jesus unto them, Verily, verily, I say unto you, Except ye eat the flesh of the Son of man, and drink his blood, ye have no life in you."* (John 6:53)

To apprehend eternal life is the imperative of Everyman and Everywoman. We will be held accountable for what we refused to know, uh, that is, for the light readily available but we preferred the darkness because our deeds were evil (re. John 3:19).

The truth of GOD's Word is that the flesh must be rent so that a way can be made for us to live. Jesus Christ condemned sin in the flesh (Rom. 8:3), a sentence of death was passed upon it. Sin must be condemned and die in our flesh, also. Children, we are made One with the gospel of Jesus Christ and him crucified, and this is an unpalatable truth to the flesh, but this is the gospel of *the Bread of Life* and *the Blood of the New Covenant.*

To eat the flesh of the Son of man fundamentally means that I have faith in the new and living way Jesus Christ has made available through the veil of his flesh to the mercy seat where his blood is applied. It means that I radically and completely accede to come the same way. It means that I identify with his sacrifice. To effectually apprehend his blood, I must press my way to the mercy seat, and to get there I must pass through the rent veil of his flesh. Have I seen his torn back and pierced side from this perspective?

Moreover, the power of sin in my own flesh must be denied and utterly abnegated and unceremoniously rent from my physical man. I must come the same way, with the same resolve. First, I must acknowledge the torn flesh of the Son of GOD and accept the astute revelation that it was my sin that rent him so mercilessly. With the revelation comes my unavoidable responsibility to forsake sin in the flesh.

Perforce I belabor the point predominantly because our laissez faire self-accommodating Christianity suggests we do not see it that way. Or, rather there are none so blind as them that refuse to see. Concisely, we have went another way. "*All we like sheep have gone astray; we have turned every one (2 words,*

KJV) to his own way; and the LORD hath laid on him the iniquity of us all." (Isa. 53:6)

Children, the revelation of Living Bread is the torn and shredded, decimated flesh of the Son of GOD. (I'm getting a little ahead of myself), but *"This is a hard saying; who can hear it?"* (re. John 6:60)

Succinctly, we want light bread and delicacies. Duh. We have turned everyone to his own way because we cannot come this way. Concisely, it is too strait (difficult, distressing), and it is too narrow. The LORD Jesus Christ said it would be (re. Matt. 7:14), and he pointedly went on to say that there would be few that find it.

I will just go ahead and say what is not being said. For many of us, the verity and reality of the analogy is that to remove sin from us it would indeed have to be rent from our flesh and wrested from our white-knuckled fists.

Know you not, Christian, that this living bread of which the LORD Jesus Christ is offering us is communion bread? And that to become One with the miracle we must become One with the sacrifice? This is what the LORD Jesus means when he says to labor for the meat (food) which endures unto everlasting life. Children, it is still the way of an old rugged cross. Concisely, there is One cross, and it is the cross of Jesus Christ and him crucified.

✳

"And he that taketh not his cross, and
followeth after me, is not worthy of me."
MATT. 10:38

*

Metaphorically, this is the meat which endures unto ever-lasting life – my acceptance by faith that Jesus Christ is the Bread of Life, and my incorporation of the revelation in all its austere implications, that sin must die in the flesh (meaning my flesh).

(If I may) this is not the "feel good about me" Sunday School of my youth. (Uh, how to say it? I can't eat this!) This is not your average benign salt-free, sugar free unleavened commu-nion wafer and unoffensive grape juice. *"For my flesh is meat indeed, and my blood is drink indeed."* (John 6:55).

Children, the miracle of the new life commands the cruci-fixion of the old one. We can come no other way but by the new and living way which Jesus Christ has consecrated (hal-lowed, sanctified) for us through the veil, that is to say, his flesh (see Heb. 10:19-20). By his blood we have this boldness to enter into the holiest. Moreover, the power of sin in our own flesh must also be rent from the top to the bottom, and by faith absolutely forsaken.

This is not superficial religious form or a perfunctory cere-monial presentation, this is the Reality of Jesus Christ and him crucified (and me crucified with him). To eat the flesh and drink the blood of Jesus Christ is to follow his example, and to have faith in every Word he has said. To be a figura-tive following, its agony is no less acute.

(Please pardon my redundancy as I cry aloud, and spare not, until the house of Jacob gets it.) This is my capitulation and acquiescence and absolute obedience to the austerity of the revelation that sin in the flesh must be rent from the top unto the bottom, and that, in my own life. Christian, this is the unequivocal meaning of our communion with the LORD Jesus Christ and the suffering association we shall share as we are resolutely being made One with the continuing sacrifice of the love of GOD for the world.

This is a fastidious diet of selfless love, perpetual sacrifice, continual intercessions for the Church and for the lost. This is the steadfast, unabating, unceremonious diet of the cross of Jesus Christ and him crucified for the souls of your unsaved loved ones.

This is the reality of the LORD's Supper they never told you about in Sunday School, and maybe not at Bible study. This is the unadorned earth-shattering revelation that the eternal life that is in the LORD Jesus Christ is that of the Eternal Shepherd, and that as long as the earth endures, ninety and nine will never be one hundred. Moreover, Christian, if indeed that eternal life is in you, then it is inciting you to seek with him also.

This is not light bread. This is not the religious ceremonies of men without real significance; you know, the loaves and the fishes and the forms of faith that leave me unchanged and unfulfilled, and uh, irrelevant. (Generally) mainstream religious services leave me unchanged because we (broadly) address the superficial. And specifically, because if any truth of GOD's Word did emanate from the pulpit with power, I refused to hear it and submit to it.

There is too often a silent, covert compromise and corporate collusion between the preacher and the congregation on just what type diet we will have. I have written of these things in other volumes (uh, extensively).

Too often, the element that tithes the best has the majority vote concerning the menu, if you follow. Too often it is donuts and weak coffee instead of the body and blood of the LORD Jesus Christ. Too often the teaching and the preaching is cursory Christian etiquette and external temporary conditions and the ceasing of a few bad behaviors.

To come this way of the broken body and the shed blood of the LORD of glory we must reckon hardy and unsparingly with personal sin. The correlative revelation of Jesus Christ and him crucified is the glaring illumination and merciless exposure of my hidden man, the corruption in my own heart, the engrained prejudices and bigotry of my own character.

The preponderance of us must be served delicacies or we will not come. We want the ceremonial loaves and fishes of the church service (and our attendance) to be qualifiers of our Christianity, but we resist the miracle of the internal transformation of our heart and mind and soul, and our character. We wander in the wilderness of religious observation much like our fathers, who did eat manna, and are dead.

Children, to be raised up in the last day unto eternal life with the LORD, I must eat his flesh and drink his blood this day. Or I shall have no life in me, Jesus said so.

I must come through that old rugged cross, through the rent veil of the flesh of the Son of GOD. This is not light bread: this is an unsparing death to the body of sin in my own flesh. This is raw and remunerative truth, the excruciating exposure and commands of the blood of Jesus, the unremitting revelation of my sin in the returns of the LORD's grace. "*This is an hard saying, who can hear it?*" (re. John 6:60).

Uh, I can't eat this. Them in the flesh, or controlled by the flesh, cannot please GOD (see Rom. 8:8). Indeed, the astute reckoning of the exceeding sinfulness of sin is an unappetizing, exacting diet of the undiluted Word of GOD, the uncompromising preaching of the cross of Jesus Christ and him crucified.

This is teaching, indeed, in the shadow and portend of Calvary. But these Jews here in the sixth chapter of John have no understanding or practical apprehension of the LORD's prophetic utterance that he must be lifted up, even as Moses lifted up the serpent in the wilderness (re. John 3:14). Their insurmountable resistance and offense to this teaching is the severe prohibitive command which GOD gave Noah to eat no flesh with the blood (the life) not properly removed from it (re. Gen. 9:4).

Christianity today, however, should not have the same compunction. We should know that the LORD Jesus is referring to his body broken for us as the veil rent into the most Holy place, and his shed blood as representative of the cup of the New Testament. After all, we are the elect and the enlightened.

Children of GOD, there is nothing like an acute (meditative, prayerful) perpetual consciousness of the cross of Jesus Christ to sustain and promote my obedience and sanctification unto the holiness of character the Word of GOD commands.

The preaching of the cross is intended to keep me close to home, as it were. It is not intended exclusively for unrepentant sinners, but for all sinners; uh, even Christian ones.

Nothing keeps me loyal quite like the astute accountability of the blood of Jesus. The Apostle Paul was intentional and impassioned to preach Christ crucified, *"the power of GOD, and the wisdom of GOD."* (re. 1 Cor. 1:24).

The blood of Jesus commands my change. The blood of Jesus Christ requires the repentance of sin for the remission of sin. Its authority over sin will be evident in my radical (comprehensive character) transformation. Words will become extraneous in the light of the miracle of redemption. *"For the kingdom of God is not in word, but in Power."* (1 Cor. 4:20).

It is the refining power of the cross of Jesus Christ which causes a Christian's light to burn brighter. GOD is bringing forth gold. It is Christ crucified that puts a relevant Christ in my Christian testimony. Only in the shadow of Calvary will I have something substantive and revolutionary to say. Words are meant to compliment the walking out of my witness – the qualifiable good works (as it were) perfecting my faith.

But (behold) the same preaching too often thins a crowd. The fervent preaching of the cross of Jesus Christ is the discomposure and acute colic of the contemporary worldly-conciliatory Christian congregation. Uh, a strong diet commands a strong stomach, and a healthy, discriminating appetite. *"For my flesh is meat indeed, and my blood is drink indeed."* (John 6:55).

And here the Holy Ghost constrains me to pause and to solemnly ask: Christian, have you seen the meek and lowly Jesus lifted up for your sin, and have you accordingly amended your behavior?

✳

"But I say unto you, that ye also have seen me, and believe not."
John 6:36

✳

This is, indeed, the indictment laid against the corporate complacent soul of corpulent Christianity: that we have seen him smitten and afflicted there, and then have still turned to our own way. We seem to esteem it a casual slight, but it is an egregious, willful denial, reckoned of the Spirit of the Living Word of God as an evil heart of unbelief.

✳

Shall a remonstrance not be made, saith the LORD, an edict cried aloud: the remunerative of Grace, the commands of Truth? shall Mercy walk alone, and Grace return empty?

Nay, but I take my prisoners, saith the LORD. Out of the crushing press of a suffering passion shall be your portion. Eat what you have trespassed upon Grace to have, son of man, and the rejoinder to your seeking. This shall you have of my hand, and all that Faith has commanded of me, angst and indignation and the great sorrow of suffering association – my intimacy, my mind, my rent heart, I tell you.

This you have of my hand, and the answer to your unbridled importunity and reckless pursuit of me; the flesh of the Son of man you have shredded, and the innocent blood you have spilled. Have you not known it? that you pass through a veil rent from the top to the bottom, and tread the blood of the covenant underfoot? Thus saith the LORD, You take Mercy and Grace from the table, leaving Truth too terrible to contemplate.

But Truth commands the remunerative of the despite shown Grace, the answer to every slander. If once you believed I AM, you would know it, and that this is your portion. Selah.

✳

Ah, but out of the crushing come a few, the faithful on the other side of the fire, the intrepid and the steadfast through a strait gate.

Children, we will partake of the very same suffering we have precipitated. This revelation I have of the LORD, receive it or not. Indeed, and what shall be our portion for the wanton pillage and misappropriation of the LORD's grace? We shall follow the LORD's death or have no part in his life. This is not light bread.

✳

"He that eateth my flesh, and drinketh my
blood, dwelleth in me, and I in him"
JOHN 6:56

✳

Children, this is the resident Christ who brings integrity and power to my Christian testimony. This transcends religious ceremony to resolutely make me a Christian from the inside out.

The Word of GOD speaks from eternity into time, foreshadowing Calvary, prophetically intimating the promise of the resurrected Christ Jesus with all power in heaven and in earth relegated into his hands. If we listen closely to the scripture above (John 5:56), we hear the LORD Jesus Christ herald the infilling and Baptism of the Holy Ghost. *"As GOD hath said, I will dwell in them, and walk in them; and I will be their GOD, and they shall be my people"* (re. 2 Cor. 6:16).

Referencing John 6:56 specifically, such is the eternal relevancy and efficacy of the Living Word of GOD, that the LORD Jesus Christ prophetically forecasts our partaking of the new covenant even before Calvary. Ah, the Word of GOD incites me to sing with Moses and the children of Israel. *"The LORD is my strength and song, and he is become my salvation: he is my God, and I will prepare him an habitation; my father's God, and I will exalt him"* (Ex. 15:2).

Correlative to the Word of GOD exalted and given a place of honor in me, even so is my faith manifested in substantive evidence. Dreams and visions become reality, the ethereal becomes tactile. The LORD solicits my singing in the Spirit. He is glorified, and I am edified and sustained by the perpetual abiding of the Holy Spirit whom GOD is.

Hear me. This is the true Eucharist: the abiding, indwelling sacrament of Holy communion, the resident sacrifice of the Lamb of GOD by faith, the perpetual LORD's Supper within the inner sanctum of my soul.

Let us hear the austerity and the terrible reality of the Word of GOD again, Jesus the Christ of GOD, uttering the amazing grace and excruciating truth of the New Covenant (New Testament).

✳

*He that eateth my flesh, and drinketh my
blood, dwelleth in me, and I in him.*
JOHN 6:56

※

This makes the LORD's Supper a living reality and a daily bread. The consecrated elements of my Holy Communion with GOD are the broken body and the shed blood of the Son of GOD. This is the true solemnity and stringency of the gospel of Jesus Christ and him crucified. To believe and accede to its conditions and enjoy its amazing grace makes me accountable to the truth of its commands.

Following GOD's promise to dwell within his people which we quoted from 2 Corinthians 6:16 several paragraphs ago, the Apostle Paul goes on a couple of scriptures later to give the following admonition. "*Having therefore these promises, dearly beloved, let us cleanse ourselves from all filthiness of the flesh and spirit, perfecting holiness in the fear of GOD.*"

Dear children, you may not have heard it expressed quite like this before, but the responsibility of GOD's people is great, even dreadful. Every Christian ought to contemplate and remain aware of the gravity and inherent obligations of calling themselves by the name of Jesus Christ. Children, the amazing Grace we enjoy (and too often think to misappropriate and misuse) answers to the Truth of GOD's comprehensive Word.

You may not have considered it as such, and the Holy Spirit is making it progressively real to me in this Bible study, but the holy communion I experience with the indwelling Spirit of GOD each and every day may accurately be likened unto my partaking of the LORD's Supper. The Eucharist is the same, that is, the consecrated (holy) elements of the broken body and shed blood of the LORD Jesus Christ. Such is the imperative of my living each day circumspect by faith, and by grace and mercy, worthy to call myself a Christian.

To live otherwise is to despise the grace of the LORD Jesus Christ and to malign his holy name. Here then is the astute uncompromising prophetic revelation of it:

✳

"Wherefore whosoever shall eat this bread, and drink this cup of the LORD, unworthily, shall be guilty of the body and blood of the LORD"
1 Cor. 11:27

✳

Children, the irrefutable inescapable portentous revelation is the consequence of living in willful sin while at the same time calling myself a Christian. (Such a condition warrants multiple adjectives). This is the persistent (pernicious) predicament of many a contemporary Christian. Someone must unapologetically say so. The author of the epistle to the Hebrews goes on to say that in such a willful disobedient state, I effectively tread under foot the Son of GOD, and count the blood of the covenant whereby I was sanctified, an unholy thing, and have done despite unto the Spirit of grace (see Heb. 10:29).

These are the consequences of such an egregious denial of the Son of GOD, the dire ramifications and reverberations of self-will, the denouement of an evil heart of unbelief – the dictates of a Holy GOD in the necessity of hell. But, contrariwise for the faithful and the diligent child of GOD, the revelation of

Jesus Christ as the Bread of Life brings (a) peace that passes understanding, and joy unspeakable and full of glory.

This teaching of the LORD Jesus Christ is the progressive revelation of the indwelling host of GOD, and the perpetual application and efficacy of the blood of Jesus Christ, the power of GOD. This is the reality of a daily bread and (an ideally) unbroken fellowship.

This is holy communion, indeed. This is the indwelling Christ of Christianity, the austerity of suffering association, the intimacy of the cross. This bread of life is not light bread, it is the reality and the tragedy of Jesus Christ and him crucified.

Let us listen once more to the Word of the LORD and take a closer look to its promises. "He that eateth my flesh, and drinketh my blood, *dwelleth in me, and I in him.*" (John 6:56).

We have already spoken of the song of Moses, and of him preparing GOD a habitation. Children, if we will make room for GOD, his promises are inexhaustible. Indeed, and how much more under the New Testament (Covenant) of the broken body and shed blood of the LORD Jesus Christ.

Here in my little home office, the Holy Ghost has, as it were, sat down upon me and enshrouded me with the peace and joy of the Holy One to share the perpetual revelation of Jesus Christ as the Bread of Life. This is my daily bread.

✳

"He that DWELLETH in the secret place of the most
High shall abide under the shadow of the Almighty"
PSALM 91:1

✳

This is the dwelling place of the Christian whose heart is upright, the godly fruit of living by faith, and the favor of GOD. The promises of Psalm 91 are too innumerable and too sweeping to include an exposition of them all right here. But they include protection and shelter, the defeat of one's enemies, divine healing, angelic companionship and safe-keeping, authority over Satan, deliverance from trouble, answered prayer, honor and long life.

Please note that all these exceeding great and precious promises are linked to what is called (I believe) a conjunctive adverb in the beginning of verse nine. I call it a conjunctive, coordinating adverb. It is the word *because,* and it is repeated twice more in verse fourteen. This Word links or unites cause and effect. Every promise in Psalm 91 hinges on the three times that this conjunctive adverb *because* is used.

If we will consider it, the entirety of verse nine is the catalyst of the promises that precede it, as well as those that follow. *"BECAUSE thou hast made the LORD, which is my refuge, even the most High, thy habitation"* (Psalm 91:9). Space prohibits the specifics, but I have already listed them generally. I will leave you to their research and application in your own life and circumstances.

An astute abiding consciousness of Jesus Christ and him crucified and an enduring awareness of the price that was paid for my ransom is the correlative of eating the flesh and drinking the blood of Jesus Christ. My faith in his sacrifice is the dynamic of our fellowship: my *dwelling* in him, and his *dwelling* in me.

This is (from every perspective) the dwelling place of the most High, and the habitation of GOD through the Spirit. We have known that GOD does not dwell in temples made with hands. Alas, but that does not prevent the preponderance of us from (too often) building our Religion upon (and basing our salvation upon) a sporadic church attendance and an external superficial ceremony. Uh, more loaves and fishes. More of the meat which perishes.

Dear children, Jesus is teaching us that Christianity is not to be something we do, but it is to be who we are. The kingdom of GOD is within us, and Jesus Christ is the Bread of Life that sustains us. "O' Holy Father, Give us this day our daily bread (re. Matt. 6:11). O thou gracious and merciful GOD, Prepare us a table in the presence of our enemies according to your Word" (re. Ps. 23:5). [paraphrase mine]

Hear me, children. Where the veil is rent, that is, the flesh of the LORD Jesus Christ, and where his precious blood is shed, is within the Most Holy place of the presence of Almighty GOD. We have spoken of the new and living way consecrated for us through the veil in Hebrews 10:19-20. Christian, it is faith that takes us there.

Listen. The revelation is broader and deeper than we had first thought, the exceeding greatness of his grace is longer and higher than anything we could hope. To eat the flesh of Jesus Christ and to drink his blood by faith is to have holy communion with GOD right there at the mercy seat above the ark of the covenant.

❋

*"And there I will meet with thee, and I will commune
with thee from above the mercy seat, from between
the two cherubims which are upon the ark of the
testimony, of all things which I will give thee in
commandment unto the children of Israel"*
EXODUS 25:22

﹡

Children, this is an expanse as far as the eye can see encompassing horizon unto horizon; the heritage, and the appointed place of a child of GOD in the bosom of his heavenly Father. It does not get any closer than this. This is unbridled reconciliation, an immeasurable mercy. This is meat and drink, indeed.

And there I will meet with thee, says GOD. There from above the mercy seat upon the ark of the covenant, I will meet you there in Jesus Christ, says the Father. Children, this (only) is the holy communion with GOD that makes me a Christian.

The infinite wisdom of GOD can bear the necessity its own redundancy, until we have ears to hear. *"And there I will meet with thee, says GOD, and from above the mercy seat, I will commune with thee"* (re. Ex. 25:22). Here is the revelation of the true LORD's Supper, and as we can receive it, here is where the kingdom of GOD is being realized within us. Here the body of the LORD Jesus Christ is broken for the believer as bread, and his blood is shed as the wine of the new covenant.

All my consolations and all my remembrances are here upon the mercy seat where the blood of Jesus Christ is effectual and perpetual and realized by faith. Here I meet with a Holy GOD: within the veil of the torn flesh of the Son of GOD, and where his blood is applied to the mercy seat. This is the secret place of the Most High (and as I can receive it), my habitation by faith. This is where I dwell in GOD, and where GOD dwells in me (re. John 6:56).

This is where all the promises of GOD are mine in Christ Jesus and where I am made a habitation of GOD through the Spirit. (Here) I eat the flesh and drink the blood of the New Covenant by faith, (here) in the astute progressive revelation (and realization) of the kingdom of GOD within me. Children, this is the most holy place on earth. This is the temple of GOD. We pass through the cross of Jesus Christ to get here. It can even be said we dwell there.

※

*"For thus saith the high and lofty One that inhabiteth
eternity, whose name is Holy: I dwell in the high
and holy place, with him also that is of a contrite
and humble spirit, to revive the spirit of the humble,
and to revive the heart of the contrite ones"*
ISAIAH 57:15

※

This is concisely the true penitent's radical reconciliation to GOD by the repentance and remission of sin. When I own my poverty of spirit, and am sorry for my sin, I can be sure that the kingdom of GOD is nigh.

Dear children, to abide in the LORD's presence we must prepare him a habitation. And, in turn, his presence shall make it a holy place. What must we do? *"Behold, I stand at the door, and knock: if any man (or woman) hear my voice, and open the door, I will come in to him, and will sup with him, and he with me"* (Rev. 3:20).

This is that bread which came down from heaven, even at the door. The altar of GOD is the penitent sinner's earnest heart. And there I will meet with thee, says GOD, and I will commune with thee from above the mercy seat (re. Ex. 25:22).

This is from where the miracle ensues, and the multiplication of loaves and fishes all the time, the perpetuation of the kingdom of GOD from the renewed mind and regenerated heart and converted souls of the sons and daughters of GOD. Christian, it is from a place of power that the witness of GOD arises, from the realization and the apprehension by faith of the kingdom of GOD within you.

Children, from where the body of the Savior of the world is broken, and from where his blood of the new covenant is applied, the hope of humanity emerges by the word of your testimony. Christian, you house treasure in an earthen vessel, and host the excellency and expediency of the power of Almighty GOD. Loose him upon the sphere of your influence and into the circumstances you occupy.

You are called to disseminate the Bread of Life within the orbit of GOD's interests in your neighborhood as you labor for this meat which endures unto everlasting life. Christian, you are confederate with the miracle now, you are the dwelling place of the Most High, and he is likewise your habitation through the Spirit.

✳

"LORD, thou hast been our dwelling place in all generations"
Psalm 90:1

✳

It is by faith that the Christian hosts the very presence of GOD, and by faith that we perpetuate the promises of GOD in Christ. We are called (every one of us) to be disciples of the LORD Jesus Christ, to bear witness of the excellency of his presence, and to wield his power in the evangelical outreach of the love of GOD. It is Jesus Christ the LORD who places the Christian disciple's mutual dwelling together with himself into the proper context.

✳

"If ye abide in me, and my words abide in you, ye shall ask what ye will, and it shall be done unto you"
John 15:7

✳

This is a sweeping inexhaustible promise, conditionally dependent upon our dwelling in GOD by faith, and by his Holy Spirit dwelling in us. This is an entirely different chapter on Jesus Christ as the true vine, but for now may it suffice to say that the indwelling Spirit of GOD looks to the interests and purposes of GOD. He has holy, heavenly expectations.

Our dwelling in Jesus Christ by faith in his broken body and shed blood (or, that is) our *eating his flesh and drinking his blood* is the effectual catalyst for the excellency of his power through the Holy Spirit. Children, whom we host (what we are freely given) we may likewise freely give to whomsoever is willing.

We effectually host the Eucharist of Christ, the bread and the wine (the flesh and the blood) of Jesus Christ. By faith we may share the sacrifice (the sacrament, the LORD's Supper, if you will) of Jesus Christ through our witness. The salvation of GOD in the LORD Jesus Christ by faith is a dynamic, enterprising phenomenon.

Let us freely give what we have freely received (see Matt. 10:8). The kingdom of GOD needs faith on the front line of the fighting. Uh, we already have enough Christians sustaining the status quo. I will have to liken them to our fathers who ate manna in the wilderness, and uh . . . well, they are dead.

Here then is the compelling dynamic (n.) of the LORD's salvation:

*

"As the living Father hath sent me, and I live by the Father: so he that eateth me, even he shall live by me"
JOHN 6:57

*

Frankly, some of us got saved, as it were, and then seemingly stopped eating. Or we are eating the same old stale bread over and over or ordering off the same old static menu of just a few prescribed dishes. As I have written (over and over), sometimes it seems that the congregation and the preacher have silently colluded on what we will eat, and what we will not. As if GOD did not have an endless, unlimited menu of the living Bread of Life in Jesus Christ.

Once more, it is the austerity and the self-denial of the cross of Jesus Christ which gives us pause. We must make that cross indelibly our own to come this way. The strictures of a strait gate and a narrow way preclude the lust of the flesh and the love of the world and the pride of life.

This is the bread which came down from heaven, and it is concisely the way of an old rugged cross. It is not all grace and gravy; it is also living in the light and the truth and the accountability of the shed blood and broken body of Jesus Christ. Succinctly said, sin must die in the flesh. Many of us cannot or will not eat this. Or, in other words:

"This is an hard saying, who can hear it?" (John 6:60).

We shall come this way, or we will not be saved. It is the way of the old rugged cross and death to the body of sin.

"Doth this offend you?" (John 6:60)

Jesus hears our murmuring remonstrance and sees our procrastination and avoidance. We like grace and sunny days, but the truth oftentimes comes with clouds and with hard and dark sayings.

It takes faith to make the Word of GOD manifest, and it is no casual endeavor. Emphatically, this is not light bread or leisure dining.

The Word of GOD does not reveal its secrets and treasures to the indifferent or the demanding, to the persnickety or the passionless, and does not indulge the particular or the petulant.

This is that eternal bread which came down from heaven for the life and soul of the world, and not to cater to earthly, transient, dainty appetites. The self-indulgent go away sorrowful.

✳

"It is the Spirit that quickeneth, the flesh profiteth nothing: the words that I speak unto you, they are Spirit, and they are life"
JOHN 6:63

✳

(Broadly), we still want the fruit that Adam and Eve lusted for in their pursuit of forbidden knowledge and self-realization. We predominantly still strive to change the truth of GOD into a lie, and society progressively worships and serves the creature more than the Creator (see Rom. 1:25).

Alas, but a genuine faith will not capitulate to the subterfuge and deception or bow to the religious forms that endeavor to supplant the commands of sanctification and holiness of true Christian living. Neither the Word of GOD nor the power of GOD will substantiate the loaves and fishes of religious ceremony without the miraculous transformation of our being radically born again.

Many of us either emulate forward momentum by forms of faith or we go away sorrowful. And the few of us find that strait gate and narrow way of genuine faith that leads unto everlasting life. This is GOD's ratio. These are the mathematics of the Holy One of God, the LORD Jesus Christ.

Children, this is the revelation of that bread which came down from heaven. Concisely, Jesus Christ has come into the world to radically change the diet of humanity.

The Word of GOD offends the flesh and was unapologetically intended to do so. Christian, it is the original sin of a willful, obdurate insurrectionist attitude that takes offense at the Word of GOD. It is a lying spirit that takes offense at the truth.

The startling reality of the revelation for some of us is that when we do not get what we want (when we want it), we go back and walk no more with him (see John 6:66). And then there is a broad element of contemporary Christianity which presumes to have their cake (or bread), and eat it, too. This is the way (let us say) of disingenuous all-permissive grace.

Jesus frankly said in John 6:64, "But there are some of you that believe not." Without having to reference it, we know that Jesus chose twelve, and one of them was a devil. In fact, even at what we call the LORD's Supper, the hand of his betrayer was upon the table with his own.

Notably, the LORD Jesus directly and specifically asks even his twelve most intrepid disciples, "Will ye also go away?" (re. John 6:67)

This particular Bible study concludes at an especially arduous time for me personally; in a season (I might add) wherein the diet is particularly austere, and the cup decidedly bitter. But even in the eye of the tempest, it is a great and unassailable joy to be able to say along with the apostle Peter, "*LORD, to whom shall we go? thou hast the words of eternal life?*" re. John 6:68

Dear Christian, the asperity and rigidity of the diet is for the true disciples of Jesus Christ. This is the fellowship of genuine faith and the suffering association of the Son of man, both the travail and the satisfaction of his own soul. As you are partaker of the cross of Jesus Christ, you are partaker of his resurrection, also. Selah.

April 9, 2020

RDB

2

I AM the Light of the World

"Then spake Jesus unto them, saying, I AM the Light of the World: he that followeth me shall not walk in darkness, but shall have the light of life"

–JOHN 8:12.

THE FIRST ORDER OF BUSINESS this morning is to confess my feelings of absolute inadequacy to the task of this exposition. Yet, with the admission of my ineptitude, I have made a beginning.

When the desires of my heart were discovered to be a writer, and specifically to write about the beauty and marvels of Almighty GOD in his Christ as revealed to me by the Holy Spirit (whom God is), the monumental fact that I did not know the first thing about writing was not an immediate consideration. Frankly, when all is said and done (as they say), whether in writing, or any other endeavor, it is GOD who has promised to give the desires of the heart to them who delight themselves in him (see Psalm 37:4).

Part and parcel of my progressive delight in the LORD is a healthy (and sometimes frightful) burgeoning trust in the Word of GOD. Christian, I do not know about your faith, but my faith develops in the episodic dynamic (oftentimes dreadful) seasons of my interminable wrestling in the midnight of my soul. Uh, I believe the Word of GOD as a little child, but I wrestle like a grown man.

As you know, there are seven distinct *I AM* statements made by the LORD Jesus Christ in the gospel as recorded by John. That is, seven specific independent times Jesus Christ definitively and unequivocally expresses his deity as GOD, as the self-existing One. It is my intent, as led by GOD, that these seven statements or scriptures comprise this manuscript naturally titled *I AM.*

As unorthodox as this is, it appears that I am interjecting a mini introduction to the entire book at what is essentially the beginning of chapter two. These seven statements that the LORD Jesus Christ makes could not have been uttered by anyone other than GOD. The introduction and comprehensive meaning and exposition of the infinite expression *I AM* is more than enough to constitute a second book. In fact, I am led of GOD that there be a second book following this one that describes in detail (by the Word of GOD) the conversation between GOD and Moses in Exodus 3:14 when GOD unequivocally tells Moses that his name is *I AM*.

It is my hope (yea) and my intention (as moved and led by GOD) that the second book substantiate and solidify the unassailable deity of the LORD Jesus Christ. It is my earnest resolution (to do my part) to contradict and countermand the noxious trend of this world system insinuating itself into the hierarchy of Christianity with the lethal intent of undermining and denying the deity of the LORD Jesus Christ.

Here in the liberty of the LORD's presence as by the Spirit of the resurrected Christ, I press into my appointed place. My portion this day shall feel the violence of my faith as I take all that has been promised me. In my pursuit of the knowledge and wisdom of GOD, I am the consternation and dread of devils, the angst and disquiet of the status quo. Darkness rightly flees my coming in Christ, contrary circumstances accede to my footsteps. Without excuse or expiation, this is matter of fact, all glory and honor to greater grace and everlasting mercy.

This is the frontline fighting of the unseen, and the next revelation of GOD. I have come to expect nothing less. It is GOD who directs me to John the beloved elder.

✳

*"This then is the message which we have heard
of him, and declare unto you, that GOD is
Light, and in him is no darkness at all"*
1 John 1:5

✳

As in the beginning, light is contrasted with darkness, but here in the first epistle of John we have the benefit of hindsight, let us say.

First, all things are relative to GOD's Omnipotence, Omniscience, and Omnipresence. Regardless the finite variables and the disputations of wise men, GOD created the heavens and the earth (re. Gen. 1:1). This is GOD's world after all.

All things evolve in the fist of the good pleasure and sovereignty of GOD. I give thanks for the grace and truth by which Jesus Christ came to declare unto us the name (the character and essence) of GOD. Relative to our manuscript, seven distinct times the LORD Jesus Christ said, *I AM.* Notwithstanding the absolute of these infinite utterances, the preponderance of us did not hear him.

Let us establish something. That is, let me make a definitive statement of the progressive (perpetual) dynamic revelation of the nature of GOD I am afforded by grace. GOD is *Love.* GOD is *Light.* GOD is *Truth.* GOD is a *Spirit* (re. John 4:24). GOD is a *Holy* Spirit. I call GOD, *Father.* I call GOD, *Jesus.* I call GOD, *Holy Spirit.*

These concise statements bring me to the *name* of GOD, and another rolling developing awe and wonder in the inexhaustible revelation of GOD. This is for me, and not for debate. I go to the source.

✳

*"And I will proclaim the name of the LORD before
thee: and will be gracious to whom I will be gracious,
and will shew mercy on whom I will shew mercy"*
Ex. 33:19

✳

Of course, we must keep in mind that GOD had already told Moses, *I AM THAT I AM.* – re. Ex. 3:14

Please bear with me. The point the Holy Spirit moves me to make (and all of this of a necessity is abbreviated) is that we cannot forget Moses and the prophets or the law. Children, all the Old Testament GOD is incorporated into the *Grace* and *Truth* of the New Testament GOD. Think upon these things.

On Sinai, the LORD descended in a cloud to where the man Moses was, *and stood with him there, and proclaimed,* (uh, this is who GOD said his name was): *"The LORD, the LORD GOD, merciful and gracious, longsuffering, and abundant in goodness and truth"* (re. Ex. 34:6).

It is GOD who *proclaimed* these things. And the New Testament equivalent for *proclaimed* is *declared.*

✳

"No man hath seen GOD at any time; the only begotten Son, which is in the bosom of the Father, he hath declared him"
JOHN 1:18

✳

Duh. *"I AM," declares* Jesus. In fact, if we are listening, he *declares* it over and over.

As if the seven specific *I AM* statements which comprise this manuscript were not enough, Jesus definitively and unequivocally tells the Jews, *"I and my Father are One"* (John 10:30). Uh, this is indivisible and incontrovertible. This is what I call one of the absolutes of GOD. Here is another, *"He that hath seen me hath seen the Father"* (see John 14:9). Indeed, GOD might very well ask us, *Have I been so long time with you, and yet hast thou not known me, ______?* Just fill in the blank.

Just a couple more, and we'll get into our text. Still talking about the name (and nature) of GOD.

Neither is there salvation in any other: for there is *NONE OTHER NAME* under heaven given among men, whereby we must be saved, (Acts 4:12). GOD is Salvation.

The LORD Jesus had forgiven a man's sins as recorded in Luke 5:20, and the Pharisees (in verse 21) said, *Who can forgive sins, but God alone?* (And as my youngest daughter was fond of saying), Duh. That quickly they had answered their own question.

None can forgive sin or give life but GOD.

✳

"Verily, verily, I say unto you, The hour is coming, and now is, when the dead shall hear the Voice of the Son of GOD: and they that hear shall live. For as the Father hath life in himself: so hath he given to the Son to have life in himself"
JOHN 5:25-26

✳

The Father and the Son are One GOD by the Holy Spirit. Not to be deliberately crass, but GOD does not suffer from a dissociative disorder or a split personality. He is not a trinity of three Gods. He is One GOD of a triune nature or essence. He is not three personalities. He is in One mind and of One personality, and who can turn him (re. Job 23:13).

The Father does not act without the Son nor the Son without the Father. Moreover, they are of the same thoughts and attributes as only One can be. There is no explication or illustration of infinity that will satisfy the disquiet of a finite mind. GOD owes me no explanation; what I have is gleaned with grace and thanksgiving. In quietness and in submission I learn. That portion received with humility has the most hope of producing increase.

The name of GOD incorporates the comprehensive character of GOD. Once more, just as God told Moses, *"I AM THAT I AM."* Children, the name that GOD has given us whereby we must be saved is the name of Jesus. GOD sent his only begotten Son into the world to declare the comprehensive character and identity of GOD from the bosom of GOD (re. John 1:18).

Jesus Christ speaks for GOD. He is the Word of GOD made flesh. As I have written before (and remember, nothing we say or write is sufficient to describe infinity), but I have said that the Word of GOD is the substance of what GOD has to say, and that the Holy Spirit is his Voice. Or the Holy Spirit is the effective catalyst (the unction) who imparts the life and essence of the Word of GOD into my deadened, blunted, finite understanding. I must always resort to the source. GOD will give me understanding, or I shall not have it.

In the context of this manuscript, it is my prayer that we receive the exposition of these enigmatic *I AM* statements of the LORD Jesus Christ with (at least) the same comprehension as these (unregenerate) Jews in the eighth chapter of John grasped the significance of exactly what Jesus meant when he said, *"Before Abraham was, I AM"* (re. John 8:58). In fact, they understood him so well that they took up stones to cast at him, but Jesus (I believe miraculously) hid himself, and passed through the midst of them (see John 8:59).

We castigate these Jews as hypocrites and haters, and indeed they were. But the correlation with contemporary Christianity that I want to draw our attention to is that we, much like them, consider ourselves GOD's chosen people and religion's best. Uh, and so we are (relatively). But the point the Holy Spirit shows me, is that even with stones in their hands, they had a more (in depth) realistic understanding of Jesus Christ's innate claim to deity than we do as GOD's contemporary chosen people.

Perhaps the most piercing (and embarrassing) element of the revelation is that the Jews in the eighth chapter of John show more fervor for the things of GOD, and more interest in the definitive identity of Jesus Christ, than we do as GOD's elect. Their passion is undeniable; the stones in their hands prove it. Sadly, the preponderance of Christianity today dismiss the very idea of the deity of the LORD Jesus Christ without enough generic interest to even investigate the matter.

Our pernicious predicament is that our self-love and world-love preclude us from having an astute (practical, hands-on, working) revelation of the Almighty GOD in his Christ. If Jesus Christ were divine, we would have to stop and worship him. Relatively, we would have to drop everything else we are doing and give him the preeminence.

Let me use myself as an example, not to let you completely off the hook, but to palliate the austerity of the revelation in the hope that you will continue looking into the matter. My self-realization (self-love) is a bigger god than my (relative) faltering concept of the One True God.

The world could not care less, and the best of Christianity is volitionally blinded to our indifference. (Oh my, slipped into the plural tense that quickly.) Concisely, if we really believed, we would begin to take care of some eternal business. If our faith went beyond a religious form or ideal, we would absolutely forsake most temporal things.

If our belief in eternity went beyond an abstraction, that is, beyond a hypothesis, and past religious idealism and the putting on of airs, we would repent of the perfunctory presentation and get down to the real business of forsaking sin. Not so much behaviors, as engrained childhood prejudices and attitudes, inveterate unforgiveness and inbred bigotry. Both hereditary and learned evil.

Frankly, we do not care enough about Jesus Christ's claim to divinity to pick up stones, or our Bibles. The only stones we cast are the metaphorical ones we cast at our neighbor. Concisely, if we really believed, we would put down our stones, or begin to remove stones from the denominational, socio-economic and ethnic walls we have erected to separate us from other peoples made in the image of the same GOD we say we love and serve.

Merging these thoughts with our text, if we really believed that GOD is Light (and that in him is no darkness at all) we would never again conceal or entertain any hidden thing.

If my faith went beyond supposition (and things heard) unto the astute earth-shaking, heart-rending revelation of Jesus Christ as GOD, I would realize that all my righteousness is truly as filthy rags, and I would repent in dust and ashes. If I had even a dim apprehension and understanding that as the LORD Jesus Christ tasted death for every man, then (correlatively) the Father tasted it also, I would have the first inkling of an incomprehensible revelation of the necessity and reality of hell. We mustn't think or presume that Father GOD stood aloof and afar (or indifferent) from the austere and terrible matters of the redemption of mankind or separate from the agonies and strictures of the cruelty of the cross of his beloved Son.

In what I call the addendum to this book, for now an idea, I hope to address these enigmatic mysteries and wisdom of GOD Almighty in his Christ.

If I knew and esteemed that (GOD is Light), I would come out of the shadows of (what I will call) my residual humanity, and uh, my religious misdirection. Some of you follow. If the light of GOD penetrated to the depths of my hidden man, that is, if I completely submitted to the irrepressible (unsparing) searching of the Holy Spirit, I would finally release that little something-something I have laid up for the proverbial rainy day, and then love and serve GOD with all my heart, mind, soul and strength.

The revelation of GOD as Light ought to redefine the terms of my absolute surrender to the deity and Lordship of Jesus Christ every day of my life. The light and illumination (uh, the irradiation and unsparing revelation) of the One commandment of Love is light and truth sufficient to render me unto (and into) a state of perpetual repentance. To love GOD with all my heart, mind, soul and strength, and my neighbor as myself, ought to be enough light to keep me from meddling in sin or transacting in the shadows.

My religious misdirection is the guy you see on Sunday morning whom I hope is smiling sincerely enough to get your mind off who I am the rest of the week. Uh, he is effectively a guy nobody knows because he does not really exist. He is a guy I send in lieu of the reality. Oh my.

In GOD's reality, he is a superficial religious sacrifice (or service). Some of you know that I have often said that anything less than the whole animal is a token sacrifice. This is fundamental Christianity, the total exposure and absolute transparency of dwelling in the light and truth of GOD's Holy Word, the abiding unbroken fellowship of living in his presence.

The carnal man has a covert disingenuous conspiratorial, as aided and abetted by the prince of this world, unscrupulous, manipulative self-promoting agenda. The lust of the flesh and the pride of life require constant surveillance, humbling and abasement, mortification, death. My natural man must be made to come out of the shadows, deny himself, and take up his cross daily. The pride of my own life is the most cunning adversary in Satan's arsenal, the one closest to home, if you will, and most adept in the ways of darkness.

❋

"But if we walk in the light, as he is in the light, we have fellowship one with another, and the blood of Jesus Christ his Son cleanseth us from all sin"
1 JOHN 1:7

❋

John has already declared that the comprehensive gospel message is that GOD is light, and in him there is no darkness at all (re. 1 John 1:5). This is an uncompromising message, an unsparing exposure. There are no gray areas or shady places in a genuine Christianity, and no bargaining with sin.

I am aware that many of my acquaintances think me too severe. The subtlety of their ways of letting me know are tweaked precisely. Often, I am treated as *holier than thou*, if you will, as if I considered myself somehow spiritually superior. Ah, if they only knew that quite the opposite is true, that I have been in the past a rival of the Apostle Paul's for *chief of sinners*.

Such is my weakness that I must live near the cross. The mandate I have accepted is of greater grace, and the standard I represent is not mine. My grace answers with rectitude and integrity to GOD's truth, or it should not be long mine. It is of a grave personal necessity that I cry aloud, and spare not.

From personal experience (I will sadly speak). For decades I subsisted in the guilt and shadow of looming character flaws that Satan had convinced me were insurmountable. Depending upon my surreptitious ability to effectively keep them off the main radar, so to speak, I was reconciled to their existence. As it was, I initially had enough trouble stopping observable unacceptable (ungodly) behaviors. Ah, there may be the term I am looking for: Observable Christianity.

For decades, I lived a life of quiet Christian desperation in the light of acceptable outward deportment, but in the bondage and despotism of a dark internal disposition. My speech and behavior were adequate, but my mind and my heart were seething caldrons of dark thoughts and dangerous temperaments.

Without getting into a lengthy diatribe to describe the childhood physical and sexual abuse which shaped my character, I want to emphasize what a challenge to redemption I was. My intention is to magnify the LORD's grace and mercy. There is no delicate (or brief) way to describe the all-consuming internal self-hatred that insidiously extends to everything and everyone externally as well, for victims of childhood sexual abuse.

Note: I really did not want to go here. But while we are here, let me qualify something. I have no qualms about discussing these things, but they would comprise a lengthy manuscript of their own. GOD wants me to say (for now) that my experience with the darkness is conditional to my calling to write about the light. Moreover, it was the darkness, and the implicit despair of it, which GOD used to drive me to the light.

Notwithstanding all variables or the particulars of circumstance, I am a vessel of grace, and a servant of mercy.

Frankly, it was when my Christian affect and righteous charade became unmanageable that hope for me was born. The anguish and the despondency which drove me out of the darkness were allowed in the permissive will and hidden wisdom of Almighty GOD. Uh, if my hypocrisy had been sustainable, I would probably still be a bond slave to sin subsisting in the shadows, running in and out of the light of a superficial Christianity. (Now you know how I am so familiar with hypocrisy). My despair positioned me to receive the gift of godly sorrow that would work repentance in the darkest recesses of my soul, driving me unremittingly into the light.

Sadly, I had no concept of the kingdom of GOD within me. The general Christian philosophy that reached me addressed (essentially) external Christian conduct and common church comportment. The old-timers in the hills of West Virginia where I am from had a saying about Christian behavior. Living for the LORD equated to "I don't drink or smoke or chew or run with them that do." Many of us presume upon stopping a few aberrant (observable) behaviors and bad habits, and regular or fair-weather church attendance, in order to qualify calling ourselves Christians.

If we will hear what the Spirit of GOD is saying to Christians in 1 John 1:7, we will realize that where the blood of Jesus Christ is effectual to cleanse us from all sin is in the light, specifically as we walk in the light as he is in the light. There are no shady places there, no sleight of hand, no surreptitious sin. Only then, in the light of nothing hidden, can we have a productive fellowship with one another.

The Word of GOD is its own quintessential system of checks and balances if you will. The grace of GOD answers to the truth of GOD. Some of us seem to think that GOD will sign off on just about anything. You have heard me call it all-permissive grace. But this is an illusion aided and abetted by the god of this world system to get us to assume that things are well with our soul when they may not be.

The Word of GOD has expectations of all of us, and we are to live up to its commands.

✳

"But be ye doers of the Word, and not hearers
only, deceiving your own selves"
JAMES 1:22

✳

I call it putting the Word of GOD into practical application, and believe it was from Oswald Chambers that I first heard this expression. When I am sincere about living for GOD, there is a Holy Spirit who accompanies this Word to help me live up to its expectations.

GOD meets genuine purpose with great grace. When I meet the inherent expectations of the truth of GOD's Word, his Holy Spirit corroborates my efforts.

✳

And it is the Spirit that beareth witness,
because the Spirit is Truth
re. 1 JOHN 5:6

✳

My comprehensive profession of faith is examined beneath the percipient omniscient eye of the light and truth of the most Holy Word of GOD. Notwithstanding that many people treat the Word of GOD as a history tome or a dead document, it is the very essence and character of GOD and a living entity.

My claim to the blood of Jesus Christ and my assertion that I have fellowship with him is scrutinized and qualified in the astute (and unsparing) light and radiance of the very character of GOD. In fact, I will not effectually walk with GOD anywhere but in the full exposure of his Holy nature. This is not my standard, it is the prerequisite of the Light of the world, Jesus Christ.

The efficacy of the blood of Jesus Christ meets my repentance, my profession of faith, and my entire Christian presentation (and persona) in the full light of the Word of GOD. To have fellowship here, I must be true.

*

*"If we say we have fellowship with him, and walk
in darkness, we lie, and do not the truth"*
1 JOHN 1:6

*

Frankly, I have had to personally reevaluate my concept and understanding of light. The light of GOD's truth, the glory and radiance of his Holy nature, is an infinite unsearchable phenomenon. Only in the Word of GOD will we behold his glory.

As I have said, GOD meets the genuine penitent with greater grace for the illumination of the interminable layers of bad attitudes and prejudices common to the human species. Yes, I speak from personal experience, from a place of explicit unsparing unapologetic exposure, and with my psyche peeled back like the layers of a large onion.

But before moving on let me say this. Fellowship in the full light and truth of GOD's Word is where the power of the blood of Jesus Christ is unleashed. Children, it is here that day by day we receive the comprehensive unparalleled cleansing that gives uncommon confidence toward GOD.

Our fellowship must be where the blood of Jesus Christ is applied, in the light and glory of GOD's character and palpable presence. This is the Most Holy place.

I just used this following scripture in the last chapter, but this exemplifies our fellowship.

❋

"And there I will meet with thee, and I will commune with thee from above the mercy seat, from between the two cherubims which are upon the ark of the testimony, of all things which I will give thee in commandment unto the children of Israel"
Ex. 25:22

❋

Here is freedom from the accuser of the brethren, and from our own conscience. This is covenant fellowship. There is no hidden thing in the light of GOD's presence, and no liberty like being completely known and absolutely accepted into the beloved.

Dear children, this is the ideal fellowship of Christianity. It should go without saying that if the individual members took care of their business, then the whole body would be full of light. Some of you follow.

Christian, the Word of GOD saves to the uttermost, but it also searches to the uttermost. That is, it searches and exposes (and liberates!) to the same degree it is willingly received and thoroughly assimilated.

As I have forthrightly confessed and alluded to, the outward (observable) behaviors and language that the LORD (by the Word and by his Holy Spirit) instructed and assisted me in ceasing, were relatively easy to resolve when contrasted with my attempts to conform my thoughts and attitudes to the character of Jesus Christ. Frankly, since I did not know where to begin, I simply and candidly confessed my absolute ineptitude. This turned out to be a propitious beginning. Duh. An explicit honesty is a prerequisite of fellowshipping with Jesus Christ in the light. Honesty with my brother and my neighbor will follow and spontaneously evolve by the Spirit of the living Word of GOD.

Children, we know that love is the commandment, and that the light of the truth has now come by the grace of the LORD Jesus Christ. Illumination and understanding are available. The wisdom and power of GOD has appeared in (and by) the gospel of Jesus Christ and him crucified. The revelation of love is an old rugged cross.

The love of GOD is the standard by which my own sentiments and disposition are measured, as I can stand the irrepressible illumination of them, that is. Concisely, GOD's Word turns the lights on.

Let us put it as simplistic as we can. (The complexities arise out of the corresponding, startling revelation of ourselves in the light and truth of GOD's holy presence by the Spirit of his living Word). But the intrepid can make a beginning.

＊

"GOD is love; and he that dwelleth in love
dwelleth in GOD, and GOD in him"
re. 1 JOHN 4:16

＊

To live there (to dwell in the light and truth of GOD's love) examines my own love espousals to the uttermost. This is a holy (and a) terrible place of scrutiny and mastery. The perfections of Christ are laid against my soul here in this place of holy fire and unsparing illumination.

Here alone with my thoughts in the light and truth of the inscrutable revelation of myself, face to face with the reality of my superficial love and facile religious form, unbearably exposed and excruciatingly naked. The love of GOD is the olive press of a great King where the oil of anointing for service is taken and given, for them that can sustain the crushing that is. Children, the love of GOD turns the lights on.

＊

"For GOD, who commanded the light to shine out of darkness, hath shined in our hearts, to give the light of the knowledge of the glory of GOD in the face of Jesus Christ"
2 Cor. 4:6

✳

But can I allow the image to take hold and prosper? Can I bravely allow the spark access and proximity to the wood, hay, and stubble of my perfunctory structured and circumscribed Christian love? You know, can I allow the true ember of the incendiary love of GOD intimacy (juxtaposition) and well, unimpeded access to the desiccated and dehydrated veneer of my religious ensemble and dry self-righteous regalia? Why, the unfiltered and unattenuated revelation of the glory and brilliance of GOD's love would render my paper Christian affections into an immediate spontaneous combustion, and all that would be left of my religious affect would be scattered ash and a quickly dissipating vapor.

The light and truth of the Holy love whom GOD is, came into the world by the grace of Jesus Christ. By the eternal mercies of the Father in the magnitude of his love, he gave his only begotten Son to redeem mankind from the curse of the law through sin, by the grace and truth of Jesus Christ.

Either I dwell in the love of GOD (which is in Jesus Christ), and the love of GOD dwells in me (by Jesus Christ), or I have no effectual life in me.

Jesus Christ is the light of the world by which the knowledge that (GOD is love) came. Jesus Christ is the continuing revelation of the perpetually unfolding prophetic Word of GOD. (Please pardon the seeming redundancy of this statement).

By the incremental, irrepressible, progressive grace and truth of Jesus Christ, I am brought into the light and knowledge (the revelation) of the glory of GOD's love. Without this love, the faith I need to be saved will not work. (All these things work together, but the Holy Spirit is introducing the elements of saving faith).

Without true love, a genuine faith will neither labor nor manifest. Without love, faith is the broken cistern of religious form. Without love, I must feign the forward momentum of faith from a static platform. The power of GOD will not substantiate (sign off on) a faith without love.

✳

*"He that saith he is in the light, and hateth his
brother, is in darkness even until now"*
1 JOHN 2:9

✳

I may say that the "light" of the knowledge of the glory of GOD in the face of Jesus Christ has reached my heart to divide the darkness (re. 2 Cor. 4:6); I may be quite vocal and demonstrative about my faith, and even ostentatious in religious dress and presentation, but without love my faith is a hollow form and the fraudulent whited face of a sepulcher full of dead men's bones. I may know all the righteous terminology (and buzz words of contemporary Christianity), and still just be another religious reproduction. I may look good on paper, but without the light of GOD's love as its foundation, my faith is a one-dimensional facsimile.

Children, a genuine faith abides in a full light, and both the faith and the light share the imperative and prerequisite of a true agape love (GOD's love).

✳

"He that loveth his brother abideth in the light, and there is none occasion of stumbling in him"
1 JOHN 2:10

✳

This unabating full disclosure is to be my dwelling place. There is no volitional delusion of just a little darkness entertained here, no secrets from God and no hidden sin, no sleight of hand or surreptitious shady business transacted here.

The love of GOD abides in the integrity of the light of GOD. Indeed. There is no self-delusion here. There is no "setting myself up" for an occasion of sin here in the Holy place of GOD's love. Some of you follow. I have written before (and I will leave it in a plural tense), that some of us seem to enjoy being overcome on a periodic (but regular) basis. We would live on the edge of the light, if there were such a place, so that we could make occasional excursions into the shadows.

My Christian love is (being) perfected in the full light and integrity of GOD's abiding presence, of whom Jesus Christ is the epicenter by the Holy Ghost. It is Jesus Christ, the Word of GOD, who incorporates my Christian love for GOD and my love for my neighbor (and my brother) (and my enemy) into the One comprehensive commandment of love.

The internal abiding Christ and indwelling Holy Ghost of GOD is the light and truth and integrity of my Christian testimony of love. And where the love of GOD abides it will unmistakably manifest.

Children, I must live in GOD to have GOD living in me. The repetition is warranted. None but GOD can show me GOD and give me GOD. I must go to the source, as I am wont to say. This is the simplicity *and* the profundity of Christ.

✳

"And we have known and believed the love that
GOD hath to us. God is Love, and he that dwelleth
in love dwelleth in God, and God in him"
1 John 4:16

✳

This is the revelation of Jesus Christ, and the light of GOD's love shined into our hearts, that the light of the commandment shines beyond the Christianity of our own heart, past our own confederated religious collaborators and our prescribed elitist denominational sect and extends to *Everyman* and *Everywoman*.

The light and truth of GOD's love is the brilliance and radiance of his glory and the essence of his character extended even unto the worst of humanity.

The parameters of his grace must have full disclosure.

Christian, the selective qualifying (elitist) nature of our denominational sectarian love attenuates (weakens) our own revelation of GOD, dims the ambient light in the sanctuary of our corporate and individual soul, as it were, where the testimony (ark) of our own covenant relationship dwells.

To pompously and presumptuously adjudicate all other denominations (and by extension all other religions and peoples) in doctrinal error, is to cast them outside the light of GOD's grace and love. The unsparing brilliance and glory in the full light of GOD's love is to have a world view. The same GOD that brings them in is the same Spirit of Truth who is able and willing to teach them all things. My purview is to love them in Christ. This is to have the mind of Christ, and the meaning of true Christianity.

GOD is seeking children and we want proselytes to our own persuasion. We want *"yes men"* to our own agenda, more weight to our denominational argument.

Jesus Christ has redeemed us unto GOD by his own blood out of every kindred, and tongue, and people, and nation (see Rev. 5:9).

Broadly, it is learned childhood prejudices that transmogrify into grown-up ethnic discrimination and religious bigotry. And then we perpetuate the species. This may be unspecified, and not adequately defined or politely expressed, but its point is made.

We may boast of the knowledge and enlightenment of our prescribed religion, but the true light of our revelation of GOD is only as radiant as the level of our love. The veil upon my heart is the same one over my eyes.

✳

"Herein is our love made perfect, that we may have boldness in the day of judgment: because as he is, so are we in this world"
1 JOHN 5:17

✳

The worship of GOD in spirit and in truth first emanates from the Christian heart. The children of GOD run in the joy and liberty of the Spirit of their Father. The temple made with hands is the sanctuary for religious elitism, most often only one denomination may worship there. The love of GOD walks openly (and unfettered) in the light; see the children run.

The love of GOD lives and proliferates in the unfiltered light of GOD, meaning the light is most radiant where love is best demonstrated. And the exemplar and unprecedented epitome of manifest love is the cross of Jesus Christ and him crucified. Notably, this is where darkness has its most definitive hour, where the love of God meets the sin of mankind. I must stand naked and exposed in its revelation.

This is the fertile ground of Christian fellowship and unfeigned faith. The freedom of nothing hidden is true religion. How is it that we have not known it?

Item. The coronavirus has shown us how small the world really is, and how insignificant our prejudices. The love of GOD still has a world vision. (March 25, 2020, rdb)

If I would have my Christian love cast no shadow, I must walk without respect to persons.

To walk steadfastly in the light of indiscriminate love promotes the perfecting of my faith, the casting out of fear and condemnation, the facilitation of answered prayer. We speak in the context of all things being relative to the love of GOD, and Jesus Christ, *The Light of the World.*

※

"The light of the body is the eye: if therefore thine eye be single, thy whole body shall be full of light"
MATT. 6:22

※

Jesus Christ is speaking of a sanctified, consecrated, unpolluted purpose. It must be put into the context of what I call John the Beloved's *short list* of the enemies of the light, and correspondingly the preeminent enemies of our soul and fundamental foes of a productive faith. That is, the lust of the flesh, and the lust of the eyes, and the pride of life. (see 1 John 2:16)

Keep in mind that this is John's short list of *all that is in the world,* and by contrast not of the Father. If we will pray and meditate upon the previous verse (vs. 15), and if we are brave enough and honest enough to embrace the revelation of it, the Holy Spirit is earnest to show us where we are at (individually) upon what I call the continuum of being radically born again. *We will be found somewhere between the antagonists (polar opposites) of the love of the world and the love of the Father.*

Concisely, the love of the Father is his Son, Jesus Christ. This is how the Holy Spirit by James can unapologetically (and radically) call anyone that is a friend of the world the enemy of God, (see James 4:4). Children, on our way to being militantly set free unto GOD in Christ, the Holy Spirit wants to show us that the prince of this present world system is the same god of this world (Satan) who collaborated with spiritual wickedness in high places, both governmental and institutional religious places, to crucify the only begotten Son of GOD. To spare you several pages rant, I will put it succinctly and bluntly. Some of us, or many of us, are somewhere between calling ourselves Christian, and being in the open hostility and unfettered fornication of an illicit love affair with the enemy of the Father of Jesus Christ.

To have a single eye speaks to the clarity and purity of my purpose in Christ – my life purpose, my eternal life purpose. GOD loves the world, but GOD loves the world in Jesus Christ. GOD wants me radically and comprehensively assimilated into his love for the world as expressed in the gospel of Jesus Christ and him crucified. In fact, he would have my love for him (for GOD), and my love for myself and for my neighbor, seamlessly coalesced into the One commandment of Love. As we have been talking about, this is the unsparing light of an uncompromising revelation.

Concisely, how bright is my purpose, how unsullied is my flame? Or conversely, how compromised or attenuated is my oil by the lust of the flesh and love of the world and the things of the world? Oh my, now we are getting real. We might just as well get the rest of it into the light. How far, or to what degree, has the love of the world and the pride of my life crept into my Christian affect and presentation? You know, into the general mission statement of my Christianity?

It is the purest oil which burns the hottest and the brightest, and uh, which gives off the least fumes. To live unsullied in the midst of a corrupt society and untoward (contaminated) circumstance is an intricate undertaking and a delicate balance, namely, to be in the world, but not of the world. Here I will honesty and openly admit to aspiring to be that Christian whom GOD can prosper but whom mammon (money) does not corrupt. We will see how well I funnel GOD's resources back into his kingdom.

Children, we cannot effectively advance the kingdom of GOD from a platform where the world, and our love for the world, still owns a controlling interest in us.

The most effective witness for Jesus Christ is him or her whom has no fear of their worldly goods and services being threatened or diminished due to the world's displeasure of their testimony of Jesus Christ.

It takes light to divide the darkness.

Frankly, them that have best apprehended the LORD's admonition to watch and pray will be the very same ones, the same soldiers, whom can be seen to overcome this world's temptations to speak boldly in the name of Jesus Christ from an uncompromised, unsullied platform of sanctification and godly living.

The disciple of Jesus Christ with a single eye to service is not easily distracted or indicted. When I have no self-interests, it is difficult for the enemy to get me off task. The name of Jesus Christ is an impenetrable tower. When there is nothing I want or need, my stewardship is unimpeachable. It is the love of GOD in Jesus Christ that sets us free to live in the light. There is no liberty quite like the complete transparency of having one purpose.

My capitulation to the Word of GOD and my willingness to have my love perfected brings me out of hiding. What it means to me to have a single eye is to have a mission statement that is above reproach, a pure motivation for doing things. It is then (Jesus says) that our whole body shall be full of light (re. Matt. 6:22)

This is, as it were, the same place that brotherly love dwells, and this place of transparency where there is no occasion (or circumstances which contribute) to stumbling in us (re. 1 John 2:9). This is the whole man and the whole body full of light, one Christian at a time. This speaks to unity as a reflection of my love for GOD and my love for my neighbor being incorporated into the One commandment of Love.

Before moving on, it behooves us to reflect upon the next verse of the LORD's teaching that contrasts the light with the darkness, and the single eye with (what Jesus says) is an evil eye. The Holy Spirit emphasizes (to me) that this evil eye is synonymous with a skewed or contaminated motivation.

✳

*"But if thine eye be evil, thy whole body shall be full
of darkness. If therefore the light that is in thee
be darkness, how great is that darkness!"*
MATT. 6:23

✳

Interestingly, before Jesus spoke these two scriptures as recorded here by Matthew about a single eye and an evil eye, he was teaching about earthly treasure and heavenly treasure, culminating in the statement, *"For where your treasure is, there will your heart be also"* (Matt. 6:21).

Concisely, the light and truth of the Word of GOD reveals whether my perspective (and my love) is earthly or heavenly, temporal or eternal. That is, if I will capitulate to the revelation. (If) I really want to know, the light and truth of GOD's Word will examine my altruism to the uttermost, and uh, reveal the narcissism and self-seeking lurking beneath the veneer of my religious service. You know. Sometimes I just want to feel better about myself. Sometimes I just want to be a bigger Christian than Brother Bob.

But are we hearing what Jesus is really saying? Frankly, if our motivation is markedly skewed in our own favor, and our own self interests are the driving catalyst of our Christian service, then there is a gaping hole in the testimony of our love. A wrong reason can summarily render our whole body full of darkness.

GOD will not countenance my introducing shady business into the light. Verse twenty-three contains one of those (seeming) incongruities that I used to quickly pass over. How can the light that is in me be darkness? Well, if my motivation is something other than I have represented it to be, then I have just presumed upon GOD's character by having the effrontery to come into the light with a hidden thing. If my intent (that is, my eye) is not pure, the Word of GOD declares that my whole body (or my entire representation) is full of darkness.

(I take) an evil eye to also mean guile and duplicity, or shrewdly evaluating a situation in hope of manipulating the elements (or persons) to my advantage. An evil eye assesses a situation for temporal gain (or earthly treasure) rather than appraise it with an eternal, discriminating eye for potential to advance the kingdom of GOD. To be untrue to the light of GOD's Word is hypocrisy, and there is no shady place to escape its revelation.

Alas, we defraud and exploit and misrepresent. It is really another clear indication of our innate pathology and the exceeding sinfulness of sin – our pernicious predisposition to hide from GOD. Christian, to have a hidden agenda is hypocrisy. And how great is that darkness!

We are congenitally inclined to hide among the trees of the garden from the presence of GOD. When GOD called unto Adam, "*Where art thou?*" well, he already knew where Adam was at. He wanted Adam to self-evaluate. Uh, in other words, "Look at yourself." Let us all stop a moment and assess the subsequent and consequent reality of not listening to the Voice of the Word of GOD: sin and death enter into our private world, and into the equation of our individual circumstances.

Let us return to our main theme and place all these things into the immediate and efficacious context of the LORD Jesus Christ being *The Light of the World*. Let us reboot.

First, GOD has always been, and he has always been light. It was the earth that was dark and without form, and void, or empty.

Some years ago now, as I was studying the Genesis of creation, the Holy Spirit showed me that as the Spirit of GOD moved upon the face of the deep, GOD was contemplating the darkness which was upon the face of the earth intently and specifically. Some interpretations say that the Spirit of

GOD was *hovering* upon the face of the deep (re. Gen. 1:2). It was Oswald Chambers who wrote that GOD was *brooding* upon the face of the deep. This gave me a visual, as it were.

The Word of GOD and the meditations of Oswald Chambers, and my own *brooding* and pondering, moved me to write in another volume that GOD's own brooding considerations of the darkness that was upon the face of the earth moved him to conclude it unacceptable to his innate light and holy character, and he spontaneously uttered, *"Let there be Light."* (Gen. 1:3)

To me, all things culminate in the deity of the LORD Jesus Christ, for so it has pleased Father GOD. Moreover, it is what the argument is all about.

※

"In the beginning was the Word, and the Word
was with GOD, and the Word was GOD"
JOHN 1:1

※

Where else could (*the Word of*) GOD have been in the beginning but with GOD. That is a statement, not a question. It is not my intention to be facetious, it is my desire to keep things simple.

That GOD spoke in the beginning (our beginning) is simply further proof that Jesus Christ, as the Voice and Word of GOD, was there. I say that Jesus Christ is the Voice and Word of GOD because:

※

"No man hath seen God at any time, the only begotten Son, which is in the bosom of the Father, he hath Declared him"
JOHN 1:18

✳

This is more of John, by the way, whom I have concluded that by revelation and personal intimacy knew the most among men about the character and essence of GOD. And the most about heaven (and GOD's throne) as well. Christian, it is no coincidence that the chapters of this manuscript, these *I AM* statements, are found in the gospel according to John. It is my intent to magnify the LORD Jesus Christ.

Sometimes I go so far as to say that the Word of GOD (Jesus Christ) is the substance of what GOD has to say, and that the Holy Spirit gives it utterance.

It is never my design to be either deliberately flippant or argumentative. It is my desire to keep things simple and to trust GOD, to radically believe all that GOD (the Word of GOD) has to say about himself.

✳

"Jesus Christ the same yesterday, and today, and forever"
HEB. 13:8

✳

The dispute, and the dissension and the discord, is ultimately about the deity of the LORD Jesus Christ: spiritual wickedness and evil having been introduced into high religious places. Yes, I am talking about the Church, we already know the world continues to deny him and spit upon him. Dear child of GOD, the enemy (Satan) knows that if he can diminish the deity of the LORD Jesus Christ in your mind, that he can then insert doubt and fear into the breach he has created.

He does not want you to have an Almighty Savior. He does not want you to know that you have the power to cast him out of your mind and out of your life. He does not want you to apprehend and assimilate the revelation that the same GOD that created you is the same GOD that saves you, that your High Priest knows and empathizes with you extending to every grain of sand (as it were) which constitutes your comprehensive being.

Satan, having insinuated himself and sold himself into the minds of the religious hierarchy of our wisest men, would cite times and seasons and dispensations to divide him who is eternal and allow you one-third of GOD at any given time, perhaps two-thirds on occasion, and rare glimpses of the three-thirds of GOD as glimpsed by the patriarchs and holy men of old, but nothing you and I could hope to have in the everyday crisis of our human condition. That is a Christian nirvana called heaven at the end of structured religious hoops and decades of compulsory ceremony and the outward observation of doctrinal and denominational bondage.

Children, that is some man telling you who GOD is. I know that is going to leave a bruise, as they say, but I was weary with forbearing, as Jeremiah expressed it, and I could not stay (re. Jer. 20:9). Frankly, if I would fast and pray and seek GOD's face as he suggested (or commanded actually), I would fall in love with my own Bible and GOD would tell me and show me who he is all by himself. Ahem, why would I prefer the religious codependency of sound bites and specified rations and the compartmentalized dribble of talking heads and tedious ceremony, when GOD concisely and extraordinarily and radically wants to set me free?

✳

*"Fear not, little flock, for it is your Father's
good pleasure to give you the kingdom"*
Luke 12:32

✳

Illumination, and revelation, has always been available. To have another man or another woman, whether counsellor, doctor, lawyer or preacher, or all of the above, tell me who GOD is and who he is not (is) not enlightenment. It is lazy. Uh, it is concisely what my dad and the old-timers up the hollow used to call *trifling.*

Not to care enough about eternity to assess the matter for myself is to be lost.

(If you are with me), not to care enough about my soul to inquire into (and secure) the matter to own my satisfaction is to be in a pronounced state of unbelief.

Not to (necessarily) be cynical, but to just go ahead and be graphic, and to get butt-naked unsparingly honest, some of us pay significant sums (sometimes called tithes and offerings) and extortion payments to persuade some preacher to tell us not only who GOD is, but also how wonderfully saved we are.

GOD wants to personally and intimately share his identity with me, to tell me the exhilarating and miraculous secrets and mysteries of his mind. In fact, he wants to take me in, and not only make me an integral part of his master plan, but to also integrate me into his very *person* and make me One with him in Christ Jesus his Son by the Holy Spirit.

What is to be said of me if I prefer a religious form to a life of faith, just to (fundamentally) save my temporal life for myself? What can be concluded of me if I would rather be told who GOD is rather than get to know him for myself?

Faith is on the front line finding out. Apathy and indifference are essentially the state of a chronic perpetual choice and a concise evidence of unbelief. Frankly, much of organized religious ceremony is the illusion and misconception of covering my bases just in case there really is a hell. There is very little of the spontaneity of a little child's worship (in spirit and in truth) inherent in a formal grownup posturing presentation.

Children, when the light comes on, as it were, having someone else tell me who GOD is will no longer suffice, or silence the nagging insecurity of my soul.

GOD is a GOD of increase: of measures, of times and of seasons, of sowing and of reaping. You have heard me say that faith is the dynamic of the LORD's salvation, and I have called it the coin of my exchange in my fellowship with GOD. By believing GOD's Word, I grow in the grace and knowledge of GOD.

✳

"For therein is the righteousness of GOD revealed from faith to faith: as it is written, The just shall live by faith"
Rom. 1:17

✳

GOD will not judge me (reward me, evaluate me) according to the enlightenment of his righteousness I have, but according to the enlightenment I could have had, but would not have.

Father GOD is a Spirit seeking true worshippers. Jesus Christ said so (see John 4:23-24). Children, faith is the enterprising passionate dynamic of the LORD's salvation by which I come to GOD in gratitude and worship. In perpetual awe and wonder, I walk faith to faith into the exhilarating miraculous depths of the living GOD. As Pastor Alph Lukau, of Alleluia Ministries International in Johannesburg, South Africa is fond of saying, "There are levels and levels."

Broadly (and tragically) in America, it appears that our religion has gradually but persistently transmogrified into an organized (or structured) system of maintaining the body of knowledge we already have. That is, we maintain what was handed down to us by our fathers and elders in a religious sense. Or, to put it more accurately, we try to sustain and perpetuate the fundamental (denominational) tenets handed down to us with minimal loss.

With varying levels of zeal, we try to preserve the integrity of what was given us. Frankly, under the guise of tolerance and open-mindedness, and in response to being indicted as unloving, what treasure we did have has been diminished with the baser alloys of worldly wisdom and carnal counsel, inundated with infidels, made confederate with foolishness.

What we have now is a religion of all-permissive grace and no accountability to the truth. The bloodline of the Spirit-filled continues to be assaulted and abated. There is little or no degree of separation between the children of GOD and the spawn of Belial. We are the hybridization and retarded progeny of wanton spiritual fornication, having sold our soul for shiny things and social acceptance.

The remnant stoically and suspiciously sustains the status quo and rigidly guards their religious ideology. Someone needs to say what everyone is too breathless and incredulous to say. We are progressively being infiltrated and overcome.

Someone must say what they will be hated for saying. I fear the kingdom of GOD is being taken from us and given to a nation bringing forth the fruits thereof.

The light that is in (many of us) is irrepressibly being revealed to be a great darkness. Ah, someone must say what we are too proper to say. We are proprietary of a privilege we have already pissed away.

Christian, it is when we resolve not to burn beneath a bushel that the next breath of revelation comes.

Duh. I do not want my religion to be the structured precisely circumscribed elusive entity that loosely defines and oversees what little I already know.

Let's you and I press up against what we do not know and what we do not have and by the violence of our faith command it to manifest. Let's you and I be the fire starters among the wood, hay, and stubble of our solemn assembly.

✳

"Why sit we here until we die?"
re. 2 KINGS 7:3

✳

Fresh revelation is available. GOD still speaks or he has never spoken. The Word of GOD is the prophetic utterance of an omnipotent, omniscient, omnipresent, living Spirit.

We have consulted within ourselves to predetermine what we will believe of GOD, and then have constructed our religions to zealously guard our finite reasoning. Our denominations are innumerable. Not even Google can tell how many there are.

We all have varying opinions of what is customer or consumer-friendly, uh, self-serving dogma. What is of the utmost importance is getting this matter of religion settled as soon (and seamlessly) as possible so that I can get back to living my life.

But some of us GOD has favored with a distinct discontent with denominational stricture and religious routine. I suspect there is something real beyond the smothering confines of this hypocritical orthodoxy, beyond these circumscribed religious horizons. Please, someone turn the lights on.

Some of us, or a few of us (commonly called fanatics) want to worship in the preeminent push-the-envelope absolute of the truth and light of GOD's Holy Spirit. Uh, moreover, *Father seeketh such* (re. John 4:23).

(Some of us are not content to sit subjected and silent in the corner of the pew assaulted with the inane repetitive man-made religious limitations unwittingly suppressing a greater enlightenment of an Almighty GOD.)

Uh, some of us occlude the portal to the next revelation of GOD, and the rest of us are glad (relieved) the way is blocked so that we do not have to get up.

Some of us are content to have someone else read our Bibles for us.

Uh, it seems some of us are content to be eternally clueless as long as we can be temporally corpulent.

Beyond the hype and the hypocrisy is the reality of the unsparing light and truth of GOD, and the startling sudden exposure of the vanity and impotence of all my convoluted dissimulation. I am going to have to see what I refused to see after all. Eternity is pressing up against my orthodox bubble of desensitization and volitional unawareness.

The LORD Jesus Christ is the Light of the World. He unequivocally said so. This is (what I call) one of the absolutes of GOD.

Children, none but GOD could utter such a thing.

Jesus Christ unambiguously and indivisibly declares who GOD is from the bosom of GOD, (see John 1:18). And not to be deliberately impertinent, but how many times must Jesus Christ say *I AM* before we believe him?

And let me say this. For them unwilling to believe, the truth cannot be expressed clearly enough or often enough.

It is the LORD Jesus Christ who declares himself the Light of the World. And as I have said, or alluded to, all argument reeks of unbelief. My desperate search to refute something Jesus Christ says is so that I do not have to live by the comprehensive commandment of *every* Word he says. Could it be that I am the unwitting tool of the adversary (and as a loyal denizen of this world system) confederate with Satan to undermine the deity of the LORD Jesus Christ? Truly, in the fullness of time, this will be revealed what the argument (and the division) has been about.

Whom but GOD could utter such an incomprehensible statement as "*I AM the Light of the World.*" It is finitely incomprehensible because it is infinite in its scope and absolute in its declaration. Children, it is by the Word of GOD that we rightly divide the Word of GOD, if you follow.

✳

In him was life; and the life was the Light of men.
JOHN 1:4

✳

With the *breath of life* man became a *living soul.* The Word of GOD says so.

Now, it is concisely my hope and prayer that you can receive it: that by the Holy Spirit of GOD, I write for GOD. I do not want to spend much time here, lest it be misconstrued I qualify myself. By the mercies of GOD, he has shown me a place of greater grace, and by the violence of my faith, I press into it.

This *breath of life*, that a friend of mine some years ago said, "hardwires us for GOD," is the resident spark of GOD, if I may say it like that.

Remembering, or remaining conscious of the fact that GOD's thoughts are not our thoughts, and that he has an infinite, eternal perspective, this *breath life* is what renders us in the image and after the likeness of GOD.

How shall I say this next point. In the past, I have said, "It takes GOD to show me GOD and to give me GOD." I will stand upon this statement. We must all go to the Source.

The Word of GOD by John says, *"In him* was life," meaning in Jesus Christ. The scripture preceding this one says, *"ALL* things were *made by him"* meaning *by* Jesus Christ (re. John 1:3). Ah, some of you see where the Spirit of GOD is going with this.

Dear children, if *ALL things were made by him*, this unequivocally makes him Creator and GOD.

✳

> *"So GOD created man in his own image, in the image of GOD created he him; male and female created he them"*
> GEN. 1:27

✳

Just because it is beyond my finite comprehension (and transcends my small-minded religious argument) does not mean that it is not so.

Moreover, why should the LORD Jesus Christ give me any more truth than I am prepared to walk in the light of. If once I decided to believe and implement what I already know, I would have to change the way that I am living. Yes, repent. I would be converted, and GOD would make me whole.

The emphasis shifts back to our primary text, and (by the Holy Spirit), I say that this *breath of life* that is the *light of men* is the internal knowledge and enlightenment of GOD, the intuitive awareness of my origins, if you will. I know that I was created by GOD and for GOD.

Now, the fact that there is a "worldwide" conspiracy to suppress this knowledge, and that we are to varying degrees volitional victims of its insidious onslaught, should go without saying. There were decades that I capitulated to the spiritual wickedness that convinced me that I did not know, uh, what I already knew. Huh?

I can almost say with accuracy that we all have more truth than we implement into practical application. How many of us, I wonder, in the middle of our complex excuses and labyrinthine dissimulation consider that what we are really trying to do is defraud GOD. You see, my natural man instinctively knows that he cannot be held responsible for, well, for what he does not know. Yeah, for decades I was one of the dumbest Christians I knew.

But I ran into a little problem. GOD, in his infinite wisdom and unsearchable mercy allowed me to be in want (and in pain) beyond the scope of my superficial Christianity. You see, along with my answered petitions for greater grace came the irrepressible revelation of greater truth. A real touch necessitates a real GOD.

(If I may), "*In him was life, and the life was the light (enlightenment) of men*" (John 1:4).

That is, Jesus Christ was/and is the Source of life, and with this life comes the understanding of its source, if you follow. That is, this *light of men* that I call enlightenment, is the instruction and knowledge and the awakening of the existence and supremacy of GOD as Creator imparted unto mankind.

✳

"For GOD, who commanded the light to shine out of darkness, hath shined in our hearts, to give the light of the knowledge of the glory of GOD in the face of Jesus Christ"
2 Cor. 4:6

✳

Christian, the Word of GOD (Jesus Christ) never ceases to declare who GOD is by progressive grace and truth.

Its perpetual prophetic revelatory nature attests to it being *a Living Word.*

It is always, always speaking. If I purpose to live according to what I hear, this Word of GOD comes with the power of the Holy Spirit to help me implement it. It is GOD who helps me (authorizes and empowers) me to live for GOD.

It was once my premise or hypothesis that every man and woman ever born knew of the existence of GOD, whether they admitted it or not. Well, I was being led by the Spirit of GOD all the while, but the Word of GOD moves beyond theory. It is fact.

I have written of these things before, and this could get lengthy, but none of us should have been under the miscon-ception that a discourse on the Light of the World would be a casual undertaking.

As I say, "The Word of God speaks best for himself."

The liability of mankind's enlightenment shall be laid against his soul.

✳

*"Because that which may be known of GOD is manifest
in them; for GOD hath shewed it unto them.*

*For the invisible things of him from the creation
of the world are clearly seen, being understood by
the things that are made, even his eternal power
and Godhead; so that they are without excuse"*
Rom. 1:19-20

✳

The Apostle Paul is speaking of them who *"hold* the truth in unrighteousness" (vs. 18), or them who deliberately suppress the truth. Of whom I was once chief, to borrow an expression from the Apostle Paul. Frankly, it is an exhausting, interminable (impossible) task to constantly convince oneself that you do not know, uh, what you know.

What may be known of GOD is manifest (or evident) in me, that is, physiologically and spiritually. After all, I was created in the image and after the likeness of GOD, and the miracle of his creative genius reflected in the marvels of the human body bear witness to this.

Concisely, GOD knows that I am not as profoundly stupid as I sometimes present to be. I have the capacity to discern between good and evil, and I know (full well) that I am a moral agent and that one day there will be a great and terrible (awesome *and* frightening) reckoning.

As hard as I tried, I could not deny the divine spark by which my soul was tethered (hard wired) to GOD. *"The life was the light of men"* (John 1:4), in other words. Children, either we acquiesce to the light, the enlightenment of our *godlikeness* and the knowledge that we are created by GOD and for GOD, or we must willfully (and tragically) close our eyes, and our hearts and minds, to what we know is true.

I deny my own spirituality and GOD's existence in a vain attempt to escape accountability. Precisely, I would rather declare myself ignorant, obtuse, oblivious, and witless, than admit understanding. Duh, I would rather be blind than capitulate to what the Word of GOD says is clearly seen since the creation of the world.

Of course, there is an element of fear involved. The power of GOD is admittedly intimidating, especially if we are not reconciled unto him in Christ. But realistically, it is not that I do not believe, but that I refuse to believe. This is willful and treasonous, insurrectionist, and from GOD's perspective, an especially odious rebellion. In such a state, the Word of GOD says the wrath of GOD abides upon me (see John 3:36), and from our present text declares me as without excuse.

We cannot live and breathe and experience GOD's amazing grace without the knowledge and enlightenment of GOD's existence (and his miraculous creative aptitude) simply overwhelming and inundating us with the corroboration of his omnipotence, omniscience, and omnipresence.

GOD's creation irrefutably and irrepressibly substantiates his existence. I'm not sure who that is for, but the LORD wants you to experience him personally by speaking to you through the magnificent light and majesty of the sun and the moon and the stars, by the radiant glory of every sunset, and the breathtaking brilliance and refreshing intimacy of every sunrise. Do you see his handiwork? Do you hear what he is saying?

✳

*The heavens declare the glory of GOD; and
the firmament sheweth his handywork.*

*Day unto day uttereth speech, and night
unto night sheweth knowledge.*

*There is no speech nor language where
their voice is not heard.*

*Their line is gone out through all the earth,
and their words to the end of the world. In
them hath he set a tabernacle for the sun.*
Ps. 19:1-4

✳

Before moving on, I wanted to note that here in Psalm 19, David expresses the glory and sovereignty of GOD with a running literary connotation and emphasizes that GOD speaks in an international language, as it were. Duh. Or as David put it in Psalm 14:1, *"The fool hath said in his heart, There is no God."*

Humanity in general, and this world system specifically, has never known quite how to deal with this level of intensity and illumination that is the ever-pressing here I AM in your face, and uh, in your lungs one breath at a time reality of GOD.

Uh, we can only take so much enlightenment. And we cannot escape our own heartbeat, or the electrical (miraculous, heavenly) spark that keeps it firing. Indeed, how to escape the correlative revelation of myself and GOD upon the continuum of his light? I have written before that I was not sure which was more agonizing: the ebullient and unquenchable revelation of GOD, or the insufferable reality of myself exposed and naked in the light and truth of the Living Word of GOD.

Oh, please, please, someone turn that light off! Dearest faithful reader, that you have followed this far attests to the fact that you have been there faith to faith. You know that I do not speak finitely of physical light, but of the inescapable indefatigable internal searching of the Holy Spirit of GOD and the excruciating enlightenment of the true character of my natural man.

It never ceases to amaze me. The correlative revelation of the righteousness of GOD faith to faith is the startling reality of the raw and merciless face-to-face with myself in the midnight of the soul: the exceeding sinfulness of sin come home, the appalling insufficiency of my religious rags, the vanity of my complex dissimulation and duplicity.

✳

And the light shineth in darkness, and the
darkness comprehended it not.
JOHN 1:5

✳

Before I give what I specifically like most of the Greek and Hebrew for the word *comprehend,* I want to share what the Holy Spirit gives me in prayer and meditation early this morning.

As is my custom, I wrote this short verse above in my journal in red ink. My very first thought (by the Holy Ghost) while contemplating this verse was: Here is opportunity not taken advantage of. Truth denied, summarily and obliviously, unceremoniously dismissed. Not even bothering to evaluate, much less value. To assimilate and take advantage of the instruction and awakening and potential of the light, not even considered. Not given an audience. We do not even suspect the value of what (enlightenment) has been made available.

Here are the notes in my Bible for the Hebrew/Greek definition of *comprehend:* possess, attain, to take eagerly, perceive through the senses, to know by experience, to seize with the mind, to gain full knowledge of, to pluck, and to take by force.

Here is another observation. In my pre-regenerative state, and even in a compromised (lukewarm) Christian condition, I intuitively perceived the unmitigated light and truth of the LORD Jesus Christ (the Word of GOD) as a clear and present danger to the status quo of my shady business. I immediately shut down and drew the black-out shades over the windows. Instantly the walls went up. The bulwarks and the ramparts and fortifications (all the same things by the way) were checked for hermetic seal, if you follow.

If light and truth are a threat, then it is "evident" that I am hiding a deception. And it is the illusion that I have accepted as the reality. It must be protected if I am to save my life for myself. (Please stay with me. And note that I am referring specifically to myself.)

The gospel according to John says Jesus Christ *"was the True Light, which lighteth every man that cometh into the world"* (re. John 1:9).

Naturally, that there is a *True* Light presupposes and (to me) inevitably entails that there is also a *false one.* Or there is a standard of knowledge and enlightenment that insists it is the reality, to wit, this world system governed (and subjected) by a standard other than the full truth and light of the Word of GOD.

This scripture verse is further proof of man's instinctive or hereditary knowledge of GOD by virtue of the *Breath of Life*, or spark of life which is in each of us that is the light (enlightenment) of men, (re. John 1:4). John irrefutably states that Jesus Christ *lighteneth* every man (and woman) that comes into the world (re. John 1:9).

We pass through this enlightenment (this knowledge of the existence and sovereignty of GOD as Creator and LORD) – we pass through this enlightenment on our way into this world as surely as we pass through our mother's womb.

By borrowing two phrases from Romans 1:19 and 1:20 respectively, it is my assertion by the Word of GOD and the Spirit of GOD that humanity is well-informed and distinctly apprised by GOD of the existence and sovereignty of GOD, *"for God hath shewed it unto them" "so that they are without excuse."*

This Word is so rich and so informative that I want to place verses four and nine in immediate succession. Dear reader, this is not to take them out of context, but to accentuate their revelatory context.

※

In him was life; and the life was the light of men. /
That was the true Light, which lighteth every man
(and woman) that cometh into the world.
JOHN 1:4,9

✳

This indisputably speaks to the deity of the LORD Jesus Christ. Children, the life that is in him is an *eternal* life.

This further confirms (to me) what we have been discussing. The initial *Breath of Life* given man is also the spark of enlightenment that not only hardwires us to GOD, but which also gives us an intuitive hereditary awareness of his existence and sovereignty as our Creator.

It is Jesus Christ who *lighteneth* (enlightens) every man and every woman that comes into the world. Dear children, there is no other *Light of the World* than He.

Sin introduced darkness and illusion into the equation, defiling and corrupting mankind's initial enlightenment, if you follow. Our *Breath of Life* was polluted by sin, and our enlightenment or vision and knowledge of GOD was sullied and distorted.

Sin removed man out of place, literally got him cast out of the Garden of Eden.

Our fellowship with GOD sustained a hit that would take a miraculous and tragic redemption to restore.

We will subsequently find, even as Christians, that sin occludes both fellowship and enlightenment. As a result of sin our vision of GOD is dimmed, and distance is put in our fellowship.

To be whole, to be an effective witness of the resurrection life that is in Jesus Christ, and to live a victorious Christian life (even a life more abundant), we need a regenerative *Breath of Life.*

None can give humanity this regenerative breath but the same GOD that gave man the original Breath of Life. This is the Promise of the Father and the Gift of the Holy Ghost, and (to me) substantiates and corroborates the LORD Jesus Christ as the Baptizer with the Holy Ghost and fire.

After all, these notebooks are all about the deity of the LORD Jesus Christ and an in-depth inquiry into the identity of GOD.

Jesus Christ says over and over for them that have ears to hear and an enlightenment that has been valued and cultivated, *"I AM."*

＊

*In him was Life; and the Life was the
Light (enlightenment) of men.*
JOHN 1:4

＊

He is the *Life* and he is *the Light of the World.*

Where there is a *True Light,* there is of necessity a false one, a clever forgery. I am thinking specifically of worldly counsel, oftentimes purporting to be founded upon the light and truth of scriptural or Christian principles but inundated with shady practices.

✳

The world by wisdom knew not God.
re. 1 COR. 1:21

✳

He was in the world, AND THE WORLD WAS MADE BY HIM, and the world knew him not.
JOHN 1:10

✳

Again, that the world was made by him makes him Creator and LORD.

They mocked him and denied him, beat him and spit upon him, and then crucified him. Children, that is the work of an insidious darkness.

Jesus Christ is the Light (enlightenment) of GOD's proprietary claim to my worship and fidelity. The blood of Jesus Christ is the demand upon my reconciliation, it must be reckoned with. Its demands must be received or rejected. There is no delicate way to put it.

When I try to give my flesh a pass or respite from the strictures of a strait gate and a narrow way it is like trying to introduce darkness into light. But there are no shady places in the light and truth and unsparing exposure of GOD's Word. Dear faithful reader, you have heard my mantra, and no doubt my rant. But you were not there with me in the midnight of the soul when the Spirit of God distinctly said, *"Bring the whole animal to the sacrifice, or stay home."*

When the prophetic Word of GOD speaks into our personal circumstances, the carefree season of our procrastination and prevarication is past.

✳

Behold, I will set a plumbline in the midst of my people Israel: I will not again pass by them any/more.
re. Amos 7:8

✳

When once the cost of Calvary is correctly counted in my personal circumstance, all rationalization and justification for willful repetitive sin rings hollow.

✳

For if we sin willfully after that we have received the knowledge of the truth, there remaineth no more sacrifice for sins.

Heb. 10:26

Christian, you may think me severe, but as I said, you were not there in the agony of my grace as I wrestled into the dawn. Such is the reality of the plumbline of a Holy GOD, and the austerity and strictures of Calvary.

Such are the commands of enlightenment (the true Light) upon my accountability and fidelity to grace. I cannot pass that plumbline with a hidden agenda or a Christianity coalesced with carnal alloys and a skewed self-serving worldly counsel.

There came a time when the truth (enlightenment) of Calvary became acute, and the correlative reality of my personal responsibility to grace became grave and dreadful. Its remunerative commands were made most heavy. I could not get a pass (if you follow) as I had in times past. There is a plumbline in the hand of the *HOLY*, and it is the cross of Jesus Christ and him crucified. It is the place I have sometimes referred to as the apex or pinnacle of time and eternity, and the epicenter of the earthquake in my revelation of GOD.

Let me interject something here. I have been reading *The Blood of Christ* by Andrew Murray (slowly and concurrently) (coincidentally) as I have transcribed from the Holy Spirit (as you can receive it) these first pages of *I AM*. Andrew Murray has been referring to the cross of Jesus Christ as the altar of GOD, and rightly so (where the Lamb of GOD is slain). He expounds upon how that altar is the Most Holy place, so Holy, that the altar sanctifies (consecrates, hallows) every gift or offering laid upon it.

Since I have begun this manuscript, and this chapter specifically, (and please pardon me if this sounds clichéd), but the lights have come on. The progressive revelatory power of the blood of Jesus Christ has turned up the index here in my humble Bible study. To use a contemporary idiom, as well as invalidate much of our interminable doctrinal disputations and ostentatious posturing, the *Power Point* is still the cross of Jesus Christ.

Once more, it resounds within my spirit man commanding urgent prophetic expression. (This is predominantly for preachers and evangelists), this is where we get a fresh Word and fresh vision and enlightenment from the Holy One for the Church of GOD.

✳

"And there I will meet with thee, and I will commune with thee from above the mercy seat, from between the two cherubims which are upon the ark of the testimony, of all things which I will give thee in commandment unto the children of Israel"
Ex. 25:22

✳

I am ever seeking GOD's palpable presence and good pleasure upon the words that I write, and upon the words that I speak at Harbor House Christian Center in Henderson, Kentucky. And upon my witness at Walmart while standing in line or in the parking lot as well. GOD keeps drawing me back personally to the place I not only get my marching orders, if you follow, but to the Holy place of his endorsement and power upon all I say and do.

Here, where the blood of Jesus Christ is shed for the remission of sin, the miracle of redemption is kept alive. (This) (Here) is the power and wisdom of GOD, the Most Holy place in the salvation of men.

This is the Most Holy place of reconciliation, of illumination and anointing, the singular enigmatic place of all knowledge and enlightenment. Here the man of GOD receives instruction, and the ministers to the heirs of the kingdom of GOD take knowledge.

Are we hearing the prophetic implications that GOD spoke to Moses? Have we perceived the potential power that awaits the intrepid? Preacher, the promise GOD gave Moses is prophetically yours.

This is the preeminent place of fellowship with GOD in the grace and truth of Jesus Christ and him crucified. This is fellowship in the Light. This transcends my own salvation. This is the Holy place where prophets and priests procure for the kingdom. That is, this is the Holy place of GOD where his prophets and priests and kings are empowered to procure the resources of heaven for their ministry on earth.

This is the unsurpassed place of efficacious intercessions. It is not only given, but it must also be pressed into.

The cross of Jesus Christ is the representative altar which sanctifies the gift that I figuratively place upon it – namely, my own life and self-interests. Here where the blood of Jesus Christ is applied to the mercy seat, my own sacrifice (the offering up of my life) is coalesced with his sacrifice.

We have covered much of this but its importance in ministry cannot be emphasized enough. Confederate with GOD's evangelical interests, I take (and receive) his anointing for service. It isn't just given, if you follow. It must also be taken.

Moses got his marching orders from GOD. His prayers and his messages to Israel (GOD's congregation), and even his songs, had the manifest evidence of GOD's favor and anointing (and subsequent power) upon them.

Correlatively, Church of GOD, the instructions for the contemporary congregation arise out of the acute intimacy of the inner sanctum, where the life is laid down for its friend.

*

There I will meet with thee, and I will commune with thee.
re. Ex. 25:22

*

This is where Christians are made. This is the Holy ground of nothing hidden and face-to-face intimacy. This is the fellowship of the life lost to find it, if you follow. This is the true fellowship of the cross, the illumination, the enlightenment and acute elucidation of love from GOD's perspective: that no greater love than the life laid down for its friend.

This is the unsparing exposure of the true Light which incites the hostility and hatred of hypocrisy (the hidden thing). This is the radical unveiling of (much) religious ceremony and the angst and disquiet of the self-righteous assembly. This is the Light of GOD right where I live and play (and fornicate) – the astute (and acute) revelation of selfless love.

In the past, I have written extensively (and too critically for many) about the necessity of religious forms to emulate the forward momentum of a dynamic, genuine faith. We erect elaborate personas and Sunday morning marionettes to send into superficial religious service – so the real me (or we) can stay home.

The *true* Light which *lighteth* every man (and woman) that comes into the world (re. John 1:9) penetrates even the most elaborate religious edifice and gingerbread fortification. Jesus

Christ speaks light and truth into even the most labyrinthine religious barricades.

He spoke light into the Judaism of the man Nicodemus. For decades I adjudicated the indictment to be for Nicodemus alone. I wonder what he has to say about our own self-serving, self-celebratory, segregated elitist religious ceremony.

*

And this is the condemnation, that light is come into the world, and men loved darkness rather than light, because their deeds were evil.

For every one that doeth evil hateth the light, neither cometh to the light, lest his deeds should be reproved.

But he that doeth truth cometh to the light, that his deeds may be made manifest, that they are wrought in God.

John 3:19-21

(please pardon the changing format).

*

We mustn't lose the context upon (or into) which this light is cast. Or forget or misunderstand that the *Voice* of the prophetic Word of GOD is perpetually uttered and forever living and illuminating. We mustn't forget that Jesus is speaking about the world generally, about religion and Judaism more specifically, and then he is speaking to the man Nicodemus narrowly and personally, if you can receive it.

We have a tendency to remove these Words of GOD from their immediate context and make them a blank indictment laid at the feet of all sinners, and only sinners. Because Nicodemus came to Jesus at night, we assume this was a private conversation, and it probably was. But does Nicodemus presume that Jesus Christ is exclusively speaking about sinners, or does he realize that the LORD is pointedly referring to him as well? I wonder at how these living Words must have resounded in the ears (and in the mind) of Nicodemus during the course of the LORD's ministry on earth.

As we study and prayerfully meditate upon the three appearances of Nicodemus in the gospel according to John (and ask the LORD for enlightenment) we cannot help but see his progressive growth in the grace and truth of Jesus Christ. I believe that Nicodemus was an ardent seeker of the knowledge of GOD. His night-time visitation of Jesus may have begun with a mixed motivation. He may well have been (on the one hand) a religious spy sent by the Pharisees. But I believe (on the other hand) he was seeking something more than outward religious routine, he was seeking something real, he was seeking an encounter.

(I believe) these Living Words continued to be rehearsed in his mind until their undying echo reached his heart and faith arose.

In my experience, these scriptures (John 3:19-21), have been taught and preached specifically as referring to the willful spiritual blindness of all humanity. Until the Spirit of GOD showed me differently, that is, and probably much the same way he showed Nicodemus.

These Words are indeed a living indictment of all humanity. But only when the indictment is made specific can it benefit me personally. We criticize Nicodemus for coming to Jesus at night, but what time of the day or night do we come and go? Notwithstanding all conjecture and criticism, Nicodemus met these Words on their level. It may have taken him a little while, but he reconciled these Words as being spoken to himself personally.

Has this living Word of GOD reached me personally? As I read these Words, do I acknowledge that the only person present representative of the entire humanity that they address is myself?

The context of the Word of GOD is now, and within the particulars of this immediate circumstance. And I am the entire audience.

These *living* Words of GOD "worried" Nicodemus, that is, they "worked" him. He heard them again and again, breath after breath, and sometimes heartbeat after heartbeat. (No, I was not there. But the Spirit of GOD takes me there).

Nicodemus gave these living Words an audience, and the power and life of them began to transform his character. The lights came on. These Words continued to instruct and enlighten him. I have found it to be so, that they will not go away.

As we have discussed, the Word(s) of GOD must be willfully and with great effort suppressed. But they will live on, and they will be back more alive and irrepressible than ever. As I have written, the Word of GOD I will not live by will be the same Word of GOD that sends me to hell.

In the case of Nicodemus, the Word of GOD reached beneath his religious cloak of Judaism and Pharisaism to touch him right where he lived. We might say the Word of GOD had begun to shed Light on the reality of his elitist religious regimen.

And as we listen, the Word of GOD radically narrows its scope. The indictment of all humanity suddenly embraces each of our sectarian cliquish schismatic multifarious religious forms. Uh, it finds me hiding beneath my religious misdirection and mindless self-righteous supposition, reaching into my superficial church service to find me anesthetized and stupefied in the corner of the pew, no more alive unto GOD than a mannequin. If I will acknowledge the light and truth of them, they will render me naked and dissimulating beneath a thin religious veil.

Christian, listen closely. It is not only "quote – unquote" sinners who will not come to the Light. There are levels and levels (thank you, Pastor Lukau).

There are levels and levels of prevarication and dissimulation like there are degrees of enlightenment and revelation. If we will listen carefully, we can hear the LORD Jesus Christ correlate hearing and doing (or applying) the Word of GOD, and degrees of illumination. (This could be lengthy, but I trust the Holy Spirit to connect this with our current text of the LORD's conversation with Nicodemus).

✳

*Is a candle brought to be put under a bushel, or
under a bed? and not to be set on a candlestick?*

*For there is nothing hid, which shall not be manifested; neither
was any thing kept secret, but that it should come abroad.*

If any man have ears to hear, let him hear.
MARK 4:21-23

᠅

There are levels and levels. There are levels of duplicity and darkness, and then there are degrees of illumination and revelation. (If I may express it as appointed of the LORD). The Word of GOD instructs the just to live by faith until their whole bodies are full of light. There is a distinct difference between working with all the light and truth I have in a specific season or circumstance and having settled somewhere short of my potential for the kingdom of GOD.

Church of GOD, I ask you: Shall the condemnation that light has come not be all-inclusive, to reach the sinner as well as the complacent and self-satisfied saint?

There is a contrast between the true Light of enlightenment of the Word of GOD and the illusion and worldly wisdom of men, much like there is a genuine dynamic faith and the religious forms that emulate forward momentum.

When I have somewhat to hide, I may necessitate an elaborate ceremony or secrete my true self within the convoluted folds of my intricate and ostentations religious cloak. We mustn't pretend or forget that Jesus Christ was speaking directly into Nicodemus's Judaism and Pharisee affect in John

3:19-21. He was the only one there much like I am the one and only designated audience when I read the Word of GOD.

The *true Light* will not spare Nicodemus, Judaism, or my own religious misdirection and pretense. What is the Word of GOD saying about my religion?

The LORD Jesus Christ unapologetically called the hidden thing by its true name.

*

Beware of the leaven of the Pharisees, which is hypocrisy.
LUKE 12:1

*

In Matthew 16:6, Jesus includes the Sadducees in the indictment. We might say that he did not want formal religion to escape the impeachment he had laid to the charge of all humanity when addressing Nicodemus in John 3:19-21.

(By the Holy Spirit), I intuit that the truly inescapable Word of GOD that the LORD Jesus spoke into Nicodemus' life, and the Word that continued to resound with the catalytic power to convict and transform was, *"Marvel not that I said unto thee, Ye must be born again."* (John 3:7)

How readest thou, Christian? Do you suspect that Nicodemus pondered and meditated upon his audience with the Living Word of GOD until he had minutely assessed not only his own spiritual state, but also the spiritual condition and suppositions (the arrogance and malevolence) of Judaism, the malfeasance and mind-numbing misdirection of the Pharisees, and then maybe feared for the verity and integrity of all organized religion and the Sanhedrin as well? Can you see him when the lights came on (if I may), tsk-tsking at how profoundly he had missed it?

Jesus Christ is indeed the Light of the World, and he searches me to the uttermost. One conversation, and I will never be the same. Notably, there is a liberty in the full light of disclosure like no other freedom.

I will love the Light that has miraculously and magnificently set me free, or I will hate it for its revelation and condemnation of me. This is a difficult Word to reconcile, that *"Every one that doeth evil hateth the Light, nether cometh to the Light, lest his deeds should be reproved."* (re. John 3:20)

Concisely, it is distasteful (unseemly) to consider that the abhorrence of the prisoner of sin directed toward the Light (Jesus Christ) is declared to be hatred. But children, the virulent hatred of the Pharisees for the LORD Jesus Christ and his subsequent crucifixion confirms it.

The Word of GOD abruptly calls the hidden thing an *evil* thing, just as it calls not trusting what GOD has said, an *evil* heart of unbelief (re. Heb. 3:12). Please bear with me. I struggle with the revelation, also, and cringe at the intensity of the illumination.

Friend, this is GOD's reality that we seek to know. These hard and difficult sayings are GOD's vocabulary, or lexicon. The Word of GOD is the estimation and conclusions and expectations of him whose name is *HOLY*. The Word of GOD is absolute. No amount of convoluted misdirection, smoke and mirrors or sleight of hand, and no clever or labyrinthine prevarication and dissimulation can diminish its utter authority.

GOD's Word flatly says that *"men loved darkness rather than Light, because their deeds were evil"* (re. John 3:19). Not only do we use darkness to conceal our deeds, but the Word of GOD declares that we *love* the darkness that aids and abets our evil.

Frankly, it is difficult to assimilate the truth of this, that even good church folk when they have something to hide, can hate like this. Yeah, in retrospect, there was something furtive behind some of them Sunday morning smiling faces, uh, something surreptitious about some of them stealthy saints. Indeed, how blatantly hubristic and privileged, how bare-assed presumptuous to assume my blackened heart is hidden behind the curtain of a superficial religious ceremony. I can hear the LORD say:

✳

"But I know you, that ye have not the love of God in you."
JOHN 5:42

✳

Oh my, the love of GOD will not cohabitate with the darkness or sign off on my shady business. (We have covered this). In fact, in him is no darkness at all (re. 1 John 1:5)

Have we (contemporary Christianity) done so much better as persons or as organized religion that this Word of GOD is summarily dismissed as belonging exclusively to the Pharisees and Sadducees?

Notably, the LORD Jesus Christ tells Nicodemus in John 3:20 that those who do evil will not come to the Light. This is distinctly paralleled in John 5:40 when the Jews were persecuting him and seeking to kill him for healing a man on the Sabbath. He told them, *"You will not come to me, that ye might have life."*

Getting abruptly back on text, to hypothesize that I have something hidden from GOD reeks of unbelief and is a glaring indication that I do not know him as well as I suggest. I may have a little religion and a lot of illusion, but I certainly do not have a loving relationship with the LORD Jesus Christ, the Light of the World.

What hidden thing is it that has me bound to a religious form to imitate the forward momentum of a genuine faith? What illusion am I clinging to, desperate to convince myself that it is the true Light that lighteth (enlightens) every man who that comes into the world (re. John 1:9)? What lie have I sold myself so I can save my life for myself?

Am I hearing that there is no Christian except a sold-out Christian? There may be some things unresolved, there may well be some idiosyncrasies or insufficiencies unfinalized, but there is nothing hidden from the omniscient eye of the Light of the World.

My character can be imperfect and my coming to Jesus Christ still be pure. There may be some things not completely conquered, yet nothing deliberately covered.

But the Word of GOD declares in John 3:20 that when I will not come to the Light it is because I do not want my deeds to be reproved or discovered, exposed. My desire for the Light, or my estimation of the value of the Light, will be directly contrasted with my desire or value placed upon the hidden thing. I have a choice to make, and it is one of first love.

Some men love the Light and other men hate it (him). This is the gist of the revelation. It will be found that I have rejected (and hated) the LORD Jesus Christ, the Light of the World.

There was a time that I lived my Christian life with the light turned down real low. It is not only bona fide sinners that have a distinct problem coming to the Light.

To place this in an ever-broadening (increasingly bright perspective) what treasure do I have hidden from GOD? (I better leave this in the first-person possessive tense for a while). What sin, whether it is a thing or a behavior or a bad attitude, do I treasure so much or want to keep so badly, that I correspondingly hate the Light for its illumination and revelation of me?

A genuine Christian will not entertain darkened corners or shady business that precludes them from having more of the light and truth of GOD's Word and the essence and nature of the LORD Jesus Christ.

✳

But he that doeth truth cometh to the Light, that his deeds
may be made manifest, that they are wrought in God.
JOHN 3:21

✳

In the life of a genuine Christian there is an identifiable quantifiable progression into the Light of God's Holy character. I sometimes call this growth the glorious progressive gradients of the grace and truth by which Jesus Christ came to declare unto us the essence of GOD.

It is as we delve deeper into the gospel of Jesus Christ and him crucified that the power of GOD unto salvation is methodically unleashed within our souls. The progression, the rising up, the transformation, is undeniable.

For therein is the righteousness of God revealed from faith to faith: as it is written, The just shall live by faith.

ROM. 1:17

We might say that we move from light to light into the exhilarating progressive revelation of GOD. We have spoken of these magnificent enigmatic things, that we have fellowship with one another and with GOD as we walk in the light, and that this is the place of our justification – where the blood of Jesus Christ is applied (re. 1 John 1:7).

A Christian with something to hide is the nonsensical counterproductive correlative of lighting a candle and putting it under a bushel. (Okay, I better go back to first-person possessive tense).

For a protracted season there was undoubtedly something cloudy and illogical about my Christian witness. Uh, and gloomy also. Alas, while there is only One *true Light* of Christianity, there are innumerable shades of Christian. Someone has to say so. We vary from a hidden agenda to no agenda. There is a lot of ungodly business transacted beneath the bushel.

The bushel is the superficial Sunday morning affect upon my smiling religious face, a Christian facade, a fellow no one really knows because he does not really exist. The bushel is to keep you from looking too closely at my flame, or at the absence thereof. Beneath the bushel (inside the reality) some of us are smoldering ash and acrid smoke.

Under the bushel, I hoard the illusion of my life for myself. Just enough light to get by on, the subsisting suspect smile you see on Sunday morning. I am the minimal and the nominal you meet with nothing to spare. But for the hidden thing I would have a viable witness of the abundant life. My surreptitious love for the world commands my silence about Jesus Christ. I consider not that the light that is in me is a great darkness called hypocrisy, or that the illusion of enlightenment causes more harm than the darkness.

✳

Verily, verily, I say unto you, Whosoever
committeth sin is the servant of sin.
JOHN 8:34

✳

I cannot cast out the devil whose rent is paid. My Sunday morning excursions into the light do not benefit me while I entertain and accommodate sin in the camp. My smiling face and my faith may appear sincere, even faultless, but in the light and consideration of the hidden thing in my heart, my religion is but a form and a façade. What I think to have hidden from GOD is the reality of a cruel servitude.

To speak with authority in the name of Jesus Christ while corruption and bitterness proliferates in my heart, I will not find. I may quote a few scriptures or spiritual truisms from memory, but with sin in my heart they are mechanical religious banalities and empty promises. I know what a Christian is supposed to look like and sound like, but without an internal light, I am an external illusion and one-dimensional facsimile.

In order to keep some bad attitudes, character flaws and even ordinary sin, the natural enlightenment that I have as being created in the image and after the likeness of GOD must be willfully suppressed. We have spoken of this, that to keep and maintain the illusion, I must deny the *true Light of the World*. His name is Jesus.

And then I must deny my denial. I go to elaborate lengths and embrace complex carnal (worldly) counsel to convince myself that the childhood prejudices or learned (ungodly) philosophies and general operating procedures of my inner man are not that big a deal or offensive to a Holy GOD.

I am effectually a prisoner of propping up the illusion that allows me the hidden thing. And at the end of the day, I am still not convinced of myself, still not persuaded that I do not know, uh, well, what I already know. You know. These perpetual nagging doubts about the integrity of the illusion must be from the devil.

✳

> *The spirit of man is the candle of the LORD,*
> *searching all the inward parts of the belly.*
> Pro. 20:27

✳

Many people believe this verse pertains to the conscience given the human animal in the exercise of self-assessment and self-control. I believe that this spirit accompanies or is coalesced with the *Breath of Life* that makes man a living soul. This is what I have called the enlightenment that all humanity receives from the *true Light* which *lighteth* every man (and woman) that cometh into the world (see John 1:10). His name is Jesus.

Dear reader, there are those who maintain that I cannot possibly know all that I declare to know. I make no excuses for myself, and no apology either. However, I do stir up the gift of GOD that is in me according to the greater grace and everlasting mercy of the LORD Jesus Christ. Some of you know how that I say it. I run my metaphorical fingers through all that I know, and by the violence of my faith press up against what I want to know. It is faith which makes the Word of GOD manifest in its season.

Children, the candle of the LORD searching the inward parts of the belly is the enlightenment of GOD pointing out all the faults in my human reasoning and worldly wisdom. He is the source of the nagging doubts I have about my own understanding. The candle of the LORD is the intrinsic light and truth of the Holy Spirit of GOD's Living Word searching me and knowing me to the uttermost.

GOD's Spirit will bear witness with my spirit when my reasoning is true, when my rightly dividing the Word of GOD is true, when my love for my neighbor is true. When the modus operandi of my heart is in tune with GOD's own, my light and enlightenment, my understanding and my reasoning is pure; not yet perfect, but pure in its season.

When my enlightenment comes from GOD instead of from the psychiatrist or from mood stabilizers, or from self-help books or talking heads, then my eye will be single. My candle will burn brighter. My Sunday morning smiling face will be genuine because its origin will be the *Light of the World* dwelling within my spirit man.

✳

Let your light so shine before men, that they may see your good works, and glorify your Father which is in heaven.
MATT. 5:16

✳

This corresponds with John 3:21 below and is a good example of the Word of GOD substantiating its (his) own self.

But he that doeth truth cometh to the Light, that his deeds may be made manifest, that they are wrought in GOD.

Deep calls to deep and truth to truth. From the inside-out, I reach. I need not strive for the life that is in me to manifest, I naturally gravitate toward the Light.

From another perspective we speak the same law of light, that to enjoy the darkness, I must suppress the Light. To have the illusion, to have the forbidden fruit, I must willfully suppress the truth to perversely and premeditatively embrace the lie. Inevitably, in every volume, we encounter what I call *The Big Lie* upon which all other lies and illusion are predicated upon or have their foundation. *"Ye shall not surely die."* (see Gen. 3:4).

Although I could never admit it, I lived my life for decades while forcefully suppressing the knowledge that there would be a reckoning one day. I cited complex and uh, nonsensical labyrinthine logic to convince myself that it was not so. You know, so that I could live my life with only a minimally disturbed conscience. I was prisoner of an interminable debate with my inner man.

This is a monumental denial, and a grievous bondage. This is a deliberate, obdurate attempt to repudiate and invalidate GOD's Word and the calculated rejection of the only begotten Son of GOD, Jesus Christ. All so I can have a lie.

Preferring the darkness to light, and a lie before the truth, is an egregious avoidance and most odious offense to the love of GOD in Jesus Christ. Although the devil aids and abets me in my self-delusion, my choice of darkness over the light is ultimately a volitional, personal choice. I am not as blind as I present to be, if you follow. *There are none so blind as those who will not see,* is attributed to John Haywood in 1546. Perhaps he was suffering the same revelation.

Satan convinces us that we are just trying to live and enjoy our lives the best we can. He uses our temporal needs and wants (and pleasures) against us as a veil that separates and desensitizes us from the eternal peril of our soul. You know. We are just trying to get by.

Dear children, the following scripture reference has been used almost exclusively to represent the state of things near the end times. But I say that even now our souls are precariously balanced upon the pinnacle of an eternal decision. Soon, time will be no more, and our temporal choices shall be eternally established.

When we willfully reject the enlightenment made available by the Word of GOD, and receive not the tender overtures and a love for the truth that we might be saved, our hearts become progressively harder and our minds more intransigent and unyielding day by day. What I am trying to say is that the delusion grows stronger and our servitude more acute. By the Holy Ghost, I declare that this prophetic Word of GOD has been perpetually unfolding since it was penned by the man of God to the Church.

＊

And for this cause God shall send them strong delusion, that they should believe a lie. That they all might be damned who believed not the truth, but had pleasure in unrighteousness.
re. 2 Thess. 2:10-12

＊

Christian, even as I write this notebook, the delusion surges and methodically mesmerizes and immobilizes us. As we deny and circumvent the Light, and deliberately suppress the knowledge and enlightenment of the truth of GOD's Word, the darkness proliferates and intensifies. Our once volitional enjoyment of just a little sin becomes a progressively cruel servitude even as it inexorably moves toward total apostasy.

We see it getting dim and do nothing to halt the pernicious waning progression and dying ember of our perfunctory Christianity.

When we turn away from the Light of the World, the LORD Jesus Christ, darkness (Satan) fills the void. I have written, we sell our souls for shiny things and an ephemeral unsustainable social acceptance. We aspire for the acknowledgement and approbation of persons more deluded than ourselves. Satan has incrementally sold himself into our minds with shady, sordid, subliminal, suggestive messages endorsing all manner of perversity as the new societal norm. (Uh, we tell ourselves we are just trying to fit in). Under the guise of being tolerant we have adulterated GOD's grace as all-permissive and unaccountable to his truth or Holy character.

We are progressively anesthetized with technological toys and inundated with godless data. *Tele*vision has supplanted our vision for GOD. We live our life tethered to an electronic device. Concisely, we worship and serve the creature more than the Creator (re. Rom. 1:25).

The mass hypnosis and pervasive pandemic apathy moves me to quote the Apostle Paul's globally fulfilling prophetic portend to the Church of God at Rome. It parallels the verse from 2 Thessalonians 2:10-12 that I listed a few paragraphs ago. Please notice the phrase *"For this cause"* in the beginning of verse twenty-six. It is the recompence from GOD upon the persons designated in verse twenty-five. The gravity of our global volitional rejection of the light and truth of the Word of GOD (and the *person* and essence of the LORD Jesus Christ) moves me to include verse twenty-five through twenty-eight.

※

Who changed the truth of God into a lie, and worshipped and served the creature more than the Creator, who is blessed for ever. Amen.

"For this cause" GOD gave then up unto vile affections: for even their women did change the natural use into that which is against nature.

And likewise also the men, leaving the natural use of the woman, burned in their lust one toward another; men with men working that which is unseemly (shameful), and receiving in themselves that recompence (penalty) of their error which was meet (due).

And even as they did not like to retain GOD in their knowledge, GOD "gave them over" to a reprobate (debased) mind, to do those things which are not convenient (fitting).
ROMANS 1:25-28

✳

Dear reader, thank you for your forbearance. This is, indeed, a lengthy indictment. Since it actually begins in verse eighteen and goes to the end of the chapter in verse thirty-two, I have nonetheless kept it as short as possible. Likewise, I hope to be brief in its exposition. However, unpleasantness not dealt with proliferates. GOD has shown me personally, and with many stripes, I add, that the only way to deal with sin is unsparingly. And as we have discussed, it is in the light of GOD's presence and holy character where our fellowship is perfected, and where the blood of Jesus Christ eradicates sin.

"For this cause" might be a suitable title for this aside. There are two more points that I want to give emphasis. The first follows directly behind *"For this cause."*

For this cause *"God gave them up"* (re. Rom. 1:26).

Now, so I do not lose the emphasis, I want to immediately direct your attention to the second point in verse twenty-eight, *"God gave them over."*

"And even as they did not like to retain God in their knowledge *God gave them over."*

Dear faithful reader, I trust that you are still with me. In fact, I hope you are following with the Word of GOD opened in front of you.

Now, for even greater accentuation:

"God gave them up." "God gave them over."

Dear children of God, we have seen the progression and the severity. We have seen the pervasive and encompassing comprehensive metastasis of sin. Indeed, we have seen (and some of us have silently welcomed) the encroaching darkness.

In the context of our chapter, we refer to the prevailing element of our society that has rejected the light and truth of GOD's holy character. Not only the rejection of knowledge and enlightenment but the willful suppression of the truth.

In such a state, it is not as if we (or I) can actually change the truth of GOD into a lie (re. Rom. 1:25), but the Word of GOD is referring to when I deliberately quell and repress the truth so that I can have the lie. So that I can live as god (little "g") and so I can serve the creature. So that I can usurp the governing authority of my life and oust GOD from the equation, encroach and infringe, trespass upon the glory and sovereignty of GOD. So that *"those persons"* can posture and preen in the pride of their life, indulging in all manner of perversity.

For decades, I attempted to live my life unaware of GOD and, uh, uninformed and unenlightened about my origins, ignorant of GOD's expectations of my acknowledgement and acquiescence to his sovereignty. The strain is in deluding myself that GOD is unaware of me, and my insurrection, as well.

We must ask ourselves, or rather, we must confess and capitulate to the truth, that when we are determined to have the darkness, GOD is justified in withdrawing his light.

As we can see from this Word of GOD by the Apostle Paul to the saints at Rome, when GOD *gives us up* to the darkness of our own desires, all manner of depravity is perpetrated. We see the prophetic implications of this living Word of GOD being fulfilled before our very eyes. We witness its progression, its plague, its pandemic, every day.

It is a dangerous thing to suppress what I already know, to persist obdurate and unrepentant, as if I had not been enlightened and instructed to the error of my ways. In such a state, this defiance will be rewarded with more of the darkness which initially incited its rebellion, until the person is overwhelmed and consumed, apostatized, and their soul forever lost.

The word, *retain,* in verse twenty-eight, conveys a responsibility to the maintenance and preservation of the knowledge of GOD. I have an accountability to the grace and truth afforded me in Jesus Christ, a responsibility to the cultivation and kingdom productivity of our relationship.

Let your light so shine before men, that they may see your good works, and glorify your Father which is in heaven.

MATT. 5:16

And, as we have said, *"he that doeth truth cometh to the Light"* (re. John 3:21). The peril is to rest upon one's laurels. To be brutally honest, I must concisely confess that for a couple of decades I could be found in the corner of the pew dozing. Not willfully suppressing the light, but avoiding exposure just the same, if you follow. I was the poster child for the minimally acceptable conscience-salving criteria to call myself a Christian. Just enough enlightenment for my circumscribed Christian subsistence beneath the bushel.

Frankly, I was embarrassingly not only a moderate Christian but also a liberal one. Well? I was a *laissez faire* Christian, and as best as I understand the term, it literally means "allow to do." From a true godly perspective, the philosophy is the erroneous notion of an all-permissive grace common to a compromised worldly-conciliatory Christianity. Under the guise of tolerance, and according to a common (attenuated) interpretation of a love without accountability, it is how much of Christianity justifies saving their lives for themselves.

For years, and to be honest it was for those decades I talk about, I surreptitiously took the inventory of those Christians around me and emulated their behavior. And I not only assimilated the presentation of common parishioners as my own if you will pardon the characterization. But I modeled my behavior and deportment and righteous affect after deacons and preachers. Uh, I wanted to be a good Christian.

This may initially seem to be amusing, until we admit that this is exactly how young Christians learn. Of course, I speak broadly.

The problem with this modus operandi is that the average congregation is too often made up of what I call minimalist and nominal Christians. Too often we do just enough to get by. I know because I was the norm.

Most folks (from my perspective then) seemed to function just fine to (what it didn't take me too long to realize) was just going through the motions. They predominantly appeared to be living successful lives. But for some odd reason (it seemed then) my own life kept going off the rails.

Concisely, I kept backsliding. We won't go into the particulars, but you can trust me on this – I was sinning. To keep this as short as possible, GOD had more in store for me than just emulating the average parishioner. In general, the average Christian's deportment, meaning both behavior and attitude, differed a great deal from who they appeared to be in church and who they were in the community. I was frighteningly becoming just like them. By the most generous estimation, I was lukewarm. GOD was not satisfied, and neither was I.

I decided to make the Word of GOD my standard. No, that's not quite right. GOD insisted that his Word be my standard. By reason of my affliction and many, many stripes, GOD would accept nothing less from me than walking in the light and truth of his comprehensive Word. What others were doing could no longer matter, but nonetheless, I could not help but make some observations. I'm not blind. What did Jesus tell his disciples?

Ye are the light of the world. A city that
is set on an hill cannot be hid.

MATT. 5:14

Let me try to write in the first-person possessive tense. First, it is Jesus who said we (his disciples) are the light of the world. To be painstakingly honest, considering that I was supposed to be the light of the world, I was a markedly shady character. The only light I had was the smiling face and religious affectation I attempted to pump up for church services. In other words, an illusion.

This is rigorous honesty, and this is what GOD was requiring of me to restore me to his grace. Uh, I tried not to pay attention to what other Christians were doing, but that is difficult when you are supposed to be members of the same body.

Frankly, I could not reconcile the glaring disparity between who I was on Sunday morning around other Christians (especially the preacher) and who I was in the marketplace and the workplace. One of those guys was an imposter and I knew who he was. I was a hypocrite, and the light I professed to have on Sunday morning was an illusion and a great darkness. Never mind that my intentions were good, I wanted to tap into the reality of GOD's Word and his expectations of me.

I emphatically was not a city on a hill. I was living beneath a bushel, a religious bushel – and in the valley. The revelation was startling, the illumination was painful. The acute explanation for my not having a witness for Jesus Christ in my community or workplace, or even among my family, became glaringly obvious. That guy in the mirror on Sunday mornings was a poser.

To be an effectual witness of the LORD Jesus Christ, I must have the light of his life. To have his resurrection life, I must first die to my own. Finally, I had begun the process. I repented not only of my sin, but also of my religious affectation and self-righteous posturing. I repented of ceremony without substance. I stepped naked and intrepid into the unsparing light and truth of GOD's Word.

The process of self-denial, and the internal assimilation of the gospel principle of losing the life to find it is painful. It is the gospel of Jesus Christ and him crucified, and the irrepressible making his cross mine. But there is no freedom that can be compared to the liberty that comes with nothing hidden or held back from GOD. And when I do not feel compelled to (attempt) hiding from GOD any longer, then I no longer feel a need to hide from man or fear man, either.

When we live the life of Jesus with integrity, we can speak in the name of Jesus with confidence. His life is the light of men (see John 1:4). This is the light of resurrection life, the light of an eternal life, and it begins the moment I surrender my old life to have the life Jesus Christ gave on Calvary. When I live in the light and truth of GOD's Word with the rectitude and accountability of the Holy Spirit, I may with boldness and power bear witness to the resurrection life that is mine in Christ Jesus. This is what makes the Christian disciple the light of the world, and it is the light and glory of the eternal life of Jesus Christ from the inside out.

It is GOD's design, dear Christian, that you and I be the light of the world (here and now). Nevertheless, and I include myself in the indictment, for Christianity to be the light of the world, it is still predominantly a very dark place. So many Christians, but so little of the selfless reality of GOD's unconditional love in the earth.

Let me be bold and bare-assed unsparingly honest. I will reference myself. There is a glaring discrepancy between the title *Christian* and the love of GOD in Jesus Christ realistically and (in practical application) reflected out of my life. To narrow the disparity globally (or in my neighborhood and family) I must begin with a painstaking personal inventory. Let me work close to home, and while it is day.

❋

I must work the works of him that sent me, while it is day: the night cometh, when no man can work.
JOHN 9:5

❋

There is opportunity enough (and evil enough) (darkness plenty) while it is called today. Even the Son of man knew his limitations and recognized that there are windows of opportunities and doors that are not always open. The evil and hatred (and unbelief) of men would bind even the hands of Jesus Christ.

The LORD Jesus Christ healed this man of blindness here in the ninth chapter of John as the occasion presented itself. In fact, verse one says that he was passing by and saw this blind man, and the entire ninth chapter is an exposition of his healing him.

Frankly, the entire chapter is an explicit instruction and revelation of the innate hostility, hypocrisy, and hatred hidden within the convoluted folds of self-righteousness and elitist sectarian religion. The Pharisees ruthlessly interrogated this poor man and his parents, also. They shamelessly indicted Jesus Christ as a sinner for healing a man on the Sabbath.

We predominantly tsk-tsk from the sanctuary of our respective denominational enclaves and fortresses without acknowledging the prophetic diagnosis and prognosis of blindness laid at our own temple door.

This entire chapter is a dissertation on the glaring disparity of light and darkness, pretense and reality, religion and love.

This blind man can be seen exponentially growing in the immediate grace and knowledge of the LORD Jesus Christ as an unprecedented healer sent from GOD, and as GOD. These, uh, good church folk, cast (him) the blind man out of the temple because of his testimony. Ahem, they are the very same righteous assembly that cast Jesus out of the temple in chapter eight.

Moreover, this man was blind from birth but was nevertheless reduced to begging in the shadow of a magnificent temple of organized religion. The Word of GOD declares that his blindness was neither a result of his sin, nor that of his parents (see John 9:2). Yet for all the sanctity and righteousness and the best of Judaism, neither enlightenment nor love had reached him there begging on the street. Still, we are predominantly blind to the prophetic revelation and connotation of the religious parameters in our own city. That is correct, we do not effectively see them begging in the shadow of our specific temple either.

✳

My little children, let us not love in word, neither in tongue, but in deed and in truth.
1 JOHN 3:18

✳

We miss the implications. You might say that we are blind. We essentially love within the constraints of our own self-celebratory religious ceremony. And them who most need the love of GOD are outside looking in.

The night is coming when no man can work. And not because of a lack of light, *per se*, but because of the evil concealed within the darkness. Opportunities to do good swiftly pass. Circumstances and Satan conspire that not one more soul is reached for Jesus Christ. Satan is conspicuously not lukewarm.

We hoard our rapidly diminishing light beneath a bushel and curse the encroaching darkness.

Without the light of the indwelling Spirit of the resurrected Christ we will not stand in the evil day. The Spirit-filled and the Spirit-baptized are the strength of our (local and national and global) body.

Without a faith that works by a genuine love (that is, in deed and in truth) we will not stand in the evil day. The night is coming when no man can work. While it is called today, we must be teaching and preaching both the infilling and the Baptism of the Holy Ghost.

This must be the urgency and the substance of our witness of the LORD Jesus Christ to our loved ones and our co-workers and friends. This must be our unsparing cry within the neighborhood of our Christian outreach and influence. The kingdom of GOD within us is his own indwelling and abiding Spirit, the internal reality of the Christ of Christianity, and not outward religious ceremony. (Perhaps) I best love my brothers and sisters in Christ within the parameters of organized religious ceremony, uh, within the "sanctuary." (Perforce) I best love sinners at the point of their need, in the community and in the marketplace and in the workplace, and in the same streets where they live.

We need the Holy Spirit to lead us into *all* Truth, and to teach us how to love. GOD is a Spirit (re. John 4:24). Jesus said so. Children, this is further enlightenment, the full exposition of the Almighty GOD in his Christ, to be filled with the Holy Ghost.

The night is coming when no man can work (re. John 9:4). We must have the fullest knowledge possible, the most comprehensive exposition and enlightenment of GOD abiding while it is day, before this world's situation becomes so dire and so dark that no man can work.

The revelation is progressive and perpetually transforming and empowering. I never tire of it. First of all, GOD is a *"Holy"* Spirit (the double emphasis is deliberate). We are not going to receive a Spirit who is Holy outside the obedience and sanctification that the Word of GOD commands. (I have covered this in depth within other volumes but am compelled to outline at least the basics here.)

We think, or presume, ("we," being the preponderance of mainstream worldly conciliated and carnally compromised contemporary Christianity) that we can have a Spirit who is Holy outside the parameters of the comprehensive Word of GOD. To make it doubly sure, that is, to make it irreconcilably irrefutable (thank you), this teaching in most of our Bibles is in red letters.

The LORD Jesus Christ made it so plain that it is difficult not to be cynical or satirical. He made it so concise and so easy to understand that the only reason for me not having the revelation is because I did not want it. Frankly, I wanted what I already had.

Personally, I could not get past the precursor of the promise. *If you love me, keep my commandments* (John 14:15). As you can see, I am incited to a glaring, brutal honesty.

In verse twenty-three of the same chapter, the LORD Jesus Christ makes it even more incisive. *If a man love me, he will keep my words* (re. John 14:23). These two scriptures were a painful and devastating revelation of my erroneous concept of Christian love. It is difficult to confess having been so shallow and self-serving about religious service.

Now, if by *keep my commandments*, I postulate that the LORD Jesus Christ means anything less than the comprehensive Word of GOD, I deceive myself. Loving GOD and loving our neighbor as ourselves precludes whom I am wont to call the preponderance of us from the promise.

Before Jesus will pray to the Father (in verse 16) to give me another Comforter, I must keep the commandments of verse fifteen. (If I may phrase it like this), this speaks to a fastidious obedience and is a command to an absolute fidelity. It is as plain as the affected piety upon our hypocritical faces.

Moreover, a Spirit who is Holy is also a Spirit of Truth *whom the world cannot receive* (see John 14:17).

This world cannot receive a Spirit who is Holy because they are driven and enslaved by an *unholy* spirit. Nor can them in love with this world receive a Spirit whom Jesus Christ emphatically says is a Spirit of Truth because they are (for the most part) volitional prisoners of a *lying* spirit.

Someone needs to tell the preponderance of us that the light that we do have (or seem to have) (or that we presume ourselves to have) will not be sufficient in the evil (and dark) day. If we think we can have a Spirit who is Holy abiding with us at the same time we serve and love an unholy spirit, we are deluded. Whether self-deluded or blinded by the god (or the spirit) of this world system, or any combination thereof, will not matter in the evil day.

> *If therefore the light that is in thee be darkness, how great is that darkness!*
>
> re. MATT. 6:23

Night is coming when no man can work. Moreover, in that day of darkness shall this saying be realized. *From him shall be taken even that which he "seemeth" to have* (re. Luke 8:18). Time and space preclude a lengthy exposition of Luke's rendering of the LORD's teaching, but we can at least touch upon it in the context of this specific notebook, *I AM the Light of the World.*

＊

No man, when he hath lighted a candle, covereth it with a vessel, or putteth it under a bed; but setteth it on a candlestick, that they which enter in may see the Light.
Luke 8:16

＊

Because we did not take advantage of the light (and enlightenment) to extend our vision, as it were; because we did not work while it was day, while we had the light and enlightenment and knowledge and wisdom in its season; because we did not take advantage of the possibilities and the potential afforded us; ah, may GOD have mercy upon us, because we did not appreciate and value *AND SHARE* the treasure that was given us, it will be taken from us. Night is coming when no man can work.

If we will listen carefully, we will hear our complacency delineated here, and our irresponsibility with the light and the vision as the prophetic correlative portend of the kingdom being taken from us and given to a nation bringing forth the fruits thereof (re. Matt. 21:43). May GOD have mercy upon us, because we would not take the light afforded us and exalt it upon a candlestick so that they which were entering in could see the light, we have effectively occluded the portal of the kingdom of GOD.

We have covered our light with a vessel, sometimes with a religious one. Sometimes we hoard our light (and celebrate ourselves) within the illusion of the sanctuary. No, I didn't use the wrong word. I speak of the illusion of security within the formal church sanctuary. The warfare rages on. There has been no cessation of hostilities. There will be no effective armistice with the god of this world. Satan lied.

Someone is going to get this. The light and truth not shared is effectively covered with a vessel. The enlightenment and revelation (I purport to have) but deliberately withhold from my neighbor and my brother, shall not benefit me either.

The light of GOD's Word is intended to be shared through my personal witness. The buck does not stop with me, that buck will be quickly spent. He who has ears to hear, let him hear. What I give away, and what I am prepared to give away, I am not only allowed to keep but also favored with its increase. What I make happen for another is not only sustained but perpetuated and increased within me and through me.

I am, as it were, a conduit of heavenly treasure. My portion is best realized as it passes through me to another.

I am, as it were, a disseminator of bread and a gatherer of fragments. My portion is realized (that is, I am fed) in the dissemination and in the gathering.

Or, to keep the analogy within this notebook, the light I have best benefits me when it is shared. That is, it burns brighter. GOD will see to it. Enlightenment begets enlightenment, revelation unto revelation. I am not trying to be deliberately mystical or cryptic, I am trying to incite one more Christian to stop burning beneath the bushel of sectarian (and elitist) religious organizations and radically and militantly take the light of their testimony of Jesus Christ into the marketplace and into the workplace. Let us resolve to take our Christian witness out of the exclusion (and seclusion) of the church sanctuary and into the streets.

The light that is in me (in a sense, the oil of anointing), or my measure of the Holy Spirit afforded me by grace, faith to faith through obedience and sanctification, best stays *topped-off* as I tell someone else about the hope that is in me. I must witness while it is called today. Night is coming when no man can work.

※

Seek ye the LORD while he may be found,
call ye upon him while he is near.
ISA. 55:6

※

Times are coming when enlightenment and revelation are going to be fixed (in their seasons). Grace will be hard to find. Light and vision will be precious. These things belong unto the *HOLY*.

※

Walk while ye have the Light, lest darkness come upon you.
re. JOHN 12:35

※

We must teach and preach and bear witness to both the in-filling and the Baptism of the Holy Ghost while it is day. We must perpetuate the light while it is still light if you follow.

※

While ye have Light, believe in the Light,
that ye may be children of Light.
re. JOHN 12:36

＊

While we have light, we must perpetuate the light. If we are not full of the Holy Ghost (and preferably baptized by fire as incendiary witnesses of the resurrection life that is in the LORD Jesus Christ), we will not stand in the evil day, and the hour of darkness even now coming upon the earth.

Night is coming when no man can work, and our enlightenment and revelation (vision) is going to be (relatively) fixed. We must seek the Baptism of the Holy Ghost while he may be found, we must tarry for him while he is near (as influenced by Isaiah 55:6).

The day is rapidly approaching that the door is going to be shut. We know the parable of the ten virgins. We know the cry came at midnight that the Bridegroom cometh (see Matt. 25:1-13). The observation that the Holy Spirit wants me to make is that it was dark well before midnight. The time to procure oil was before the evening progressed into night, and before darkness fell. I have already referenced the following scripture, and its second half many times, but the urgency and severity of our spiritual pandemic can sustain the redundancy.

I must work the works of him that sent me, while it is
day: the night cometh, when no man can work.

JOHN 9:4

We have also covered this, but it will not go away, as it were. Even the LORD knew that his opportunities to restore sight to the blind and preach the gospel to the poor were limited by times and season. Church of GOD, my cry is that he has made provision for you and I to do even greater works than these (re. John 14:12). He has sent us the *Expediency* and the *power* of his own glorified *person* and essence to enable us.

My loved ones and my neighbors must have the Holy Ghost before darkness falls, and well before midnight, if you follow. The opportune time, the expedient time, is now.

Children, I will answer to GOD for the illumination afforded me. There will be an astute reckoning of my stewardship of the light, of my sharing revelation when the opportunity arose. There will be an accounting of the light I have shared within the sphere of my immediate influence, of the grace and truth and hope and faith which works by love perpetuated within the orbit I occupy.

Seasons change. Some things become fixed. There are times and seasons which the Father hath put in his own power that are not for you and me to know (re. Acts 1:7).

We are to occupy with what we have and where we are while it is called today. There will be variables over which we have little or no control; capricious, unstable circumstances will arise. As we are good and faithful stewards of the LORD's resources, he will give them increase, (and give us increased opportunity), in the season of his sovereign good pleasure and self-determinate will.

A genuine faith would have both hands full. The maintenance and integrity of the light and truth afforded me is laid to my soul's account. The Word of GOD I have abiding sets the specifications for my lifestyle. The enlightenment I have is required of me, if you follow. Many times, I have said that the Grace of GOD answers to the Truth of GOD. Faith works by love within the constraints of holiness.

Children, the goodness of GOD has a just expectation of my gratitude, of thanksgiving, of praise and worship. The enlightenment and revelation of the Word of GOD given me is the holy criterion of both my liberties and my restrictions.

Thy Word is a lamp unto my feet, and a light unto my path.

Ps. 119:105

Darkness must be permitted, and sin given place to have any power. Dear reader, you may disagree, but this I have of the LORD. Darkness is allowed to encroach upon the light when I have something to hide, in a spiritual, figurative sense. It is I who lets the darkness in, that is, my carnal nature opens the door. Succinctly, I willfully sanction the darkness when I have some shady business to conduct.

And this is the condemnation, that Light is come into the world, and men loved darkness rather than Light, because their deeds were evil.

John 3:19

At some critical juncture, I have capitulated. I may call it *being overcome of temptation* or, as I have referenced it before, "Oops, overcome again." For all my tsk-tsking and feigned righteous indignation, I am a genial prisoner of willful sin. At some crossroads, as it were, I consented to the darkness so I could volitionally endorse (and enjoy) some evil.

There is a liability to the light I have, and it shall be laid upon my soul for all eternity. The grace and truth given me belong to Jesus Christ. I have a solemn responsibility for the preservation and the perpetuation of the vision, for its clarity and continuity, for its integrity, for its unalloyed rectitude and purity.

We all should be familiar with the prophet Samuel's calling, beginning with his mother Hannah's testimony, and her faith and prayer. We all should know of the corruption of Eli's sons, Hophni and Phinehas, who defiled the office of the priest. The first four chapters of 1 Samuel are rich and revelatory, terrible and eternally prophetic, contemporarily pertinent.

Space prohibits an exposition of the entire four chapters. They contain a veritable unfathomable and inestimable wealth of living prophetic wisdom, but they are also full of foreboding, and an infinite exacting knowledge.

For the last few pages of this notebook, I will use the first three verses of chapter three for our primary text. Then I can paraphrase or interject portions of other pertinent scriptures as the LORD leads. Before I list our current text, please let me emphasize that the exposition and revelation which follows is exclusively my own as afforded by GOD in prayer and supplication, always by great grace and an immeasurable mercy, and never of merit.

*

And the child Samuel ministered unto the LORD before Eli. And the Word of the LORD was precious in those days; there was no open vision.

And it came to pass at that time, when Eli was laid down in his place, and his eyes began to wax dim, that he could not see.

And ere the lamp of GOD went out in the temple of the LORD, where the ark of GOD was, and Samuel was laid down to sleep. (1 Samuel 3:1-3)

✳

Although it is not critical to our text, we notice that Samuel was in the temple under Eli's supervision, but it was the LORD that he ministered unto.

First, the ark of the covenant is representative of GOD's manifest presence. By the Spirit of the LORD, I assert that the lamp of GOD in this context, and the fact that it is about to go out, is an accurate measure of GOD's disfavor with the state of affairs as pertains to the office of high priest.

The narrative bluntly states that the sons of Eli, Hophni and Phinehas, are *sons of Belial* (concisely Satan), and even reinforces it with the statement *they knew not the LORD* (see 1 Sam. 2:12). The historian, Josephus, maintains that Eli was effectively retired because of his advanced age and that his sons were officiating as high priests in his stead. Notwithstanding, as we know, GOD not only holds his sons responsible for their corruption, but Eli as well for not putting a stop to it.

Concisely, the sons of Eli were misappropriating the best portions of the people's sacrifices for themselves and fornicating with the women who served in the sanctuary. Eli confronted them with their evil and went as far as to tell them that they were sinning against the LORD. Nevertheless, they did not obey him, and the LORD help him responsible as well as his sons.

The LORD sent a man of GOD to confront Eli with these evils, and the following is part of the formal indictment.

*

Wherefore kick ye at my sacrifice and at mine offering, which I have commanded in my habitation; and "honorest thy sons above me" to make yourselves fat with the chiefest of all the offerings of Israel my people?
1 SAM. 2:29

*

Of course, I want to put all this into the context of the Word of GOD as a lamp unto our feet, and a light unto our path (re. Psa. 119:105), as enlightenment and knowledge, as vision and wisdom in the preservation and perpetuation of the kingdom of GOD.

There was no fresh Word of GOD and no active or enterprising (passionate) vision to rally around. Because of malfeasance and corruption in the office of the priesthood, GOD had withheld both the light and the rain.

But it also behooves us to address the responsibilities (and accountability) of them who minister to the LORD in any capacity. Notably, Hophni and Phineas *knew not the LORD*, or in contemporary vernacular, if we may, they were not saved. Notwithstanding their ignorance, GOD held them responsible for what they (claimed they) did not know, but what they could have (and should have) known.

The light (enlightenment) was available but they preferred the darkness (ignorance) because their deeds were evil. This is a volitional blindness, a willful ignorance, a self-delusion.

With a closer consideration, Eli did, in fact, strongly admonish his sons about their behavior. His strong reprimand clearly testifies to his own enlightenment and knowledge of the LORD's holy character. In the following portion of scripture, we hear his awareness, his fear and dreadful portentous warning that GOD was going to hold Hophni and Phinehas responsible for their evil. Although the text does not explicitly reveal it, Eli should have known that the LORD was going to hold him liable for not putting a stop to it as well.

＊

Ye make the LORD's people to transgress (probably refers to the fornication with the female servants of the temple). *If one man sin against another, the judge shall judge him: but it a man sin against the LORD, who shall intreat for him?*
re. 1 Sam. 2:24-25

＊

In a figure of speech, if you can receive it, the Word of GOD concisely and distinctly describes Eli's negligence. *Eli was laid down in his place* (re. 1 Sam. 3:2)

Now, I know Eli was old and he was tired. He may have even considered himself retired, as Josephus suggested. But GOD held him responsible for the place he had been given and the duties he had assumed. And he was *laid down in his place.*

The Word of GOD does not directly indict Eli as it does his sons for purloining the sacrifices of GOD's people, but it does include him in the unambiguous rebuke for making himself fat with the *chiefest* of the offerings of GOD's people (see 1 Sam. 2:29). In other words, all three of them had gotten fat on the office of the priesthood. There is no delicate way to say it.

Moreover, GOD took it personally, you might say, that Eli did not put a stop to the impropriety and the evil. He impeached Eli with honoring his sons before him. Especially dreadful is that (from GOD's perspective) this evil continued to be perpetrated *in my habitation* (re. 1 Sam 2:29).

This was a terrible state of affairs in the house of GOD, the infiltration of wickedness into the temple, a salacious and insatiable evil appetite having insinuated itself into the very priesthood. This is indicative of the perpetual fervent readiness of darkness to encroach upon the light. There is nothing lukewarm about evil.

This situation is an unmistakable example of spiritual wickedness in high (religious) places. There is not a politically correct (or, as I say, delicate) way to say it. Within contemporary Christianity, religious personages continue to get fat (and rich) off GOD's people.

However, the preeminent prophetic portend that I glean is that if we are *"laid down in place"* (notwithstanding Eli's age) our *"eyes begin to wax dim, that we cannot see"* (re. 1 Sam. 3:2). When the light and truth of GOD's Word that we have available is not taken full advantage of, it may justly be withdrawn from us. The light within us is revealed as a great darkness, if you follow, (see Matt. 6:23).

Child of GOD, you and I are that temple now. We are the habitation of GOD through the Spirit (see Eph. 2:22). Moreover, the mature disciples of Jesus Christ are his priests in the earth.

We must "live up to" the Word of GOD afforded us in its season, that is, we are expected to walk in the practical living application of the light and truth that we have. We are expected not only to take full advantage of the enlightenment (and vision) that we have, but to also perpetuate it through our witness.

The Word of GOD becomes most precious during circumstances of encroaching darkness and oppressing evil, especially when under the virulent assault of spiritual wickedness in high (and even religious) places. If we capitulate to the darkness, we displease GOD. Duh. If we lay down in the place that has been entrusted to us because of social pressures or unpleasantness. If we turn a blind eye to evil.

Capitulation to evil always occludes vision. We are commanded to let our light shine for good reason. Otherwise, darkness will fill the void.

We are enlightened, imbued with the knowledge and wisdom of the Word of GOD to actively push back the darkness. When we burn for GOD, he taxes heaven and earth to fuel the dynamic enterprise of our faith. He releases more light and revelation and increases vision. This is the simplicity and the profundity of Jesus Christ, the Light of the World.

Profoundly (and not to frighten you) but the lamp of GOD in the temple of the LORD where the ark of GOD dwells is entrusted to every one of us who call ourselves by the name of Jesus Christ. This is, as it were, inspired by 1 Samuel 3:3.

Although it is an infinitely enigmatic seemingly incomprehensible concept, Christian, you and I are the temple of GOD now where the presence of GOD dwells, the ark of the covenant.

We have a covenant presence of GOD by faith, the indwelling Holy Ghost of the resurrected glorified Christ Jesus. He is *the lamp of God in the temple of the LORD.* That is, you and I are the temple, and the Holy Ghost is the resident fire of GOD.

Such is the accountability of grace in the true light and total exposure of the life of Christ. It is the constancy of self-evaluation and undivided consciousness of the indwelling Spirit of the risen Christ Jesus, truly to live and move and have our being in him (re. Acts 17:28).

The Spirit of GOD serves the purposes of GOD, and the expenditures of his grace (and my stewardship) shall suffer an astute reckoning. In the middle of our murmuring remonstrance, it behooves us to remember that the Father spared not his own Son. The revelation renders me an unprofitable (or unmeritorious) servant. My duty does not decide my portion. Indeed, mercy will.

Both my light and my vision emanate from the kingdom of GOD within me; ah, even as I work out my own salvation with fear and trembling (see Phil. 2:12). As the word *fear* is used here it can also mean *reverence*, but fear is really the more accurate translation. The word *terror* could have also been accurately used. I add this in order to say, "such is the nature (and holiness) of the Light whom we have been studying." His name is Jesus.

Honestly, I have had to redefine my "working" definition, or uh, decoding of the word *transparency.* Concisely, my working definition of *light* is finitely stuck. My rendering has always permitted me at least one "hole card" if I may use a poker analogy here. You know, be honest, but always, always hold something back.

Granted, I have some distance to go. If I may use the same analogy (and relax, saint, I do not play poker anymore), I have never played poker with anyone who has all their cards on the table.

This is the absolute of Jesus Christ, the Light of the World, in whom is no darkness at all (see 1 John 1:5).

Now, this is going to upset some religious apple carts, and turn over some doctrinal tables (and I may lose what few friends, and readers, I have) but I must give you what the Holy Spirit shows me and compels me to share.

When John wrote this portion of 1 John 1:5 as inspired by the Holy Ghost, *"GOD is Light, and in him is no darkness at all,"* well, he knew exactly who he was referencing.

Moreover, when John recorded the following scripture as anointed and ordained by the Spirit of him who is Holy, he knew exactly who he was talking about.

That was the true *Light, which lighteth every man that cometh into the world.* (John 1:9)

Finally, when John recorded the following verse as moved upon by the Holy Ghost, he was not confused about the deity of the LORD Jesus Christ or the identity of GOD.

Then spake Jesus again unto them, saying, *I AM the Light of the World: he that followeth me shall not walk in darkness, but shall have the Light of Life.*

JOHN 8:12

Selah.

3

I AM the Door

"I AM the Door: by me if any man enter in, he shall be saved, and shall go in and out, and find pasture."

–John 10:9

Here in the tenth chapter of the gospel according to John, we have what will comprise both the third and fourth chapters of this manuscript being birth out of my Bible study. Like all of these powerful and enigmatic *I AM* utterances of the LORD Jesus Christ, they will naturally overlap and interrelate; perhaps these two more than others since they are given in the immediate context of the same teaching. Moreover, Jesus Christ as the Door may also have a tendency to naturally overlap with Jesus Christ as "the Way," which will be a main component of chapter six, *I AM the Way, the Truth, and the Life* (re. John 14:6).

As the Holy Spirit dictates and permits, I will try to minimize repeating myself, but in defense of my inevitable redundancy, our subject matter is One LORD. It is as broad as it is deep. His name (meaning his character and essence) is Alpha and Omega.

✳

And he is before all things, and by him all things consist. For it pleased the Father that in him should all fulness dwell.
re. COL. 1:17 & 19

✳

And when the Father says all fullness, he infinitely means nothing lacking. This transcends the finite like eternity eclipses time, and like the heavens overshadow the earth.

Concisely, there is but One Door in the kingdom affairs of a Holy GOD and fallen sinful humanity.

✳

*Neither is there salvation in any other: for
there is none other name under heaven given
among men, whereby we must be saved.*
Acts 4:12

✻

There are twelve gates in that heavenly city, New Jerusalem, but there is only One Door into the kingdom of GOD.

Not to be deliberately contentious or divisive, but I call him (GOD) "Father" and I call him "Holy Spirit." But to be precise, his name is *Jesus*.

Now, I did not know I was going here this morning, but the Holy Spirit did. Our text needs a preface or a precursor (which could be a play on words), meaning "forerunner." But what I meant was both a preamble and a prerequisite.

Most of you know by now that I call them the "absolutes" of GOD. (To me) they preclude or interdict and nullify all subsequent argument or possible misinterpretation. I was only going to trouble you with two, but the Holy Spirit moves me to give you three. The first is:

✻

I and my Father are One.
John 10:30

✻

This one is especially fitting because it is found in the same chapter as our main text. Many theologians and wise men wish this statement were not in the Word of GOD, and others try to qualify it with oblique and obscure semantics and assorted complex religious-speak and doctrinal palaver desperate to make GOD three persons. And then they assign them different offices and different duties, and three distinct personalities.

If you have sensed some cynicism on my part, then your discernment is indeed correct. The doctrine of the trinity is the last bastion of the wisdom of this world as spiritual wickedness in high religious places. Yes, that is a strong statement. Hear me. It is the world system and organized religion in collusion to impart and confer or ascribe finite characteristics upon GOD to undermine the deity of the LORD Jesus Christ, to make him less than GOD, less than Almighty.

As the Son of man, our faithful High Priest was touched in all points with the feelings of our infirmities (re. Heb. 4:15), but this did not make him any less than One with the Father. This made GOD even more understanding and empathetic with our plight.

By the grace of GOD, Jesus Christ tasted death for every man (re. Heb. 2:9), and by the same grace (and as One), the Father tasted it also. That the Creator was made in the form of the creature, and as a servant experienced sin and death in Christ, exacerbates our offense and elucidates the severity and necessity of hell.

I believe in the Father, the Word (Jesus Christ, the Son of GOD), and the Holy Ghost, and I believe that these three are One according to 1 John 5:7. But I do not believe that they are three persons, or three personalities. God is distinctly not a person. *God is a Spirit* (re. John 4:24). I believe the Father and the Son are One LORD by the Holy Ghost. In fact, I wrote a book about it. I believe that Jesus Christ is One with the Father just like he said. Christian, he could not have said it any plainer.

Jesus Christ is so much GOD that he is One with the Father. Believer, the god of this world system (Satan) is desperate that you never know just how Almighty your Savior is. He goes to great (doctrinal) lengths to diminish his deity. He who has ears to hear, let him hear. Welcome to my Bible study.

No, I will not take it back. I do not care (too much) about how many books, uh, that I am not selling.

Of a matter of note, I am not interested in debunking anyone's doctrinal theory. I am interested in accentuating and apprehending (and assimilating) the GREATEST conceptualization and realization of GOD that I possibly can. I simply want to know him whom my soul loves.

Children, the more grace I grasp by the Word of GOD, the more his Voice resonates in the barrens and backrooms of my uncultivated spirit man. Here is another absolute. I have read this Word for decades, but I have just (relatively) (recently) *heard* it.

*

All things that the Father hath are mine
re. JOHN 16:15

*

Both worldly men and religious men scramble to attenuate this Word also, but there is no effective mitigation of the word *"all."* But, dear children, I ask you, who would endeavor to diminish the deity of the LORD Jesus Christ but a devil?

Whose doctrinal or denominational design would allow me only one-third of GOD at any given time? Some of you act like you do not know what I am alluding to. Granted, I would rather be discussing something less divisive and distasteful, as well. Welcome to the Holy Spirit's Bible study.

There are those who would maintain that Jesus means positionally here, or representatively, you know, as the Son of the Father, kind of like all that belongs to the husband (technically) belongs to the wife. But no. Jesus Christ means precisely what he says. *"All"* that the Father has is also his. Alas, the most obvious conclusion is that they concurrently share all because they are One (entity or essence / actually, One Spirit) as the LORD Jesus previously stated in John 10:30.

Here in John 16:15 he is talking to his disciples, to persons invested. He has no reason to speak obliquely or in parables here, as was his custom when speaking to the indifferent and the one-dimensional (the self-invested or self-interested). Neither is he beating around some doctrinal bush or skewed religious agenda common to contemporary wise men and witch doctors, not really meaning what we say, or deliberately taking other men, and even the Word of GOD out of context.

(If I may paraphrase the LORD), *"All things that the Father hath are mine because we are One just as I have said."* Oh my. If the children realized just what was theirs in Christ Jesus, they would be even more difficult to control (and subjugate). That is, if we realized we could have more than the one-third of GOD that our earthly fathers and religious leaders allocated us in any given circumstance. (Why, we would come out of the pews.)

Now, here is a third absolute, which in the light and revelation and the truth of, it causes me to wonder how we can still limit the Holy One of Israel. It attests to the hardness of our heart and the dedication of devils to diminish the omnipotence of the LORD Jesus Christ.

*

ALL Power is given unto me in heaven and in earth.
re. MATT. 28:18

*

It seems that we (relatively) have the same problem grasping the absolute of the word "all" as we do grasping the implications of the word "One." Putting this in its proper context will only seem to complicate our conundrum of keeping GOD contained and prescribed within the parameters of our presumptuous doctrinal box.

As we have already mentioned, there is but One Door to the kingdom of GOD by which a man or a woman may enter in to be saved. Likewise, and as we have said, when GOD says "all" he pointedly means "infinitely all." But this does not hinder wise men and witch doctors of various religious persuasions from imposing finite characteristics and limitations upon the absolute deity of the LORD Jesus Christ.

We patronize and imperiously postulate finite restrictions upon the Almighty One. We delight to tell him who he is. (Broadly) we have church tenets delineating what we will condescend to accept of him. The very word "finite" means limited.

We must go to the Source. *GOD is a Spirit* (re. John 4:24). The LORD Jesus Christ says so. This is my first fundamental, my first prerequisite absolute in forming the mind of Christ. The beginning of my understanding is to capitulate to the revelation that all my finite conclusions of him who is *infinite* fall short. To confess my ignorance, this is the beginning of wisdom.

GOD will show me, or I shall not have it. By way of an example of how GOD sometimes colors outside the lines of our doctrinal strictures, John saw him in the midst of the throne of GOD as a Lamb that had been slain, having seven horns and seven eyes, which are the seven Spirits of GOD sent forth into all the earth (see Rev. 5:6).

By way of a personal example, in prayer and fasting and in the awe and wonder of a little child, I saw the hand of the LORD bearing a candlestick with three candles burning, and the face of Jesus Christ through the flames. In a moment of pure worship and absolute surrender, GOD expressed himself by grace.

You already think me deranged or under the influence of mind-altering substances (but I assure you, I am not), so I might as well tell you the rest.

Some of this, I wrote of in another volume. There was a distinct season in Lexington, Kentucky that I attended two churches at the same time, the First Assembly of GOD, and a church by the name of Greater Faith. To be accurate, this season lasted about eleven and a half months.

First Assembly of GOD dismissed about 12:15 p.m. or so, and the Sunday school at Greater Faith began at 12:45 p.m. and the worship service and the preaching began at 2:00 p.m. Subsequently (and consequently), I attended two Sunday school classes, two worship services, and two sermons every Sunday. Moreover, most Sunday evenings, I attended Harvest Worship Church of GOD at 7:00 p.m. Yes, GOD had me in school, and as I have written, in special (or alternative) education, as it were.

To be concise, the Assemblies of GOD are staunch believers in the trinity, and they are Pentecostal, of course. Greater Faith are stalwart and avid believers of what is sometimes called the "oneness" Pentecostal doctrine. I did not know it at the time, but it was a *setup*, as it were, cleverly designed by GOD to specifically teach me some things about his identity (for lack of a better finite expression).

Succinctly (and sadly) we Pentecostal Christians are zealous champions of one of these two camps, trinity or oneness. We love GOD dearly, but we will not dare fellowship with one another. GOD emphatically did not want me ensconced or entrenched (and indoctrinated) by either faction, to use an almost militant term to describe the animosity that exists between these two (GOD loving) camps.

It was just a couple of weeks before GOD initiated my attendance at these two churches simultaneously, that the LORD Jesus Christ appeared to me in a vision bearing this candlestick and peering at me (almost) humorously through the flames. Dearest reader, whether you believe it or not, it does not diminish either my grace or my joy, or my love for you in Christ, either. For the record, I was on my feet praying at the time, in worship (wide-awake), walking back and forth as I often do. Jesus stopped me in my tracks.

Moreover, this is the first time (ever) that I have relayed the following, but here goes. About ten days later, I was lying in bed praying. At the time, I lived in an efficiency apartment in the shape of a large "L." My bed was in the shorter leg of that "L-shape," and I was laying there praying while facing my desk on the other side of the room, about ten feet away.

Directly above the chair at my desk and suspended about two feet below the ceiling were nine blue translucent globes, three by three by three; diagonally, horizontally, vertically. They were about the size of tennis balls and were almost see-through, gossamer, an incandescent resplendent cerulean blue. They possessed an *"other worldly"* radiance. Had I been seated at my desk they would have been just over my head.

I was astounded, transfixed. One of the first thoughts I had was to evaluate and establish my level of consciousness and to confirm that I was, indeed, awake. Christian, I did not know what to think. It has been over eight years and I can only now articulate what I saw. Meaning, dear reader, that I can only now take a chance on you.

Now, I know that the LORD our GOD is One LORD (re. Deut. 6:4 & Mark 12:29). Moreover, I know that there are three in heaven (the Father, the Word, and the Holy Ghost) that bear record of One LORD, or as the Word of GOD says, *"these three are One"* (see 1 John 5:7).

Dear children, it is the Word of GOD that says he is three and he is One; yes, simultaneously. As I was contemplating the Lamb of GOD in the midst of the throne having seven horns and seven eyes, the LORD moved me to relay the vision of the nine globes suspended above my desk chair. I am not sure what the number nine represents except that every way I looked at those globes, I saw three. Ah, but these eight years I have heard GOD say, "Do not circumscribe or restrain me, and do not limit me to what you understand."

Christian, that Lamb in the midst of the throne is the LORD Jesus Christ, and he is the One and only Door to the kingdom of GOD.

✳

> *I AM the Door: by me if any man enter in, he shall be*
> *saved, and shall go in and out, and find pasture.*
> JOHN 10:9

✳

Jesus Christ is the ingress and egress of GOD, the One Door of our effectual fellowship at the mercy seat (inside the veil) where the blood of the Lamb is applied.

✳

> *Behold the Lamb of GOD, which taketh*
> *away the sin of the world.*
> re. JOHN 1:29

✳

Jesus Christ is the Passover Lamb of GOD. The Door of my soul's reconciliation with GOD is by way of the cross of Jesus Christ and him crucified, through the veil of his flesh to the mercy seat where the blood of that Lamb is applied. Children, the rent flesh of Jesus Christ is the Door. This is the astute reality of the love of GOD, and the acute necessity of the physical existence of a horrible place called hell for those who deny him.

Moreover, the One Door represents the one commandment of the love of GOD for one world and one humanity, and we will come the same way, or we will not enter in. The Word of GOD expresses it like this:

✳

For thou wast slain, and hast redeemed us to GOD by thy blood out of every kindred, and tongue, and people, and nation.
re. Rev. 5:9

✳

This slams the door on our elitist denominational distinction. Frankly, our segregationist religious preference and privilege is representative of thieves and robbers trying to come up some other way, some other way than the one commandment of GOD's love.

The preponderance of us want to have the privilege of calling ourselves Christian and to have heaven as our eternal home but we want to keep and save what we consider the best of our temporal lives for ourselves. I am not talking (specifically) about mammon, or wealth. I am referencing the (predominantly) hidden riches that we have, our secret cache of clandestine personal (both individual and group) preferential prejudices and engrained judgmental attitudes toward other peoples. I (especially) include our ethnic and racial prejudices toward peoples of not only our own nation, but of the world.

(Leaving it in the first-person possessive tense) for decades I preserved and hid both the best and the worst of the "wealth" of my life for myself. I skimmed off the top and dealt off the bottom. There was good that I could have (and should have) done that went undone. There were bad attitudes and character flaws that should have been freely surrendered to the fire but which I clung to with the (relatively) same tenacity as I hoarded the good.

Succinctly, this is not the heart and mind of the meek and lowly Son of man, Jesus Christ, the Lamb of GOD. This is, rather, trying to come up some other way. Some other way than the total surrender and absolute transformation of the assiduous light and unsparing truth of the Word of GOD.

The Door is effectually (and correspondingly) the strait gate and narrow way of the Word of GOD. I mustn't think that I am going to get through that sedulous and punctilious door clutching the baggage and treasure chest of the natural man. The love of GOD in Christ Jesus is the omniscient eye of the *HOLY*. It is the figurative (but no less precise) eye of a needle, as it were. To love like that, to love anywhere resembling that, I must pass through the comprehensive (refining) gospel of Jesus Christ and him crucified.

The resurrection power of the LORD Jesus Christ comes by the strait gate and narrow way of Gethsemane, Pilate's Hall, Calvary, and three interminable days and nights in the belly of the earth (or sheol), until I have left the body of sin in the grave, and only then by way of an empty tomb. Alas, woe is me. I would come up some other way.

✳

*Verily, verily, I say unto you, He that entereth not by
the Door into the sheepfold, but climbeth up some
other way, the same is a thief and a robber.*
JOHN 10:1

*

The negative aspects of the Truth must be addressed, uh, you
know, the disease and the diagnoses and the excising of gan-
grenous or leprous flesh. (I can almost hear the righteous remonstrance of delicate spiritual sensibilities.) Our abhorrence
of correction and exhortation, of injunction and admonition,
is duly noted, and moreover, documented in GOD's books.
Child of GOD, he has them (see Rev. 20:12, 15), including one
called *the Book of Life.*

Here in the tenth chapter of John, the LORD Jesus Christ
speaks in parable and in allegory, as was often his practice.
GOD is hid in Christ (please allow the tense), and Christ is hid
in the Word. Sometimes the truth must be veined or mined
like gold and silver. It takes faith to make the Word of GOD
manifest the greater graces and deeper, purer, more precious
stratifications of truth. Only the intrepid come this way. The
indifferent and the apathetic, the slothful and the pretender,
oftentimes fall volitional victim to forms of faith, captivated
by mechanical religious ceremony yet remaining fundamentally unchanged in character.

The pure in heart see GOD (re. Matt. 5:8). Them with a single
eye and a sanctified purpose plumb the depths and scale the
heights and make the Word of GOD produce. Some things
must be hidden from the wise and prudent, and revealed
unto babes. Many of us are not docile or pliant (or obedient)

enough to understand and apprehend the ways of sheep, or to think like the Lamb of GOD. Oh my. Or to have the Shepherd's heart and mind, and vision.

The sheepfold in John 10:1 is normally an enclosure which contains several flocks of sheep, having their own respective shepherds. The walls are ordinarily made of stone and thorns are commonly placed on the top to discourage predators. There is only one Door into the sheepfold.

Now, much of the tenth chapter of John is parable and allegory, and the teaching and the exposition of the LORD Jesus Christ as the Good Shepherd. We shall proceed as the Holy Spirit leads. The "thieves and robbers" mentioned in verse one, are notably mentioned again in verse eight, and must be addressed.

✳

All that ever came before me are thieves and robbers: but the sheep did not hear them.
JOHN 10:8

✳

Dearest faithful reader, perhaps much like yourself, I would rather be talking about lying down in green pastures, still waters, or of being seated comfortably at a table prepared in the presence of mine enemies. However, the LORD Jesus Christ did not circumvent the reality of thieves and robbers. His custom was to confront unpleasantness and distastefulness directly. He seems to have had a distinct dislike of hypocrisy and pretense in all its varying shades of religious duplicity. Just saying, (as they say).

We like our religion unoffensive, tolerant. I have a label for our most popular contemporary righteous contingent of mainline Christians. I call our current *laissez-faire* worldly conciliatory commercial Christianity the fashionable denomination of *"all-permissive grace."* Concisely (and someone has to say it), if the Holy One were here, he would turn over some tables and drive the Pharisees and the pretenders (and the money changers) out of the House of Jacob.

We know that when Jesus Christ refers to "all" that ever came before him as "thieves and robbers" that he is speaking relatively. That is, he is not speaking about Moses and the prophets.

After prayer this morning, when I first sat down, I asked the LORD for his help with this exposition. We know that Satan is a thief and a robber, and a murderer as well. The LORD Jesus Christ explicitly singles him out for consideration a few verses later, and we will have plenty of time to discuss both his personality (to use a finite term) and the methodology of his evil.

As soon as I asked the LORD's help, and at the instant he gave me the word "relatively," he also gave me this precise word: *"Let GOD be true, but every man a liar"* (re. Rom. 2:4).

As we discussed in Chapter 2, The Light of the World, there may be (as it were) many sources of illumination in the world, but only One *true* Light of the World. GOD has appointed men to help you and I along the way, but like John the Baptist, they were not *that Light,* but they were sent to bear witness of that Light (re. John 1:8).

By way of comparison, there may be many nutritious meals on the Christian's menu, but only One Bread of Life. There are roads that have to be traveled and corridors that must be trod, but there is only One Door into the sheepfold; there is One Good Shepherd, One Resurrection Life, One Way to the Father, and One True Vine. His name is Jesus.

✳

Neither is there salvation in any other: for
there is none other name under heaven given
among men, whereby we must be saved.
Acts 4:12

✳

We must go to the Source. None speak for GOD but the Word of GOD. By way of comparison, there really is no comparison. There is no substitute for the absolute of the Word of GOD.

✳

GOD is not a man, that he should lie; neither the son of
man, that he should repent: hath he said, and shall he not
do it? Or hath he spoken, and shall he not make it good?
Num. 23:19

✳

The LORD our GOD never said anything he had to later retract or recant, has never reneged on a promise or a judgment. Nevertheless, GOD has made a way in the wisdom of his omniscient sovereignty and foreknowledge for the prayers and intercessions of men and women as priests, and as his sons and daughters, to influence times and seasons and circumstances by faith. Christian, he wants you and I to step up.

In the immediate context of Jesus' teaching here in the tenth chapter of John, let us address the Pharisees as first on the list of the LORD's indictment of thieves and robbers. We know about their defrauding the pilgrims in the temple who came to Jerusalem for the three annual festivals of Judaism. We know of Jesus cleansing the temple and driving the money changers out. Concisely, we know how that the works and the words of Jesus Christ revealed their mendacity and perfidy, their hypocrisy and virulent hatred of truth – and how that his explicit holiness convicted them of sin.

There are actual lists of the "*Woes of the Pharisees*." Eight are recorded in Matthew and are appropriately referred to as "*the eight woes*." Six are listed in Luke and are therefore called "*the six woes*." Matthew's version is found in Chapter twenty-three, verses 13-16, 23, 25, 27, and 29. (Ah, I wish we had the time and the space.)

Especially relevant to our study of Jesus Christ as the Door to the sheepfold (or as the Door to the kingdom of GOD), is that the scribes and Pharisees are effectively occluding the portal to the kingdom of heaven. As we will see, this tops the list of woes given by Matthew.

✳

But woe unto you, scribes and Pharisees, hypocrites! for ye shut up the kingdom of heaven against men: for ye neither go in yourselves, neither suffer ye them that are entering to go in.
Matt. 23:13

✳

What a dreadful charge to have laid against one's soul, but that you have hindered the soul of another. Whether deliberately or indirectly, hypocrisy impedes my neighbor's or my brother's ingress into the house of GOD, and into the kingdom of heaven. Perchance, I have neither purloined money nor possessions, and still be indicted as a thief and a robber indirectly.

When my misrepresentation of light steals your attentions and affections from the One *true* Light, I am a thief and a robber. When the message from the pulpit does not contain the unadulterated ingredients and power of the Bread of Life and the Blood of the New Covenant, that preacher is a thief. The teacher who compromises and mediates the austerity of the gospel of Jesus Christ and him crucified to give his flesh and my flesh a pass is a robber.

When I teach or preach *all-permissive grace*, or when I suppress the truth, to give both myself and my audience a pass, I am a thief and a robber. The severity of the allegation can bear its own redundancy. When I sit on the Word of GOD I cannot life by, when I will not stir up the gift of GOD that is in me, when I will not launch out into the deep and let down my nets for a draught – when I am standing in the Door, indecisive, whether afraid or just malingering, I am still obstructing the portal to the kingdom of heaven.

As you can receive it, the Holy Ghost shows me this morning that this is the "first" woe. The first woe is not teaching all the truth I know. Well, my first admonition is to live it, so that I can then teach it with integrity and under the auspices of GOD's grace, and in the power of his anointing. The Apostle Paul expresses it so much better.

＊

I kept back nothing that was profitable unto you.
Wherefore I take you to record this day, that I am pure
from the blood of all men. For I have not shunned
to declare unto you all the counsel of GOD.
re. ACTS 20:20, 26-27

＊

When speaking to the men at Harbor House and having what may be termed as a less than enthusiastic audience, there have been times when I have wanted to abruptly say, "*I'm not here to necessarily make friends, running for office, or trying to win a popularity contest.*" To qualify somewhat, my audience for the past seven years has not been made up of novices or debutantes. Most of you know that I primarily teach and speak as a lay minister to the homeless, whom in turn are often predominantly chronic addicts and alcoholics, sometimes mentally ill. Many are also felons and/or on parole.

My, um, *parishioners*, are not playing church. Most of them have been to multiple rodeos. All of them are hurt, broken, angry. Notwithstanding, I am sure most of them have also left hurt people in their wakes. We never want to intentionally offend, and always take care not to further alienate. But to preach Grace and withhold Truth is not the love of GOD in Jesus Christ. Succinctly, the Door is the way of an old rugged cross. "*My Father worketh hitherto, and I work*" (re. John 5:17).

The first woe directed at the scribes and Pharisees listed in Matthew 23:13 is that they have *"shut up the kingdom of heaven against men."* Although they are related, this specific woe is in two parts. 1) *"for ye neither go in yourselves,* and 2) *"neither suffer ye them that are entering to go in."*

To obstruct the portal to the kingdom of heaven or impede the free access of others is enough to make me a thief and a robber. The indictment is so dreadful that I dislike even using myself as an example by writing in the first-person possessive tense.

To have a "woe" directed at you personally by the LORD Jesus Christ (the Living Word of GOD) is indicative that one's behavior or attitude has already been laid in the balance and found wanting, to use an expression from the Book of Daniel. To follow in the same example or allegory, these woes being proclaimed over the scribe's and Pharisee's malfeasance of their position is symbolic of the handwriting on the wall that king Nebuchadnezzar saw. It essentially means that judgment has already been passed, and that manifold sorrow and chastisement are imminent.

As we mentioned, this first woe spoken to the scribes and Pharisees is found in verse thirteen. To be concise, I will just say that their offenses were cumulative and aggravating. Ten of the first twelve verses delineate their multiplied corruption. The comprehensive list of their impropriety and dishonesty extends all the way to verse thirty-six. It is a scathing and exhaustive description given by the LORD Jesus Christ of the absolute moral turpitude and dissolution (and dissimulation) which had spread like a cancer beneath the self-righteous cloak of the scribes and Pharisees.

As was common, there was a great multitude gathered around the LORD Jesus Christ and his disciples. He begins his charge and impeachment against the scribes and Pharisees by solemnly citing the honored position that has been entrusted unto them.

The scribes and the Pharisees sit in Moses' seat.

re. MATT. 23:2

If we will consider it, the gravity, influence, and prestige of their office explains and justifies the LORD Jesus' exacting critique of their behavior and attitudes. Frankly, it should cause the preacher and the deacon board to tremble. Everyone involved in the ministry of the Word of GOD should remain aware of the solemnity and eternal value of the souls whom we serve. And it is not only the size of the gathering that gives it such gravity, it is also the character and virtue of him in whose name we gather.

For where two or three are gathered togeth-
er in my name, there am I in the midst of them.

MATT. 18:20

O dear children, let us not gather to practice religion or celebrate ourselves, but to attend to kingdom business in the astute consciousness of the Holy One in our midst.

Jesus Christ is the Door of the sheep, in (and through) whom all kingdom business is transacted. *"By me"* says Jesus, *"if any man ENTER IN, he shall be saved"* (re. John 10:9). Moreover, *"to go in and out, and find pasture"* is indicative of a healthy, burgeoning relationship of a sheep with a good appetite.

Now, we have covered the following scriptures at some length, but the Holy Spirit wants to reiterate their significance and authority, their magnificence and excellency in the context of Jesus Christ as the Door to the sheep, and as access unto the Father for all the kingdom business of our soul.

✳

Having therefore, brethren, boldness to enter
into the holiest by the blood of Jesus.

By a new and living way, which he hath consecrated
for us, through the veil, that is to say, his flesh.
Heb. 10:19-20

✳

Christian, this is the way we must come. To get to the mercy seat where the blood of the Lamb of GOD is applied for the remission of our sin, we must pass through that rent veil, *"that is to say,"* the torn flesh of the Son of man and Son of GOD, Jesus Christ. This is the Door.

This is the acute reality of Calvary, and the absolute of Christianity.

✳

Verily, verily, I say unto you, Except you eat the flesh of the
Son of man, and drink his blood, ye have no life in you.
re. John 6:53

✳

This is not playing church or practicing religion. This is not ceremonial self-preservation or self-celebration or seeking the honor one of another. This is not superficial religious form, but this is the agony of grace and the truth about real love – this is covenant faith.

This is the portal to the kingdom of heaven. We pass (as it were) beneath the blood of the Lamb of GOD upon the door posts of the portal, and through the pierced and rent flesh of GOD's only begotten Son, Jesus Christ. The weight and the consequence in the manner of our coming lies in the rectitude and preeminence of the Holy One of GOD as we esteem the value of the sacrifice.

This is no casual undertaking or superficial religious ceremony. The flippant and apathetic way we (often) go about it (sadly) attests to the lack of eternal value we place upon it. In fact, if you will consider it, it is actually an accurate reflection of the faith we have, or the lack thereof.

Faith has respect unto the sanctity and holiness of the sacrifice. Ostensibly we are going to offer worship unto a great King, and to receive the Words of Life by the mouth of his servant, the man of GOD. Many of us simply go through the motions. Our GOD is no more real (and no more revered) than the faith we have.

What does it say about our own character (and Christianity) that we too often come indifferent or preoccupied, busy about earthly things, minds and hearts glutted with earthly material things, hypnotized, obsessed, enslaved by earthly things?

Moreover, we unabashedly and bare-assed approach a Holy GOD on Sunday as if he did not know how we lived the other six days of the week. (Please pardon the expletive as you can.) As if the phony smiling face mitigates the hatred for our neighbor and/or our brother in our heart, the resentments and unforgiveness and bad attitudes we hoard.

We come having other lovers: self, the world, mammon and status. We offer a Holy GOD pretense and leftovers. Where would GOD spend our subterfuge and dissembling, or the phony sticky-sweet, fabricated love of our artificial religions form?

*

Leave there thy gift before the altar, and go thy way; first be reconciled to thy brother, and then come and offer thy gift.
MATT. 5:23

*

Many think me severe, but I defy them to read the entirety of the LORD's formal indictment of hypocrisy in the twenty-third chapter of Matthew, and throughout the comprehensive gospel, in fact. They thought the LORD severe, also. Concisely, a Spirit who is a Holy Spirit convicts of sin. Frankly, coming up any other way than "real" makes me a thief and a robber.

The omniscient eye of a Most Holy GOD oversees the blood and body of his only begotten Son. To think that I can enter in behind that veil with a hidden thing not only makes me a thief, but a fool as well. And GOD is not going to meet me anywhere else. We have covered this at some length, but what some think is redundancy simply delights my soul.

*

And there I will meet with thee, and I will commune with thee from above the mercy seat, from between the two cherubims which are upon the ark of the testimony, of all things which I will give thee in commandment unto the children of Israel.
Ex. 25:22

❋

Christian, this is where the man of GOD, Moses, got his marching orders. All things being equal, or ideal, this is where your pastor receives his also, and this is where you are to receive yours.

To presume or endeavor to enter in behind that veil with unrepentant sin is not boldness, but impudence and delusion. *"If I regard iniquity in my heart, the LORD will not hear me"* (re. Ps. 66:18).

In the context of our discussion, if I give sin a place in my heart, I cannot gain access into the Door. Children, the scribes and the Pharisees were playing church. Just like much of contemporary Christianity, they were attempting to climb up some other way.

My will must be in agreement with GOD's will, that sin has to die in the flesh for me to make my way to that mercy seat. (Let's just keep it real.) Sin must die in the flesh for me to be alive in Christ (in the Door). The price is too high (and too Holy) to allow willful sin, the blood is too precious.

❋

*For if we sin willfully after that we have received knowledge
of the truth there remaineth no more sacrifice for sins.*
HEB. 10:26

✳

We are not talking about sinless perfection. That, of course, is a place of Christian nirvana called heaven. The word "willfully" here in Hebrews 10:26 corresponds to the word "regard" in Psalm 66:18 which we quoted a few paragraphs ago. To "regard" iniquity in my heart is to give it place, or in other words, to give it a pass. This means to willfully allow it or give it permission. (This also gives it power.)

This giving sin a pass is willful. The Word of GOD says there is no more sacrifice for it, meaning it is not under the blood, it is not upon the mercy seat. Pertinent and agonizingly relevant to contemporary Christianity, this pokes a gaping hole in the erroneous notion of all-permissive grace. Concisely, grace is for them who resist this sin and trust the power of the blood of Jesus Christ for their ultimate victory over it. The same grace that saves my soul from sin, teaches me and empowers me to stay out of sin.

To be saved, I must enter into the sheepfold by the Door, the LORD Jesus Christ. I enter into the covenant accountability of the shed blood and through the rent veil of the flesh of Jesus Christ. Both outward behaviors and internal attitudes are meticulously assessed in the light and truth of the Word of GOD, the LORD Jesus Christ. Indeed, I am evaluated to the uttermost because I am saved to the uttermost.

I am to live and move and possess my being in the intimacy and integrity of the abiding fellowship of Jesus Christ. I am not to be a practitioner of religion, but a Christian by virtue of the indwelling Holy Spirit of the resurrected Christ of GOD.

(To redirect) frankly, the first woe is the hypocrisy of not being real, and the pride and egotism of self-righteousness. The scribes and the Pharisee's malfeasance was compounded or exacerbated by the position of honor which they held. That is, they sat in Moses' seat, or wielded his authority. They were responsible for the interpretation and administration of the Law.

To be concise, their glaring comprehensive evil was perpetrated through hypocrisy and pride. They abused their position of trust through oppression, exploitation and extortion, and through misdirection and fraudulence.

Their preeminent sin in the astute percipient estimation of the Holy One was occluding the portal to the kingdom of GOD and of heaven. I repeat it for emphasis, what I called the "first woe" of eight. But let me go on record here and now, I did not count them.

✴

But woe unto you scribes and Pharisees, hypocrites! for ye shut up the kingdom of heaven against men: for ye neither go in yourselves, neither suffer ye them that are entering to go in.
MATT. 23:13

✴

To place this in the context of our chapter, and to state their primary infraction in contemporary vernacular, *"they were standing in the Door."* The Pharisees were the preeminent righteous standard for the religion of Judaism. They considered themselves the religious aristocracy, you might say, of GOD's chosen people, Israel.

The Pharisees governed the temple, interpreted and administered the Law of GOD given to Moses. They effectively represented themselves as the only genuine means of access to a "right" or righteous relationship with GOD. They bluntly represented themselves as the Door. Well, to be fair, perhaps it was not so much that they represented themselves as the Door, as it was, but that they were blocking the portal. This definitively put them at odds with the LORD Jesus Christ.

Broadly, along with the Sadducees, they were part of the religious and political body of the Sanhedrin in Jerusalem. This was the seventy-member council which ruled the Jewish people, and the temple high priest was their leader.

In all communities with a significant population there will be a group of people (or several different groups) which represent themselves as the religious standard for godly living. To varying degrees, they feel that their particular doctrine is the only appropriate way to establish a viable (or righteous) relationship with GOD.

As you can see, I am proceeding circumspectly. To be fair, most of these religious peoples (or denominations) do point to Jesus Christ as the Door, or as the Savior of the world. Uh, but they have the exclusive access (meaning their specific church tenets and doctrine) to the only corridor. They can tell you who GOD is and precisely how to get to him. Their way, or essentially no way.

Our first inclination is to respond that we do not feel that way, that is, considering ourselves the exclusive righteous avenue to GOD. But I have visited different denominations within the same town which each, in turn, are convinced of their own singular spiritual superiority. The preponderance of us (that is, each denomination) are persuaded that the members of the other two, three, or ten other churches in town are unfortunately irrevocably lost.

Many of us are too spiritually refined to admit it, but if we are painstakingly, brutally honest, we know them folk over there are going to split hell wide open. Indeed, and all the evidence suggests that we are resigned (and somewhat smugly satisfied) about the fact that they are lost. We are certainly not trying to reach them. Some of us bid them Godspeed.

What does it mean to "*shut up the kingdom of heaven against men?*" Jesus is plainly telling the scribes and Pharisees that they are not trying to get any closer to GOD, and that they are hindering those who want to. Essentially, they are satisfied with the status quo. They oversee the temple, they have (as it were) arrived at the pinnacle of religious prestige and authority.

Let us define the indictment in some of Jesus' own words. Jesus warned the multitude and his disciples about both the hypocrisy and the pride of the scribes and the Pharisees.

✳

Do not ye after their works: for they say, and do not.
re. MATT. 23:3

✳

In other words, do not emulate or base your religious deportment and behavior upon their example. They are not genuine, or true. They say one thing and do another, (or do nothing).

They are not the gold standard they are representing themselves to be. Moreover, they abuse their authority. They put religious duties upon others that they themselves will not perform. (Don't do as I do – do as I say.)

※

For they bind heavy burdens and grievous to be borne,
and lay them on men's shoulders; but they themselves
will not move them with one of their fingers.
MATT. 23:4

※

Jesus is basically saying that these scribes and Pharisees, from the positional authority of Moses' seat, under the auspices and accreditation of the Sanhedrin and the high priest, instruct the common people (if you will) to do one thing, but they do another. *"For they say, and do not."* (re. Matt. 23:3)

These scribes and Pharisees are misrepresenting themselves as the preeminent standard for godly living. The Word of GOD teaches that this misrepresentation is hypocrisy, and effectively a type of fraud. This fundamentally makes them the same as a thief and a robber.

Let me personalize this in an attempt to make a point. My own aspiration or passion to attain some position must be sanctified unto GOD. That is, my seeking and my ambition must be singular, holy, pure. Indeed, if my faith is genuine it will be perpetuated and sustained by love.

My ambition must be for GOD's honor and glory. I am offering myself as a living sacrifice for service, and not as a candidate for office. As a disciple of Jesus Christ, GOD redirects my love for him into the service and love for my neighbor. And remember, my neighbor is anyone whose life in in crisis.

The following words of Jesus Christ also expose and exemplify the pride of the scribes and Pharisees that is the catalyst of their self-seeking and self-righteousness.

✳

But all their works they do for to be seen of
men: they make broad their phylacteries, and
enlarge the borders of their garments.

And love the uppermost rooms at feasts, and
the chief seats in the synagogues.

And greetings in the markets, and to be
called of men, Rabbi, Rabbi.
MATT. 23:4-6

✳

The pride of life in a religious context is the corpulence and the cancer that gluts and occludes the portal to the kingdom of heaven. Religious pride says, *"look at me,"* when I should be saying, *"look unto Jesus."*

Sometimes our organized religious service is more about the costume and the self-celebration and the ceremony than about Jesus Christ. We become an end to our own means in the honor one of another. Whom are we really worshipping? For whom are we gathering, for whose ultimate benefit?

The eternally pertinent Word of GOD has reached us here on the periphery of self-veneration and posturing piety. The LORD Jesus Christ could accurately tell the preponderance of us, *"Ye worship ye know not what."* (re. John 4:22)

We hide behind the ostentatious borders of our religious garments. Beneath the shady cloak of self-righteousness and pride (and covetousness) all manner of evil ensues. Rather than a radical character transformation (repentance), we have a light show and a large (and loud) band. We teach and preach superficial Christian etiquette rather than the austerity and strait gate of the Word of GOD.

Broadly we are stuck in a religious form to emulate the forward momentum of a genuine faith. The rant is indeed mine, but the indignation and vexation of Spirit belong to Jesus Christ. The LORD justly takes exception to them that impede passage into the kingdom of GOD.

Sometimes extravagant costume and elaborate religious pretentions and theatrics distract from the absolute of One Door. The counterfeit extorts and defrauds (and frankly steals) from the genuine, detracts from and attempts to devalue the original. Sometimes the focus of the righteous assembly becomes the ceremony, and having church becomes all about us.

Relative to contemporary Christianity, the Holy Spirit gave me this term early this morning to designate a phenomenon that obstructs the portal to the progressive grace and truth of the LORD Jesus Christ in the dynamic (unending) revelation of GOD. He called it *"positional complacency."*

We have already touched upon positional pride: the ascendancy of self-righteousness and presumed personal piety, the predisposition of religious pride to stand in the Door – to covet the honor and recognition of the congregation, to purloin and misappropriate the glory of GOD. Rather, the steadfast servant of GOD is vigilant to keep the corridor unobstructed and direct the attention and loyalty of his audience to the LORD of glory. The good and faithful servant facilitates unimpeded access to the One true Door to the kingdom of heaven, the LORD Jesus Christ.

Some folk proprietarily pose as having an exclusive patent on the portal to the kingdom of GOD. (I speak broadly but no less concisely if you follow.) There are multitudinous wannabe denominational monopolies out there. You know, our way, or hell is going to be hot.

Notwithstanding our particular church or charter tenets and body of religious knowledge, our comprehensive denominational disciplines delineating the identity, characteristics and expectations of GOD; organized church leaders have a tendency to reach some vague pinnacle of nebulous know-it-all accomplishment. What I am struggling unsuccessfully to say is that we plateau, and then begin to teach out of a box.

There are certain doctrinal questions and perhaps some hard sayings for which we have prepackaged or prefabricated facile (often perfunctory) answers on the run. We then worship together with like-minded (and close-minded) folk. Most often we dress alike and sound alike.

There are what could be called doctrinal fault-lines which often delineate and circumscribe religious camps. It is imperative to know on which side of each of these lines that you are going to pitch your tent (if I may stick to the camping metaphor). These are where major earthquakes occur. You can probably even feel the tremors as I list a few. Some of them concern water baptism, the baptism of the Holy Ghost, the doctrine of "oneness" or that of the trinity, "pre," "mid," or post-tribulation rapture, that sort of thing.

Of course, these things are very important. And it is important to pray and research and meditate upon all of these, and to know where I stand on each. The point I want to make is, it is okay to believe I am correct, but it is in condemning the next fellow as wrong that the earthquake ensues. Too often we not only denounce these persons who believe differently than ourselves as wrong, but as hell-bound heretics. Irrevocable harm is done.

Broadly, each denomination indoctrinates neophyte believers into our specific church tenets. (I nearly used the word *convert* for *neophyte* but converted is what the Apostle Peter was after Satan had sifted him as wheat for a season. After he betrayed everything he had been taught and denied the LORD three times in quick succession – bested by a servant girl, warming himself around the devil's campfire.)

Frankly, these neophytes must be ruthlessly brainwashed into our denominational tenets, or some wolf in sheep clothing from another denomination (you understand) will snatch then away. In fact, the LORD Jesus Christ describes this process of elitist sectarian indoctrination in his list of woes upon the Pharisees that we have been considering. And as we shall see, it is directly related to "the first woe" of shutting up the kingdom of heaven against men.

✳

Woe unto you, scribes and Pharisees, hypocrites! for ye compass sea and land to make one proselyte, and when he is made, ye make him twofold more the child of hell than yourselves.
MATT. 23:15

＊

The Pharisees were obviously quite proficient at this inimical process of religious indoctrination. They devoutly tutored and uh, inculcated their neophytes into being twice the devils as themselves.

Relatively, religious indoctrination (or brainwashing) has not changed. These specific denominational church tenets which I have termed "*fault-lines*" run right beneath our surface Christianity. On the surface are smiling self-righteous faces and shallow Christian smarm. But tread upon one of these fault-lines and suddenly you will see the smoke and lava, and the incendiary religious devil beneath the superficial form of faith.

Once we have settled into the strictures of our specific denominational brands, digging around these doctrinal fault-lines is surreptitiously but ardently discouraged. The Holy Brethren and the Sisters of Sanctity like to have things settled. They are not only above reproach but also exempt from the inane questions of common parishioners and johnnie-come-lately(s).

The Church tenets are inviolable and unimpeachable (and uh, immaculate). Please, call before digging here. Stay off the grass. Do not trouble the waters or ask the deacons and the preacher any embarrassing or controversial questions. Of course, many contemporary churches conveniently dismiss with the most potential dissension or debate by having one primary doctrine – that of all-permissive grace. Surface Christianity.

Some of us are fortunate enough to have a certain body of knowledge or a list of general doctrinal tenets settled centuries ago. We have entered into the perpetual peace of positional complacency and ultimate spiritual poise, totally desensitized and unreachable by either discussion or dissension, effectively dead in the pew.

Let's get honest. There is church etiquette and structured ceremony, and then there is the real me without the Christian accoutrement and trimmings.

Religious routine never reached me where I really live. It takes the Holy Spirit of a living Word to transform my irascible character into a viable reflection of Jesus Christ. It takes a miracle to eradicate childhood prejudices and adult bigotry. Only the Word of GOD can change a heart and transform a mind.

I can precisely emulate Christian deportment and spontaneously reproduce all the religious jargon and trite spiritual euphemisms and even quote scriptures in a pinch, but can I love my neighbor as myself and pray for them that despitefully use me? When deep calls to deep can I answer with unfeigned faith from the heart? Do I know who Jesus is when my loved ones are in the midnight of their soul?

Jesus Christ is the revelatory Door of progressive grace and truth that affords me glimpses of the Almighty GOD. My external Christian aspect and general deportment may be tweaked perfectly, but have I fallen in love with the Word of GOD, and is there a fire in the inner sanctum of my soul?

Beyond the honor one of another is an opened Door into the depths of GOD, an enterprising dynamic encounter awaiting the intrepid.

Through that veil, mercy awaits to embrace the bold and the needy with amazing grace. On the other side of the Door, (Jesus Christ). *"There I will meet with thee, and I will commune with thee from above the mercy seat"* (re. Ex. 25:22).

It is in Christ Jesus that I cry, *"Abba Father."* Dear Christian, it is Jesus Christ (the Door) by the Holy Spirit that you and I are made One with the Father.

Through that veil, I move into the next quadrant of a new horizon; with fresh vision, still waters, green pastures – Holy communion. I am a Christian nowhere else but at that mercy seat. Here, on this side of the Door, I am incrementally and resolutely made a disciple and then a priest.

This is beyond superficial ceremony and religious stasis, here where critical encounters occur in the light and truth and astute transparency of the presence of GOD. We must leave all pretense and grandiose Christian delusions on the other side of the Door, sequestered and solemn in the sanctuary of positional complacency. Here at the mercy seat it is sinners saved by grace only.

The world sees plenty of Christians, and so little of Jesus Christ. We must go *"into"* Jesus Christ to tap into his power to transform and equip us into ardent disciples. His own virtue and anointing delegate and empower us to bear witness to his resurrection life because we are made partakers of his essence and authority.

This world desperately needs to see the effectual power of Jesus Christ to radically transform a life, but I cannot show you what I do not have, or (sadly) introduce you to someone I really do not know.

Many Christians subsist on the wrong side of the Door (Jesus Christ). We believe "*on*" him, but we do not progress "*into*" him.

✳

Then said Jesus to those Jews that believed on him, If ye continue in my Word, then are ye my disciples indeed.
JOHN 8:31

✳

(Broadly) (I ponder) if we believe on Jesus Christ with any more substance or depth than these Jews did here in the eighth chapter of John. These last eight years that I have been writing consistently out of my Bible study, it has caused me significant consternation for the comprehensive soul of the contemporary Church. (The status quo of the saints is disconcerting.) And, frankly, without debate or expiation, I have the mind of Christ.

John makes a definitive point that these Jews "believed" on Jesus. He (seemingly, to me) emphasizes the fact. In fact, he states it twice in quick succession. Here is verse thirty, the verse preceding the one I quoted.

As he spoke these words, many believed on him.

JOHN 8:30

It is inevitable that these Jews enter into about everything that I write. Their religious predicament (and paradox) concisely parallels my own personal experience. They trusted that their religious heritage as the physical offspring of Abraham established them as GOD's elect. Succinctly, I was the preacher's son. Both they and I trusted the body of religious knowledge we possessed, as well as our positional righteousness. We were both "in the Church."

They "heard" Jesus' words (his doctrine and teaching) and believed on him. I had listened to good sound Bible teaching and preaching all my childhood and much of my adulthood. And I "believed" on Jesus, but to be brutally honest, the level of my believing (for decades) could not prevent my uh, well, my perpetual (habitual) periodic backsliding. And if you will read the remainder of John, chapter eight, it becomes starkly evident that the words (or the teaching and preaching) that these Jews heard from Jesus did not truly benefit them any more than the teaching and preaching that I heard (or the level of my believing) prospered me. We both explicitly fell into the following category.

✳

But be ye "doers" of the Word, and not hearers
only, deceiving your own selves.
JAMES 1:22

✳

Both they and I trusted in the aggregate body of (head) knowledge of GOD that we had accumulated over the years, and what (tradition and ceremony, religious ritual) had been handed down to us. Both they and I were Bible historians, you might say. Yet it is obvious that the head knowledge we possessed had not penetrated our hearts.

We had not transitioned into "doers" of the Word, we were "hearers only" and unfortunately (in such a state) we were deceiving our own selves. Each of us may have been misinformed or were unsure on certain points, but the bulk of the knowledge we possessed was sound, potentially beneficial, even life-transforming knowledge. We just were not "doers" of the Word.

We had not implemented it to our hearts or allowed it to change our behavior, or we had not submitted to the genuine repentance that the Word of GOD commands. James would have said, *"Faith without works is dead"* (re. James 2:26). The author of the Epistle to the Hebrews puts it as follows.

❋

For unto us was the gospel preached, as well as unto them: but the Word preached did not profit them, not being "mixed with faith" in them that heard it.
HEBREWS 4:2

❋

We know that the Word of GOD here is referring to that entire generation of the children of Israel who were relegated to wandering in the wilderness for forty years. They provoked GOD and grieved his Holy Spirit.

Yea, they turned back and tempted GOD, and limited the Holy One of Israel.

Ps. 78:41

GOD had repeatedly admonished them. His miraculous delivery of them from the hand of Pharaoh and from bondage and servitude had not genuinely transformed their minds or moved (and softened) their hearts to serve the living GOD. They habitually and impudently defied GOD's longsuffering love and eventually evoked GOD's wrath. Because of their rebellious and irascible character and recalcitrant (unrepentant) behavior they were denied access into the promised land.

※

Because all those men which have seen my glory,
and my miracles, which I did in Egypt and in the
wilderness, and have tempted me now these ten
times, and have not hearkened to my Voice.

Surely they shall not see the land which I sware unto their
fathers, neither shall any of them that provoked me see it.
Num. 14:22-23

※

Although we (as contemporary Christianity) have not comprehensively received (and assimilated) the prophetic revelation, we have much in common with this generation. In fact, this generation here (on the wrong side of Jordan), as well as the Jews in the eighth chapter of John, *and* contemporary Christianity, are of the same general (garden variety) religious genre.

Church folk have not fundamentally changed. (I speak broadly.) Many of them who consider themselves GOD's chosen (elect) people have not radically changed or been regenerated. Predominantly, we have not entirely and utterly been converted.

※

Marvel not that I said unto thee, Ye must be born again.
JOHN 3:7

＊

This Word of GOD was spoken to (arguably) the most religious (and perhaps the wisest) man alive at the time. He had plenty of head knowledge and observed copious traditional church ceremony and much religious ritual, but he had not been radically changed (or radically repented). Judaism was replete with formal religious ceremony, but also surfeited with hypocrisy and hatred simultaneously. Just saying.

We resist the prophetic correlation. We are reluctant to look too deeply into the mirror of the Word of GOD to make the associative connection, and uh, to draw the revelatory religious parallel: to humbly accept the prophetic implications – that the LORD Jesus Christ (the Word of GOD) is speaking explicitly to us.

The Word of GOD is not a history tome. It is piercing revelatory prophetic implication. GOD is talking to me.

＊

Now these things happened unto them for ensamples:
and they are written for our admonition, upon
whom the ends of the world are come.
1 COR. 10:11

＊

Christian, we are that generation upon whom the ends of the world are come. And we have more in common with the children of Israel in the wilderness than we are willing to admit and accept. In fact, the Holy Spirit draws a three-fold parallel or collateral if you will. I am moved to rephrase a statement made a couple of paragraphs ago. We (as contemporary Christianity) are the religious equivalent and counterpart of both the children of Israel in the wilderness, and the Jews in the eighth chapter of John.

Amazingly, the children of Israel in the wilderness, *"drank of that spiritual Rock that followed them:* (and miraculously and prophetically and phenomenally) *that Rock was Christ!* (re. 1 Cor. 10:4)

Yet when ten of the twelve spies that were sent out to spy the promised land brought back an evil report, the children of Israel received this bad report, rather than believe what GOD had promised. Rather than fight for what GOD had promised, they indulged in defeatism and self-pity.

✳

> *And all the congregation lifted up their voice, and*
> *cried; and the people wept that night.*
> Num. 14:1

✳

Christian, it is GOD's sovereign prerogative to test his people; for exceedingly abundant is the promise, and most precious the price that was paid. We must by faith in Jesus Christ, our Rock, overcome temptation and adversity, or we will be overcome of them and fall short of the promise.

✳

*But with many of them GOD was not well pleased:
for they were overthrown in the wilderness.*
1 Cor. 10:5

❋

Bluntly, they would not fight for what GOD had promised. In this life there will always be another giant possessing what GOD has promised. GOD could remove them, but he wants me to vanquish them. He wants me to correctly esteem the value of the promise, and to experience the exhilarating joy of faith in ascendancy.

Here is another parallel or analogy for them who can receive it. We know that Christ was the figure of that Rock which the Word of GOD says followed the children of Israel in the wilderness. GOD instructed Moses to smite the Rock at Horeb and water came out of it (re. Ex. 17:6). They drank of that spiritual Rock (see 1 Cor. 10:4), *and that Rock was Christ.*

Jesus Christ is that Rock that was smitten, and that brings forth *Living Water.* He is the *Gift of GOD.* (I am compelled to expound just a little.)

GOD often speaks in type and figure and shadow. Jesus Christ often taught in parables, and in dark and hard sayings. Jesus Christ is the Living Water representative of the Gift of GOD, just as he related to the Samaritan woman at Jacob's well (re. John 4:10). He is the Living Water by which a man must be born again, just as he related to Nicodemus in the third chapter of John. Christian, he is *"rivers of Living Water"* as he related to the Jews in John 7:37. Moreover, Jesus Christ is representative of that *"River of Life"* that John saw proceeding out of the throne of GOD and of the Lamb (see Rev. 22:1).

Jesus Christ is not only the Rock of Christianity upon which the Church of GOD is built, but he is also the Door of the sheepfold and of the kingdom of heaven. Just as his pierced and broken body is representative of the rent veil which affords me access into the most Holy place of communion and fellowship with GOD, even so, *He is the Door.* His is the blood and his is the body of the Host, the sacrament of the New Covenant. All glory and honor to our LORD and Savior, Jesus Christ.

For as many as receive it, I offer the LORD's parallel. As Christ is the Rock of the Living Water of GOD, even so, he is the Door which afforded the children of Israel access across the Red Sea, and also across the Jordan River. Moreover, he is our access into the Holy of Holies, not only to be saved, but also to go in and out as his priests in the earth.

I AM the Door: by me if any man enter in, he shall be saved, and shall go in and out and find pasture.

JOHN 10:9

All believers in Jesus Christ are to progressively transition into disciples and ardent witnesses of the resurrection life that is in the LORD Jesus Christ. Children, through that Door (that veil) (that rent flesh of the Son of man) is the place of our communion with a Holy GOD, above the mercy seat where the blood of the Lamb is applied. This is a place for disciples to transition into priests. This is where we enter in to be saved, but this is also where we enter into the intercessions of Jesus Christ for the lost. (We will return to this.)

When Moses stretched forth his hand and his rod over the Red Sea, then GOD parted the waters, *"and they were a wall unto them on their right hand, and on their left"* (see Ex. 14:22).

(If you follow), GOD created a corridor through the midst of the Red Sea. The parallel I offer (and as you can receive it), this I have from the Holy Ghost; that is, it is GOD's parallel or analogy, his figure or type. As Christ is the spiritual Rock from which the children of Israel drank (and the Word of GOD attests that he is), then Christ is also the Door through which the children of Israel entered to pass through the Red Sea upon dry ground.

Moreover, we know that when the next generation was prepared to cross the Jordan River, the ark of the covenant of the LORD passed over before them into the promised land. As soon as the feet of the priests that bore the ark entered into the water, the LORD caused the waters to stand up in a heap, and the children of Israel crossed over on dry land (see Josh. 3:11-17).

Some of you follow. Jesus Christ is the figurative Door across the Jordan River just as he is the analogous Door across the Red Sea. However, to speak in the figurative does not diminish the reality of my personal ordeal: the correlative necessity of my entering into the Door, or the imperative of my passing over. Do you follow?

Let us look at four distinct groups of God's people, and then trust the Holy Spirit of GOD to draw his own parallels, and to place each of us into the group which most accurately corresponds to our present spiritual state. Where are we on the Holy continuum of GOD's salvation by faith in the LORD

Jesus Christ? To qualify, all four of the following groups consider (or considered) themselves GOD's chosen people.

The children of Israel at the Red Sea.
Concisely, (and to be honest), with Pharaohs armies in fierce pursuit, they did not have much of a choice but to cross the Red Sea. What a dreadful predicament in which to be found. Surely, they heard Pharaoh's chariots and horsemen in close pursuit. (I have a good imagination.) I imagine the noise was cacophonous. And I wonder what the level of fear must have been like.

How high (and how foreboding), were those walls? How wide was the corridor? Wow. Talk about being between the proverbial "rock and a hard place!" Notwithstanding how dreadful these circumstances were, there was no alternative to crossing the Red Sea other than death by the hand of Pharaoh's armies. The children of Israel passed through the Door that GOD had provided across the Red Sea, just as they would later drink water from the Rock that he made available. And as you can receive it, both that Door and that Rock are the Christ of GOD.

The children of Israel at the Jordan River.
Here we have two subgroups, if you will, as delineated by the Word of GOD: the generation that murmured against GOD and against Moses because there were giants in the promised land, and their children.

It was GOD that distinguished the parameters of these two generations. Those from twenty years old and up which had murmured against GOD would die wandering in the wilderness (until their "carcasses" fell). Then GOD would bring their children across Jordan.

Whom I will call the first generation are they who wept the night they found out there were giants in the promised land (Num. 14:1). To summarize their sentiments and mental disposition, they said they had been better off in Egypt, and suggested that they make themselves a captain to lead them back there. The following verse summarizes their soul's dilemma, and uh, you might say, their being abruptly stopped at the Door.

So we see that they could not enter in because of unbelief. (Heb. 3:19) It takes faith to enter in.

As the LORD leads, we will speak more about each group and their relevance to contemporary Christianity. For now, we see that the generation which murmured against GOD, and refused to fight for what GOD had promised, are distinguished by the Word of GOD for their unbelief. And it is written, *that without faith it is impossible to please GOD* (re. Heb. 11:6). Moreover, unbelief incited them to murmur and revolt. Subsequently, they were not only denied access to the promised land, but they had evoked GOD's wrath.

Notably, the giants whom the older generation feared and refused to fight had not gone anywhere. The younger generation, under the leadership of Joshua, still had to vanquish them from Canaan, the land GOD had promised. Faith is a fight every time. (I believe I first heard this from Oswald Chambers.)

We must speak briefly of this "subgroup" of the younger generation of the children of Israel at the Jordan River. The following scripture exemplifies what their faith embraced and engendered.

※

Behold, the ark of the covenant of the LORD of all the earth passeth over before you into Jordan.
Josh. 3:11

※

Faith is the dynamic of salvation that evokes the presence and favor of GOD. Faith responds (acts upon) the goodness of GOD's love and the integrity and faithfulness of his character.

※

For by grace are ye saved through faith, and that not of yourselves: it is the Gift of GOD.
Eph. 2:8

※

As Christ was the spiritual Rock from which the children of Israel drank (re. 1 Cor. 10:4), even so he is the Door by which they entered in and were saved. Christ was the portal of access upon dry land through both the Red Sea and across Jordan. It is the Almighty Christ of GOD who makes a way in the wilderness.

We see at Jordan that both subgroups of the children of Israel (both generations) were given more of a choice than they had at the Red Sea, if I may put it like that. Bluntly, the choice was to fight the giants in the promised land or to turn back, relatively (and prophetically) the same choice contemporary Christianity has.

There is much to say about these examples that were specifically given us in the Word of GOD through all that the children of Israel experienced. But for now, we must keep the narrative or exposition moving, and name all the principles, if you will.

The Jews (children of Israel) in the eighth chapter of John.
The Holy Spirit moves me to accentuate and prioritize what John has already emphasized (the urgency of the revelation warrants multiple adjectives).

As he spake these words, many believed on him.

Then said Jesus to those Jews which believed on him, If ye continue in my Word, then are ye my disciples indeed.

JOHN 8:31-32

The Word of GOD affirms that these Jews believed on Jesus. John asserts it (by the Holy Spirit) twice in short order. This brings us acutely to the fourth principle group of those who distinctly consider themselves God's chosen people.

Contemporary Christianity.
Now, it must be emphasized that we believe on Jesus also. The preponderance of us are good church folk.

(How shall I express it.) This believing brings me to the Door. Believing, I stand at the portal to the kingdom of GOD. Let us see where this believing places me or positions me in the Word of GOD – for the Word of GOD is the Reality of GOD, and the only perspective that matters.

＊

*(But) as many as received him, to them gave he
power (authority) to become the sons (or daughters)
of GOD, even to them that believe on his name.*
JOHN 1:12

✳

First, we must address the difference between *believing* on Jesus Christ and *receiving* Jesus Christ. It is a propitious place and a good beginning to believe on Jesus Christ, to believe that he is the Son of GOD and the Savior of the world, but I must also receive him to be saved. To receive him is to accept him into my heart as my Savior, and to also submit to his authority as LORD. I go through the Door.

Personally, I have experienced all four of these categories. But to be explicitly (rigorously) honest, I must confess to being most closely identified with the children of Israel at the Red Sea. Satan, much like Pharaoh's armies, was in hot pursuit of me and I was nigh unto being completely consumed. As much as I may wish it were otherwise, or that my testimony made me appear at least a little valiant, alas, it was not so. I stood at the precipice of total destruction and had no choice but to enter into the Door, which is Jesus Christ.

Concisely, it was all of grace and mercy and unmerited love. I had always believed in Jesus. Indeed, I was a Baptist minister's son. But I had never submitted to Jesus Christ as LORD – I had never stepped across that portal. I had never entered into the Word of GOD and passed into that relational threshold of personally and radically living for GOD. Frankly, I had not been born again.

To receive Jesus Christ as LORD is to submit to every Word that proceeds out of the mouth of GOD and agree to live accordingly, to become a *"doer"* of the Word, and not a *"hearer"* only, deceiving my own self (re. James 1:22). For years (for those literal decades I talk about), I believed on Jesus Christ, but I stood at the Door deliberating, hesitating. We must *enter into* the Word of GOD to be saved.

To believe on the name of Jesus Christ gives me the *authority* (or power) to become a son of GOD. But I must assume the responsibility for that authority. I must utilize it for the reason it was intended and enter into the Door of the kingdom of GOD and the responsibility of all that entails. Jesus Christ is the dynamic threshold between this natural life and the reality of the kingdom of GOD and living by faith.

For a distinct and protracted season, I was identified with the children of Israel at the Jordan river. Yeah, the generation that murmured against GOD because there were giants in the promised land. I was right at the Door, as it were, but there were giants possessing what GOD had promised.

Well, much like the congregation of Israel, I wept that metaphorical prophetic night (yeah, another protracted season). By my gross cowardice and what the Word of GOD calls an evil heart of unbelief, I limited the Holy One of Israel. By my fear and inaction, by my skepticism and my wavering, I demonstrated that I did not trust GOD to perform with his hand what his mouth had spoken. By my unbelief, I effectively called GOD a liar.

Oh my. This is indeed the perspective of GOD and the only pertinent reality, the defining reason why the Word of GOD adjudicates this unbelief in my heart as evil. It is slanderous of the integrity and righteous character of GOD. By my behavior and attitude (and inaction), I suggest that GOD cannot make good on his promise.

It is an explicit faith in GOD's Word and astute trust in his holy character that keeps me in the portal of the kingdom of GOD. By faith, I am made secure in this grace. Jesus Christ is the Door GOD has provided. It is by the Christ of GOD that I enter in and am saved.

GOD has made a way where there was no way. He has set a Door of deliverance and salvation in the midst of his people. (But I am getting ahead of myself.)

As I was saying, there was an extended season that I was identified with the older generation of the children of Israel. In a metaphorical sense, I was camped right there with them at the Jordan River, immobilized by fear and unbelief and murmuring against GOD.

Notably, I had no functional awareness or understanding that I was offending GOD by doubting him, or at least I was unconscious at the time of the magnitude of my offense. With what I will call 20/20 retrospection, it was because I had no real relationship with the Word of GOD, the LORD Jesus Christ. I believed *on him,* but I did not fundamentally *know him.* To be honest, offending someone we do not functionally have a working relationship with (someone we basically do not know) is not that big a deal.

Well? Someone must get honest. We are often patently diffident and generally insensitive to a person's feelings whom we have not taken the time or made the effort to get to marginally know. We are the relationally nominal and the minimal. The preponderance of us are on the wrong side of the Door. Or, as in the case of the older generation of the children of Israel, on the wrong side Jordan.

GOD had promised to go over before them, he had promised to fight their battles and be an enemy to their enemies. GOD had promised to drive out all the other people (nations) that were possessing the land he had promised. And as we know, because of their unbelief they were consigned to wander in the wilderness until they perished.

GOD had brought them out of the bondage and cruel servitude of the Egyptians by a strong hand, with gold and silver, and there was not one feeble person among their tribes (re. Ps. 105:37). Notwithstanding such a great and miraculous deliverance and all the signs and wonders of GOD's sustaining power, unbelief would decimate their ranks and destroy an entire generation. Such is the trespass and outrage of unbelief in the estimation of the Holy One. GOD distinctly called it a breach of his promise (see Num. 14:34).

Figuratively, wistfully, I peered across Jordan at a land flowing with milk and honey; and at the giants that were possessing the land GOD had promised. Some of these giants (I felt) were common to humanity, and others (I knew) were specific to my case, if you follow. Uh, some (I suspected) were particular to my personal (and very private) pathology. Yes, the grandsons of Anak were there.

Concisely, my hesitancy and passivity are indicative of unbelief, of fear. In fact, it is undeniable evidence of my believing an evil report rather than what GOD has said. That is correct, my apathy and indolence and emphatic lukewarm state is a distinct indication that I have been listening to the adversary, the devil. Someone suggested that I was but a grasshopper in the relative sight of such giants, and I summarily accepted it.

Stay with me. Jesus Christ is the Door (the way, the access) across this metaphorical Jordan. But because I will not enter in, I am relegated to wandering in the wilderness on this side.

Tarry with me, please. Because the kingdom of GOD occurs and transpires (and is) within me, all these dynamics are taking place internally. This is the relative existential state of my spirit man. And for all intents and purposes (since I am essentially a spiritual being) this is my practical reality.

The temporal decisions I make which effect my eternal destination is the true reality. Only Jesus Christ, the Word of GOD, can effect an eternal change in the state of my spirit man. Only by Jesus Christ can I transition from Egypt, through the wilderness of my unregenerate nature, and into the promised land of peace and joy and rest.

Frankly, I was lost in trespasses and sin, with the sentence of death upon my soul. Only Jesus Christ can change that eternal reality.

Jesus Christ is the Door, the threshold of progressive grace and truth across these barrens and badlands of my unregenerate soul, across the forbidding desolate abyss of my natural man's bottomless depravity. To believe on him is a propitious beginning, but I must enter in to be saved.

The children of Israel at the Red Sea did not have much of a choice but to go on across, they had to go immediately or be killed. But when they came to the Jordan River, they no longer had Pharaoh's armies in hot pursuit. They had time to listen to their own reasoning, as it were, and a little time to lean unto their own understanding. Rather than fight, they suggested making themselves a captain to lead them back to Egypt.

We look for loopholes to elude the self-denial and austerity of the gospel of Jesus Christ and him crucified, and the laying down of our own life in the same selfless love. This is the contemporary correlative of our malingering procrastination (and dissemination) at our own figurative Jordan. GOD has made a way across the barrier of my sin and unregenerate nature which represent the giants in my personal promised land. Jesus Christ is the Door. These giants must be vanquished, and they are not going anywhere without a fight.

As we have said, believing on Jesus Christ is a good beginning, but we must enter in to be saved. A few pages ago, we referenced the Jews in the eighth chapter of John as a preeminent representative of a people that believed on Jesus, but did not continue in his Word, and therefore did not effectively *enter in* to be saved (re. John 8:30-31). We hesitate and malinger (and rationalize) on the wrong side of the Door. This is where a great many of us stop and have *Church*: at the very threshold of the miracle. The kingdom of GOD is not about the ceremony, but about the transformation, about being converted.

For about three years now, I have been referencing these Jews in the eighth chapter of John. (In a quick aside) this is the fourth manuscript in which they have pointedly pressed their prophetic (perpetually unfolding) revelatory presence into. (I am trying to get your attention.) Because I am persuaded that these Jews are emphasized for our acute contemporary example, just like the children of Israel in the wilderness.

As we mentioned a few pages ago, immediately after John records (two distinct times in a row) that these Jews *believed on Jesus* (see John 8:30-31), the LORD Jesus Christ clarifies something for them concerning their adamant claim to being GOD's chosen people. Again, there is, as it were, mandatory conditions to legitimately calling myself a Christian disciple:

> *"IF" ye continue in my Word, "then" are ye my dis-*
> *ciples indeed. And you shall know the truth,*
> *and the truth shall make you free"*
>
> re. JOHN 8:31-32

*

Believing (faith) positions me at the portal to the kingdom of GOD and gives me the power (or authority) to become a son of GOD (re. John 1:11). The urgency of the message and the exigency of the soul of contemporary Christianity shall sustain and justify my redundancy.

*

> *I AM the Door: by me "if" any man enter in, he shall*
> *be saved, and go in and out, and find pasture.*
> JOHN 10:9

*

The *"If ye continue"* of John 8:31 equates and parallels the *"If any man enter in"* of John 10:9. And they are both acute examples of what we have also quoted from James 1:22. *"But be ye doers of the Word, and not hearers only, deceiving your own selves."*

We must enter into the Word of GOD to be saved. That is correct, we must read our Bibles and live accordingly.

For every man's Word shall be his burden.

re. JER. 25:36

The difficulties and impediments of entering into the kingdom of GOD are relatively and primarily the same for the peoples of GOD in every era. Even in this, our dispensation of (what I call) the erroneous notion of all-permissive grace.

The perplexities and peculiarities (and perennial predicaments) of the lust of the flesh and the pride of life are common and evocative expressions of the human condition.

For all have sinned, and come short of the glory of God.

ROM. 3:23

✳

There are obstructions congesting the portal and giants possessing what GOD has promised. In contemporary vernacular, there is an evil entity and spiritual design to discourage and frustrate, preempt, suppress, avert or deter you from reading and prayerfully studying and meditating upon the Word of GOD.

GOD has an earnest and loving aspiration and assiduous sovereign objective to transform every believer on Jesus Christ into an ardent witness and incendiary disciple of Jesus Christ. All obstacles and adversaries are to be systematically and resolutely overcome. Of course, this is easier said than done. Concisely, this is what the warfare is about.

GOD has used these Jews here in the eighth chapter of John to distinctly show me the peril in which my soul had subsisted for decades. Just like an inestimable number of Christians in every era, I believed on Jesus and was convinced that, what amounted to a superficial faith was sufficient to call myself saved. I attended church faithfully and I listened attentively when the Word was preached, but on a personal, intimate level, I did not enter into the Word.

Concisely and honestly, I believed on Jesus, but I did not know him. I did not enter in. I had made his acquaintance, but neither associated with his sufferings nor acutely identified with his cross. Dear Reader, I was on the wrong side of the Door. This consequently left me on the wrong side of the bloodline; fundamentally untransformed, unconverted, essentially unregenerate – frankly, lost.

My predicament was the specific prerequisites to the promised land. In other words, the prophetic correlative of the giants the children of Israel encountered were my own lust and pride, and the general dysfunction of my aberrant perplexing personality and anomalous idiosyncratic attitudes. You get the idea.

The devil had convinced me that my personal giants were insurmountable. Such was the weight and complexities of my emotional baggage that I could not envision it ever being opened in the light. To fight these giants, I would have to face them.

Consequently, I settled overwrought and uneasily on this side of the Door (if you follow) and tried to convince myself that my superficial religion and mechanical church attendance would suffice to qualify me as a Christian. Maybe if I said it forcefully enough.

Wistfully and disconsolate, I would contemplate the Door in the astute and percipient awareness of my dilemma on its other side. Believing on Jesus without entering into Jesus (the Word of GOD) left me fundamentally unchanged. Melancholy and regret were not going to mitigate my cowardice. Oh my. I was going to have to enter into the Door to be saved.

Referencing the children of Israel once again, the Word of GOD says that the younger generation was consigned to wander in the wilderness with the older generation (essentially because of the older generation's unbelief and murmuring remonstrance against GOD).

✳

And your children shall wander in the wilderness
forty years, and bear your whoredoms, until
your carcasses be wasted in the wilderness.
Num. 14:33

✳

GOD wants me to keep positioning this example in application to my personal circumstances in the past. He wants me to preserve the remembrance of the explicit peril in which my soul took its uneasy rest in religious service and ritual to supplant the rigors of a real relationship. Playing church, feigning persuasion, pretending I was in the promised land;

suppressing the reality of my own giants, and bearing the generational whoredoms of all I had erroneously been taught.

But for mercy, I would have wandered until my own carcass dropped in the wilderness of my intractable personality and engrained impenitent attitudes, on the wrong side of Jordan, if you follow. The Word of GOD says "IF" I would enter in, I would be saved. To enter into Jesus Christ (the Word of GOD), I was going to have to get honest for the first time in my life.

✳

> *For the Word of GOD is quick (alive), and powerful,*
> *and sharper than any two-edged sword, piercing*
> *even to the dividing asunder of soul and spirit,*
> *and of the joints and marrow, and is a discerner*
> *of the thoughts and intents of the heart.*
>
> *Neither is there any creature that is not manifest*
> *in his sight: but all things are naked and opened*
> *unto the eyes of him with whom we have to do.*
> Heb. 4:12-13

✳

Although I had no legitimate reason for not reading and studying and meditating upon the Word of GOD, I at least had a quasi-explanation for my profound reluctance. I pretty much knew (or at least suspected) what horrors lurked in the catacombs and secret hallways on the other side of that Door, if I may put it like that.

The Word of GOD unsparingly turns the lights on. The first order of business would be admitting the size and the nature of the giants possessing the promised land, and uh, the sin I had allowed to proliferate over there. You know, the progeny (the children and incestuous descendants) of my runaway lust and unbridled pride, the fugitives and refugees of gross wantonness and insurrection. As I alluded to, the grandchildren of Anak roamed unchecked over there.

But for mercy, even as I said. It was grace that brought me back around to Jordan again and again. Staying with the same metaphors and allegory, I wandered forty years bearing my own whoredoms and obstreperous personality, my irrepressible rampageous hurt and pride. This was not my first rodeo.

As I have mentioned, I identify more closely with the children of Israel at the Red Sea, although I can relate to every group that I referenced. To enter into Christ requires radical change, (that most dreaded word of the self-righteous congregation) – repentance. GOD wants us to yield to a miraculous transformation and we give him superficial, patronizing, imperious ceremony. Well. Someone has to say so. Let us stop feigning surprise at what is obviously necessary.

Marvel not that I said unto thee, Ye must be born again.

JOHN 3:7

The Word of GOD searches us to the uttermost. It is a reader of minds and a revealer of the secrets of the heart. Only the intrepid enter into that Door. Only a genuine faith can confront and fight the giants and mutants spawned from sin and pride. GOD fully intends that I not only confront them, but defeat them in Jesus' name, that is, in the power and the essence of his abiding nature through the Holy Spirit.

✳

*Then said David to the Philistine, Thou comest to
me with a sword, and with a spear, and with a shield:
but I come to thee in the name of the LORD of hosts, the
GOD of the armies of Israel, whom thou hast defied.*
1 Sam. 17:45

✳

In order to have a victorious testimony, there must first be
a test. For my good, GOD intends that I know (and feel) the
deleterious, inimical nature of my own sin. Succinctly, I shall
fight for the promises of GOD in Christ, or I shall not have
them. Of course, sin is a defeated foe, but there are residual
personality giants (namely Behemoth and Leviathan) occupying the peace and joy GOD has promised. Children, often it
is just inside the Door that the most virulent warfare ensues.

The Word of GOD strips me bare and streamlines me for
battle. Moreover, it reveals and illuminates (what I will call)
generational giants: learned childhood prejudices and biases, bad attitudes and behaviors. Just as I said, the great, great
grandchildren of Anak are proliferating over there, and all
sorts of incestuous interbreeding and outbreeding and cross-
breeding has been going on, producing multifarious personality quirks and peculiar ogres.

Children, sin has consequences. I am, as it were, an active
combatant in the dynamic collaborative of the LORD's salvation: a warrior. (I do not know about you) but such is the
nature of my faith that the promise is as much taken as it is
given. I will fight or I will not have it.

Stark and unsparing the revelation that I am a soldier now. There are giants occupying what GOD has promised. Hear me. Such is the interminable warfare in (what I call) the season of my humanity, that there is always another personality flaw to fight, another grandchild or nephew or third-cousin of the progeny of Anak to overcome, if you follow. Ah, indeed, might I say that I press toward the mark of a total unchallenged occupancy of the promised land, as in this life, I fight for my daily bread.

As mentioned, GOD shows us that he would have every believer on Jesus Christ transition into a disciple of Jesus Christ; indeed, such is the nature of living by every Word that proceeds out of the mouth of GOD. We know this. Notwithstanding the command, not everyone follows.

Moreover, the Word of GOD is the only means to be freed from the insatiable demands and cruel servitude of sin, and to be radically delivered from the tyranny of my own personality flaws. The LORD addresses this to the Jews in John 8:31. He prefaces his statement with the prerequisite "if." John recorded what Jesus told the Jews for posterity if you follow. This Word of GOD is prophetic or perpetually fulfilling, and it is Now. What shall we say.

"If" ye continue in my Word, "then" are ye my disciples indeed. And ye shall know the Truth, and the Truth shall make you free.

JOHN 8:31-32

✳

Only the Word of GOD (Jesus Christ) can effect this fundamental radical change (repentance) in my irascible and incorrigible character. I must enter in to be saved, and there is only One Door. His name is Jesus.

Children, this is what makes reading and studying and meditating upon the Word of GOD so difficult (initially). It is the austerity and the self-denial of the commands it requires of me – the rigors (and the sweat and the tears) of repentance. It is much easier to pause and procrastinate and play church on what I will call the unregenerate (and unconverted) side of the Door. There is no more delicate (but accurate) term for the condition unless I simply call it "unsaved."

Some of you summarily refuse the revelation, or the suggestion, that many of contemporary Christendom (or Christianity) that believe on Jesus have subsequently gone nowhere (or not very far). This is my premise, as pressed by the Holy Ghost, and as you can receive it. Many of us are on the wrong side of the Door (Jesus Christ). We must enter (into) the Word of GOD to know GOD.

To enter the Door entails taking up my cross. I must daily deny myself and follow the LORD Jesus Christ through a strait gate and upon a narrow way of sanctification and true holiness. This is concisely why Jesus Christ prefaced discipleship with a stipulation.

First, if we esteemed and valued the Word of GOD as a living entity (the LORD Jesus Christ) we would hear his Voice and acknowledge the prophetic implications. If we do not continue in the Word of GOD, we remain fundamentally unchanged. For emphasis, I repeat the dreadful portend: "*IF*" we do not enter in, we remain unregenerate, unconverted (and subsequently, not healed, not whole), unfortunately but realistically lost.

Jesus intuitively knew that these Jews in the eighth chapter of John had no intention of continuing in his Word. They had taken the Word that GOD had already spoken through Moses and the prophets and the psalmists by the unction of the Holy Spirit and stopped short of allowing it to radically transform their characters.

Old Testament and New Testament, the Christ of GOD is the Door, which is the Word of GOD (the LORD Jesus Christ). Just as the Christ of GOD is the spiritual Rock that followed the children of Israel in the wilderness from which they drank (re. 1 Cor. 10:4).

We must enter into the Word of GOD to be saved. (In fact) . . .

It is written, Man shall not live by bread alone, but by every Word that proceedeth out of the mouth of GOD.

re. Matt. 3:4

✳

Many peoples believe on Jesus and go no further. Many Hindus and Muslims believe on Jesus. The devils also believe (re. James 2:19).

For special emphasis, John recorded two distinct times (successively) that the Jews in the eighth chapter of John believed on Jesus. They evidently had also superficially believed Moses and the prophets and the psalmists but had not *"entered into"* that Word of GOD to allow it access to their heart. Instead, they had effectively stopped on the wrong side of that Word of GOD and founded a religion which we know as *Judaism.* The LORD Jesus Christ described their religious predicament as he was explaining why he spoke unto them in parables.

For this people's heart is waxed gross, and their ears are dull of hearing, and their eyes have they closed; lest at any time they should see with their eyes, and hear with their ears, and should understand with their heart, and should be CONVERTED, *and I should heal them.*
MATT. 13:15

Approximately 50 or 60 years later, while writing to the Church of GOD at Corinth, the Apostle Paul explains the religious predicament of the Jews from a slightly different perspective. Moreover, there is a prophetically relevant parallel with church folk in any era who do not allow the Word of GOD access to their heart and mind and soul.

But their minds were blinded: for until this day remaineth the same vail untaken away in the reading of the Old Testament; which vail is done away in Christ.

But even unto this day, when Moses is read, the vail is upon their heart.
2 COR. 3"14-15

The Word of GOD must be allowed access to my heart and mind and soul. I must enter into the Door of it (the Christ of GOD), to be saved.

The Jews in the eighth chapter of John were the custodians and administrators of the Law of Moses and interpreters of the prophets and the psalms. They were proud descendants of Abraham and religious zealots. (If I may) the Pharisees were the gold standard of Judaism and the religious elite of their time. Notwithstanding all the Word of GOD that they were the proud overseers of, the remainder of the eight chapter of John clearly distinguishes them as hypocrites and haters. Jesus concisely told them that they were children of the devil (re. John 8:44).

They had Religion without any life or transforming power in it. The tense of it cannot be changed. The revelation is so acute that I am exposed as a dullard. The Word of GOD is so rich and so lovely that it exacerbates my inadequacy and baseness. I shall require greater grace. It is my desire to give voice to the heart and mind of Jesus Christ. All else is platitudes and vanity.

Thank you for listening. We know that the letter killeth; that only the Spirit can give life (see 2 Cor. 3:6). It is as I read and study the Word of GOD with singleness of purpose and with the unembellished intent to submit to its commands that the Spirit of GOD accompanies and quickens (gives life to) my efforts. Otherwise, it is as if I am reading a history book or a self-help manual. When I read with godly intent, I step inside the Door, and the *Paraclete* is called alongside to help me as both my Advocate and my Counselor.

The Apostle Paul wrote the following Word while referencing Judaism, but I receive its prophetic application as mine. My hope and prayer are that contemporary Christianity receives and assimilates the revelation also.

＊

Nevertheless when it (Judaism) (contemporary Christianity) shall turn to the LORD, the vail shall be taken away. Now the LORD is that Spirit: and where the Spirit of the LORD is, there is liberty.
2 Cor. 3:16-17

＊

This brings us distinctly to an appointed place where the Holy Spirit wants to make a point by concisely comparing and contrasting Judaism and Christianity. Judaism is roughly 6,000 years old as a religion, and Christianity about 2,000 years old.

Just to give us a foundation, I will review some generally accepted facts. According to tradition, the Hebrew calendar started at the time of Creation. The current year (2019/2020) is the Hebrew year 5780. The Jewish people believe that the seventh millennium will correspond to the Messianic Age. Based upon their cumulative religious works (writings, the scriptures, some traditions, et.al.) the Jewish people believe that the "deadline" by which the Messiah must appear is 6,000 years from Creation, or 2240.

According to Hebrew scholars and theologians, we are living in the Messianic Age. The LORD Jesus Christ could return at any time. Without getting too deeply into the subject or complicating things, Christianity generally agrees with this hypothesis.

However, it is my premise, (yea) moreover, it is my assertion by the Holy Spirit and by the Word of GOD that Jesus Christ was with GOD in the beginning, and that Jesus Christ was GOD in the beginning (*primary reference,* John 1:1).

Jesus Christ the same yesterday, and today, and forever.

HEB. 13:8

✳

(Concisely) Jesus Christ was with GOD, and was GOD, as the heavens and the earth were created. Jesus Christ was with Moses on Mount Sinai, just as Moses was with Jesus Christ on the Mount of Transfiguration. Just saying.

We have mentioned that Christ was the Rock that was with the children of Israel in the wilderness.

And did all drink the same spiritual drink: for they drank of that spiritual Rock that followed them: and that Rock was Christ. (1 Cor. 10:4)

Here is a good place to declare (as I have in other works) that I believe that the Christ of God is *"both"* the Father and the Son (Jesus Christ) by the Holy Spirit. This is what Jesus taught and what John the Beloved described as the doctrine of Christ. I will list the primary references.

First, I must quote (again) a couple of what I call the absolutes of GOD. Of course, all the Word of GOD is absolute, but I believe you will get my point. Jesus Christ emphatically and unambiguously told the Samaritan woman at Jacob's well that, *"God is a Spirit"* (re. John 4:24). Many times, I have also called this my *first fundamental* in understanding and assimilating the essence and identity of GOD. This never fails to reboot and settle my ruminations and meditations. Here is another absolute: *"I and my Father are One"* (John 10:30). This is taken from the same chapter of John as our primary text for this notebook, and Jesus Christ as the Door to the kingdom of GOD.

And here is the primary text (the first fundamental) (and the absolute of GOD) whose perpetual revelation moves me to declare that the Christ of GOD is *"both"* the Father and the Son by the Holy Spirit.

✳

And Jesus answered and said unto him, If a man love me, he will keep my words: and my Father will love him, and "we" will come unto him and make "our" abode with him.
JOHN 14:23

✳

Children, this is what makes you and I a Christian from the inside out. This emphatically places a manifest (visible and tactile) Christ in the middle of our Christianity. This is the Christ the world needs to see.

Moreover, this is the doctrine (teaching) of Christ. This is not denominational dogma or the duplicitous self-serving doctrine of wise men and witch doctors. John the Beloved describes its absolute nature and urgent necessity.

✳

Whosoever transgresseth, and abideth not in the "doctrine of Christ" hath not GOD. He that abideth in the doctrine of Christ, he hath "BOTH" the Father and the Son.
2 John 1:9

✳

Now, concerning both Judaism and Christianity, and indeed, the whole world, Jesus Christ is the Door to understanding the scriptures. He was (and is) there the whole time. He is eternally the Christ of GOD. He is One with the Father by the Holy Spirit, and the same in the Old Testament and in the New. He is the comprehensive absolute of the cumulative Word of GOD: the Law and the prophets and the psalms of the Old Testament, and the Grace and Truth of the New Testament.

A few pages ago, we quoted the Apostle Paul referencing Judaism, that their minds were blinded, and that unto this day there is a vail upon their hearts (see 2 Cor. 3:14-16). Moreover, much of contemporary Christianity must be included in the Word of GOD's diagnoses relative to the state of our hearts and minds.

The good news is that (that) vail is done away in Christ (re. 2 Cor. 3:14). We must pass through that veil (switching to the contemporary spelling), or into that Door, if you will. This is the same veil that was rent in twain from the top to the bottom when the LORD Jesus Christ yielded up his ghost (his Spirit) on the cross of Calvary (see Matt. 27:51).

Here is the Word of GOD's explicit expression of our access unto GOD through that veil (and that Door) which is representative of the blood and body (the flesh) of the LORD Jesus Christ.

※

Having therefore, brethren, boldness to enter into the holiest by the blood of Jesus. By a new and living way, which he hath consecrated for us, "through the veil," that is to say, his flesh.
HEB. 10:19-20

※

Ah, all doctrine and all disputation (and all notebooks) culminate here in the revelation of the LORD's salvation by grace and truth unto the mercy seat. There is only One Door, and he is the Christ of GOD and the Word of GOD.

Concisely, both Judaism and (certain elements) of Christianity have settled on the wrong side of the Door. It is here that religions are born to supplant and replicate a true relationship with GOD. You have heard me speak of *"forms of faith"* that emulate the forward momentum of a dynamic genuine faith.

This is going to leave a bruise, as they say, but the mandate of the mind of Christ upon me compels me to speak. On this side of the Door is where the preponderance of us pause and have *Church*. That is correct, religious services.

Only in Christ Jesus (the Word of GOD), only through that Door is the miracle of the new birth progressively (and perpetually) perpetrated on the sovereign continuum of the revelatory grace and truth of GOD in Jesus Christ.

I AM the Door: "by me if any man enter in," *he shall be saved, and shall go in and out, and find pasture.* (John 10:9)

Dear children, this is relatively why I use the word "preponderance." The majority of (what I call) mainstream Christianity presumes to be saved outside the Word of GOD. Not to deliberately offend or to hurt anyone's delicate spiritual sensibilities, but we must not assume we are going to be saved "outside" the Word of GOD. Uh, you know, lingering or malingering in the hallway or in the lobby, or ahem, occluding the portal.

Well, someone has to say something. Mankind is commanded to *"live by"* ever Word that proceeds out of the mouth of GOD (re. Matt. 4:4). A casual perusal does not qualify as *"living by."* The preacher reading the Bible for me and expounding upon the scriptures on Sunday is not going to equate to my *"living by"* the Word of GOD.

We must enter into the Word of GOD to be saved. *"By me"* says Jesus, *"IF" any man enter in, he shall be saved.* Inside that Door is where the transformation ensues. Uh, not to be intentionally obtuse or annoying by my redundancy, but:

Marvel not that I said unto thee, Ye must be born again.

JOHN 3:7

✳

"By me" says Jesus (if I may paraphrase for the LORD) if any man (or woman) enter in, they shall be made fit to have an audience with a Holy GOD. By the blood of Jesus Christ, we enter into the holiest through the veil of his torn flesh (re. Heb. 10:19-20).

Whether in Judaism or Christianity, only in and by Christ is the veil done away with, which then brings understanding of the scriptures. As I like to say; None speak for GOD but GOD.

※

No man hath seen GOD at any time; the only
begotten Son, which is in the bosom of the
Father, HE HATH DECLARED HIM,
JOHN 1:18

※

None speak for GOD but the Word of GOD. Outside the constraints and parameters and commands of the Word of GOD, removed from the grace and truth by which Jesus Christ came to *declare* him, I will not know GOD. Detached and indifferent, apathetic to the reading of my own Bible, I am as lost as I ever was.

If I say that I love Jesus Christ but I am careless and dismissive of my own Bible, or cavalier and dispassionate of the preaching of the Word of GOD, I am a liar and the truth is not in me. Moreover, my hope of all-permissive grace to be forgiven for what I continue to allow is in vain.

Only inside the veil and at the mercy seat where the blood of Jesus Christ is applied can I be saved. A Holy GOD will not meet with a sinner like me anywhere else. (I never tire of this following Word.)

※

And there I will meet with thee, and I will commune
with thee from above the mercy seat, from between

*the two cherubims which are upon the ark of the
testimony, of all things which I will give thee in
commandment unto the children of Israel.*
Ex. 23:22

✳

Whether Judaism or Christianity, or garden variety sinner, to circumvent the austerity and self-denial of the gospel of Jesus Christ and him crucified, we effectively pitch our tents on this side of the Door (if you follow) and have church. To avoid the rigors of the forbidding and unrelenting transformation of our innermost character, we desperately resist entering into the Word of GOD.

Necessity truly being the mother of invention, religious forms and placebos are born, elaborate ceremony and multifarious service to supplant the self-denial of a living sacrifice. We disseminate and posture and muddy the waters rather than submit to the exacting evaluation of the omniscient eye of the Word of GOD.

*For the Word of God is quick (alive), and powerful, and sharp-
er than any two-edged sword, piercing even to the dividing asunder of soul and spirit, and of the joints and marrow,
and is a discerner of the thoughts and intents of the heart.*

Heb. 4:12

Here, then, is the unequivocal reason for my hesitancy to enter into the Door. It is concisely and fastidiously the Door of a Holy man. The Word of GOD is the essence and character of GOD, and the express image of the invisible GOD. To enter into the Christ of GOD, I must be clean, and unencumbered of other things and other loves. *God is a Spirit* (re. John 4:24), and he is a *Holy* Spirit.

The Word of GOD is purposefully and irrepressibly determined to separate me from sin and self and world love, from the lust of my flesh and the insurrectionist and treasonous pride of my life. Children of GOD, no willful or premeditated sin shall pass unchecked beneath the punctilious omniscient eye which watches over that portal.

GOD watches over his Word. It is the Door into the kingdom of GOD. That rent veil into the most Holy place is representative of the torn and bleeding flesh of the Son of GOD, the LORD Jesus Christ. This is what it means to be *"in Christ:"* absolute fidelity to the blood and body of the LORD Jesus Christ.

✻

And, Let everyone that nameth the name
of Christ depart from iniquity.
re. 2 TIM. 2:19

✻

Duh, as my youngest daughter was fond of saying. Let everyone who calls themselves a Christian, stop willfully sinning. This is what it means to be *"in"* Christ: to follow my Savior and LORD through a strait gate of sanctification upon that narrow way of obedience and true holiness. The Word of GOD is the astringent which streamlines and cleanses my spirit man from the excesses and perennial (chronic) sin of my natural man.

The Word of GOD is the *Sword of the Spirit* and the character of GOD in Christ Jesus severing me from self-love and self-rule, from worldly love and a subservient mentality. The Word of GOD is the progressive grace and truth by which Jesus Christ came to declare the nature and holiness of GOD. I must be found on its dynamic continuum perfecting holiness in the godly fear and reverence of a developing discipleship in the LORD Jesus Christ.

I must *"enter in"* to be saved (double emphasis mine). To enter into the Door (the LORD Jesus Christ) equates to entering into the Word of GOD. I must be found *dwelling* in the Word of GOD (the LORD Jesus Christ) and the Word of GOD *dwelling* in me. GOD must see me *"in"* Christ Jesus in order for me to be saved. Now, this should go without saying, but without reading and studying and meditating upon the Word of GOD, I will not be saved.

To live by every Word that proceeds out of the mouth of GOD is not some religious ideal or arcane (and meaningless) platitude, it is the very salvation of GOD hid in the mysteries and wisdom of the LORD Jesus Christ. The Word of GOD is the acute and exquisite expression of the heart and mind, and the grace and truth, of GOD from the bosom of GOD, declaring GOD, (re. John 1:18).

The Jews and the Pharisees in the eighth chapter of John were the overseers and interpreters of the law and the prophets and the psalms. They were distinctly and unarguably the one element of society that knew the most about the Word of GOD. They are whom the rest of Hebrew society deferred to when it came to the rigors and intricacies of Judaism.

These Jews considered themselves to have a proprietary claim to the Word of GOD, and (as such) also regarded themselves as the descendants of Abraham and the patriarchs. They esteemed themselves the elect (chosen) of GOD. But as the LORD Jesus Christ would show them, they indeed had a claim on the Word of GOD, yet the Word of GOD had not effected a quantifiable change in their characters. Until we get the prophetic implications to our religious ceremony:

✳

Then said Jesus to those Jews which believed on him, If ye continue in my Word, then are ye my disciples indeed. And ye shall know the truth, and the truth shall make you free.
JOHN 8:31-32

✳

Of course, the Jews take an immediate exception to this admonition and insist that they are already free. As we know from the remainder of the chapter, the conversation quickly deteriorates from here, culminating in these religious people (and good church folk) calling Jesus a Samaritan and accusing him of being possessed by a devil. (see John 8:48)

The Holy Spirit frequently moves me to use these Jews here in the eighth chapter of John as the preeminent example of a religious contingent or faction that I compare to contemporary Christianity to make a point. *We can have the Word of GOD, and the Word of GOD still not have us.* As we have noted:

But be ye DOERS of the Word, and not hearers only, deceiving your own selves.

JAMES 1:22

The Word of GOD must be applied to my innermost be-ing, and its commands laid up against my soul eliciting and expecting change. The dynamic progressive nature of the LORD's salvation by the Holy Spirit of a living Word cannot be emphasized enough. Jesus said, *"Follow me."*

To reiterate, the scribes and Pharisees sat in Moses' seat, (re Matt. 23:2). They were custodians and administrators of the Word of GOD, but they were not living by the Word of GOD. Jesus warned his disciples of them.

Do not ye after their works: for they say, and do not. (re. Matt. 23:3)

The Word of GOD must be allowed to have its way, it must be allowed unfettered access to the unregenerate thoughts of my mind. When I read the Word of GOD with an intent to apply its commands, it comes accompanied with the pow-er to effect the very changes it requires of me. To enter into the Word of GOD is to allow it unrestricted admission to my heart.

The Word of GOD never ceases to effect change in my character.

✻

Not as though I had already attained, either were already perfect: but I follow after, if that I may apprehend that for which also I am apprehended of Christ Jesus.
Phil. 3:12

✻

Dear reader, I do not know about you, but the Word of GOD never ceases to exhort me to love my neighbor as myself, and to pray for those who despitefully use me and persecute me. Perpetual and interminable is the admonition I need to love my enemies, eternal the exhortation to bless them that curse me. Just saying.

Concisely, either I am ceaselessly and progressively entering into the Door which is the Word of GOD and the essence of the LORD Jesus Christ, or I am effectively obstructing the portal. Stark and acute the revelation that I had not already attained some obscure ethereal nirvana of untouchable self-righteousness, but that I must endure unto the end to be saved (re. Matt. 24:13).

Quite often, I reference literal decades of subsisting by superficial religious ceremony and specious self-serving works of the flesh, volitional prisoner of a contrived Christianity. I was not the Lone Ranger. There was a horde of us.

Like the Jews in the eighth chapter of John, we can consider ourselves in charge of the Word of GOD and still obdurately persist unchanged, impenitent and unconverted. And here comes a carpenter's apprentice and itinerant preacher with a radical gospel concept and compulsory command of the Word of GOD:

Marvel not that I said unto thee, Ye must be born again.

JOHN 3:7

✳

Rather than surrender my life absolutely and in a living unabating sacrifice, I require some external religious ceremony to represent or supplant what I am desperate to save for myself.

If you think the dying is theoretical, then you have never submitted to the gospel of Jesus Christ and him crucified. The first thing I find *"in"* Christ is a cross. There will be no being born again a new creature in Christ Jesus without the acute and absolute death of my natural man.

I must genuinely capitulate to a Holy GOD's adjudication of sin in the flesh, that the body of sin must die. Religious ceremony and service work is not a sustainable substitute. I must yield (give up) the body of sin to be crucified with the LORD Jesus Christ. There is no other way to know him and the power of his resurrection except to fellowship with his sufferings and be conformed to the death of his cross (see Phil. 3:10).

It is one thing to have the Word of GOD, but it is an altogether different dynamic for the Word of GOD to have me (if you follow). Not to be deliberately mystical, but to enter into Jesus Christ is to enter into the Door of the supernatural, and to live (as it were) otherworldly. My being born again is just such a miracle.

To enter into the Word of GOD is to willingly submit to its perpetual washing and cleansing of my body, mind, and soul – to surrender my comprehensive nature and character to the supernatural transforming power of the Holy Spirit of the Almighty GOD in his Christ.

✳

For in him we live, and move, and have our being.

re. ACTS 17:28

The words *"in him"* are the functional nucleus of this spiritual phenomenon called *"being"* born again. To enter into Jesus

Christ is to enter into the Door of the kingdom of GOD. Christ is effectually my chrysalis, and the safe place of my transition. Outside Christ (outside the Word of GOD), I am lost and undone, exposed to the elements, prey to the adversary.

This is what I often call *"Christ-consciousness."* It transcends ceremonial religious service. It is expressive of the kingdom of GOD emanating from the secret place of the indwelling Christ in my soul, his mind and his breath and his heartbeat coalesced with mine; ideally the image of the invisible GOD pressing to the front of my life – that the world might see Jesus.

Whether Jew or Greek, bond or free, whether Judaism or Christianity, the proprietary (and self-promoting) elitist declaration or claim that I presume to have on the Word of GOD is in vain if the Word of GOD does not, in turn, have my allegiance and absolute capitulation to its commands.

> *For in Christ Jesus neither circumcision availeth anything, nor uncircumcision, but a new creature.*
>
> GAL. 6:15

✳

Only by the Door can I enter into the kingdom of GOD. He is the Word of GOD, and the LORD Jesus Christ. Notwithstanding my denominational slant or doctrinal pontification, am I a new person? Concisely, new creatures are those whom the Word of GOD has radically and miraculously converted.

Unfortunately, innumerable persons, circumventing the austerity and self-denial that the Word of GOD unsparingly and realistically and justly commands, stop on this side of the Door (and someone has to say it) and have church. Hence, we have contemporary mega-congregations of the unconverted calling themselves Christians, playing church.

The Jews in the eighth chapter of John are the startling, inescapable prophetic correlative of contemporary Christianity. Of course, the children of Israel are contemporary Christianity's prophetic example throughout the entire Word of GOD. Unfortunately, we quite vocally and predominantly are openly critical of them, but without turning the critique toward our own spiritual evaluation. Broadly, we (pretty much) mercilessly take the spiritual inventory (and temperature) of others but spare ourselves the same meticulous examination.

The Jews in the eighth chapter of John vociferously defended themselves as GOD's chosen by virtue of being direct descendants of Abraham. However, a substantial conversation with the Word of GOD made flesh, the LORD Jesus Christ, revealed them as the hyper-religious self-righteous hypocrites and unadorned haters that they really were. By the end of the chapter, they take up stones to cast at Jesus Christ (see John 8:59).

Someone must ask these things. What might a lengthy conversation with the Word of GOD reveal about our Christianity? Broadly, we posture as GOD's Spirit-filled elect, but are we radically born again and comprehensively, fundamentally and totally transformed disciples of Jesus Christ? Are we essentially and emphatically the converted of Jesus Christ? Notwithstanding the Christianity I claim, does my character reflect the virtues, grace and truth, longsuffering love and faithfulness of the LORD Jesus Christ?

✳

For the kingdom of God is not in word, but in power.
1 Cor. 4:20

✳

You are probably weary of hearing me say it, but we settle for religious form to emulate the earnest forward momentum of a genuine faith. True faith unsparingly compels me into the cleansing stream and washing of the water by the Word. This is distinctly (and inescapably) how the LORD Jesus Christ both cleanses and sanctifies his Church:

That he might present it to himself a glorious Church,
not having spot or wrinkle, or any such thing; but
that it should be holy and without blemish.

Eph. 5:27

✳

This transcends a written or vocal testimony and eclipses and overshadows all religious ceremony. This is the defining and making of Christian disciples from the inside out. This goes beyond the pretty and surpasses all religious presentation and pumped-up pious affect; this is the living sacrifice of a genuine Christian.

This is what it means to be in Christ Jesus, the Door – allowing the Word of GOD to have his way with me. This is the agape love of GOD in Christ Jesus, and that no greater love of the Christian laying down their life for another; to wit, GOD's sanctified instrument and holy vessel in the outreach of his love for the next sinners soul.

This is to be *"in"* the faith. A genuine faith perpetually holds me up to the consuming and sanctifying fire of the Holy Ghost. My chronic, perennial bad attitudes and persistent character flaws must be subjected to a Holy Fire. I call this my wood, hay, and stubble, my idiosyncrasies and eccentricities. Dear Christian, the refiner's fire is pitched in the soul of the sanctified, and it is (as I am) *"in"* Christ Jesus that I shall know it best. Indeed, often I have said that the refiner is seeking the gold of a genuine faith, but actually the trial of our faith is much more precious than gold:

Receiving the end of your faith, even the salvation of your souls.

1 PET. 1:9

✳

All the palaver and the pious prattle, the babble (Babel), all the posturing and the pontification and sometimes even the preaching is inconsequential to the indwelling fire of the Holy Ghost. Christ in me (and me in Christ) is the Hope of Glory. The Apostle Paul goes on to define the sovereign purposes of GOD in the inexorable irrepressible process of my being refined.

> *Whom we preach, warning every man, and teaching every man in all wisdom; that we may present every man perfect in Christ Jesus.*

COL. 1:28

✳

This is the perfecting of holiness in the fear (reverence) of the LORD. This is the perfecting of the saints by the obedience and sanctification of the Word of GOD, the LORD Jesus Christ, the Door unto the salvation of GOD and our acceptance in his presence. This surpasses playing church and exceeds religious ceremony; this only gives substance and evidence to my Christian testimony.

This, only, is the reality of GOD and the salvation of mankind:

I AM the Door: by me if any man enter in, he shall be saved, and shall go in and out, and find pasture.

JOHN 10:9

＊

The key to all knowledge is Christ. From the foundation of the world, Jesus Christ is representative of the veil which separates sinful humanity from a Holy GOD. Or, as the writer to the Hebrews expresses that veil, *"that is to say, his flesh"* (re. Heb. 10:20).

Or, as the Apostle Paul says, *"We preach Christ crucified . . . the power of GOD, and the wisdom of GOD"* (see 1 Cor. 1:23-24). To enter into Christ is to acquiesce (agree and surrender) to the comprehensive gospel of the cross of Jesus Christ, that his cross is effectively my cross, and that my natural man (and the body of my personal sin) must be crucified with him there.

My repentance of sin is the precursor and prerequisite of the remission of sin. Only True penitents are permitted behind the veil to the mercy seat where the blood of Jesus Christ is applied. I must pass through the torn and pierced flesh of Jesus Christ to have an audience with a Holy GOD and receive forgiveness of sin. *"By me"* says Jesus, *"if any man enter in, he shall be saved." "I AM the Door."*

✳

(Thus saith the LORD), "*By me you pass beneath the omniscient eye of the Holy One. I AM the portal into the promised land, the avenue to green pastures, the source and the oasis of living water. On this side of the Door, you lay down all claim to self-love and self-rule, all world-love and the lust of your flesh and the aggregate pride of your life.*

I AM the Door, the demarcation of the life lost to find it, the astute delineation of them of the world, and them not of the world. Today is the day of salvation, and your defining moment of mercy is Now.

I AM the Door, and your desperation to come up some other way, concisely, your dissimulation and duplicity, your misdirection and dishonesty, designate you as a thief and a robber.

I AM the Door at which the wedding garments of a great King, (and a fastidious Bridegroom) are checked, and I AM the perfecter of holiness in the reverential fear of GOD.

I AM the veil into the most Holy place where the eternal business of souls is transacted. Selah.

✳

(To me) the last part of the LORD Jesus' statement as recorded in John 10:9, *"and shall go in and out and find pasture,"* is indicative of a believer's progressive growth in the grace and knowledge of GOD in Christ. To *"find pasture"* is expressive of the righteousness of GOD being irrepressibly revealed *"faith to faith"* by the Word of GOD. As it is written, *"The just shall live by faith."* (see Rom. 1:17)

As we shall see in chapter four, Jesus Christ is not only the Door to the sheepfold, he is also the Good Shepherd. Not to get ahead of myself, but as is apropos of a moment of greater grace: *"He maketh me to lie down in green pastures: he leadeth me beside the still waters."* (Ps. 23:2)

Psalm 23 is so rich and so powerful that it is tempting to go immediately there, but the Holy Spirit is leading in another direction. Relative and eminent to the preponderance of (whom you know I call) contemporary mainstream Christianity, we are on the wrong side of the Door.

First, let me establish something. My frequent use of the word *preponderance* is not my initial idea, meaning there are things that I write that did not originate in my mind. That is correct, (as you can receive it), I write for GOD out of the mind of Christ by the Holy Ghost. Again, not to be mystical or egotistical, I am not looking for a job or for notoriety or for a position, I am already given *place*. I seek nothing above my portion.

(That being said), the innumerable quantity represented by the word *"preponderance"* is not my number or proportion. The ratio of the *"few and many"* is not mine either, it belongs to GOD. He who has ears to hear, let him hear:

> *Enter ye in at the strait gate: for wide is the gate, and broad is the way, that leadeth to destruc-tion, and "many" there be which go in thereat.*

> *Because strait is the gate, and narrow is the way, which leadeth unto life, and "few" there be that find it.*

> MATT. 7:13-14

＊

The preponderance of us are on the wrong side of the Door; (or, if you will) on the wrong side Jordan. There is a promised land of green pastures and living water in this life, but we must pass through the portal to assume its possession. Therefore, I sometimes say, *"The promise is as much taken, as it is given."*

Concisely, the giants in the promised land have precluded the preponderance of us from passing over into the abundant land of peace and joy and rest, in this life. *"The kingdom of GOD is within you,"* (re. Luke 17:21). The LORD Jesus Christ speaks this Word. It is a Word for the *living*. And it is *Now*.

Jesus Christ, the Word of GOD, says, *"Follow me."* This is the dynamic fundamental of a genuine faith, my forward momentum. Real faith is paralleled by a demonstrative love for the Word of GOD. It can not be otherwise. It is, concisely (and precisely), my love for the LORD Jesus Christ.

We know (intellectually) that everything that befell the children of Israel in the wilderness is written for our example and for our admonition (see 1 Cor. 10:11). We shall (ourselves) be seen pursuing the promises of GOD in this life if we are to inherit the promises of GOD after this life: that is, eternal life. The promise is not for those who believe, and then sit down; the promise is for those who believe, and then follow (or continue).

A genuine faith continues to follow. The redundancy is warranted by the preponderance of contemporary Christianity in the wayside of worldly love, wanton materialism, and the rabid pursuit of mammon. A Christian who says they believe on Jesus Christ but then do not follow him will fall short of the promise. A genuine faith can be seen entering into the Door, the Word of GOD. A genuine faith can be seen crossing Jordan and fighting giants. Or not.

So we see that they could not enter in because of unbelief. Let us therefore fear, lest, a promise being left us of entering into his rest, any of you should seem to come short of it.

Heb. 3:19-4:1

✳

(If I may), Let us fear, lest any of us be found lingering (indifferent and languid) on the wrong side of the Door. To borrow an expression from the parable of the ten virgins, *"at midnight there was a cry made,"* *'Behold, the Bridegroom cometh; go ye out to meet him'* (see Matt. 25:6).

✳

Children, when GOD shuts the Door to this dispensation of his exceeding grace and mercy and longsuffering love extended toward us in the LORD Jesus Christ, then it will be irrevocable, unalterable, irremediable and eternal. (One or two adjectives were not sufficient to express the immediate urgency and acute peril of our loved one's souls).

My fear for contemporary mainstream Christianity is that we have persuaded ourselves that a superficial believing on Jesus equates to our being born again (somehow), even while we remain fundamentally unchanged, untransformed in attitude, unconverted in character.

We effectively settle short of the promise, persuaded we have enough oil to endure. Some of us are going to be gravely disappointed in the evil day, overtaken and overthrown by darkness, on the wrong side of a closed Door. Church attendance, singing in the choir, holding a religious position such as deacon or Sunday school teacher, and even the most elaborate church ceremony and service work is not the same dynamic as entering into the Word of GOD.

Only by the Word of GOD can I confront and overcome my personal giants occupying what GOD has promised. Notably, some of mine were mutant oddities and various deviants and monstrous descendants of the children of Anak, Goliath's inbred cousins. Concisely, I will fight for what GOD has promised, or I shall not have it.

By the Word of GOD, I enter in to do battle. As a young Christian, this was not adequately explained to me. In retrospection, I realize that was because the preponderance of my religious forefathers settled on the wrong side of the Door.

It is when we refuse to fight that forms of faith are born. They evolve out of our religious posturing as if we had overcome. This leaves us a lot to hide. We check our self-righteous cloak in the superficial religious reflection of one another. Instead of the factual tooth and nail fighting of giants that is fundamental of a genuine faith, we have ostentatious religious services, questionable entertainment and elaborate ceremonies, and we make a lot of noise. Uh, but there is a glaring problem with that, and a gaping hole in my Christian affect.

*

*Though I speak with the tongues of men and of
angels, and have not charity* (love), *I am become
as sounding brass, or a tinkling cymbal.*
1 Cor. 13:1

✳

For all my religious posturing and pious prognostications
and pontification (and prostitution), if I have not learned to
love like GOD loves, then I am a pretender and a player of
a part in a shallow religious production and a fabricator of
noise. If I do not know how to love, if I have not been radically converted to know how to love as GOD loves, then I am
just making noise, and (sometimes) perhaps just drawing attention to myself.

An extravagant and flamboyant religious ceremony can leave
me feeling positively righteous. Unfortunately, too often we
go home with the same learned childhood prejudices and
contrived or presumptuous societal biases and hatreds that
we arrived with. Only worse, because now the innate malevolence of our natural man (or woman) is hidden behind a
smiling religious face.

We have preconceived estimates and notions of how much
oil will suffice until the Bridegroom gets here, and we have
settled for the show. Too often we rest upon tradition or an-
cestry or ceremony. The Jews in the eighth chapter of John
had all the bells and whistles, they were the religious aristocracy that sat in Moses' seat. Notwithstanding, the remainder
of the chapter reveals them as hypocrites and haters. They
had not (themselves) entered into the very Word of GOD
that they were custodians and administrators of. The chapter

concludes with the best of them (religion's finest) with stones in their hands.

By the progressive grace and revelatory truth of GOD in the LORD Jesus Christ, I am methodically transformed into an ardent disciple and living witness of the resurrection life that is in him. My radical transformation is evidence of the miracle. Fighting giants is part of the process, an integral and sovereign part of the promise, a necessary discipline. After the sifting, as it were, and after the testing of my faith, I can be trusted with kingdom business and with strengthening my brethren (see Luke 22:32).

There remaineth a rest to the people of God.

HEB. 4:9

✳

The murmuring (and weeping) of the children of Israel at the Jordan river was revealed to be unbelief. It leads to a wilderness experience, a restless wandering repetitive hardship and cyclical sorrow until we drop (on the wrong side of Jordan). It takes faith to fight, and it takes faith to follow. We must enter into the Word of GOD (*Jesus Christ, the Door*) to be saved.

Let us beware of complacency (and of becoming part of the problem) (occluding the portal) (procrastination), impeding the next fellow's progress.

✳

Let us labour therefore to enter into that rest, lest
any man fall after the same example of unbelief.
HEB. 4:11

✳

The kingdom of GOD comes with the radical transformation of my character from the inside out. The indwelling and abiding Christ Jesus makes me a Christian. The kingdom of GOD (and the day of salvation) and the perpetual militant transformation is Now.

Children, when the LORD Jesus Christ returns, we must be found to be already in the house, as it were. We are going to transition from this natural, temporal life, directly into our supernatural, eternal life. Even now, we are purposefully being made One with GOD in Jesus Christ. He is the Door to the supernatural reality of GOD. I wonder if you have heard his Voice.

✳

Let not your heart be troubled: ye believe in GOD, believe also in me. In my Father's house are many mansions: if it were not so, I would have told you. I go to prepare a place for you.
JOHN 14:1-2

✳

Notably, the word *mansion(s)* is also interpreted *rooms* or *apartments.* Christian, you are given *"place"* in the body of Christ. You are specifically and individually, wonderfully and mysteriously made and placed by divine appointment into the kingdom of GOD.

By the violence of their faith, the stalwart and the intrepid take their portion. Nevertheless, when the LORD Jesus Christ returns, will he find me having pressed my way by faith into my appointed place? (inspired by Luke 18:8)

The opposition to my entering in is expressly designed and sovereignly allowed for the perfecting of my faith. The following scripture can relate to both my personal salvation and ministry endeavors as a viable disciple and minister of Jesus Christ. It is written by a man of GOD who lived a life of dynamic faith:

> *For a great door and effectual is opened unto me, and there are many adversaries.*

> 1 Cor. 16:9

＊

The Word of GOD (Jesus Christ) is the progressive (perpetual) prophetic revelatory grace and truth by which we enter into the kingdom of GOD, systematically deeper into the mysteries and wisdom of GOD. It is those who overcome that possess the promise. (Though there is an evil designed to impede your progress), faith pleases GOD:

> *And this is the victory that overcometh the world, even our faith.*

> re. 1 John 5:4

＊

The Father is seeking true worshippers whose faith is the spirit of their life. Faith is the inner sanctum. Faith distinguishes and delineates the children of promise from the posers and players of religious presumption and performance, or those just having church, malingering in the outer courts:

*I know thy works: behold, I have set before thee an open
Door, and no man can shut it: for thou hast a little strength,
and hast kept my Word, and hast not denied my name.*

REV. 3:8

✳

A dynamic faith in Jesus Christ is a perpetual opened Door to the kingdom of GOD. The intrepid can be seen entering in. Notably, in the very next verse, specifically contrasted with the faithful, are them *"which say they are Jews, and are not, but do lie"* (see Rev. 3:9). Alarmingly, this is the second church of seven that is pointedly given this portentous sobriquet of *"the synagogue of Satan"* (see also Rev. 2:9).

In contemporary vernacular, this is, of course, them who say they are Christians, but are not. I do not need to be Hebrew to understand this. I do not have to be a student of the Greek or Latin or Aramaic to know that the Word of GOD is distinguishing true Christians from pretenders and hypocrites, from those who presumptuously take the name of the LORD Jesus Christ upon themselves, but do not surrender their lives or their love of the world unto him. They do not enter into the Door.

In the first example, the Word of GOD ominously declares (again, in contemporary vernacular) that if I call myself a Christian, but I am not, it is blasphemy (see Rev. 2:9). Unregenerate in mind and untransformed in heart, unconverted in character, I am relegated to the outer court. Only true penitents are permitted to enter into the Door, for without a definitive repentance of sin, there will be no genuine remission of sin.

The access through that rent veil to the mercy seat of GOD is by way of the cross of Jesus Christ and him crucified. Concisely, I must take it up, because it is my cross, too.

Religious ceremony shall not supplant (or suffice) for a radical and comprehensive character conversion, and a genuine heart transformation. Much of contemporary Christianity is having church in the outer court, purposefully saving their lives for themselves.

*

When once the master of the house is risen up, and hath shut to the Door, and ye begin to stand without, and to knock at the Door, saying, Lord, Lord, open unto us; and he shall answer and say unto you, I know you not whence ye are.
LUKE 13:25

Selah. / rdb

I AM THE DOOR

4

I AM the Good Shepherd

"I AM the Good Shepherd: the Good Shepherd giveth his life for the sheep."

–John 10:11

AFTER MUCH PRAYER and meditation, my first assertion in this chapter must be relatively the same as what the LORD Jesus Christ is declaring with this teaching (or doctrine) of the Good Shepherd here in the tenth chapter of John. Indeed, it is more of the absolute deity of the LORD Jesus Christ. There is definitively One Good Shepherd in the comprehensive Word of GOD, Old Testament and New Testament, and the LORD Jesus Christ is indubitably declaring for those who have ears to hear, "I AM *He.*"

Once more, I reiterate the unassailable revelatory assertion of the Word of GOD that Jesus is the Christ. And by the Christ, I emphatically mean that the Father and the Son are One LORD by the Holy Ghost. (For now) I offer two absolutes from the Word of GOD for this indisputable conclusion. The first is, "*I and my Father are One*" (John 10:30). This is, of course, uttered by Jesus Christ, the Word of GOD made flesh, and the express image of the invisible GOD. The second is spoken by the man of GOD, Moses, as moved and inspired by the Holy Spirit. *"Hear, O Israel: The LORD our GOD is One LORD"* (Deut. 6:4).

Moreover, without shame, I advance (and promote) that I wrote a book titled *One LORD* and recommend that every Christian read it. Born out of my personal Bible study, what began as a tentative premise transmogrified into an impregnable revelatory truth. (I have found) that when I seek the truth of GOD's Word with no preconceived notions or hidden agenda, a veil (if you will) is lifted from my heart and my mind.

GOD showed me (by the Word of GOD) that Jesus Christ met and embodied (at least) the following two immutable prerequisite specifications of deity. 1) Only GOD has power over life and death (resurrection power), and 2) Only GOD can forgive sin, or has power over sin.

Well. This certainly transcended the Christmas story. Not to be deliberately facetious (or insulting), but these two revelations eclipsed all my painstakingly accumulated religious ideology, (you know), all the manmade restrictions that I had placed upon the deity of the LORD Jesus Christ so that he would be more lenient and accommodating for my natural man to live with. Without naming (denominational) names, I am just trying to keep it real.

Relative to the two "immutable prerequisite specifications of deity" listed above, GOD added these following two points. 1) Only the same GOD who gave man life in the first place could give him resurrection life or make him a new creature. (Perhaps some of these should be sub-points, or their own points.) Only the same GOD who gave mankind the initial Breath of Life could give him the regenerative breath of the Holy Ghost (if you follow). 2) Only the same GOD who initially gave mankind the commandment not to sin could forgive him for sinning against that commandment.

This is not common sense; this is GOD-sense. This is the revelatory grace and truth of the Word of GOD, and the express deity of the LORD Jesus Christ. This is what he came to declare about both the identity and the deity of GOD.

✳

For if ye believe not that I AM "He," ye shall die in your sins.
re. JOHN 8:24

✳

We must believe that Jesus Christ is *He*, the Almighty GOD who has this resurrection life and the forgiveness of sin to give, even as he says.

✳

*I AM the resurrection, and the life: he that believeth
in me, though he were dead, yet shall he live.*
JOHN 12:25

✳

This scripture above, of course, will be chapter five. Relative to our present chapter is the Good Shepherd giving his life for the sheep. This is how the LORD Jesus Christ describes his authority over life and death in our current text.

✳

*Therefore doth my Father love me, because I lay down
my life, that I might take it again. No man taketh it
from me, but I lay it down of myself. I have power to
lay it down, and I have power to take it again. This
commandment have I received of my Father.*
JOHN 10:17-18

✳

Absolute acceptance and acquiescence of the Father's will in selfless love and total obedience elicits the Father's honor and reciprocal love. Jesus Christ executes the Father's will as one yet accomplishes and fulfills all things in what he calls the "testimony of two." This is integral to the doctrine of Christ, that the Father and the Son (the Word) are One by the Holy

Spirit. They are in the agreement of One mind and will. These things must be touched upon, and each man and woman left to the burden of their own prayer and fasting and meditation, and their own research.

*

For I am not alone, but I and the Father that sent me. It is also written in your law, that the testimony of two men is true. I am one that bear witness of myself, and the Father that sent me beareth witness of me.
re. JOHN 10:16-18

*

That the Father and the Son are One by the Holy Spirit is an infinite phenomenon. John the Beloved definitively and concisely called it the *Doctrine of Christ*, (see 2 John 1:9). We separate them to our own detriment, unwittingly diminishing the deity of the Holy One. Once more, I must reiterate the following absolute.

*

All things that the Father hath are mine.
re. JOHN 16:15

*

GOD keeps and fulfills his own Law, establishes his own authority. In our current text, for them with eyes to see and ears to hear, we have the *Giver of Life* revealed as the Good Shepherd. None have such unmitigated authority over life and death but the Almighty GOD.

To lay down life and to take up life is the exclusive purview of the Almighty GOD. The Word of GOD and the essence and character of GOD are inseparable. That is, or in other words, the Father and the Son are indivisible.

We must not think that the Father was aloof or dissociated from all that the Son suffered at Calvary. The revelation is excruciating and explicit, that by the grace of GOD, Jesus Christ should taste death for every man, (re. Heb. 2:9). As One LORD and One indivisible essence, it therefore invariably emerges that everything the Son experiences, the Father experiences also.

You ask, am I saying that GOD died for our sins? And I answer that, it cannot be otherwise. None but the Almighty GOD can restore mankind from where he fell. None but the Author of the Law can fulfill and satisfy the Law.

He who has ears to hear, let him hear. If we will listen in spirit and in truth, we can hear the answer to the Pharisee's rhetorical question hiding in plain sight (if you will), within the very question.

✳

Who can forgive sins, but GOD alone?
see LUKE 5:21

✳

Let us make it plain. That is, let me make what I believe as unambiguous as the reality that the LORD Jesus Christ is expressing here. Jesus Christ not only forgives sin, but heals the sickness and disease caused by sin.

It was a memorable and blessed day when my feeble faith began to draw some inexorable conclusions about the deity of the LORD Jesus Christ as revealed here in this small portion of the Word of GOD. His authority has no limits in the affairs of men, and this reveals him as the Almighty GOD.

Let us heed the Pharisee's negative example and be careful not to repeat their mistake. Notably, they were reasoning some of these same great things in their heart (see Luke 5:22), yet it left them unchanged (that is, unrepentant).

According to my faith, the forgiveness of sin will spontaneously elicit the healing of my body. I have experienced the phenomenon in body, mind, emotion, and to the depths of my very soul, all glory and honor and praise to the LORD Jesus Christ. (All things being equal, as we say), they equate to the same thing, or the same divine miraculous phenomenon. Indeed,

✳

> *Whether is easier, to say, Thy sins be forgiven*
> *thee; or to say, Rise up and walk?*
> LUKE 5:23

✳

Concisely, this is the Almighty GOD expressing his desire and his authority to both heal of sickness (or disease) and to forgive sin. Two other scriptures immediately come to mind. They are precise and applicable (and I must add) contemporarily relevant. Ah, when a truth is so magnificent, so divine, multiple adjectives are warranted.

✳

*And the prayer of faith shall save the sick, and
the LORD shall raise him up, and if he have
committed sins, they shall be forgiven him.*
James 5:15

❋

What a singular privilege and inestimable favor to be led of the Holy Spirit to write about such unfathomable truths as these. My faith grows exponentially. Child of GOD, what manner of greater grace is this in the ever-changing supernatural seasons of GOD, to see hope transition into faith, and faith transmogrify into trust. To borrow an expression of the Apostle Paul, *"O the depth of the riches both of the wisdom and knowledge of GOD! how unsearchable are his judgments, and his ways past finding out!"* (Rom. 11:33).

This account of the paralytic man here in the fifth chapter of Luke is also recorded by Matthew and Mark. We know it is when Jesus saw the faith of the man's friends that he declared the man's sins as forgiven. Notably, remarkably, the faith of the paralytic man is not mentioned. This is the divine dynamic of the *"prayer of faith"* that James is also describing, and he does not specifically reference the sick person's faith either. Children, here is not only hope when we are too sick to pray, but an explicit encouragement and admonition to pray for the sick when we are well.

The other scripture(s) that I wanted to reference before returning to our main text is taken from a Psalm rich in the essence and character of GOD. As is fitting, let us bless his name.

❋

*Bless the LORD, O my soul: and all that
is within me, bless his holy name.*

Bless the LORD, O my soul, and forget not all his benefits.

Who forgiveth all thine iniquities; who healeth all thy diseases.
PSALM 103:1-3

✳

This is the same dynamic (n.) throughout the Word of GOD, the same methodology of faith – the same miracle formula. That is, *according to your faith, be it unto you.*

Uh, my faith grows exponentially with the exposition of faith, if you follow. My faith escalates with the inquiry. Faith burgeons and proliferates before an opened Bible.

✳

*So then faith cometh by hearing, and
hearing by the Word of GOD.*
ROM. 10:17

✳

The truth is so radiant and so imperial, the revelation so majestic and royal that my redundancy is warranted:

Whether is easier, to say, Thy sins be forgiven thee; or to say, Rise up and walk?

LUKE 5:23

This divine question is remarkably and dramatically asked before Calvary. But it is astoundingly and solemnly (and inarguably) foreshadowed. Jesus Christ was utterly prepared to lay down his life for this man's sins, as well as for his paralysis. What an extraordinary total redemption and astute definition of being made whole. What love.

This is the pronouncement of him who had written the Law, meeting and fulfilling the requirements of the Law. This is an irrefutable declaration of deity, an indubitable expression of the Ancient of Days, the explicit testimony of Alpha and Omega; this is the concise witness of him having neither beginning of days, nor end of life (re. Heb. 7:3). This is the Word of GOD speaking.

*

I lay down my life, that I might take it again.
re. JOHN 10:17

*

The Law had to be satisfied before mankind could be restored to the place from which he fell. When man and woman sinned, GOD *"drove out the man"* from the Garden of Eden and pronounced sorrow and manifold labor upon mankind. Unless the soul of man could be redeemed, then after his physical death, the soul of man would experience what the Word of GOD calls *"the second death"* of eternal separation from GOD in the lake of fire.

No, I am not going to preach hell (at least not right now). I want to be as concise and uncomplicated as possible, and within the scope of my limited understanding, I want to attempt to express what the Holy Spirit has comprehensively shown me in prayer and fasting and meditating upon GOD's Word.

Most of you know that what I call my *first fundamental*, and the Word of GOD that never fails to *reboot* and redirect my focus, is the LORD Jesus Christ declaring, *"GOD is a Spirit"* (re. John 4:24).

This is what I call an unadorned absolute of GOD. Markedly, the LORD Jesus Christ did not make this startling, straightforward incisive statement to the man, Nicodemus, one of the most preeminent religious persons alive at the time, but he spoke it to an unnamed sinner woman at Jacob's well. Often, we are much too wise in our own human estimation to be trusted with percipient (heavenly) revelation. Jesus would sum it up on another occasion as follows:

✴

I thank thee, O Father, LORD of heaven and earth,
that thou hast hid these things from the wise and
prudent, and hast revealed them unto babes: even
so, Father; for so it seemed good in thy sight.
see LUKE 10:21

✴

This is going to upset someone's theology, but GOD is a Spirit, and decidedly not a person. Jesus Christ was made in the *likeness* of men (see Phil. 2:7), just as men were made in the image and after the likeness of GOD (see Gen. 1:26).

These heavenly things are for us to ponder and meditate upon in spirit and in truth, and not for disputation and argument. No human mind is sufficient for such divine revelation. GOD will impart them unto me by his Holy Spirit or I shall not have them.

The immediate context of any given Word of GOD is the domain and milieu of the comprehensive Word of GOD. That is, one scripture cannot be removed from the province, atmosphere, frame of reference or environment of the entirety of the scriptures.

*

I and my Father are One.
JOHN 10:30

*

This is another unembellished absolute of GOD. Search the scriptures. Jesus Christ took upon himself *"the form," "the fashion," "the likeness of men"* (see Phil. 2:7-8). He never ceased to be GOD, was never less than deity.

We must think outside the religious and doctrinal box of our forefathers. If GOD does not show me, I shall not have it.

*

*Let this mind be in you, which was also in Christ
Jesus. Who, being in the form of GOD, thought
it not robbery to be EQUAL with GOD.*
PHIL. 2:5-6

*

Christian, let us humble ourselves as servants and become like children, and become obedient unto death, even the death of the cross. This, only, is the gospel principle of the life lost to find it, the precept and prerequisite for the resurrection life of the LORD Jesus Christ. This only will open our understanding of the scriptures.

Adam and Eve questioned GOD's Word. This always results in an opened door for the adversary and a dialogue with the devil. I am being deliberately elementary. Mankind was structurally and essentially entrusted with the breath of life, GOD's own Spirit, and man became a living soul. Sin radically defiled GOD's constitutional image and likeness within man. Self-seeking and egotism opened a forbidden door, and lust and pride entered in.

The humility and obedience of Jesus Christ as the Son of man and the Son of GOD, and his submission as the blood sacrifice and the Lamb of GOD that would satisfy the Law, positioned him to receive all glory and honor and power (all authority) from the Father. No, I was not there to see what transpired, I did not overhear their conversation, but if you can receive it, I write by the Spirit of GOD, for GOD. To him who hears the Word of GOD and keeps it, to him it is given, as it were, to read between the lines. Dear reader, either I am anointed of GOD to write, or both your reading and my writing is in vain.

Concisely (once more), the Father and the Son are One LORD by the Holy Spirit. Let us look at what precipitated the Father's glory in honoring Jesus Christ to be the Baptizer with the Holy Ghost.

✳

*Therefore doth my Father love me, because I lay
down my life, that I might take it again.*
JOHN 10:17

✳

The Good Shepherd's life was not taken, it was freely given. The meekness and obedience in which it was given exacerbated its value and its glory.

Finite words are not sufficient to describe it, but the Apostle Paul relates it as follows. But it must first be noted and emphasized that the Apostle Paul did not see the *form* or the *fashion* or the *likeness* that Jesus Christ had taken upon himself to fulfill the Father's commandment, he saw the very *"reality"* on the Road to Damascus. And the reality was above the brightness of the noonday sun (re. Acts 26:13). Here, then, is how the Father honored and glorified the Son for his obedience.

✻

Wherefore GOD also hath highly exalted him, and
given him a name which is above every name.
PHIL. 2:9

✻

Christian, Jesus Christ has left us an incisive example of humility, obedience, and sanctification as pleasing unto GOD. We know the comprehensive gospel teaches that for us to share his glory, we must first share his sufferings and his separation. These things are just so. The gospel principle of losing the life to find it is found only in the cross of Jesus Christ and him crucified. Ironically, it surprises many religious folk when the reality (or the revelation) comes home to them, that we must first radically die unto sin and self, the love of the world, the lust of the flesh, and the pride of life, et. al. before we can genuinely share the grace of resurrection life and power.

*

Marvel not that I said unto thee, Ye must be born again.
JOHN 3:7

*

Concisely, we need this regenerative breath of GOD, this Holy Spirit of resurrection life. The breath we have from Adam, as it were, is defiled. Bluntly, we are essentially unregenerate and predominantly unconverted. We feign to have received the LORD Jesus Christ by grace through faith, and then (somehow, miraculously) remained fundamentally unchanged in heart and mind.

The life of GOD in Jesus Christ will manifest radical fundamental change. It will not be otherwise. Genuine faith commands forward momentum; that is, my progressive and irrepressible becoming more like Jesus Christ. It may sometimes be incremental and agonizingly slow, but genuine faith will inevitably engender evidence and substance.

Our contemporary mainstream multitudes and mega-congregations of the unregenerate and unconverted casually calling themselves Christians must be addressed. I will use myself as an example.

Young Christians are not taught to wait upon GOD, and for their expectation to be upon him only. (I speak broadly.) Too often, young believers are pressured to conform to the forms of faith of their forefathers, predominantly religious ritual and ceremony, and sparse emphasis upon the Holy Spirit. We are not taught to wait on GOD; we learn to wait on men. We learn to covet (and compete for) the honor one of another.

We learn to depend upon the ceremony, and precisely document and celebrate our religious service while persisting fundamentally unchanged. We learn to tweak the presentation perfectly, and stuff our imperfections deeper. We present before one another, but we do not operatively present our true selves before GOD. The altar has become antiquated.

To realistically have the resurrection life and power of the LORD Jesus Christ, I must also effectually fellowship with his sufferings, and radically conform to the death of his cross. This is a fundamental gospel principle and an acute prerequisite of the life of a dynamic faith. The Apostle Paul expresses it as follows:

＊

*That I may know him, and the power of his
resurrection, and the fellowship of his sufferings,
being made conformable unto his death.*
PHIL. 3:10

＊

This is elementary, and should be glaringly obvious, that it is only dead men (and women) that can be born again and raised to newness of life. Nonetheless, our natural man goes to elaborate and ingenuous lengths to circumvent the self-denial and austerity of the cross. In the desperation to save our lives for ourselves, what the Apostle Paul calls *forms of faith* are born: basically, various religious exercise and service to emulate the forward momentum of a genuine faith. (I will repeat it until mainstream contemporary Christianity gets it.)

Only GOD has power over life and death. By virtue of his humility, and the laying down of his life in obedience and in the ultimate sanctification, and by reason of being the first-born from the dead, the LORD Jesus Christ has this resurrection life to give.

✳

For it pleased the Father that in him should all fullness dwell.
COL. 1:19

✳

It pleased the Father that his Son, the LORD Jesus Christ, have the glory and the honor and the power of being the Baptizer with the Holy Ghost and with (what I call, evangelical) fire. The *promise of the Father* was first made to the Son. This *Holy Ghost* (I declare) is the regenerative breath of GOD. Humanity must have this regenerative breath and Spirit to be born again because the initial breath of life given Adam was defiled by sin.

Both the Father and the Son (as we shall see) are said to send this Holy Spirit upon obedient and sanctified believers in Jesus Christ. This is also expressive of the Doctrine of Christ, that the Father and the Son are One LORD (whom I call by the Holy Ghost) the Christ of GOD. The following scriptures delineating what I am struggling to say are within the following text.

First, (to paraphrase) Jesus says if we love him, we will keep his commandments and then he will pray to the Father to send us another Comforter (re. John 14:15-16). Later in the chapter is where Jesus says that the Father sends this Holy Spirit.

*

But the Comforter, which is the Holy Ghost, WHOM THE FATHER WILL SEND in my name, he shall teach you all things, and bring all things to your remembrance, whatsoever I have said unto you.
JOHN 14:26

*

It behooves us to immediately reference where the Word of GOD also states that it is the LORD Jesus Christ who sends us this Holy Spirit of GOD.

*

But when the Comforter is come, WHOM I WILL SEND UNTO YOU from the Father, even the Spirit of Truth, which proceeded from the Father, he shall testify of me.
JOHN 15:26

*

The Word of God refers to the Holy Spirit as "*the Promise of the Father,*" the "*Spirit of Truth,*" the "*Holy Ghost,*" and "*the Comforter.*" This is the same (One) Spirit of GOD. Here is its explicit incisive expression, and a few of what I call the absolutes of GOD:

I and my Father are One.

JOHN 10:30

GOD is a Spirit.

re. JOHN 4:24

*For there are three that bear record in heaven, the Father,
the Word, and the Holy Ghost: and these three are One.*

1 JOHN 5:7

It is by the comprehensive (unabridged, unconditional) Word of GOD, and by the Holy Spirit of that Living Word, that I declare that the Father and the Son are One LORD. This is what John the Beloved concisely calls the *Doctrine of Christ*. I list the scripture in its entirety (again) that there be no error, and that we may observe its portentous admonition.

✳

Whosoever transgresseth, and abideth not in the [Doctrine
of Christ], *hath not GOD. He that abideth in the* [Doctrine
of Christ], *he hath "both" the Father and the Son.*
2 JOHN 1:9

✳

Although I have written of these wonderful mysteries of the Almighty GOD in his Christ at length in other volumes, the Holy Spirit deemed it expedient that I reference this revelatory (prophetic) and radical Word of GOD here as well. Children, it is by the Word of GOD (as it were) that we rightly divide the Word of GOD. As I have said, all specific scripture(s) must be considered in the immediate context of the comprehensive Word of GOD.

Before returning to our main text, I want to share the one scripture (I believe) best exemplifies this phenomenon that John the Beloved calls *the Doctrine of Christ*. And, uh, markedly, it is spoken by Christ:

✳

*If a man love me, he will keep my words: and my
Father will love him, and "WE" will come unto
him, and make "OUR" abode with him.*
re. JOHN 14:23 (emphasis mine

✳

Now, to abruptly return to our main text, these scripters which specify and characterize the Holy Spirit of GOD are concisely expressive of the life of the Good Shepherd that he willingly lays down for his sheep. Moreover, amazingly and miraculously, the life that he takes back up is the glory and power of resurrection life that he has the authority to pour out upon (and into) his obedient and sanctified disciples. This is concisely and explicitly the *Gift of the Holy Ghost,* the *Promise of the Father,* our *Comforter* – this is incredibly *the Breath and Life of GOD!*

This Spirit of Resurrection Life is *"both"* the Spirit of the Father, and the Spirit of the Son. This is the *Gift of the Holy Ghost.* He is the *"we"* and the *"our"* spoken of in John 14:23 as explicitly taught by the LORD Jesus Christ, that is, this is the *Doctrine of Christ.*

But I must not get ahead of myself. We are sure to talk about this resurrection life that the Good Shepherd takes back up in chapter five of this manuscript, *I AM the Resurrection and the Life.* For now, the point which the Holy Spirit wants me to emphasize concerns this commandment that Jesus Christ has received from the Father. This power (authority) over life and death makes him One with GOD, coalesced and indivisible from the Father. This is *He* with authority to forgive sin and impart eternal life, this is the comprehensive (and incomprehensible) *I AM THAT I AM.*

All of these chapters are going to naturally overlap and coalesce into the continuing revelation of One LORD, and as the Holy Spirit assists me, magnify the deity of the LORD Jesus Christ as GOD. The life that the Good Shepherd takes back from the powers of death, hell, and the grave is the Spirit of Resurrection Life. It is the Spirit of the Glorified Christ. Amazingly, this is the life that he gives his obedient and sanctified disciples. This is the *Gift of the Holy Ghost.*

By the same Holy Spirit, I am moved to emphasize (and re-emphasize and belabor) that there is no distinction between the deity of the Father and the deity of the Son. It has pleased the Father to commit all judgment and authority to the Son, *"that all men should honor the Son, even as they honor the Father"* (see John 5:22-23).

The Holy Spirit wants there to be no misunderstanding. The same Spirit of an endless life is *both* the Spirit of the Father, and the Spirit of the Son. None but the Almighty GOD has this eternal life to give. As the LORD Jesus Christ frequently does, he will state a Truth, and then a few verses later, restate that same Truth from a slightly different perspective. Such is the case in the following two verses:

*

For as the Father raiseth up the dead, and quickeneth (gives life unto) *them; even so the Son quickeneth whom he will.*
JOHN 5:21

*For as the Father hath life in himself; so hath he
given to the Son to have life in himself.*
John 5:26

✳

GOD sent his Word to heal us body, mind, and soul. This is
the joyful sound and exceeding good news of the gospel of
Jesus Christ, the Voice of the Word of GOD that raises the
dead. This is, concisely, GOD speaking:

✳

*Verily, verily, I say unto you, The hour is coming, and
now is, when the dead shall hear the Voice of the
Son of GOD: and they that hear shall live.*
John 5:25

✳

There is sure to be much more about this power of Resurrection
Life in our next chapter. Let us talk about the Good Shepherd.
First, he is both the Door to the sheepfold, and the Shepherd
that stands vigilant in the portal. His gaze is all-knowing, incisive, percipient, what I often call the *omniscient eye* of the
HOLY. He intuits all things unto the perimeter and past the
horizon, and no thought can be withheld from him (re, Job
42:2). His reach extends into the margins of society, and his
grace esteems the worst of humanity. There is none beyond
redemption; no, not one.

Each of these enigmatic and inscrutable *"I AM"* statements of
the LORD Jesus Christ affirm and authenticate and magnify
his deity. We reach into the divinity and identity of the *"Most
High."* On the perimeter of our faith we press into the next

striation of glory, into the next gradation of Greater Grace. Nigh unto trespass I press, thirsty and hungry for the Truth of GOD, desperate for one more encounter, one more taste.

That the LORD is my Shepherd is a fresh vista, another astounding, inexplicable perspective of the unfathomable mysteries and wisdom of GOD. Finite words fail me. For glimpses of grace I live.

GOD is "hid" in Christ, and I must find him there, in every Word that proceeds out of his mouth. Or, as Job puts it, *"I have esteemed the words of his mouth more than my necessary food"* (see Job 23:12)

But have we esteemed this Good Shepherd who gives his life for the sheep as the Almighty GOD, as One with the Father, just as he says? Concisely, our Creator and King, Redeemer and Savior, are One LORD.

✳

I, even I, AM the LORD, and beside me there is no Savior.
Isa. 43:11

I AM the LORD, your Holy One, the
Creator of Israel, your King.
Isa. 43:15

✳

The comprehensive Word of GOD substantiates that GOD was manifest in the flesh. He has always been the Good Shepherd. The same GOD that created humanity, redeems humanity.

✳

O come, let us worship and bow down: let us
kneel before the LORD our maker.

For he is our GOD; and we are the people of
his pasture, and the sheep of his hand.
Psa. 95:6-7

✳

The crowning grace of the aggregate or composite virtues of the Good Shepherd is, of course, the eternal life he gives. GOD gives himself away in Jesus Christ. The gift of GOD is the gift of himself, the Spirit of an endless life.

I have repeatedly stated that (none) but GOD can forgive sin and impart life. The implications and comprehensive parameters of exactly what Jesus Christ is attesting to here in the tenth chapter of John are astounding. There were many shepherds in Israel during this time. But this was no ordinary Shepherd that Jesus Christ was contending and (in fact) asserting to be.

Of course, the Old Testament, and specifically the Psalms, endorse and validate *"the"* Good Shepherd as being the LORD, or Yahweh (YHWH). Every good Hebrew alive during the time of Jesus Christ knew that it was GOD that delivered the Israelites from the cruel bondage of Egypt, and that led them by signs and wonders through the wilderness, and by a strong and mighty hand into the promised land.

✳

Thou leddest thy people like a flock by
the hand of Moses and Aaron.
Ps. 77:20

✳

Let there be no misunderstanding of the magnitude and exceeding significance of exactly what Jesus Christ is asserting when he says *I AM the Good Shepherd.* Precisely, Moses and Aaron were *under-shepherds*, and the Chief Shepherd is Yahweh (YHWH), or Jehovah.

Concisely, the Good Shepherd is the GOD who conscripted Moses to lead his people out of Egypt by engaging him from the midst of a burning bush. Exodus 3:2 states that *"the angel of the LORD appeared unto him in a flame of fire out of the midst of a bush,"* and then verse 4 goes on to say, *"GOD called unto him out of the midst of the bush."*

It is my testimony by the Holy Ghost that this is GOD in his Christ speaking to Moses out of the fire from the midst of this bush. This I have from GOD, that Jesus Christ was with GOD in the middle of that bush just like the Word was with GOD in the beginning (re. John 1:1). The LORD Jesus Christ makes it even plainer when he says, *I and my Father are One* (John 10:30). This GOD out of the midst of that bush is the very same GOD that a few verses later tells Moses his name is *"I AM THAT I AM."*

This is the GOD who forgives sin and gives life. Our Creator and Redeemer is One LORD.

✳

Know ye that the LORD he is GOD: it is he that
hath made us, and not we ourselves, we are
his people, and the sheep of his pasture."
Ps. 100:3

*

The Jews and the Pharisees in the tenth chapter of John knew exactly who Jesus Christ was claiming to be by adamantly stating that he was the Good Shepherd. The Jews revered GOD as their Shepherd, both Creator and Redeemer. Midway through the chapter, there is a division among the people because of this teaching (vs. 19), and toward the end of the chapter the Jews take up stones once again to kill him (vs. 31). They understood his testimony perfectly. As already mentioned, it was the verse before this one, that when the LORD Jesus spoke it, removed all doubt, *"I and my Father are One."* None could utter such a testimony but GOD.

To these Jews, the claims of Jesus were so fantastic (and unimaginable) that they kept provoking him to repeat them. Duh, this was not his first *I AM* statement. It was his fourth as we count them, meaning as seven direct or definitive ones in the gospel according to John. Our LORD's additional (indirect) references or allusions to deity are incalculable. Moreover, innumerable signs and wonders and miracles of healing had already corroborated his words.

Children, our spiritual predicament shall be the prophetic correlative and mirror image of these Jews and Pharisees if we, too, doubt or deny the Word of GOD. Contemporary Christianity has more in common with these Pharisees and posers than we care to confess. (Bluntly), we are both the predominant religious contingent of our respective time. You know, religion's best.

The revelation of the Holy One is here. The sudden exposure reveals my religious dilemma, uh, meaning my prevarication and procrastination, and, ahem . . . my pretending and pontification and prostitution. If I concur with the deity of the LORD Jesus Christ, I will have to forsake self-love and world-love and turn to the One True GOD in absolute surrender and obedience and sanctification.

The revelation presses up against the religious ideology of my theoretical Jesus and glaringly illuminates my playing church, commanding reality of my uh, conceptual, hypothetical, speculative idea of GOD. That is, the reality that Jesus Christ is GOD eclipses and overwhelms my abstract idolatrous conceptual presumptuous GOD of all-permissive grace and self-inflating self-celebratory religious ceremony (if you will pardon the grammatical largesse).

The sudden revelation of Jesus Christ as the Good Shepherd strenuously adjures and acutely requires me to present as a docile and obedient sheep. Frankly, the revelation exposes all my religious posturing as self-serving vanity. Duh, everything beyond hearing his voice and following him is kind of extraneous. How to get through that strait gate with all my religious paraphernalia and impedimenta, I cannot find.

The deity of Jesus Christ in theory makes no life-changing, ego-bashing, attitude-transforming, sin-eradicating commands of me (you get the idea). But the reality sure does.

A philosophical Jesus can be served by superficial service and perfunctory religious ceremony. The expectations of a hypothetical Jesus can be satisfied with an academic presentation. You know what I am saying. If Jesus Christ is not GOD, then my guilty conscience can be salved by a cursory religious routine. Yes, by a one-dimensional mechanical church attendance. Uh, in other words, a form of faith.

The reality on the other hand, requires a radical life-transforming, pride-shattering regeneration. Yep, a radical being born again. (Or, as we used to say it up the hollow, "*borned*" again.)

The power is in believing what the LORD Jesus Christ declares about who GOD is. Concisely, (he declares), *I AM.* My believing what the Word of GOD says about . . . well, about himself, is called faith, the catalyst and sustaining impetus of salvation. This is what I often call the dynamic of salvation, or the gospel principle of living by faith. Anything else is going through the motions.

Few of us are interested enough (and invested enough) in the eternal state of our soul to painstakingly investigate Jesus Christ's assertions of deity. *"The many and the few"* is not my ratio, if you follow. It is the Word of GOD's ratio. See Matthew 7:13-14.

This defines our prophetic contemporary Christian conundrum as identical to the other elitist (elect) religious population to whom this Living Word of GOD was originally spoken, essentially Judaism. *"For if ye believe not that I AM (He), ye shall die in your sins"* (re. John 8:24).

The power (authority) to transform and regenerate and convert my life is found in my believing the revelation – faith in what GOD has said. GOD is hidden here in Christ, and by faith, I see him.

Succinctly, (by the Holy Ghost) I say that the preponderance of us are not invested enough in eternity to fundamentally care what the Word of GOD says, or we would read and study our Bibles. It would be evidenced by a marked reformation of behavior, attitude, and character. Concisely, we would be converted. The love of GOD would abound. It could not be otherwise.

Conversely, the preponderance of us are convinced of our casual Christianity, the smarm and smiling faces and all the phony trimmings of the comprehensive church ceremony. We do church very well. The presentation is tweaked perfectly. And internally we remain principally unchanged.

For my faith to be engaged, and for me to be empowered (and transformed), I must investigate the revelation. I must see GOD for myself. By faith, I encounter the Almighty GOD in his Christ (the Word).

Do I believe what Jesus Christ says about himself, or do I believe in church ceremony and the religious pretender I present on Sunday mornings for the preacher and the righteous congregation, all so I can save the real me for myself?

If I look into the Word of GOD, the Word of GOD looks into me. But if I have a linear, one-dimensional, conceptual Jesus, then he has no righteous expectations of me. He is no more real than I am.

The revelation of Jesus Christ as the Good Shepherd startlingly and disconcertedly designates me as an ordinary, uncelebrated, garden-variety sheep. Consequently, all these years, I have been thinking too highly of myself and my religious persona and presentation. *"Follow me"* is relatively all I need to know, as it were. Uh, I complicate the simplicity that is in Christ by my ostentatious elaborate Christian affectation and uh, righteous airs. Concisely, Jesus Christ is looking for sinners to save by grace.

(Broadly) the piercing, irrepressible prophetic (and progressive) revelation of the deity of the LORD Jesus Christ upsets our structured gingerbread all-permissive grace and serpentine religious form (our cardboard Christianity) as profoundly as it disconcerted and discombobulated the labyrinthine and extravagant Judaism of these Pharisees. Yet, there is at least one significant difference between their flamboyant religious pretention and our contemporary Christian theatrical posturing. They were at least committed or zealous enough about their religion to ask, *"Who art thou?"* (re. John 8:25)

Concisely, Jesus Christ came to declare the Grace and Truth (and identity) of GOD, and to meet and satisfy the Law. He told us who GOD is and what he wants.

✻

The hour cometh, and now is, when the true worshippers shall worship the Father in spirit and in truth: for the Father seeketh such to worship him.

JOHN 4:23

*[inspired by the Holy Spirit]

Come unto me without pretention or excuses, saith the LORD; follow me in sincerity and rectitude, and I give you the Spirit of Life. Allow my Holy Spirit to be your guiding impetus in the way, and faith in me, the dynamic that awakens you before the dawn. Follow me, and you shall know that *I AM THAT I AM.*

Greater Grace is for the genuine, and deeper truths for the intrepid. The astute revelation of *I AM* is the acute correlative of the reflection of your own soul. When I show you who you are, then you shall know that *I AM.*

Hear me, son of man, I AM he that parts the waters for them that follow. I AM a pillar of a cloud by day, and a pillar of fire by night.

I AM the Bread of Life, and *I AM* the Light of the World; *I AM* the Door to the sheepfold, and *I AM* the Good Shepherd who stands vigilant in the portal.

I AM the Holy One of Israel. How many times must I tell you *I AM?*

❋

The Apostle Peter calls the LORD Jesus Christ the *Chief Shepherd* (re. 1 Pet. 5:4). We are going to be looking at this reference in conjunction with the LORD's teaching on thieves and robbers, and hirelings, in the tenth chapter of John.

Pointedly, the LORD Jesus Christ did not excuse or mitigate hypocrisy in any of its forms and did not give pretenders and wannabe prophets and priests a pass. There is no compromise with evil. To bargain or accommodate sin and deception is like attempting to interject darkness into light. Unfortunately, some of us seem to like these theoretical shady places.

The Truth innately and unapologetically confronts all illusion and misconception, all duplicity and fantasy. Succinctly, genuine truth reveals religious form. GOD is a Spirit (re. John 4:24), and he is a *Holy* Spirit. Three distinct times in the gospel according to John, the LORD Jesus Christ called the Holy Ghost which was to come and dwell within his sanctified and obedient disciples, *the Spirit of Truth*, (see John 14:17/15:26/16:13).

Speaking the truth in love is going to unavoidably upset religious affectation and self-righteous posturing, and (as I say), inevitably hurt the pretender's delicate spiritual sensibilities. Jesus Christ went about the Father's business with a grave and foreboding determination. This Good Shepherd is the same GOD that drowned Pharaoh and his armies, and the same GOD who sometimes turns over tables. The LORD Jesus Christ does not compromise with them just playing church or placate pretenders and hypocrites.

When I investigate the Word of GOD, the Word of GOD investigates me. Genuine faith recognizes and exposes religious form, casts illumination upon the fallacies and fables of some of our forefathers. The Word of GOD has much to say about those that would presume upon the calling and office of pastor or shepherd. He who has ears to hear, let him hear. To preach to GOD's people is not by personal aspiration, but by the appointment of GOD.

✳

> *And no man taketh this honor unto himself, but he that is called of GOD, as was Aaron.*
>
> *So also Christ glorified not himself to be made an high priest; but he that said unto him, Thou art my Son, today have I begotten thee.*
> HEB. 5:4-5

✳

Once more, he who has ears, let him hear. The old-timers used to say, "Some are sent, but some just went." In addition to the Good Shepherd's denouncement of thieves and robbers and hirelings in our current text, the Word of GOD has much to say about under-shepherds or pastors, and about both prophets and priests. Before we look at what the Apostle Peter wrote about elders and shepherds as he was inspired by the Holy Ghost, let us look briefly at his own precise calling and commission from the Chief Shepherd.

One day, when the LORD and his disciples entered Caesarea Philippi, Jesus asked his disciples what may correctly be termed a cardinal tenet and critical question of the Christian faith. *"Who do men say that I the Son of man am?"* (see Matt. 16:13)

This is a living, prophetic, indispensable question for every ensuing disciple of the LORD Jesus Christ. As we should already know, the Church of GOD is founded upon the answer given that momentous day by the Apostle Peter. *"Thou are the Christ, the Son of the Living GOD."* (re. Matt. 16:16)

Every Christian should possess the same living revelation as the foundation of a zealous and enterprising faith. Furthermore, (and as you can receive it), the Holy Spirit has shown me that the Christ of GOD is One LORD by the Holy Spirit. That is, the Father and the Son (Jesus Christ) are One LORD by the Holy Spirit. Its scriptural equivalent, as it were, is spoken by the LORD Jesus Christ, the Living Word of GOD, *"I and my Father are One"* (John 10:30).

This living (perpetual, progressive, prophetic) revelation is the Rock upon which Jesus Christ has built the Church of GOD. Moreover, the Christ of GOD has always been GOD.

He is the eternal Word of GOD and the Rock of our salvation. The Christ of GOD was with the children of Israel in the wilderness.

※

For they drank of that same spiritual Rock that
followed them: and that Rock was Christ."
re. 1 Cor. 10:4

※

It was the Father in heaven who revealed this mysterious wisdom unto the Apostle Peter. Neither (flesh nor blood) nor theology school can reveal it unto me. Only the diligent and the intrepid come this way. Only by the grace of GOD and the violence of our faith does that Rock still release Living Water.

Much has been made of the LORD Jesus Christ's singular statement unto Peter when he told him he would give him the keys to the kingdom of heaven. That is, much religious presumption and pontification has been perpetrated (without naming names, as they say).

Concisely, the revelation is that Jesus is the Christ, the Almighty GOD, both the Father and the Son by One Holy Spirit, the Alpha and Omega of GOD. Precisely, GOD is a Spirit (and as you know I like to say, he is a *Holy* Spirit), and the Apostle Peter was favored to introduce him on the Day of Pentecost when he suddenly came from heaven as a rushing mighty wind and as cloven tongues like fire (see Acts 2:2-3).

The Apostle Peter is still criticized for his having publicly denied the LORD Jesus Christ three times in short order. But it must be specified that this was a compulsory (inevitable) prelude to the power that would be entrusted unto him. His preaching on the Day of Pentecost would prove it, when about three thousand souls were saved and added to the Church, (see Acts 2:41).

Notably, while Peter was being sifted as wheat by Satan, and while his faith was being tried to the uttermost simultaneously, the rest of the disciples except for ostensibly John, were (more or less) cowering behind locked doors. Concisely, it was the confrontation of the Apostle Peter's faith which was the effectual catalyst of his conversion. Bluntly, the LORD Jesus Christ orchestrated the specific circumstances that would occasion Peter's denial of him three times.

I ask you, saint of GOD, "Have you ever been set up like that?" Jesus frankly told Peter that Satan desired to have him that he might sift him as wheat. Outside the auspices and sanctuary of the LORD's grace, we all would be swiftly and summarily overcome of evil. What appeared to be the utter failure of the Apostle Peter's faith was the fiery trial which would help fashion him into a soldier.

✳

> *That the trial of your faith, being much more*
> *precious than of gold that perisheth, though it be*
> *tried with fire, might be found unto praise and honor*
> *and glory at the appearing of Jesus Christ.*
> 1 PET. 1:7

✳

My testimony of faith is tempered by fiery trial, and my character progressively converted into the image of Christ by suffering association. As I have often said, if I do not suffer some type of persecution as a Christian, then the world does not know that I am one. Moreover, if the world does not hate me, then there is no viable or definitive reflection of Jesus Christ in me, or out of me, and the world is essentially seeing one of her own. As they say, "There is no testimony without a test."

Circumstances (seemingly spontaneously) conspire to confront all viable or measurable faith. If the image and Holy Spirit of Jesus Christ is being birthed into me, then Satan has heard about it as surely as King Herod was apprised of the Christ-child being born in Bethlehem of Judaea. Satan will come for you just like that. If you have endeavored to witness to your neighbor or loved one, or dared to speak in the name of Jesus Christ, then you know these things are so.

Unfortunately, contemporary (mainstream superficial) Christianity presumes an indirect or oblique, or silent, denial of the LORD Jesus Christ will not be laid to our charge. Well? What does it say (or not say) about my faith if I am a Christian on Sunday, but silent on Monday? Duh, we are much too wise and prudent to place ourselves in the precarious circumstances that Peter foolishly exposed himself to. No, we cower behind metaphorical (but no less real) locked doors, fundamentally unconverted. Well, these days, sometimes literal ones.

If we only knew what we were missing. If once we appreciated the potential of our testimony and the accompanying power of the Holy Spirit released upon our witness, we would speak in the name of Jesus Christ with a progressive boldness in the market places and the work places of this world. Our spiritual strength and vigor would be increased exponentially. We would proportionally and rapidly be converted from lukewarm, minimal and nominal Christians into virulent and incendiary witnesses of the resurrection life and power of the LORD Jesus Christ, as we were intended to be.

Let us realize and functionally apprehend the following Word of GOD to release the radically transforming power of the Holy Spirit upon our witness of Jesus Christ in the earth.

✳

Whosoever therefore shall confess me before men, him will I confess also before my Father which is in heaven.
MATT. 10:32

✳

Returning to our main text, we can only imagine the despair and humiliation that the Apostle Peter experienced after denying the LORD Jesus Christ the third time, and then immediately hearing that rooster crow. From excruciating personal experience, I can commiserate. To extract and mortify pride from my character, the LORD still periodically choreographs adverse circumstances which command my having to utterly humble myself. Ah, the Holy One presses his own olives, and crushes his own grapes.

At the absolute end of himself, and after going out and weeping bitterly (re. Matt. 26:75), the Apostle Peter understood the grace of humility.

✳

*Humble yourselves therefore under the mighty hand
of GOD, that he may exalt you in due time.*
1 Pet. 5:6

✳

We come to the occasion of the LORD Jesus Christ restoring the Apostle Peter to his grace, and an especially relevant Word of GOD to our discussion of the Good Shepherd. Each of the four gospel accounts have a distinctive and urgent (evangelical) ending. We generally and traditionally take what we call *The Great Commission* from the closing in the gospel according to Matthew. All four accounts are indispensable, as well as astounding, but the close of the gospel according to John is especially pertinent to our present text.

We should all know this Word of GOD well. John the Beloved is moved by the Holy Spirit to close his gospel account (in large part) with the LORD Jesus Christ specifically commissioning the Apostle Peter to *"Feed my sheep."* This is definitively the Good Shepherd speaking here, and there is no misunderstanding his directive or the preeminent desires of his heart. (If I may) and as the LORD concisely expressed it earlier in his ministry, *"My Father worketh hitherto, and I work"* (re. John 5:17).

As long as the earth endures, ninety and nine sheep will never be one hundred, and the Holy Spirit of the Good Shepherd is still urgently seeking the lost. The LORD Jesus Christ is still entreating and petitioning (and commissioning) his sons and daughters.

He who has ears to hear can still hear his Voice. *"If you love me, feed my sheep."*

*

The Holy Spirit of GOD is still transforming and empowering (and converting) servants and stewards into sons and daughters, and into efficacious witnesses of the saving and delivering and healing power of Jesus Christ.

But have we understood the utter implications of this austere commission for every ensuing or subsequent disciple of the Good Shepherd?

*

This spake he, signifying by what death he should glorify GOD.
And when he had spoken this, he saith unto him, Follow me.
JOHN 21:19

*

Each one of us that believe on the LORD Jesus Christ are expected to transition into disciples of the LORD Jesus Christ. Or, as I have expressed it in the past, we grow spiritually grace for grace and faith to faith by obedience and sanctification (all, working by love), incrementally but substantively *"changed into the same image from glory to glory, even as by the Spirit of the LORD."* (re. 2 Cor. 3:18)

As we see with the Apostle Peter, it is love for the LORD Jesus Christ which is the preeminent qualifier for the office of under-shepherd, or for any viable (fruit-producing) aspect of ministry, for that matter. Our faith will only work by this love. Gospel truth is sheathed within this love of GOD in Jesus Christ. It is the highest grace.

The love of GOD is other-worldly. That is, it had to be sent into this world. Its exemplification is the selfless austerity of Calvary.

Love is the weapon of GOD in the warfare for the soul of humanity. Such is its imperative that our faith will not work without it. Such is its indispensable command that the LORD Jesus Christ asked Peter three consecutive times to affirm his love as genuine, once for each time he had previously denied him (perhaps).

There is a natural affection we often call love, but when exposed to the fire, or in the crushing press of adverse circumstance, and if afforded an opportunity, it will escape with its life intact. The love of GOD distinguishes between the impetuous boasting of the natural man and the soul of a genuine faith founded upon the bedrock of the true love of GOD in Jesus Christ.

It behooves us to ruminate and meditate upon the LORD's deliberate and systematic preparation of the Apostle Peter to be a shepherd. Notably, before we move on, he was not the only disciple who impulsively boasted that he would go to death with Jesus Christ before he denied him. *"Likewise also said ALL the disciples"* (re. Matt. 26:35).

However, he was indisputably the one individual whom the LORD Jesus Christ extraordinarily designated as the recipient of the keys of the kingdom of heaven (see Matt. 16:19). Moreover, just as he was the singular individual with the ignominious designation of having denied the LORD Jesus Christ three times, likewise, and after his public humiliation, he is the exclusive disciple to be subjected (if you will) to the

LORD's, uh, inquisition or acute assessment of his love. And then, astoundingly, he is given the dreadful portend signifying by what death he should glorify GOD. Finally, he is given the command of the Good Shepherd for every subsequent disciple, that is, *"Follow me"* (re. John 21:19).

This Word of GOD is prophetically (and perpetually) fallen out unto you and I, and all comprehensive Christianity, all who call themselves by his great name. This is no casual undertaking or shallow religious observance or ceremony, this is the life and death of the love of GOD in the gospel of Jesus Christ and him crucified.

Genuine love is a dreadful and a glorious item. Moreover, the Apostle Peter would tell you that the way to honor is humiliation, and in order to have the life of the LORD Jesus Christ, we must first willingly surrender our own. I wonder how many of us are prepared to love like that. Children, by the Holy Spirit, I contend that only the converted can traverse the abyss of life and death in the love of GOD like that. A *few* of us follow to find that resurrection life, and *many* of us fall away into forms of faith. And once more, I stipulate that the ratio is not mine. It is the Word of GOD's.

Concisely, we examine the specifications and criterion for shepherding. Succinctly, the Great Commission is *"Feed my sheep."* Jesus Christ is eternally the Good Shepherd, and my love for him is expressly indicated or illustrated by my feeding his sheep. He could not have conveyed it any clearer, that this is what is most dear to his heart. Moreover, it can reasonably be concluded that the Apostle Peter would know it best. Writing specifically to the elders in the Church of God in Christ, he expresses it as follows:

Feed the flock of GOD which is among you, taking the oversight thereof, not by constraint, but willingly; not for filthy lucre, but of a ready mind.

1 Pet. 5:2

✳

The (first) priority of the Good Shepherd, and the first prerequisite of the pastor or under-shepherd is that the sheep are being fed. The Apostle Peter would always acutely remember the LORD Jesus' query of his love for him, and his three consecutive admonitions to ensure that the sheep are being fed and cared for. In fact, it is a nonnegotiable sacrosanct command of the LORD Jesus Christ.

If we go back just one verse, (1 Pet. 5:1), as mentioned, we see that the Apostle Peter is writing specifically to the elders of the Church, which (to me) implies that it is to be the business of every mature Christian to feed and set an example for the flock. Regardless of our position or calling, we are to set a positive example in conversation and godly deportment, and in our comprehensive attitude and behavior. The elders are to give themselves away in the service of the flock, and in a demonstration of losing the life to find it. That is, as a manifest example of laying their life down for their friend, and in their love for the LORD Jesus Christ by answering his explicit command to care for the flock.

Frankly, what first comes to mind is taking the entire flock before the throne of grace in earnest, intercessory prayer. And specifically, not (striving) or vying for position or notoriety, or for the honor one of another. Nothing promotes brotherly love and the unity of the body in the bond of peace quite like my praying in Spirit and in truth for the entire assembly. Unity and peace are immediate and measurable by-products of earnest, fervent prayer.

The Apostle Peter also writes that we are to take the oversight willingly, which concisely means voluntarily, readily. It is not a chore, but a privilege. When it is undertaken in love for the LORD Jesus Christ, it is a great honor. Moreover, the giving of one's life in the service of the LORD has its inestimable return in the grace and power of his resurrection life. All who willingly fellowship with the sufferings of Jesus Christ shall also share his glory (re. 1 Pet. 5:1).

Notably, the elders are not to take the oversight of the flock *"for filthy lucre, but of a ready mind"* (re. 1 Pet. 5:2). *"Filthy lucre"* specifically means illicit gain. Any combination of money, power, or control as motive(s) is not only inappropriate, but deleterious, and probably some aberrant outgrowth of religious pride and/or greed.

I have a premise concerning preachers getting paid which many (especially preachers) may find peculiar. Nonetheless, the Holy Spirit induces me to present it. Now, I know that the LORD has ordained that they which preach the gospel should live of the gospel (re. 1 Cor. 9:14). But I also know the summary of the Apostle Paul's discourse here in the ninth chapter of his first epistle to the Church of GOD at Corinth, as well as his documenting the providing for his own needs laboring as a tentmaker (re. Acts 18:13).

The Apostle Paul understood he could have legitimately (and sensibly) expected the gospel to meet his needs. Yet, he was exacting and scrupulous about his reputation for integrity, especially concerning monetary matters and gospel principles (or religious ethics, you might say). To avoid a lengthy diatribe defending my postulation that preachers ought not accept any pay for preaching the Word beyond immediate necessity, I will allow the Word of GOD to speak in representation of my (peculiar) premise.

Succinctly, evidently others were getting paid to minister to the flock at Corinth, but practicing self-denial even in ministry, it was the Apostle Paul's and Barnabas' custom to work in order to provide for themselves (see 1 Cor. 9:6). The Apostle Paul consciously chose not to exercise his prerogative or liberty to partake of the gospel for personal recompence but expended himself in the love of Jesus Christ for the Church (the flock).

Nevertheless we have not used this power (or privilege, authority) (see 1 Cor. 9:12).

The entire ninth chapter of 1 Corinthians is presented as the model for a pastor's explicit personal example of self-denial when ministering to the Church of GOD. The Apostle Paul considered the very thought of profiting from his care of the LORD's flock as abhorrent. A rich preacher ought to be an anomaly, or an oxymoron. I am talking about extravagance, and specifically extravagance at what may be construed as at the flock's expense.

To spend one's self, or to lose one's life in the service of the LORD's sheep, is the preeminent privilege and honor of the Chief Shepherd bestowed upon selected individuals, a highly esteemed sovereign appointment. Jesus Christ has specifically placed apostles, prophets, evangelists, pastors and teachers in the body as pleases him *"for the perfecting of the saints, for the work of the ministry, for the edifying of the body of Christ"* (see Eph. 4:11-12).

We address or delineate hirelings and imposters from genuine shepherds because the Word of GOD has much to say about them, (fat preachers and phony pietists). The LORD Jesus Christ did not circumvent unpleasantness, and he certainly never excused or mitigated hypocrisy in any form. Dear children, wolves in sheep's clothing is a reality of our religious service and prettiest church ceremony. Might we not, then, liken tares among the wheat, even as goats among the sheep?

The Apostle Paul concurs with the Apostle Peter about the care and maintenance of the flock.

✳

Take heed therefore unto yourselves, and to all the flock, over the which the Holy Ghost hath made you overseers, to feed the Church of GOD, which he hath purchased with his own blood.
ACTS 20:28

✳

It is the Holy Ghost who moves men to minister to other men. It is the Holy Spirit who is the dynamic power and essence of Almighty GOD, who appoints and empowers apostles and prophets and priests into the body of Christ. It is the Holy Spirit of GOD who imparts the selfless (sovereign, divine) love of GOD which is in Jesus Christ unto men appointed to minister to the sons and daughters of GOD.

It is the Holy Spirit of GOD who gives an individual the heart and mind of the Good Shepherd. If we sincerely ask and earnestly seek the heart and mind of Christ, GOD will give them and much more besides. The agonizing intimacy and acute suffering association of the cross of Jesus Christ is progressively (and seemingly spontaneously) made mine. (Some of you get it.) Grandma said be careful what you ask for.

※

For unto whomsoever much is given, of
him shall be much required.
re. LUKE 12:48

※

Tradition and history record or hold that the Apostle Peter was crucified upside down, and that the Apostle Paul was taken from prison and beheaded. These two men are the preeminent representative under-shepherds of the LORD Jesus Christ, the Good Shepherd, who exhort us by the commandment of the LORD to feed the flock of GOD. In selfless love and irrepressible service, these men laid down their lives both figuratively and literally, leaving us a dreadful and illustrious example of the gospel principle of laying down their life for their friend.

We know these things, but it is fitting and profitable that they be revisited. Contemporary Christianity must be brought to an astute conscious awareness and personal reckoning of the reality of the cross of Jesus Christ and the explicit truth of its suffering fellowship.

※

Greater love hath no man than this, that a
man lay down his life for his friends.
JOHN 15:13

＊

Children, this is the reality and severity of the truth about the love of GOD in Jesus Christ. This they do not teach you in contemporary mainstream "feel good about me" Christian Sunday school. This is the penetrating reality and dreadful consuming absolute of the love of GOD as revealed in the cross of Jesus Christ. This is the concise prophetic reality of the Word of GOD that has reached me right where I sit, languid and complacent and anesthetized in the pew. The prophetic implication of this love of GOD is the loss of my life.

＊

Lovest thou me more than these?
re. JOHN 21:15

＊

The splendid and sometimes extravagant experience of playing church and all that convoluted religious routine and complex form of faith is eclipsed by the reality of the love of GOD and the, uh, loss of my life. Some of you know that I call this *"the agony of greater grace"* and the astute terror of midnight truths. This is the reality of *"Feed my sheep,"* and the absolute of *"Follow me."* For now, in America, at least, this is the figurative loss of my life in the love of GOD for the soul of the world. If I am invested, that is, meaning if I am really a living sacrifice in the suffering association of the love of GOD in the gospel of Jesus Christ and him crucified.

Only by this love will the world see Jesus; that is, by the gospel of his cross made mine.

※

*Always bearing about in the body the dying of the LORD Jesus,
that the life also of Jesus might be made manifest in our body.*
2 Cor. 4:10

※

Christian, that the death is metaphorical (at least for now), does not make it any less acute. The reality of love is a living sacrifice, and the gospel of a perpetual cross.

As this relates to being under-shepherds of the LORD Jesus Christ and overseers of the LORD's flock, the Church of GOD, just about anyone can teach general Christian principles and traditional religious platitudes (or tell stories), but only the living sacrifice of selfless love can show the world Jesus.

The love of GOD in Christ is not a natural species. Only the genuinely converted can show the world a new creature in Christ Jesus. Only a genuine faith is the effectual catalyst for this miraculous transformation, everything else is (relatively) religious form and ceremonial routine. Only GOD has this love. (Or rather) this is the love that GOD is. His name is Jesus.

This is the reality of Chapter 4, and the life (and the love) we have gathered to discuss:

*I AM the Good Shepherd: the Good Shepherd
giveth his life for the sheep.*

John 10:11

*

Concisely, this selfless love, and this sacrificial laying down of one's life for the sheep (that is, its prophetic correlative), is what precipitates the hireling to flee. Some of us think this lets us off the hook because we are not formal pastors or ordained preachers. Ah, but this is the very same love (and the same loss of one's life) by which GOD desires to reach the soul of my neighbor.

This is the same gospel and the same acute suffering association of the cross of Jesus Christ, the surrogate sacrifice of selfless love and the perpetual loss of my life, in attempting to love my (essentially unlovable) neighbor. Oh my.

But, dear children, the reality is that nothing can change the unregenerate mind or touch the hardened impenitent heart of a person but the love of GOD in Jesus Christ. Only the genuine selfless love of the gospel of Jesus Christ and him crucified can save the soul of humanity. Love is GOD's weapon of choice.

This is the life the Good Shepherd gives for the sheep, and the unmistakable fruit of my genuine conversion is the same selfless love.

This surrender of one's life in selfless love is the impetus which induces the hireling to flee, the truth which forces the imposter to hide behind religious form. Ah, but this same selfless love can convert a young shepherd boy into a champion. Yes, I am saying that the Spirit of Christ, the Spirit of the Good Shepherd, was upon David.

And the Spirit of the LORD came upon David from that day forward. (see 1 Sam. 16:13)

✳

As the Holy Spirit leads me into all truth, and in this, the specific season of my humanity on this date, June 23, 2020, I attest to believing the following. That the LORD our GOD is One LORD who is both the Father and the Son (Jesus Christ) by One Holy Spirit as expressed by the comprehensive Word of GOD.

(Perforce) unlike you and I, and the best of us, all of GOD is invested in the love of Jesus Christ for the soul of humanity. The Word was with GOD in the beginning, and the Word *was GOD* in the beginning.

Whom I call the Christ of GOD is both Father and Son (Jesus Christ) by the One Holy Spirit of GOD. This is the Spirit that came upon David, and the same Spirit that raised Jesus Christ from the dead. *"God is a Spirit"* (re. John 4:24), and this is *He.*

This is the Spirit of life (and selfless love) of the Good Shepherd that came upon David as the prophet Samuel anointed him with oil. This is the Holy Spirit of GOD who gives a young boy the heart and the mind of the Good Shepherd. This is the Spirit of GOD who transforms ordinary men into zealous and courageous (and loving) shepherds of sheep. Here is its expression in David:

✳

And David said unto Saul, Thy servant kept his father's sheep, and there cane a lion, and a bear, and took a lamb out of the flock. And I went out after him, and delivered it out of his mouth: and when he arose against me, I caught him by his beard, and smote him, and slew him.
1 Sam. 17:34-35

This is the Spirit of extraordinary valor in the face of the adversary. David was incensed at the impudence and defiance of Goliath and mortified at his insults and at the reproach upon the armies of the living GOD. The same brave heart and unwavering percipient mind which made him a steadfast defender of his father Jessie's flock, also incited him to Israel's defense and GOD's honor.

GOD was pleased to choose the youngest of the eight sons of Jessie to be king over his people, Israel. Notably, the three eldest sons were with King Saul as the armies of Israel were cowering from Goliath and the Philistines. Eliab, the eldest, perhaps as a result of his own impotence and embarrassment (and well, cowardice) in the face of battle, directs his anger at David, indicting him with pride and inordinate curiosity. He accused him of neglecting the sheep in his care, but David had risen early in the morning and left the sheep with a keeper (re. 1 Sam. 17:20).

Goliath had disgraced and dishonored the armies of Israel morning and evening for forty days (re. 1 Sam. 17:16). We can only imagine the consternation and sense of shame that surely enveloped King Saul, the armies of Israel, and the three eldest sons of Jessie. David was obeying his father Jessie's instructions in delivering corn and bread and cheese to the battlefront, but it was GOD who orchestrated these untoward and untenable circumstances.

The Spirit of the LORD that was upon young David is none other than the Spirit of the Good Shepherd. David's heartbeat was in tune to the same rhythm as GOD's own. He also possessed the mind of Christ as it pertains to sheep. How dare a lion or a bear presume to take a lamb from his father's flock! His determination to eradicate the predators of sheep extended to his assessment of the enemies of GOD's people.

＊

For who is this uncircumscribed Philistine, that he
should defy the armies of the living GOD?
re. 1 SAM. 17:26

＊

David thought it unconscionable that any enemy could withstand and ridicule the armies of the living GOD. He considered it abhorrent and inexcusable that the chosen people of GOD should cower from someone who has no covenant relationship with GOD.

The Holy Spirit of GOD makes all the difference. We see its astute expression as a young shepherd boy boldly approaches King Saul.

＊

Let no man's heart fail because of him; thy
servant will go and fight with this Philistine.
re. 1 SAM. 17:32

＊

Christian, as long as the earth endures, ninety and nine sheep will never be one hundred, and in this, the dispensation of the fullness of time and the end of the world drawing suddenly nigh, this is the orientation and disposition the Good Shepherd is ardently seeking.

The LORD hath sought him a man after his own heart, and the LORD hath commanded him to be captain over his people.

re. 1 SAM. 13:14

✳

GOD is seeking men whose hearts beat to the same rhythm and cadence as his own. The Holy Spirit of Christ, the Spirit of both the Father and the Son, (the Holy Spirit whom GOD is); the Spirit of the Good Shepherd, is in the earth actively and earnestly seeking lost sheep. And GOD is still passionately seeking pastors and under-shepherds to seek them out among the barrens and the badlands of a lost and disillusioned world.

I ask you, Church of GOD, *"Is there not a cause"* (re. 1 Sam. 17:29)? Is there not an enemy of GOD, and of his people, prophetically and sedulously defying the armies of the living GOD? Is there not a giant in the land whom has effectively silenced our witness of the LORD Jesus Christ, and rendered us impotent and immobilized and cowering in the corner of the sanctuary that this world and its pervasive evil threat has graciously allotted us?

Verily, we placate ourselves with the ceremony and the presentation and pretend that the wolf is not at the door. We are anesthetized and entertained by religious routine and distracted and mesmerized by materialism while our adversary the devil, as a roaring lion, walks about seeking whom he may devour, (re. 1 Pet. 5:8).

Every Christian is meant to be a priest and surrogate sacrifice of the love of GOD in the continuity of the gospel of

Jesus Christ and him crucified. Every Christian is to have a cross. I will fellowship with the sufferings of Jesus Christ and conform to the death of his cross, or I will not know him and the power of his resurrection, (see Phil. 3:10).

Or, let me see, Jesus Christ ever lives to make intercession for the saints (re. Heb. 7:25), but, uh, I ever live for myself. (I am trying to make a point.)

Everyman and *Everywoman* is intended to be a priest and an earnest intercessor in the love interests of GOD for their neighbor's soul. In the love of GOD, *Everyman* is his brother's shepherd. Christian, you and I see the roaring lion, the wolf and the bear and the serpent – we see the predator. Are we cowered in the corner of the sanctuary in a false or elusive sense of safety, or are we in the trenches, and on the frontline of the good fight of faith, steadfastly standing down the adversary in the interests of GOD's love for our neighbor's soul?

The outward religious presentation may be tweaked perfectly, but only the heart and mind aligned with the purposes of GOD's love will stand in the evil day to face down the adversary.

✳

For the LORD seeth not as man seeth; for man looketh on the outward appearance, but the LORD looketh on the heart.
re. 1 Sam. 16:7

✳

We might say that the three eldest sons of Jessie that followed Saul to the battle were representative or figurative hirelings.

But when push suddenly came to shove, as they say, GOD had to send for a shepherd boy.

These three eldest sons of Jessie, Eliab, Abinadab, and Shammah, must have been impressive and formidable looking specimens of superior manhood. But when Goliath began to roar, they were all summarily included in the following comprehensive indictment:

> *And all the men of Israel, when they saw the man (Goliath), fled from him, and were sore afraid.*

> 1 Sam. 17:24

*

(As you can receive it) the Holy Spirit shows me that *"all the men of Israel,"* including King Saul and the three eldest sons of Jessie, were looking on the forbidding and dreadful, and intimidating, outward appearance of Goliath. But the shepherd boy, David, was seeing something else. Now, I do not know how to articulate it precisely, but he was seeing as GOD sees. He was looking on the heart of the matter.

Now, I do not pretend to know that he saw anything specifically about the heart of Goliath, but I postulate that he looked upon the comprehensive dynamic of the matter. David intuitively understood that this Philistine was uncircumcised. That is, he did not have a covenant relationship with the One True GOD.

Moreover, David understood the essence and character and the omnipotence of the GOD with whom he (himself) had a personal and intimate covenant. That is, by the Spirit of Christ upon him, he understood the *"name"* of GOD.

✳

*Then said David to the Philistine, thou comest to me
with a sword, and with a spear, and with a shield:
but I come to thee in the name of the LORD of hosts, the
GOD of the armies of Israel, whom thou hast defied.*
1 Sam. 17:45

✳

David is offended for the honor of GOD, appalled at the impotence and fear of the armies of GOD. By the Spirit of Christ upon this young shepherd boy, he sees beyond the outward appearance to the spiritual reality of the forces arrayed in combat. Concisely, David is a type of Christ here, and Goliath is representative of Satan. Relative to contemporary Christianity, David's heart and temperament is the character of the shepherd GOD still seeks. GOD still seeks men after his own heart to shepherd his people, men in whom to form the mind of Christ to seek that which is lost.

David aligned himself with the purposes of GOD's anointing upon himself to champion and uphold the character and notoriety of the LORD's name, *"that all the earth may know that there is a GOD in Israel"* (re. 1 Sam. 17:46).

Child of GOD, your adverse circumstances must answer to GOD's love for you in Jesus Christ. It would us well to remember that the grace of GOD answers to the truth of GOD, and that even love and mercy indivisibly dwell within the holiness of GOD. This all-permissive grace of mainstream Christianity in America is an aberration and an adulteration and a deliberate misconception of the love of GOD, that I can somehow, some way (please) be forgiven for all the sin I continue to allow. The name of Jesus Christ is not a magic wand. His name is *HOLY.*

His name *"is called Faithful and True, and in righteousness he doth judge and make war"* (re. Rev. 19:11). Moreover, *"his name is called the Word of GOD"* (re. Rev. 19:13). His name is the integrity and honor of every Word that proceeds out of the mouth of GOD that we are commanded to live by.

David apprehended the comprehensive name of GOD and stepped out to meet the giant Goliath in the absolute unwavering trust and confidence that GOD would uphold and utterly substantiate the rectitude and preeminence of his own great name. It causes me to earnestly and wistfully desire the ability to completely acquiesce to the Holy Spirit of GOD, to (somehow) absolutely empty myself of any and all illusion and misconception of my own abilities and allow GOD to be all in all.

✻

And all this assembly shall know that the LORD saveth not with sword and spear: for the battle is the LORD's, and he will give you into our hands.
1 Sam. 17:47

✻

David drew no distinction between a lion and a bear that would dare to take a lamb from his father's flock, and this uncircumcised Philistine that would impudently defy the armies of the living GOD. Goliath had impugned the name (the honor, integrity, the righteousness and the holiness, the flawless character) of GOD. Frankly, (I believe) that David was appalled and outraged (and astonished) at the immensity of Goliath's manifest arrogance.

Concisely, David dwelt in the secret place of the Most High and abided under the shadow of the Almighty (re. Ps. 91:1). Moreover, all the relevant promises throughout this powerful Psalm belonged to David by virtue of his knowing the name of GOD. He exemplified the LORD's prowess in battle as the astute realization of an internal Champion.

✳

Thou shalt tread upon the lion and adder; the young
lion and the dragon shalt thou trample under feet.
Ps. 91:13

✳

Once more, I must reiterate and resolutely emphasize that the Spirit that was upon David was whom I call the Christ of GOD. He is the same Spiritual Rock from whom the children of Israel drank in the wilderness. *"And that Rock was Christ,"* (re. 1 Cor. 10:10).

The Christ of GOD is One LORD who is both the Father and the Son by the Holy Spirit. Moreover, he moves me to expound briefly, while the responsibility to research and meditate upon the reality (and what I call) the absolutes of GOD, rest upon the individual.

✳

But unto every one of us is given grace according
to the measure of the gift of Christ.
Eph. 4:7

*

Dear reader, relevant to our current text, and as the Apostle Paul may express it: David apprehended the Spirit of him by whom he was also apprehended. We might say that David assimilated the anointing of Christ unto practical (and miraculous) application – he incorporated the power of GOD into his adverse circumstances and released it upon Goliath. Here, then, is the New Testament (covenant) correlative for every disciple of Jesus Christ who can receive it by faith.

*

Behold, I give unto you power (authority) to tread on serpents and scorpions, and over all the power of the enemy: and nothing shall by any means hurt you.
LUKE 10:19

*

This same Holy Spirit (who GOD is), and that rested upon David, now abides with and indwells the spirit man and spirit woman of the obedient and sanctified disciples of Jesus Christ. Jesus Christ called him the Holy Ghost, and the Comforter, and the Spirit of Truth. I refer specifically to chapters fourteen through sixteen of the the teaching (*doctrine*) of the LORD Jesus Christ found within the gospel according to John.

It must be emphasized (and reemphasized) that the "worldly" cannot receive this Holy Spirit of Truth. And it must be distinctly delineated that this includes the innumerable multitude of contemporary carnally compromised persons calling themselves Christians today.

*

*Even the Spirit of Truth; whom the world cannot receive,
because it seeth him not, neither knoweth him: but ye
know him; for he dwelleth with you, and shall be in you.*
John 14:17

✳

Only those distinctly separated (sanctified) from the delusion and deception which governs this world system can receive a Spirit who is True and Holy. This next scripture is the LORD Jesus Christ's answer to Judas' (not Iscariot) question of how he (Jesus) was going to manifest himself to his disciples, but not to the world (see John 14:22). It is the preeminent scripture which expresses the phenomenon of the *Doctrine of Christ*, that the Father and the Son are One LORD by the Holy Ghost.

✳

*Jesus answered and said unto him, If a man love me, he
will keep my words: and my Father will love him, and WE
will come unto him, and make OUR abode with him.*
John 14:23

✳

This is the One Spirit who GOD is. The following is expressive of (what I call) an absolute of GOD, spoken to a Samaritan woman at Jacob's well one glorious day: *"GOD is a Spirit"* (re. John 4:24). The comprehensive (exhaustive) body of the Word of GOD attests to the immutable fact that this Holy Spirit is One LORD who is *"both"* the Spirit of the Father, and the Spirit of the Son. (Once more), this is who I frequently call the Christ of GOD. And when I use this expression, I mean absolutely "all" of GOD.

Before returning to our main text, I must say that this is the Holy Spirit who Jesus said will lead (guide) us into "all" Truth, (see John 16:13). I am also moved to include that this teaching of Jesus Christ, specifically in the gospel of John between chapters fourteen and sixteen (that I mentioned), is what John pointedly describes as the *Doctrine of Christ*. By the Holy Ghost, I add this definitive codicil in lieu of a lengthy exposition: We must have (possess and teach and preach) all of GOD. The redundancy is indicative of our hardness of hearing.

*

Whosoever transgresseth, and abideth not in the doctrine of Christ, hath not God. He that abideth in the doctrine of Christ, he hath BOTH the Father and the Son.
2 John 1:9

*

Here, I must unabashedly refer you to a book that I wrote (by the Spirit of GOD) expounding upon the portentous warning within this specific Word of GOD. It is titled *One LORD*, and within it, I also tried to capture the Holy Spirit's teaching on both the plural and the singular nature of GOD's identity or essence. Dear faithful reader, GOD wants to teach you himself. The urgency of GOD's love for the soul of mainstream contemporary Christianity is such that this teaching (doctrine) of the LORD Jesus Christ pervades everything I am moved to write.

Yes, it is not only my premise, but my wholehearted conclusion by the comprehensive Word of GOD, that there is One Holy Spirit expressive of the absolute nature and being of Jehovah GOD, and that this is the same Spirit of GOD that was upon David from the moment the prophet Samuel anointed him with oil.

> *And the Spirit of the LORD came upon*
> *David from that day forward.*

> re. 1 SAM. 16:13

Lest I be indicted with even the suggestion of placing doctrinal or expository constraints upon the omnipotent, omniscient, omnipresent Spirit of the living GOD, I must insist that the Spirit of GOD is unchanged from Old Testament to New Testament. To qualify that statement somewhat, I will add that while GOD does not change, the times and the seasons (and the dispensations) within his own power belong unto GOD to alter as pleases him. Occasionally, I have said: Sometimes GOD colors outside the lines. And I mean outside the lines of our doctrinal tenets and close-minded presumptions and denominational strictures of the unfathomable One. I mean, who do we think we are?

To perhaps expiate our misunderstanding somewhat, I add the following. While it is true that there is a season or dispensation wherein *"the Holy Ghost was not yet given, because that Jesus was not yet glorified"* (re. John 7:39), I simply want to draw our attention to a notable exception, or three exceptions in one, as it were.

John the Baptist was filled with the Holy Ghost, even from his mother's womb (see Luke 1:15). And to this, I will add the immutable addendum and binding codicil of the LORD Jesus Christ who proclaimed that John the Baptist was not only a prophet, but much more than a prophet (see Luke 7:26). Moreover, John the Baptist's mother, Elisabeth, was filled with the Holy Ghost (see Luke 1:41), and spoke a blessing over Mary, and magnified the LORD. His father, Zacharias, was also filled with the Holy Ghost, and prophesied mightily of the salvation which was come to Israel, and attested to John being the prophet of the Highest that would prepare the way of the LORD (see Luke 1:67-80).

It seems that this entire family was experiencing an inexplicable epidemic of being filled with the Holy Ghost, and well before the Day of Pentecost. Just saying. There are some things that we will not know until GOD reveals then unto us. As I sometimes say, it takes GOD to show me GOD, and to give me GOD. Frankly, I am a little bit afraid of these doctrinal wise men and denominational witch doctors who tell GOD what he can and cannot do. Well, not afraid *of* them, but afraid *for* them.

All of that (I say) (and leave much unsaid) in order to say the following: I make no inane or unlearned (uninspired) determinations of the Spirit that was upon David, except to say it was the Spirit of the Good Shepherd. And from that, I must attest that this was the Spirit of Christ.

Now, the Holy Spirit of Christ is *both* the Spirit of the Father, and the Spirit of the Son, Jesus Christ, coalesced into One LORD.

Concisely, this was the Spirit of GOD upon David, the Spirit of the Good Shepherd still in the earth, and still seeking the lost. Moreover, this is the Holy Ghost who fills and indwells the obedient and sanctified disciples of Jesus Christ. This Spirit, this anointing, still comes upon men and women and baptizes them with evangelical fire and passion (love) for the worst of humanity.

*

This is the "Promise of the Father" (saith Jesus), which ye have heard of me.

For John truly baptized with water; but ye shall be baptized with the Holy Ghost not many days hence.
Acts 1:5

*

Notwithstanding the fact that we predominantly have mis-appropriated this Gift for personal (spiritual) self-promotion and religious posturing, this Spirit is intended to make us ear-nest and loyal (and sanctified) witnesses of the LORD Jesus Christ. Instead, we (broadly) expropriated the Spirit of GOD to enhance our religious persona. That is correct, much of our dancing and signification is a thinly veiled religious pos-turing, and an attempted plundering of the resources of GOD for personal benefit – you know, to be Bigger Christians, but not necessarily better ones. You know, *"feel good about me"* Christian or religious ceremony.

Jesus Christ is soliciting disciples to baptize with fire and make them virulent witnesses of his saving and redeeming power, and we want to dance and pontificate in the vain re-ligious reflection of one another. GOD shows me that the Spirit of the Good Shepherd seeks the lost. But where are we on the acute revelation of GOD's love for the next sinner's soul? We need to get over ourselves. Someone has to say it.

Please pardon my verbose grammatical largesse, as it were. Here is the concise spontaneous explicit expression unaffectedly describing and delineating the Spirit that was upon David: *"The LORD is my Shepherd; I shall not want"* (Ps. 23:1).

There is much excellent and inspirational exposition of this Psalm already available, and I would love to run the metaphorical fingers of my mind through its magnificent expanse, but the Holy Spirit leads me in another direction. Of a necessity, we must talk about the thief. As the Spirit of the Good Shepherd is still in the earth actively seeking to save lost sheep, so is the spirit of the adversary, as a roaring lion, seeking to devour them. The Word of GOD has much to say about hirelings, thieves and robbers, and wolves in sheep's clothing. This is the reality of GOD in the shepherding of souls, the Old Testament and New Testament dynamic phenomenon of the LORD's salvation sent into the heart of the humanity.

(In an aside, I must say what lays heavy upon my soul.) The Holy Ghost and fire of an earnest witness of the incendiary resurrection power of the LORD Jesus Christ alienates and scatters the lukewarm much like cucarachas. Frankly, and sadly, the Spirit of the Good Shepherd is not upon every professing Christian. Pointedly, not every mainstream contemporary professing Christian seems to have been baptized with the evangelical fire and passion of GOD for the lost. But to be fair, the majority of us do write a check for conscience and commandment sake.

Well? (Again) *someone* must say something. These things must be considered in the context of shepherding. The LORD Jesus Christ was always conscious of the urgency of fields white unto harvest and the critical need for laborers.

> *Pray ye therefore the LORD Of the harvest, that*
> *he will send forth laborers into his harvest.*

MATT. 9:38

(To me) it is inexplicable that (yes) the preponderance of (us) mainstream contemporary Christianity, specifically those of us who testify to being Spirit-filled and sanctified, do not experience the same urgency. It is my personal experience that if we ask for the heart and mind of the Good Shepherd, GOD will liberally give them, and much fire, also. But we better mean business. Grandma said be careful what you ask for.

The heart and mind of the Good Shepherd is in the field. We know that the Good Shepherd is solicitous to the needs and security of the ninety and nine, but the acute consciousness of his mind and the loving urgency of his heart is upon the one still lost.

He wants our heart and mind to be coalesced with the same evangelical fire and radical outreach of his love for a world still lost and desperate. Christian, when it was your soul or my soul that was the one balanced precariously between this life and a sudden eternity, suspended over hell by a thread, as it were, we were glad that the LORD of the harvest had laborers in the field with the indomitable heart and mind of the Good Shepherd.

The LORD of the harvest is zealous to give us the same heart in the continuity of his love, and he is resolute to give us the same mind of Jesus Christ to make us compelling witnesses of his resurrection life. He gives us his own Spirit to empower us to perpetuate and testify of the wonders of his salvation through our personal witness. I deliberately abbreviate the following scripture to illustrate the LORD's (irrepressible evangelical) purpose. *"Ye shall receive power . . . and ye shall be witnesses unto me"* (re. Acts 1:8).

The Holy Spirit of GOD serves the purposes of GOD. Yes, of course GOD wants me to feel good enough to shout and sing and maybe even dance a few steps, but isn't that kind of superfluous or extraneous in the immediate interests of the next sinner's soul? Especially if I do not have a vocal and behavioral testimony of the saving power of the LORD Jesus Christ at my place of employment Monday morning.

My celebration ought to rest upon (or be relative to) my corresponding evangelical outreach. I mean, since there is more joy in heaven over one sinner that repents, more than over ninety and nine (just) persons who need no repentance (re. Luke 15:7), where should *our* focus be?

My worship must be mingled with mercy, and my celebration should be in the awareness of the next lost soul.

✳

But go ye and learn what that meaneth, I will have
mercy, and not sacrifice: for I am not come to call
the righteous, but sinners to repentance.
MATT. 9:13

✳

Him (or her) who will not share that which is entrusted to their care, can (relatively and situationally) be construed as a thief and a robber.

To worship in Spirit and in truth is to be apprised and enlightened and absolutely acquiescent to the perfect will of the love of GOD for even the worst of humanity. There ought not to be margins or levels to One Love. How does a GOD who is not a respecter of persons really feel about our spirit of exclusive spiritual superiority and our self-inflating, self-sustaining, self-celebratory religious service?

✳

I hate, I despise your feast days, and I will not smell in your solemn assemblies. Though ye offer me burnt offerings and your meat offerings, I will not accept them: neither will I regard the peace offerings of your fat beasts. Take thou away from me the noise of thy songs; for I will not hear the melody of thy viols. But let judgment run down as waters, and righteousness as a mighty stream.
Amos 5:21-24

✳

First, we must acknowledge and accept the prophetic relevance of the Word of GOD in every era. The Word of GOD is a living entity. His name is Jesus, and he is the express image of the invisible GOD. He is the Christ of GOD in every era, and whom I attest as being One LORD who is both the Father and the Son by the Holy Spirit. *"God is a Spirit"* (re. John 4:24), and this is He. (He) is the Holy Spirit of this *living* Word.

GOD experiences us in Christ Jesus, and we experience GOD in Christ Jesus. We cannot come to GOD except in Christ. Likewise, GOD experiences you and I comprehensibly and absolutely in Jesus Christ. Christian, you are the masterpiece of GOD's creative genius, and he loves you so much that he ardently desires to experience you to the uttermost. This is what brings him joy. No detail is too small.

The Word of GOD declares, that by the grace of GOD, Jesus Christ tasted death for every man [and woman] (re. Heb. 2:9). And since Jesus Christ and the Father are indivisibly One by the Holy Spirit, the Father tasted (or experienced) it also. Notwithstanding, many of us are so disconnected from the relevance and reality of the Word of GOD that we are not conscious or appreciative of the fact that (in Christ) GOD not only tasted death for us, but as the prophet Amos declares by the inspiration of the Holy Spirit, GOD also knows what our solemn assembly smells like.

That we have not internally or cognitively assimilated the indisputable reality that GOD can taste, see, hear, smell and feel us, speaks volumes about our inveterate unbelief and ubiquitous hardness of heart. *"Ye worship ye know not what"* (re. John 4:22). Our smart phones and automobiles and flat-screen high-definition TV's and laptops and notebooks and assorted electronic technological devices and toys are more real than the GOD many of us gather to purportedly worship.

We still reference the heart and the mind of the Good Shepherd and see that the prophet Amos was anointed to acutely express the innermost thoughts and feelings of GOD. The revelatory indictment ought to give every church assembly pause and reason for an astute and exacting introspection.

This prophetic Word of GOD is portentous enough to provoke a scrupulous self-evaluation of every individual in the righteous congregation.

Hypocrisy smells the same in every era or dispensation. The heart and mind of the Good Shepherd is the fire and passion of the Holy Ghost for the lost; not for the convenience and compromise of the self-celebratory exclusivity of the congregation of the ninety and nine righteous with no consideration for the one still lost.

We have no realistic comprehension that our modern-day worship and contemporary church ceremony is comparable to the burnt offerings and meat offerings of the Old Testament. GOD can, concisely, smell and taste our posturing piety and self-inflating superficial religious service.

The world is going to hell, (and at the same time) we have no viable witness outside the four church walls. Whereas a genuine faith would be aware that GOD sees our heart reserved covetously for ourselves in world-love, material possessions, and carnal entertainment.

❋

This people draweth nigh unto me with their mouth, and honoreth me with their lips; but their heart is far from me.
MATT. 15:8

❋

If our GOD were real, our religion would follow. The heart and mind of the Good Shepherd for the one still lost would be revealed to be among the righteous assembly. We would not have to pretend that he was among us. We would not only see the evidence of the transformed lives around us, we would be one of them. A genuine conversion will not and cannot be concealed or its fire quenched.

We think to serve GOD with unwashed hands and unsanctified hearts, to sing praises from unhallowed lips. (By the Spirit of GOD) the prophet Amos is effectively saying that GOD does not want to hear it. The melody is gone out of our song. There is one missing in the House of Jacob and none take it to heart; for as long as the earth endures, ninety and nine will never be one hundred.

The taste of my offering upon the altar is correlative to the secret corruption in my heart, the hidden unforgiveness I have for my brother, the covert hatred I have for those different than me, childhood prejudices and hasty judgmental attitudes. The melody of my song is mingled with the clandestine small-minded ethnic (and religious) bigotry of the moral majority, the surreptitious malice of the self-righteous congregation.

If my faith is genuine, I will appreciate the acute cognitive reality of how GOD truly feels about (both) what is lukewarm, and what is fundamentally fraudulent. I would know how GOD feels; I would have the mind of Christ. It is by faith that I may feel after GOD and find him (re. Acts 17:27). It is by faith that I may taste and see that the LORD is good (re. Ps. 34:8).

GOD showed the prophet Amos a plumbline. Christian, GOD is zealous for what is true.

✳

*Behold, I will set a plumbline in the midst of my people
Israel: I will not again pass by them anymore.*
re. Amos 7:8

✳

Grace and mercy and love answer to truth and light and holiness. There is going to be a great and effectual, eternal reckoning, and GOD holds the scales in which the soul of humanity is measured.

✳

*That is the dispensation of the fullness of times he might
gather together in one all things in Christ, both which
are in heaven, and which are on earth; even in him.*
Eph. 1:10

✳

The cross of Jesus Christ is the measure of GOD's love for the world he created. It is the line of demarcation and delineation, and the eternal determinant in the righteous judgment of GOD for the soul of every man or woman ever born. The erroneous notion of all-permissive grace will be revealed for the illusion and deception that it really is. You know what I mean, the specious idea that I can be forgiven for the sin I willfully and continually allow.

Grace answers to Truth in the acute revelation of the Holy character of GOD.

✳

I will not again pass by them anymore.
re. Amos 7:8

✳

There will be an abrupt end to my spiritual pandering and religious posturing, an astute reckoning of all forms of faith.

✳

For the time is come that judgment must begin at the House of GOD: and if it first begin at us, what shall the end be of them that obey not the gospel of GOD?
1 Pet. 4:17

✳

The prophet Amos and the Apostle Peter concur. Church folk are relatively the same in every generation. The implacable and uncompromising (portentous) preaching of the prophet Amos had reached unto the bulwarks and strong places of Bethel. Study the scriptures. Repetitive and willful offenses try the limitations of mercy and justice. Children, there comes a time in the annals of grace when conscious (volitional) sin answers to Calvary.

I will not again pass by them anymore.

re. Amos 7:8

All things inevitably answer to Truth. His name is Jesus. We have the children of Israel in the wilderness for our example. Those who incur GOD's wrath through willful sin, and through ingratitude and murmuring, will not enter into his rest.

GOD had been trying to get Israel's attention for some time. Amos testified repeatedly of the necessity of the LORD laid upon him, that in the day when the LORD visited Israel for their transgressions, that he would also visit the altars of Bethel in judgment, (see Amos 3:14). In contemporary vernacular that means that he would also visit the House of GOD, or the Church of GOD, in judgment.

By the Holy Spirit, I attest that it was the heart and mind of the Good Shepherd upon Amos which provoked him to prophesy and spare not. GOD's prophet shall share the concise and unabridged perspective of the Good Shepherd and shall not be silenced by the opposition of the priest, or peer, or even the fear of the king. The Spirit of the Good Shepherd upon the man of GOD does not compromise or capitulate to either civil or religious opposition. Indeed, it is even as Amos said: *"The LORD GOD hath spoken, who can but prophesy"* (re. Amos 3:8)?

The straightforward unapologetic preaching of Amos had earned him the distinct disfavor of the priest of Bethel, Amaziah, who promptly reported him to the King of Israel, Jeroboam.

※

Then Amaziah the priest of Bethel sent to Jeroboam King of Israel, saying, Amos hath conspired against thee in the midst of the House of Israel; the land is not able to bear all his words.
Amos 7:10

※

Principally, because of Israel's unfaithfulness and their love and worship of other gods, and because of their defrauding and oppressing the poor, the judgment of GOD was being pronounced upon both the civil government and the institutions of religion in the land. It is the nature of sin and evil to virulently proliferate and pervade the entire society. Often, it is the prayers of GOD's people and his own presence representative among them that withstands the judgment of GOD and elicits his mercy and forgiveness. Amos had steadfastly been interceding for Israel, and many times GOD had deferred his wrath because of his (Amos') mediation and prayers.

Corruption was rampant. Neither Israel's worship nor their offerings were pleasing to GOD because of the impenitent state of their heart. Praise (and prayer) not only becomes perfunctory and superficial, but it is in vain when my character is not being progressively converted. Frankly, GOD told them that their worship stunk. He did not even want to hear their songs.

Grace and mercy can be overextended or taken for granted. Children, the longsuffering love of GOD has its astute and exacting remuneration promised within the commands of his righteousness and in the rectitude of his holy character. *"I will not again pass by then anymore"* (re. Amos 7:8 & 8:2).

GOD's appraisal and eventual reckoning of his people is as comprehensive as his omniscient nature. The requital of grace is laid up in the balances of truth and holiness, and its redress shall be satisfied in equity and righteousness. Both the priest and the king are assessed in the equanimity and percipience of the righteousness of GOD.

※

And the high places of Israel shall be desolate, and the sanctuaries of Israel shall be laid waste; and I will rise against the house of Jeroboam with the sword.
AMOS 7:9

✳

The eye of the Good Shepherd corresponds to the singular nature of his heart, as grace and love answer to truth and holiness. To be laid in the balances of God (and to be found wanting) is to have despised grace and shown contempt for merciful and repetitive room to repent. Amos was not on a fool's mission or preaching to hear the sound of his own voice – he had been sent by GOD.

The short conversation between the priest of Bethel, Amaziah, and the prophet of the LORD, Amos, is some of my favorite scripture in the Word of GOD. Evidently, Amos had come from the south, from Judah, but was sent from GOD to prophesy unto Israel. Amaziah assertively (and seemingly, even aggressively) admonished Amos to go back to Judah and prophesy there.

Amaziah was probably being apprehensive and possessive of his own position as the priest at Bethel, but under the guise of being loyal and proprietary for the king. His stern censure of the prophet Amos was a thinly veiled threat to get him into trouble with the king if he persisted with his uncompromising preaching.

✳

> *But prophesy not again any more at Bethel: for it*
> *is the king's chapel, and it is the king's court.*
> AMOS 7:13

＊

"Bethel" means *"House of GOD"* in Hebrew. Jacob named it. It is where GOD appeared to him and renewed the covenant he had made with Abraham and Isaac, promising Jacob that many nations and kings would be his descendants. Obviously, the king (Jeroboam) had made Bethel his private sanctuary, but Amaziah was being imperious and domineering in the interests and security of his own position within the hierarchy of Israel's theocracy.

Amaziah essentially told Amos, *"You can't preach that here."* But like the children of Israel in the wilderness, encamped and ensconced at Jordan, and paralyzed by fear, they had repeatedly and willfully trespassed upon grace and done great despite to GOD's longsuffering love. The message of GOD was not going to be suppressed or silenced, and neither was his messenger. Ah, dreadful and inescapable the declaration of God's righteousness at the boundaries of his grace.

> *I will not again pass by them anymore.*

> re. AMOS 7:8 & 8:2

Amos had seen GOD's plumbline set in the midst of his people Israel. Oftentimes, Amos had resolutely interceded for Israel's transgressions, and GOD had stayed his hand. But, alas, there is no deviation or allowance made in the precise measurement of a plumbline. Anything even incrementally to the left or the right of that plumbline is what a carpenter calls *"out of true."*

Children, grace and longsuffering love are for error-prone lambs in their determined aspiration to develop into ardent disciples and obedient adult sheep. A plumbline is for the obdurate and the recalcitrant, the insubordinate and the rebellious. Grace must be grasped (and guarded) as it is given. The times and the seasons are in GOD's own power.

The point is, that God can see, hear, smell, taste and feel our worship and allegiance. We are altogether known. Notwithstanding, we transfer our own attitudes upon GOD and concisely (but silently) conclude him as indifferent (and lukewarm), and as uninvested as ourselves. If we truly believed GOD is real, we would sit up a little straighter and listen more attentively. We would pray and read our Bibles and our growth in grace would manifest.

Apparently, King Jeroboam had made Bethel his headquarters and main sanctuary. Being his court, it was probably where he conducted selected kingdom business, and perhaps where he entertained or received visitors. Being that the priest, Amaziah, also called Bethel the king's chapel, it may well have been his designated place of worship. But then again, if the king was a steadfast and fervent worshipper (in spirit and in truth), then the kingdom would have subsequently and naturally been in a more godly or favorable disposition.

At any rate, we may safely conclude from Amaziah's comments that Bethel was the place of the king's respite, or the place he resorted to in order to find peace and where he felt most secure. Notwithstanding the walls we erect or even the citadel we build to insulate ourselves from trespass or trouble, the Word of GOD can reach into our hiding place, and into the inner sanctum of our soul.

Amos was not deterred by the priest's proprietary posturing, or his threats of the king's wrath. When we have trespassed upon grace and shown contempt for multiple pardons, GOD sets a plumbline in the midst of our obdurate pontifications and headstrong histrionics. When we will not have mercy, we may have judgment. I wonder if contemporary Christianity has grasped the correlative prophetic portend?

✴

The end is come upon my people of Israel. I will
not again pass by then anymore.
Amos 8:2

✴

It is the Spirit of Christ who makes a mortal man fearless and resolute. It is the heart and mind of the Good Shepherd in the earth seeking the lost, inexorably and irresistibly drawn to them whose lives are in crisis.

The self-important prognostications and attempted intimidation of the priest Amaziah did not discombobulate Amos, he moved under the mantle of a higher authority than the approbation or endorsement of mortal men. Uh, he was neither subject to the priest's dominion nor to the king's jurisdiction.

✴

Then answered Amos, and said to Amaziah, I was no
prophet, neither was I a prophet's son; but I was an

"herdman," and a gatherer of sycamore fruit. And the LORD
"TOOK ME" as I followed the flock, and the LORD
said unto me, Go, prophesy unto my people Israel.
AMOS 7:14-15

✳

(If I may paraphrase Amos in contemporary vernacular, as it were): "I was not looking for a job – I already had a job. In fact, I was minding my own business, just trying to scratch out a living. It was not my idea to come here, and not my life's aspiration to prophesy. But the lion has already roared. The LORD GOD has spoken, who can but prophesy?" (re. Amos 3:8)

Notably, the LORD found Amos (relatively) in the same place he found David.

✳

Thus saith the LORD of hosts, "I TOOK THEE"
(David) from the sheepcote, from following the
sheep, to be ruler over my people, over Israel.
re. 2 SAM. 7:8

✳

Markedly, in both instances, the Word of GOD uses the word *"took"* to describe or designate both Amos' and David's assignation and investiture as the LORD's instruments and messengers. Uh, bluntly and concisely, the sovereign pleasure of GOD is spontaneous, irrepressible, and compulsory. When GOD sets his heart upon you, to send you, what are you going to do? Duh, just ask the prophet, Jonah?

✳

Indeed, is not the burden of the LORD's prophet predetermined to be the LORD's people? Thus saith the LORD, One of a hundred I cannot find, the faithful and the intrepid among the sons of men. Whom, then, shall I send but a keeper of sheep, and a follower of the flock? Whom to apprehend the contractual and incumbent statues of covenant love, and whom to give my heart and mind, saith the LORD?

✳

Christian, the Spirit of the Good Shepherd is still in the earth, seeking not the perfect, but the prepared and the purposeful. He sends whom he can trust with the integrity of his Word, to speak the truth in love. In fact, Jesus Christ is seeking under-shepherds to declare the same grace and truth as himself, in the same Spirit and power of resurrection life.

The Good Shepherd is irrepressibly single-mindedly interested in the security and the sustenance of the sheep. Concisely, if you love me, feed my sheep (see John 21:15-17).

It saddens me to leave Amos so abruptly, but the Holy Spirit has much more to say about shepherding, and much of it is ominous and uncompromising; and all of it is prophetic (meaning presently fulfilling and eternally pertinent). The Word of GOD does not circumvent the awkward or the uncomfortable, it confronts sin right where it lives and commands integrity and accountability out of our irresponsible laissez faire proclivities. Cautions and injunctions for pastors (or shepherds) are particularly portentous.

✳

And the Word of the LORD came unto me, saying. Son of man, prophesy against the shepherds of Israel, prophesy, and say unto them, Thus saith the LORD GOD unto the shepherds; Woe be to the shepherds of Israel that do feed themselves! should not the shepherds feed the flock?
EZEK. 34:1-2

✳

At this point, I am constrained somewhat to digress and/or qualify (and perhaps expiate) my testimony of the LORD. Let me say this: the text of this manuscript thus far, by its un-abridged austerity and the depth of its revelation, ought to attest to my earnest and intrepid seeking of the heart and the mind of the LORD Jesus Christ.

Concisely, I have no other motive or aspiration than to un-apologetically express the heart and mind of GOD in his Christ upon the page. Frankly, I have no other reason (or love) for living except to magnify the wonders of his grace and truth. As I have said many times, I neither covet wealth nor position, I am already given place. My portion is that of greater grace and overwhelming sufficiency, even before I sell the first book. He who has ears to hear has already heard.

The Good Shepherd's heart and mind is preoccupied with the security and the diet of the sheep. We might even say that to procure a nutritious diet presupposes security; that both health and safety are integral to a good diet. In the words of the Good Shepherd, and as we have noted, "If you love me, feed my sheep" (re. John 21:15-17). This naturally entails their safety, as well as their being fed.

Naturally, the love of the Good Shepherd is the flock, but the Word of GOD differentiates between the ninety and nine (righteous), and the "one" that is lost. Or, as I have frequently said: As long as the earth endures, ninety and nine will never be one hundred. It is the Father who will let us know when it is the fullness of time, and when the very last sheep has been found (re. Matt. 24:36). He will send Jesus Christ to go get his children.

(I say that to say this): Out of the heart and mind of Jesus Christ, I unequivocally attest that the love of the Good Shepherd is the "ninety and nine," but his obsession is the "one" still lost. Indeed, and when we were the one whose soul was suspended over hell by a thread, we were glad it was so. Christian, inevitably and irrepressibly, the command "*Follow me*" eventually means for each one of us to (ideally) progress grace by grace and faith to faith, to have developed the heart and mind of the Good Shepherd and his unquenchable love for the lost.

The Spirit of the Good Shepherd upon (and indwelling) a pastor and his (or her) respective congregation will be evidenced by an ardent and indisputable love for the lost. You know, sinners. The Spirit of the Good Shepherd is indicated by a measurable and impassioned love for the lost. The Holy Spirit of the LORD Jesus Christ will be found among them.

❋

Then drew near unto him all the publicans and sinners for to hear him. And the Pharisees and the scribes murmured, saying, This man receiveth sinners, and eateth with them.
LUKE 15:1-2

✳

Yes, when love is genuine, even a Spirit who is a *Holy* Spirit, can be found among sinners. Concisely, if both a pastor and his congregation are getting fat, and yet there is a large population within their inner-city of poor and hungry that are not being ministered to on a daily basis, then there is something suspect about their religious testimony. The church service or ceremony should always be held in the consciousness of those still lost and poor and sick.

Frankly, we posture as if we had to protect the LORD Jesus Christ's reputation from the proximity of sinners. Let's just say it, Christian. It is you and I, and the righteous brethren and the sisters of sanctity, that are too holy to eat with sinners.

(Broadly and fundamentally, and with embarrassment and ignominy) we do not teach or preach the manifest selfless love of the Good Shepherd that was demonstrably upon (and within) the Church of GOD in the Acts of the Apostles.

✳

And the multitude of them that believed were of one heart and of one soul: neither said any of them that ought of the things which he possessed was his own; but they had all things common. And with great power gave the apostles witness of the resurrection of the LORD Jesus: and great grace was upon them all.
ACTS 4:32-33

✳

Here we see that the Word of GOD speaks best for himself. These believers *"were of one heart and of one soul."* I guess it goes without saying that they were of One mind, as well. This is the heart and mind of the Good Shepherd that we have been talking about, exemplified and personified. These believers were Christians from the inside-out. Our myriad excuses for not wholeheartedly loving one another, or loving the lost, are too innumerable to list. We generally skip over the above passage in the Book of Acts as if it were a failed (and embarrassing) socialist experiment that could not be sustained. We pass over it as quickly as possible, knowing that we cannot love like that.

As I said, it is the Word of GOD that differentiates between the ninety and nine who have no need of repentance, and the one still lost. (As you can receive it), it is by the Holy Spirit that I predicate that the preponderance of the righteous congregation have no "conscious" need of repentance – that they are self-sufficient and self-sustaining, and self-congratulatory.

As I have asserted, the LORD Jesus Christ loves the ninety and nine, but the one still lost is his passion. This is definitively how you can identify the pastor or the disciple or the apostle who has the heart and mind of the Good Shepherd.

We must take the time to note that it is amazing how quickly your average Christian transitions from a sinner saved by grace into a saint with no need of repentance. And then sadly, and too often, the more righteous we become, the less grace we can afford the next fellow.

Again, we see that the Word of GOD answers best for himself.

✳

Why eateth your Master with publicans and sinners?
But when Jesus heard that, he said unto them, They
that be whole need not a physician, but they that are
sick. But go ye and learn what that meaneth, I will
have mercy, and not sacrifice: for I am not come to call
the righteous, but sinners to repentance.
re. MATT. 9:11-13

✳

A sincere demonstration of longsuffering love and mercy in the interests of the next sinner's soul is more than all burnt offering and sacrifice. Genuine love eclipses religious ceremony and takes up an old rugged cross.

It is the Word of GOD that qualifies and substantiates the Good Shepherd's passion for the one still lost. The Spirit of GOD establishes the criterion for a good sinner, as it were. Jesus Christ concisely evinces why he has come.

✳

The Spirit of the LORD is upon me, because he hath anointed
me to preach the gospel to the poor; he hath sent me to heal
the brokenhearted, to preach deliverance to the captives, and
recovering of sight to the blind, to set at liberty them that
are bruised. To preach the acceptable year of the LORD.
LUKE 4:18-19

✳

In another volume, while describing the contemporary mainstream Christian congregation (you know, the righteous assembly), I effectively said that, notably, there was not one poor, one brokenhearted, one captive, one blind or one bruised among our saintly assembly. Why, we do not even require an altar anymore.

Once again, it is Jesus (the Word of GOD), who bluntly and unapologetically says that there will be *few* to find the strait gate and narrow way which leads unto life (see Matt. 7:13-14). The majority of us, the many upon the broad way to destruction, pressing our resolute way into the wide gate of an illusory fantastical all-permissive grace, also have a fabricated form of faith. And our righteousness is, frankly, a figment of our own pious imagination.

We have predominantly left off earnest prayer and have cunningly circumvented forthright repentance. We are much too pretty, too spiritually poised, and too religiously presumptuous and privileged to submit to the rigors and austerity (and honesty) of a studious repentance. Church ceremony and religious routine have supplanted genuine conversion. We leave the same way we came, convinced we have worshipped well.

(We know that) according to the parable of the lost sheep as recorded in Luke 15:1-7, the shepherd Jesus is describing is fundamentally himself. This parable embodies and personifies the heart and mind and unquenchable love and irrepressible passion of the Good Shepherd for the lost. This Holy Spirit of urgency is decidedly difficult to find among the contemporary laissez faire righteous congregation.

When Jesus leaves the ninety and nine in the wilderness to go after the one lost, I advance that the wilderness he is referring to is the wasteland and quagmire of our self-righteousness, the entanglement of our religious ego and inflated spiritual estimation of ourselves. Too often, the righteous congregation are the anesthetized and volitionally desensitized by the opiate of outward religious routine, remaining fundamentally (internally) unchanged. Jesus Christ came to seek and to save the lost, and we are already found.

Too often, the ninety and nine righteous are contained by a superficial religious diet and mere form of faith. (Broadly) we are not being led into the depths of the sanctification and holiness at the heart and mind of the LORD Jesus Christ, and into the intricacies of his character and the suffering association of his cross. We are not being purposefully led into the Baptism of the Holy Ghost. Pastor and congregation alike (predominantly) circumvent the rigors and commands of a genuine faith, which concisely demands and expects of me the austerity of a true character conversion. Superficial religious stasis has satisfied the preponderance of us.

The Good Shepherd must go outside the camp seeking. He who has ears to hear, let him hear. GOD is seeking a people honest enough to admit (or confess) that there is something fundamentally wrong with them. But cursory religious ceremony serves both the congregation's and the pastor's compromise and complacency.

✳

Woe be to the shepherds of Israel that do feed themselves! should not the shepherds feed the flocks? Ye eat the fat, and ye clothe ye with the wool, ye kill them that are fed: but ye feed not the flock. The diseased have ye not strengthened, neither have ye healed that which was sick, neither have ye bound up that which was broken, neither have ye brought again that

which was driven away, neither have ye sought that which was lost; but with force and with cruelty have ye ruled them.
re. Ezek. 34:2-4

✳

In these solemn scriptures we get another acute glimpse of the heart and mind of GOD for the lost. Alas. A pronouncement of woe from GOD is a prophetic adjudication of imminent calamity. This is for them teaching and preaching surface and peripheral moral virtues and external Christian etiquette (and all-permissive grace) without the accountability of the truth, without delving into the intimacies of the holy character of GOD. Without taking up the cross of Jesus Christ, without fundamentally denying oneself the lust of the flesh, the love of the world, and the pride of life: without the gospel dynamic of losing the life to find it, without the radical transformation that being born again inherently entails (and commands).

In these solemn and dreadful scriptures, we get a glimpse of how GOD really feels about a pastor (or shepherd) getting fat at the expense of his flock. Not feeding the flock (to me) concisely means not leading them distinctly and boldly into the depths of Jesus Christ's crucifixion and death, and then into his thoroughly transforming resurrection power. We are led as far as the portal to the kingdom of GOD, and there stop and have church. We are not being taught to die unto sin and lust and pride, and unto the love of the world.

(Broadly) we are not being led into a revolutionary transformation. Children, it is the converted who have been sifted, and shaken, and led through the purifying and sanctifying fire and Baptism of the Holy Ghost. Only the militant and the radical have the heart and mind of the Good Shepherd in the continuity and outreach of GOD's love for those whose lives are still in crisis.

At present, the world has been unable to see past our presumptuous self-righteous affect and empty pious posturing. Only the radically converted reflect the genuine love and true character of Jesus Christ; they can be seen seeking the lost. Only them that possess a realistic appreciation and earnest apprehension of their lost condition in the first place progressively transition into ardent disciples of the LORD Jesus Christ. Only them that have been saved from something, if you follow.

It is distinctly and formidably difficult to renew the already righteous to repentance. Them that have no functional appreciation of their (once) lost condition will never adequately comprehend the militant urgency in the heart and mind of the Good Shepherd. Only them raised from the dead have a viable (and virulent) witness of the resurrection power of the LORD Jesus Christ. The rest of us go to church. The ceremony reminds (some of us) that we are Christians.

Yes, this is cynical, for I have seen (by faith and by the Holy Ghost) the prophetic portend of the children of the kingdom cast out into outer darkness, and a people appreciative of the LORD's salvation taking their place.

✳

*Therefore say I unto you, The kingdom of
God shall be taken from you, and given to a
nation bringing forth the fruits thereof.*
MATT. 21:43

✳

The type and genre of the lost sheep that the Word of GOD lists in Ezekiel 34:4 remarkably resembles the list of those the LORD Jesus Christ gives in Luke 4:18 as specifically them to whom he is anointed to preach and minister healing and deliverance and liberty. It will take the heart and the mind (and the same anointing) of the Good Shepherd to reach them where they subsist on the margins of society. Someone must have a witness of the resurrection power of the LORD Jesus Christ. And that someone (of a necessity) must have first died to what they would rather do and taken up their cross.

Christian, dear faithful reader, is that you? Ah. Having tested its weight for a little while, I shall inevitably and irrepressibly discover that it is the same cross that Jesus Christ bore.

Preacher, have you ever read the thirty-fourth chapter of Ezekiel objectively? It is part and parcel of the comprehensive Good Shepherd that (perforce) you did not hear about in the attenuated processed exposition of the twenty-third Psalm. Indeed, the twenty-third Psalm ought to be read and studied in the immediate context and urgency and prophetic portend of the thirty-fourth chapter of Ezekiel. It is, after all, just another perspective of the same Good Shepherd.

Christian, did you realize that your conduct and deportment as an average parishioner will be astutely evaluated and judged by the Good Shepherd, and that your heart and mind and comprehensive character will be minutely assessed by the omniscient Spirit of the living GOD? Whom have you hindered or pushed or did your part to scatter abroad? (see Ezek. 34:20-21)

✳

Seemeth it a small thing unto you to have eaten up the good pasture, but ye must tread down with your feet the residue of your pastures? and to have drunk of the deep waters, but ye must foul the residue with your feet? And as for my flock, they eat that which ye have trodden with your feet; and they drink that which ye have fouled with your feet.
Ezek. 34:18-19

✳

The disdain and contempt (and uh, how we really feel) about the unfortunate or the outcast is upon the altar with our gift, or our extortion payment for the illusion of all-permissive grace; you know, so that we can continue to volitionally delude ourselves that we are forgiven for all that we perpetually allow. The Good Shepherd knows how we really think and feel about the poor and needy: *Let them get their own.*

We give the poor day-old bread and conclude ourselves righteous and generous. We give the poor what we do not want and what we will not eat and assess ourselves as altruistic and downright holy. Just saying.

Church of GOD, have we, without the religious bias of a self-favoring slant, equitably read and accepted (assimilated) the ominous prophetic foreshadow of the thirty-fourth chapter of Ezekiel? Strikingly, and unsparingly, when the Good

Shepherd has despaired at the discriminatory and negligent methodology of his under-shepherds (uh, pastors), and when he resolutely goes after the one that is lost or was driven away, he will also fastidiously evaluate the entire flock.

✳

I will seek that which was lost, and bring again that which was driven away, and will bind up that which was broken, and will strengthen that which was sick: but I will destroy the fat and the strong; I will feed them with judgment.
Ezek. 34:16

✳

Yes, that is correct, the righteous congregation (the ninety and nine), you know, them that have no (conscious) need of repentance, shall be astutely graded beneath the omniscient eye of the Holy One. *And I will judge between cattle and cattle* (re. Ezek. 34:22). *Behold, I, even I, will judge between the fat cattle and between the lean cattle,* (re. Ezek. 34:20).

Indeed, in that day, the ninety and nine shall be evaluated in the context of the one missing. Alas, my prosperity shall be minutely assessed in the light of my brother's abject penury. Ah, and my fullness shall be judged in the consideration of the multiple seasons I have ignored my neighbor's hunger and left them empty-handed.

The Good Shepherd has watched the ninety and nine conduct religious business as if one of their own was not missing. That is, he has watched us preen and prance and posture (and prostitute) as if we were all that. You know, as if we were whole.

It was with infinite wisdom and intentional percipient fore-thought that the LORD Jesus Christ incorporated my love for GOD and my love for my neighbor into One commandment.

It grieves the grace of the Good Shepherd when we celebrate ourselves, insentient and unsympathetic of the one still missing, indifferent to the need in our own neighborhood, cavalier or oblivious to the crisis in our own city. Dear Christian, there is one of our number being preyed upon amid the calamity, and whose soul is in immediate extremity. You know the one of whom the Good Shepherd has persistently made you acutely aware. Concisely, sometimes someone must go into the lion's den. (Do not go alone or unprepared.)

*

And other sheep I have, which are not of this fold:
them also I must bring, and they shall hear my voice;
and there shall be One fold, and One Shepherd.
JOHN 10:16

*

As long as the earth endures, ninety and nine will never be one hundred. Christian, our dispensation is today, the time for our testimony is now, the arena of our witness is the whole world. Children, there is concisely One fold, because GOD is in the One mind and One purpose of One LORD. He is the Good Shepherd. I call his name, Jesus.

The LORD Jesus Christ, here in the tenth chapter of John, parallels the thirty-fourth chapter of the prophet Ezekiel. That there is only One fold, kind of nullifies our denominational proprietary one-upmanship and totally invalidates our religious elitism, and uh, rescinds our sense of spiritual superiority. Duh.

We are all just ordinary (ornery) garden variety sinners saved by grace. Christian, that we have all these multitudinous (opinionated) close-minded motley flocks is a reflection of how far we have missed the commandment of One Love. If we still insist that this Word of GOD (Ezekiel, chapter 34), is exclusively for Israel, then we (in essence) are refuting the prophetic nature of the comprehensive Word of GOD, and we have effectively not heard a Word he said. Frankly, the revelation is humbling.

Concisely, (in what I call) the season of my humanity, the state of my eternal sanctification is being incrementally (day by day), irrepressibly set. The assessment of the ninety and nine is as sure as that of the one, and the time is eternally now. He who has ears to hear has already heard.

＊

When the Son of man shall come in his glory, and all the holy angels with him, then shall he sit upon the throne of his glory. And before him shall be gathered all nations: and he shall separate them one from another, as a shepherd divideth his sheep from the goats.
MATT. 25:31-32

＊

Now, of course, this Word of GOD must be considered in the objective context of the comprehensive Word of GOD. Notwithstanding the elements and specifics of other scripture, this precise teaching here in the twenty-fifth chapter of Matthew attests that my eternal state will be astutely decided by virtue of my treatment of *"the least of these"* the LORD's brethren. Notably, my eternal sanctification here at the LORD's throne will have already been progressively and irreversibly decided by how I treated *"the least of these"* day by day. In other words, was *love* my Christian modus-operandi?

When love is genuine, the heart and mind of the Good Shepherd is being resolutely perfected in me grace for grace and faith to faith, day by day. To be converted is to be *"changed into the same image from glory to glory, even as by the Spirit of the LORD"* (re. 2 Cor. 3:18).

The *"least of these,"* the LORD's brethren, will eventually and conspicuously be revealed to have essentially been the one lost sheep whom the preponderance of the ninety and nine go to great lengths to be unaware of.

✳

> *For I was an hungred, and ye gave me no meat; I was*
> *thirsty, and ye gave me no drink. I was a stranger, and*
> *ye took me not in: naked, and ye clothed me not:*
> *sick, and in prison, and ye visited me not.*
> MATT. 25:42-43

5

I AM the Resurrection and the Life

*"I AM the Resurrection, and the Life: he that believeth
in me, though he were dead, yet shall he live.*

*And whosoever liveth and believeth in me
shall never die. Believest thou this?"*

–John 11:25-26

THIS IS AN UNPARALLELED declaration of deity. The LORD Jesus Christ is unambiguously asserting that he can restore humanity from where we have fallen, that he has power (or authority) over death, hell and the grave. He is authoritatively pronouncing that he can make all things new.

Moreover, there is no greater (or more pertinent) question presented unto mankind than *"Believest thou this?"* The forthright answer to this question will irreversibly decide the eternal fate of every man or woman born.

Jesus Christ is audaciously and frankly attesting to have the utter authority to reverse the wages of sin (if I may put it like that). Well, concisely, it was sin that had killed Lazarus.

✳

For the wages of sin is death: but the gift of GOD
is eternal life through Jesus Christ our LORD.
ROM. 6:23

✳

We have touched upon this perspective. Jesus Christ was/ and is so much GOD that he forgave sin(s) before Calvary. This undeniably corroborates him as Alpha and Omega, free from the constraints of time; GOD of the past, present, and future: *"him which is, and which was, and which is to come, the Almighty"* (re. Rev. 1:8).

(If I may), Whether is easier to say, "Thy sins be forgiven thee; or to say, Lazarus, come forth?" (as inspired by Luke 5:23)

It is even as each of these *"I AM"* statements of the LORD Jesus Christ substantiate: *None but GOD can forgive sin and impart life.*

It is the Christ of GOD who breathes new life into my dead situation. Only GOD can redeem a soul from the curse of sin and death upon it.

Before we delve into our main text of the (physical) resurrection of Lazarus, the Holy Spirit moves me to revisit the absolute sovereignty and dominion of the LORD Jesus Christ to impart eternal life. As I have phrased it before, I want to run my metaphorical fingers through what I know, and by faith press up against the next measure of glory in the progressive dynamic revelation of the LORD Jesus Christ. Someone must stir up the water. I wonder how many of us have heard and received the LORD's command. That is, how many of us take the Word of God personally?

✳

Launch out into the deep, and let down your nets for a draught.
re. LUKE 5:4

✳

Deep calls to deep, as it were, and incites me upon the edge of faith, challenges me upon the precipice to expand my horizons; sometimes takes me where I would rather not go. These are the ways of death and life in the dynamic of being born again. My soul abhors the safe place. Welcome to my Bible study.

The alternative is religious stasis and another self-celebratory church service, smiling faces, religious smarm, vanity and inane posturing piety – the ninety and nine laid heavy and malodorous upon my consciousness.

Thank GOD this is only one perspective: like the view of a brick wall out the bathroom window, a dead end.

But I digress.

Nothing defines and distinguishes the deity of the LORD Jesus Christ more than his unmitigated authority over death. Nothing attests to his deity and identity as GOD and Creator more than his undeniable supremacy to bestow eternal life.

✻

For as the Father raiseth up the dead, and quickeneth (gives life unto) *them, even so the Son quickeneth whom he will.*
JOHN 5:21

✻

This Word of GOD is one of many principals, or part of an infinite comprehensive (as it were), that convinces me of the absolute divinity of the LORD Jesus Christ. I see no separation of duties or offices or personalities here; I see and hear the Father and the Son in the One mind and One purpose of One Spirit here. It is even as the LORD Jesus Christ says, *"I and my Father are One"* (John 10:30).

In this chapter, we are still essentially discussing the life that the Good Shepherd voluntarily laid down for the sheep, and with great power and unmitigated authority took back up.

Indeed, I have no effectual presumptive limitation or circumscription of this eternal being with power over sin and death, and with the unparalleled authority to bestow life and favor unto sinners lost in trespasses and sins. All my doctrinal postulations and finite religious pontifications fall short, and echo hollowly. Who can raise the dead but GOD?

Try as I might, I draw no viable doctrinal distinction, to intellectually divide this infinite being with power over life and death into three persons. Rather, I must conclude that it is even as the Word of GOD (Jesus Christ) says: *"GOD is a Spirit"* (re. John 4:24).

Moreover, it is even as John the Beloved bore witness of GOD's own record: *"For there are three that bear record in heaven, the Father, the Word, and the Holy Ghost: and these three are One"* (I John 5:7).

✳

Please listen. The Father and the Son (Jesus Christ) are whom I often call One LORD by the Holy Spirit. Now, this is not presumption or supposition on my part, this is not religious posturing or some aberrant product of the pride of life. It is the Word of GOD who calls GOD (and who refers to GOD) as One LORD. Indeed, it is even as I frequently say: "The Word of GOD speaks best for GOD."

✳

Hear, O Israel: The LORD our GOD is One LORD.
DEUT. 6:4

✳

Dear reader, it behooves us to revisit this specific Word of GOD to demonstrate that the life the LORD Jesus Christ gives is the very life of GOD. Its significance cannot be emphasized enough. These words of Deuteronomy 6:4 are the introductory words of *"The Shema,"* the Jewish call to prayer and worship. Jesus Christ (himself) quoted these words as the introductory injunction of the first (and great) commandment.

This is (as it were) a lengthy aside, but a critical exhortation of the Holy Spirit. One of the scribes had asked Jesus which was the first commandment of all, and I cite his entire answer.

＊

And Jesus answered him, The first of all the commandments is, Hear, O Israel; the LORD our GOD is One LORD.

And thou shalt love the LORD thy GOD with all thy heart, and with all thy soul, and with all thy mind, and with all thy strength: this is the first commandment.

And the second is like, namely this, Thou shalt love thy neighbour as thyself. There is none other commandment greater than these.
MARK 12:29-31

＊

Now, this is paramount, and extraordinary grave. Please listen. The LORD Jesus Christ is exhorting us and cautioning us, that before we embark upon loving GOD and loving our neighbor, it is imperative that we pause and *hear* something. In the past, I have referred to this admonition as a compulsory (indispensable) preamble or prelude to the first commandment. It is that important. Jesus Christ prefaced the first and great commandment in the context of its conscious contemplation, that before I even commence worship, or enter into prayer, that I pause and consider its command.

The Word of GOD gives us a crucial and integral element in the progressive intimacy and comprehensive identity of GOD, and it is as if we did not hear a Word he said.

It is Jesus Christ who says GOD is a Spirit and that he is One LORD. Jesus said it. The Word of GOD says it. Present prophetic tense.

The Word of GOD says, *"Hear, O Israel."* The prophetic equivalent of this is naturally and unavoidably, *"Hear, O Christianity."*

We fundamentally disregarded this prerequisite preamble and missed our very first instruction to a deeper understanding of GOD. And to this admonition, I must add another precise one from the gospel according to Mark.

※

Take heed what ye hear: with what measure ye mete, it shall be measured to you: and unto you that hear shall more be given.
MARK 4:24

※

If we have not structurally and elementally heard the first thing GOD said, how are we going to effectually comprehend and assimilate the next thing GOD says? What (or whose) foundation are we building upon?

Jesus Christ distinctly and purposefully quoted Moses. When he says, *"Hear O Israel,"* he is effectively saying, *"I want you to get this."* Duh. This is an obligatory prerequisite to prayer and worship. The redundancy is deliberate.

The statement, *"The LORD our GOD is One LORD"* is intended to be our first fundamental in comprehending the identify of, and understanding the commandments of, the LORD. In other words: Before you do anything else, before you consider any other teaching (or doctrine) or commandment, *hear this.*

Of course, the aggregate teaching of the Word of GOD reveals the Father and the Son as One LORD by the Holy Spirit. We spoke of this in our last chapter (and perhaps every chapter). It is concisely, *the Doctrine of Christ.* The Holy Spirit has me list its primary reference once more. This is an indication of its critical nature in our progressive apprehension of the essence of GOD.

✳

Whosoever transgresseth, and abideth not in "the Doctrine of Christ," *hath not GOD. He that abideth in* "the Doctrine of Christ," *he hath both the Father and the Son.*
2 John 1:9

✳

Now, the exhortation to *hear* (and/or grasp and comprehend) that *"the LORD our GOD is One LORD"* is given in the immediate context of what we call the first and great commandment.

By the Holy Spirit, I predicate and attest that the revelation of One LORD is given in the admonition (and revelation) of One Love. Concisely, it is the love of GOD in Christ. It is the LORD Jesus Christ who prefaced the commandment of One Love with the revelation of One LORD. It is the Word of GOD who gives it this place of urgency and preeminence. But have we effectively heard what he said?

My love for GOD and my love for my neighbor is to be as indivisible as my conceptualization of GOD as One LORD. It is the LORD Jesus Christ (the Word of GOD) who merges or incorporates my love for him into my love for my neighbor. It is the love of GOD in Christ Jesus. I am to love my neighbor with the same love that GOD loves me with. No other love will do.

Alas, this is unconditional love. There is no schism to One Love or One LORD, or to One Spirit. Just this past Sunday, I told the men at Harbor House Christian Center in Henderson, Kentucky, that this One commandment of Love should be sufficient to keep me busy. In fact, I should be too busy to be overly inquisitive or entangled in anyone else's business.

This (finitely) incomprehensible Spirit of Resurrection Life of which we desire an exposition and better understanding, is inseparable from the acute revelation of the love of GOD in Jesus Christ. As we have said, it is the glorified (resurrected) life that Jesus Christ freely gives for the life of the world. It is most clearly revealed in the context of the Spirit and exchange of love that exists between the Father and the Son, and in Jesus Christ's humble acquiescence and obedience to the will of the Father.

*

Therefore doth my Father love me, because I lay down my life, that I might take it again.
JOHN 10:17

*

Incredibly, this is the life that Jesus Christ gives – the life he first laid down. Now, we have said that it is given in the context of the exchange of love between the Father and the Son, accentuated and glorified by his (Jesus Christ's) meekness and humble obedience and absolute submission to the will of the Father. It is love which elicits and perfects this obedience. This is the Spirit of Life, of Resurrection Life, which Jesus Christ intends every Christian be progressively and resolutely coalesced into.

Love and obedience work together to meet and fulfill the commandment. This is the Resurrection Life with which we (the faithful) are merged. Here is its exemplification:

※

*This is my commandment, That ye love
one another, as I have loved you.*

*Greater love hath no man than this, that a
man lay down his life for his friends.*

*Ye are my friends, if ye do whatsoever
I command you.*
JOHN 15:12-14

※

My love for GOD (is) (to be) inseparable from my love for my neighbor, Jesus Christ has made it so. This necessitates the laying down of my life in obedience and submission (and sanctification) to the commandment of love. This looks easier on paper than it proves to be in practical application. We must look at the gospel principle (and then the process) of *"losing the life to find it."* For it is only dead men (and women) that can be raised unto newness of life, that is, unto Resurrection Life.

Christian, GOD wants to make you and I a capable host and reservoir and conduit of this gift of eternal (resurrection) life. Now, *"GOD is a Spirit"* (re. John 4:24), and as I like to say, his first name is *"Holy."* GOD is a Holy Spirit of love and light and truth. And I do not know about you, but the earthen vessel of my spirit man was in dire need of cleansing and regeneration. And as I occasionally say at Harbor House, introductions happen, but relationships *develop*.

Frankly, no one warned me of this inexorable process of *"losing the life to find it."* There are many elements to this dynamic, that is, the fact that I was not cautioned and forewarned of the hardships and opposition I would encounter apprehending this Resurrection Life. But the primary reason would grudgingly be revealed to be that not many of my forefathers had risen (or grown) beyond a perfunctory form of faith, to apprehend the reality (and overcome the obstacles) of a genuine faith. Well? Someone must get painstakingly honest.

The Word of GOD that was the effectual catalyst and genesis of my radical transformation and irrepressible conversion, is found within the same teaching (or doctrine) of Jesus Christ as recorded in the fifth chapter of John. (That is), I heard the Voice of the Word of GOD.

※

Verily, verily, I say unto you, the hour is coming, and
now is, when the dead shall hear the Voice of the
Son of GOD: and they that hear shall live.
JOHN 5:25

※

If I may be glaringly (and graphically) transparent and brutally honest, this may have been the precise moment that I began to believe in spirit and in truth. Notably, I had been posturing as an (adult) Christian for some time. From a certain perspective, I kind of wish I could say that this is the very instant when my faith overwhelmed all fear and unbelief and wrought a great and final victory. But, alas, such was not the case.

This (may have been) the moment I believed, and the process began. This (may have been) the first awakening of my finite awareness of eternity pressing its way into (my) time. Pardon me as I ruminate and run the metaphorical fingers of my finite mind through the wonders and mysteries of the Almighty GOD hidden in the infinity of his Christ. I am lost in the awe and contemplation of him who is Alpha and Omega. Glimpses of greater grace, I call them, these incremental progressive encounters, and my having begun to experience eternity. The Resurrection Life of which we speak is (from one perspective) already here.

Now, there is going to be a physical resurrection of the dead: some unto the resurrection of life, and some unto the resurrection of damnation (see John 5:29). But when I speak of first hearing the Voice of the Son of GOD in John 5:25, I am referring to the process of losing my life in order to find it, or, that is, the process of losing my life in order to have the life of the LORD Jesus Christ. I was *Dead* in trespasses and sins (re. Eph. 2:1). I am referring to the process of *being* born again or *becoming* a son of God. This *becoming,* I sometimes call "perpetual present tense." Pointedly, I am not there yet. It is he that endures unto the end that shall be saved (re. Matt. 24:13).

To be explicitly honest, it was while meditating upon John 5:25 that I first began to suspect that the LORD Jesus Christ was a living entity. This goes deeper than religious ceremony or a form of faith, or just calling myself a Christian; this is the genesis of genuine faith commanding change, taking control of circumstance.

The misconceptions I had formed of GOD and of salvation as a young and tentative seeker of knowledge must be addressed. Frankly, the religious traditions and ritual, the teaching and the preaching, the presumptions and the illusions which were allowed to develop, the nuance and innuendo and even the silences which suggested things that were not true, and which contributed to the fallacy and forms of faith which had supplanted the reality, must be brought to light.

The foundations and religious traditions our forefathers have handed down to us, and all that we have further engineered and fabricated and concocted upon them, will be exposed and tried by fire.

✳

Every man's work shall be made manifest: for the day
shall declare it, because it shall be revealed by fire; and
the fire shall try every man's work of what sort it is.
1 Cor. 3:13

✳

All my inventions will be found out. You know, my labyrinthine contrivances and circumvention of the light and truth my compromised Christianity cannot coexist comfortably with. This is what I often call my wood, hay, and stubble.

The Word of GOD commands conformity, transformation, conversion; repentance unto remission of sin. A genuine faith is its own self-assessing fire, exposing the foundations. The Word of GOD commands radical character conversion. The Voice of the Son of GOD resolutely reverberates within the caverns of my unregenerate man until my heart beats to the rhythm of his name. Only what is real is eternally relevant.

*

And they that hear shall live.
re. JOHN 5:25

*

Outside of grace and mercy, I am undone and immaterial. Everything I know is an inconsequential vanity and rapidly dissipating vapor. Everything I know got me here. In great mercy am I made to wait upon GOD, and in great grace am I given ears to hear.

*

*So then faith cometh by hearing, and
hearing by the Word of God.*
ROM. 10:17

*

It was a momentous, lucrative revelation, the day I realized that I would be best served to go to the Source. The Word of GOD has no hidden agenda or denominational slant and has no inane argument to win. Moreover, and as I have often said: GOD shall show me, or I shall not have it.

He who has ears to hear, let him hear. It is the Word of GOD who rightly divides the Word of GOD. Moreover, it is the Spirit that *quickeneth* (or gives life), (re. John 6:63). To covet the honor one of another by a self-serving, self-inflating religious ceremony profits nothing. To wait upon the approbation of a man more confounded than myself is to waste the LORD's time. (No, I will not mitigate or attenuate or expiate what the Holy Spirit has given me. I am not sure who that was for.)

I cannot breathe this same old malodorous religious misdirection, I must have the reality of GOD; for without holiness, I shall not see the LORD. I must have the Voice and understanding (and essence) of the Son of GOD. Only the Word of GOD has the regenerative breath of Resurrection Life that I need.

✳

For "therein" is the righteousness of GOD revealed from faith to faith: as it is written, The just shall live by faith.
Rom. 1:17

✳

Christian, we are (every one of us) intended to grow in the grace and knowledge of Jesus Christ, and irrepressibly transition into ardent disciples and incendiary witnesses of the resurrection life and power that is in him. GOD has no children malingering idle in the marketplace, no true servants or stewards or sons circumventing the field. There is no imaginary wayside for the diligent disciple of the LORD Jesus Christ, no stasis and no waste in the perpetual outreach of GOD's love for a world still perishing.

Persons who believe on the LORD Jesus Christ, but who do not continue in his Word to become passionate and capable disciples, is a recurring theme in everything the Holy Spirit has me write. Such is the urgency of every soul in the continuity of the gospel of Jesus Christ and him crucified, that as long as the earth endures, ninety and nine will never be one hundred.

Such was my repetitive trespass upon grace, that GOD transformed me into a proponent of grace. But such was the LORD's mercy, that he first restored me to his grace before he showed me the truth about my trespass and grievance upon grace, and the true extremity and peril in which my soul had subsisted for literal decades. As much as I wish it were different, and that relapse or backsliding were not part of my story, alas, such is not my testimony. I was a preacher's son, but I was not a choirboy, as they say.

The grace and truth Jesus Christ came to declare is progressive and gradational. Indeed, sometimes, incremental. But there is no stasis in a life lived by faith in the LORD Jesus Christ. Even the waiting is work.

To be (essentially) figurative or metaphorical, the cross of Jesus Christ is inexplicably and agonizingly real. The Word *allegorical* is insufficient to describe the actuality and anguish of its death. Some of you know what I am talking about.

Such is my portion to write about the process. Please pardon my inevitable and (even requisite) redundancy. My only defense in the past has been to cite that there are four gospel accounts, and nothing redundant or boring about them.

(Ideally) a Christian grows grace for grace and from faith to faith into obedience and sanctification which works by love. All things are indeed made new, but it has been my experience that things do not happen overnight.

To use myself as an example, and to keep it simple, the Holy Spirit took me aside, as it were, and showed me that everything that the Son of GOD experienced actually, I was to experience relatively. Notwithstanding, and as some of you know, the acuity of the suffering association is remarkably real. As I said, the word *allegorical* does not suffice to describe the agony of such great grace.

Such is the prophetic nature of the Word of GOD in following Jesus Christ by faith, our high priest and forerunner within the veil. It has been my experience that to share this glory, there shall inexorably be an acute suffering association and excruciating intimacy with the sacrifice of GOD upon the cross. My apprehension of the gospel truth, that only dead men (and women) are raised up to the newness of resurrection life, was agonizingly slow.

Alas, in the annals of the longsuffering love of GOD, I hold the world's record as the epitome of mercy and grace. It was Oswald Chambers who said, *"There are some things that I have not done, but there is nothing that I am not capable of."* Dear Christian, I do not know about you, but the depths of my depravity, of a necessity, were exposed, and by grace I saw the acute revelation of myself in the unsparing light of GOD's truth.

✳

Wherefore I abhor myself, and repent in dust and ashes.
Job 42:6

✳

Henceforth, I shall despair of the depravity of no man, for I have seen the reach of GOD's love and heard the rhythm of his heartbeat for the worst of humanity. (And it was me.)

The Holy Spirit definitively and indisputably showed me, that for me to share the glory and power of the LORD's resurrection life, I would also have to share his death. And as I have said, to be in allegory or in a figure, it is excruciatingly real. Children, there is no other way, and no effectual religious loopholes.

Frankly, I was a mastermind of misdirection and dissimulation, an expert in clandestine prevarication and procrastination and various attempts to escape with my life intact. But to have the life of Jesus Christ, I was going to have to lay down my own.

✳

Marvel not that I said unto thee, Ye must be born again.
John 3:7

✳

This is, after all, the gospel. This is also the critical juncture where forms of faith have been invented to supplant the forward momentum of a genuine faith. You know, various religious facsimiles and assorted solemn assemblies and church ceremony. My cynicism is an accurate reflection of the peril in which my soul subsisted in religious ceremony to supplant and emulate the austerity and rigors of a genuine faith and real repentance.

Succinctly, it was the painstaking astute revelation of my real self that I was ultimately circumventing. Radical transformation and genuine (bone-deep) character conversion require a militant repentance, self-denial, and an old rugged cross.

✳

If any man will come after me, let him deny himself, and take up his cross daily, and follow me. For whosoever will save his life shall lose it: but whosoever will lose his life for my sake, the same shall save it.
LUKE 9:23-24

✳

GOD's promises come with inescapable binding codicils or caveats if your will. In the past, I have described GOD's Word as being its own innate and fastidious system of checks and balances. Perhaps, this is why the LORD Jesus Christ told Nicodemus to *"Marvel not."* Frankly, I was surprised too. Shocked even. Although we should not be astonished that, to have the life of Jesus Christ, we must first surrender our own. This is integral to the immutable gospel principle of being born again.

To *deny myself* means to simply (but painfully) tell myself no. The Word of GOD harrowingly streamlines me for a strait gate and a narrow way.

Now, granted, I have met Christians who (apparently) (ostensibly) were transformed from sinners into saints instantaneously. Every church has a few, I have decided. But, alas, such was not my case. It may be that the difficulties I encountered were related to the depth of my depravity, as it were, because I was a professional, industrial-strength sinner. But, frankly, I did not, and have not, experienced that elusive Christian nirvana of transcendental spontaneous righteousness common to many of the Sisters of Sanctity and Holy Brethren that I have met.

The reason I know so much about forms of faith and religious posturing to mirror or mimic the rigors of true repentance, is because I became quite proficient at the mainstream contemporary Christian phenomenon. I knew all the religious jargon and self-righteous doublespeak. When we will not deny ourselves, and take up our cross, we must imitate the power of resurrection life because (concisely) we have not first died to have it. Someone must get honest.

Here we have the primary reason the Spirit of GOD has called me to write books to the Church of GOD. He took me from preening and prevarication, from presumption and pious pontifications and convoluted religious posturing, and moved me to testify to contemporary Christianity. He took my shame for having been a poser and an imposter, and by suffering association with the cross of Jesus Christ, saved my soul.

The comprehensive process of losing the life to find it, and the miracle of being born again, is enough to make you marvel. The astute (and acute) reality of the gospel of Jesus Christ and him crucified is that his cross is my cross. (Bluntly) it is not only enough to make you marvel, but it is sufficient to make a grown man cry.

Some of us (apparently) think that Jesus Christ suffered and died to make us exclusively Bigger Christians. (I include myself to take some of the sting out of my comments.) Indeed, *many* of us lust to be Bigger Christians, and a precious *few* of us die to the flesh to become better ones. The scriptural caveat, as it were, of our current text of *losing the life to find it* is that we surrender our life *"for my sake"* says the LORD Jesus.

The life of Jesus Christ is not given me so that I can prance and preen (and prostitute myself) before the righteous assembly, essentially seeking the honor and approbation one of another. (If so be) that I have effectually died to myself so that I might have the resurrection life and power of the LORD Jesus Christ, it is to make me an ardent disciple and incendiary witness of that same resurrection life.

Because the austerity and self-denial are real, and because the cross is indeed heavy, we compromise and cut corners and collude to sustain the status quo of mediocrity. And we then perpetuate the species.

"For my sake" is the indispensable prerequisite to Resurrection Life. The Word of GOD sees, hears, smells, feels, and tastes my living sacrifice: my prayer, my worship, my praise, my thoughts. My motivation is minutely assessed, the thoughts and intents of my heart acutely discerned (re. Heb. 4:12). The Word of GOD is more infinitely alive than I could ever imagine. Indeed, his name is Jesus.

The correlative reality or equivalent of the prerequisite *"for my sake,"* is the evangelical *"ye shall be witnesses unto me"* (re. Acts 1:8). Ah, but we presume to have misappropriated the promise of the Father, and the power of the resurrection life of the LORD Jesus Christ, to dance and sing and posture in a self-celebratory religious ceremony. Sometimes we call it Church, sometimes we call it Camp-meeting. Meanwhile, the poor and the oppressed and the homeless and the mentally ill are perishing within the very orbits we occupy, going to hell in the shadow and proximity of our religious posturing.

There is a natural (but infinite) progression to the dynamic of a genuine faith, a restless reaching forth. Finite words are insufficient to adequately describe the impetus of Resurrection Life; the ethereal essence and aggregate virtue of GOD, (in short), his Glory.

The Resurrection Life of the LORD Jesus Christ is its own self-sustaining, self-perpetuating *"Witness"* who keeps the miracle of redemption alive, a living, breathing entity – in short, the same self-contained fire that the man Moses saw in the midst of the burning bush on the backside of the desert.

(I experience eternal life Now), the earnest of my inheritance Now; in (this) "the season of my humanity," as I am wont to call the phenomenon of this heavenly treasure that I have in an earthen vessel.

Christian, this Resurrection Life within you yearns for expression. This urgency you feel is (concisely) the continuity of the love of GOD in the gospel of Jesus Christ and him crucified. He is whom I call *"the Witness."* Actually, I apprehended and assimilated (and acclimatized), or borrowed the expression from John the Beloved.

✳

And it is the Spirit that "beareth witness,"
because the Spirit is Truth.
re. 1 JOHN 5:6

✸

Concisely, this is him (*He*) that death could not hold. This is the Witness of GOD. This is whom the sanctified host. He who has ears to hear has already heard.

Now, I am not trying to be mystical. If "*the Witness*" is in you, then you already know; and if he is not, then prayer and fasting and meditating upon GOD's Word are in order.

(Bluntly) (rigorously and painfully honest), this is the predominant reason that the (preponderance) of mainstream contemporary Christianity has no viable or demonstrative (both vocal and behavioral) witness of the saving power and resurrection life of the LORD Jesus Christ in the market-place and in the work-place. And it is because we do not effectually have "*The Witness*" living and abiding within the temple of our spirit-man or spirit-woman. Someone must candidly and brusquely say so.

Jesus is here and he is Now. This is the Witness of GOD still in the earth, and he is the witness of Resurrection Life housed and hosted in the earthen vessel of the sanctified disciples of Jesus Christ.

✸

And there are three that bear witness in earth, the Spirit, and
the water, and the blood: and these three agree in One.
1 JOHN 5:8

✳

The Witness of the Resurrection Life of the LORD Jesus Christ will not sit silent and anesthetized and dumbfounded in the corner of the pew, amused and distracted and entertained by the religious theatrics of contemporary wise men and witch doctors and peddlers of all-permissive grace. The Witness of GOD will not suffer the religious stasis common to the saints of the status quo. The Witness of GOD is going to tell someone about the Resurrection Life and power of the LORD Jesus Christ.

This *Witness* is concisely the Spirit of a Living Word who can neither be contained nor silenced. He is an evangelical Fire. He is enthralled by them whose lives are in crisis. He is ardent to raise the dead to newness of life.

He is the witness of an empty tomb and the regenerative Breath of GOD, the gift of the Holy Ghost. He is the heart of God for the lost, and the concise living expression of perfect love. He is the unction of the Holy One, the *"endowment"* of GOD.

To realize Christ, we must follow Christ. To operatively and productively apprehend the grace and truth and power of Resurrection Life, we must first die to sin and to self and to our love for the world. We must die to all that is in the world through the lust of the flesh and the pride of life, to all that is not of the Father (re. 1 John 2:15-16).

Jesus Christ ever lives to make intercession for both the saints and the lost, and we (mainstream Christianity) essentially live for ourselves. Some of us want to sit together with Jesus Christ in heavenly places and look holy, and pretty, and to point our self-righteous finger down below. Some of us just want to sit here and not do anything, and we (pretty much) do not care about how we look. The preponderance of us circumvent the austerity of the self-denial and reality of the cross. (Broadly) we have no witness of Resurrection Life because we have (basically) refused to die.

(It has been my experience) that there is a definitive progression of the grace and truth by which Jesus Christ came to declare unto us the essence and comprehensive identity of GOD. My own experience is the only one that I can describe or relay with verity and rectitude. Therefore, as much as possible, I try to write in the first-person possessive tense.

My own salvation and transformation into a witness and disciple of Jesus Christ is a perpetual dynamic evolution, a continuing development, an enduring, unremitting breakthrough. Concisely, I am a sinner saved by grace in the continuity of the gospel of the longsuffering love and mercy of GOD. By the living gospel of Jesus Christ and him crucified, and by the effectual unceasing power of his blood upon the mercy seat, I am in a constant state of radical character transformation.

Borrowing several expressions of the Apostle Paul from several different scriptures, and in no particular order, let me say that I count not myself to have apprehended, but I press toward the mark, if by any means I might attain unto the resurrection of the dead (see Phil. 3:11-14). I will attempt to expound upon the same Word that GOD gave me to assist me in understanding the process of (what I call) my *"becoming"* a son of GOD.

*

*That I may know him, and The Power of His
Resurrection, and the fellowship of his sufferings,
being made conformable unto his death.*
PHIL. 3:10

*

As a young Christian, resurrection power appealed to me, but I did not understand the acute level of intimacy that this scripture not only implies, but commands. First, I had to understand (accept and assimilate) the prophetic nature of the entire Word of GOD, that it is a living perpetual revelation without horizons. His name is Jesus.

All the types and shadows and figures within the Word of GOD, and their application to the peoples of GOD (in every era), are of an immediate (living) relevancy to me. It applies to me: *Every Word that proceeds out of the mouth of GOD.*

The Word of GOD is here, and the Word of GOD is now. Frankly, there will be no forthcoming expiation (atonement) for the Word of GOD that I refuse to live by.

For literal decades, I emulated (the best I could) the resurrection power of the LORD Jesus Christ, because I had neither fellowshipped with his sufferings nor conformed to his death to apprehend it. These statements are, perhaps, generalities, but I must also try to be concise, and acute. I will not and cannot mitigate my own fraudulence and dissimulation. I was a poser and a hypocrite, convinced my artifice was harmless.

It may help to list some fundamental gospel principles that I was blissfully (but oftentimes willfully) unaware of.

(Bluntly), I equated being born again with stopping a few (observable) offensive behaviors. Since I would not read and study my Bible, my ignorance was essentially a volitional one. Uh, I was stupid of the things of GOD by choice, if the truth must be told.

I feigned nonchalant ignorance that GOD expected every Christian to transition into a disciple. I was not (exactly) sure what it meant to fellowship with the sufferings of Jesus Christ, or to be conformed to his death, but I intuitively suspected the unpleasantness and austerity of its nature. I knew nothing about the gospel process of losing the life to find it. I had no effectual understanding of what it entailed to be a servant, steward, and then a son of GOD. I did not understand what it meant, nor did it appeal to me, to be made a priest and a king unto GOD.

(In short), I was taught external Christian etiquette and church protocol, not radical character conversion. This is what I mean when I say that we perpetuate the species. The bloodline is being attenuated, and the ranks of the Spirit-filled believers within the contemporary Christian congregation are being decimated. In an age of instant gratification, nobody wants to wait upon GOD. In an era of all-permissive grace, nobody wants to die unto sin.

I was taught (by nuance and innuendo and unspoken implication), Christian civility and deportment, and to feign a holy affectation and righteous posture. (Yes, a delicate endeavor.) You know, smiling faces.

Instead of my becoming an integral member of a living entity (the Church of GOD), church became something I did, a performance, a pretension, a formal pageant of posturing pietists and self-righteous phonies. Although I am attempting to speak only for myself, it must be assumed that I was not the Lone Ranger among the assembly. Precisely, I was not the only one who dutifully and dispassionately went through the motions of an external religious routine while remaining fundamentally (and blissfully) internally unchanged.

The *process* the Apostle Paul is referring to in Philippians 3:10-11, which goal is eventually to attain unto the resurrection of the dead, is (actually) the dynamic phenomenon of our being born again by grace through faith in the LORD Jesus Christ. It is the marvel and the wonder (and the mystery and the wisdom) of the LORD's salvation. The LORD Jesus Christ (relatively) delineates the identical process when he says, *"Follow me."*

Following the LORD Jesus Christ is an indispensable command of discipleship, and the imperative (and the prerequisite) codicil of my radical character conversion. To experience and enjoy and to prosper in the resurrection life of Jesus Christ, the body of sin must first be figuratively (but operationally) crucified with Jesus Christ, and then left in the grave. The LORD Jesus Christ is the preeminent example and explicit forerunner of this definitive process of living and dying and being risen again.

✳

I am crucified with Christ, nevertheless I live; yet not I, but Christ liveth in me: and the life which I now live

*in the flesh I live by the faith of the Son of GOD, who
loved me, and gave himself for me.*
Gal. 2:20

✳

Children, this distinct process naturally commands my qualifiable death to sin. This is what the fight is about. This is the expedient suffering fellowship and irrepressible conformity to the death of the LORD Jesus Christ that the gospel of his cross commands.

This is the scope and imperative of my perpetual message, book after book. Contemporary Christianity has become expert at circumventing the suffering association and acute death unto sin which the cross of Jesus Christ commands. This is the gospel. There will be no definitive resurrection life without a demonstrable death unto sin.

✳

Marvel not that I said unto thee, Ye must be born again.
John 3:7

✳

The Apostle Paul would also further qualify this inexorable gospel process with the statement, *"I die daily"* (re. 1 Cor. 15:31). (If I may), these are the tumultuous redemptive conditions of the Christian's suffering fellowship and radical conformity to the death and resurrection of the LORD Jesus Christ. This is my measure from the LORD. These are my wages.

The Apostle Paul would tell you, *"I do not take day off from the gospel of the cross of Jesus a Christ."* Likewise, I concur. In fact, I personally attest that I cannot and will not afford to spend one day indifferent or dispassionate. The love of GOD in Jesus Christ constrains me to testify of that same immeasurable love.

This inexpressible never-ending revelation of the love of GOD in the LORD Jesus Christ constrains me to write book after book. A prominent (and perpetual) theme of my writing is contemporary Christianity's evasion of this process of dying unto sin so that we may be raised to newness of resurrection life. Frankly, this evasion, and the interminable (rabid) seeking of religious loopholes, is as old as that old rugged cross. And I unapologetically and transparently confess that I was often chief among the self-righteous assembly.

As I have written many times, the primary reason that I am so familiar with the *forms* of faith we initiate and sustain to emulate the forward momentum and radical personality transformation of a genuine faith, is that I was an ardent practitioner and religious poser of these forms for literal decades. Mainstream contemporary Christianity in America is inundated and surfeited with proponents and masters of perpetuating a doctrine (that I call) all-permissive grace. It is based upon the misconception of the love and mercy of GOD without the accountability of truth and holiness. Concisely, it is the erroneous notion that I can be forgiven for the sin I willfully and repeatedly continue to allow.

Without submitting to the death of the LORD's cross, I shall not share the glory of his resurrection life and power. In order to effectually save my life for myself, I must feign a formal submission to the suffering association and conformity to the death of the cross. This pretense is a superficial Christianity.

The state of affairs described above is what I have often called not having a Christ in the middle of my Christianity. Where there is no cross, there is no actual death to sin; where there is no death to sin, there is no realistic (life transforming) resurrection life and power, and no effectual conversion.

Perilous times are upon us. Our Christianity is going to be tried by fire. He who ears to hear has already heard. Yet, it behooves us to fill up the places left behind of this prophetic portend, and to take an unabbreviated look at its fulfillment before our eyes. This generation's children are even now in the street.

✳

This know also, that in the last days perilous times shall come. For men shall be lovers of their own selves, covetous, boasters, proud, blasphemers, disobedient to parents, unthankful, unholy. Without natural affection, trucebreakers, false accusers, incontinent, fierce, despisers of those that are good. Traitors, heady, high-minded, lovers of pleasures more than lovers of GOD. Having "a form" of godliness, but denying the power thereof: from such turn away.
2 Tim. 3:1-5

✳

Here, then, is a concise and explicit description of the religious phenomenon that I call not having a Christ in the middle of my Christianity. (Using myself as an example), my Christianity is reduced to a mere form because I have denied its power, that is, I did not *submit* to its life-transforming power. I resisted the tender overtures of the Holy

Spirit's solicitous endeavors to elicit my unconditional surrender. I insisted upon saving my life for myself.

Fundamentally and principally unconverted, I will not experience nor apprehend the resurrection life and power of the LORD Jesus Christ. I did not die to have it. (Bluntly), the lust of the flesh and the pride of life (I insist upon) have precluded the obedience and holiness and sanctification that the gospel of the cross of Jesus Christ commands. Frankly and unapologetically (if such is my state), then I am revealed to be a lover of pleasures more than a lover of GOD.

A genuine love would have elicited my total and joyful capitulation to every Word that proceeds out of the mouth of GOD. His name is Jesus. Oh my. That is correct, it will eventually be revealed that I loved myself more than I loved the LORD Jesus Christ. Children, this makes me an idolater. All my other (multifarious and innumerable) other little sins are symptoms of my original sin, and my insisting upon being my own god. Little "g" of course.

My Christianity is reduced to an abridged and superficial formality and a spurious religious presentation. All fluff and no substance. The ceremony may be loud and ostentatious, and still not have a heart. I go through the motions to salve my conscience in a vain attempt to convince myself that my worship is real. Unpersuaded of myself, I subsist in fear and unbelief, a denizen and a prisoner of a minimal and nominal religious routine.

We are sustained by cursory self-celebratory service and mutual collusion in the self-righteous reflection of one another. We are the righteous assembly, and beyond reproach, the gold standard for contemporary Christian living. Sunday afternoon, we are convinced we have worshipped well, and return to our lives Monday morning unconverted.

✴

Ever learning, and never able to come
to the knowledge of the Truth.
2 Tɪᴍ. 3:7

✴

(Predominantly) we perpetually affirm one another's perfunctory Christian affect with the repetitive teaching and preaching of peripheral (and oftentimes worldly) principles and general ethics. Uh, Christian etiquette. Just be nice. GOD forbid we should gaze too deeply into the reality of our unregenerate character to see where we actually live, and who we really are.

Ever learning, and never really being transformed. Christian, that is a politically correct (polite) religious way of saying, *not born again.* Ever learning general Christian deportment, but never really dying unto sin. Well? Someone must reach inside our cursory Christian cloak to the cancer breeding and proliferating deep inside.

Ever learning, but always holding back. Dealing off the bottom and skimming off the top. Ever learning to tweak the external presentation, but never being radically and internally transformed. Ever learning but never getting real. Ever learning to be a Bigger Christian, but never really being a better one.

Ever learning all-permissive grace, and never able to apprehend the knowledge of the Truth, and repentance unto remission of sin.

Ever learning the religious platitudes and pious phrases of my forefathers, and never fully persuaded of these forms of faith, living in fear. (Essentially) ever learning to extort and misappropriate the grace and mercy of GOD, and perpetually circumventing the truth about my prevarication and dissimulation.

Thus has the Spirit of the *HOLY* shared with me the multitude (and the many) pressed into the wide gate and fleeing upon the broad way of religious collusion and compromise, contrasted with the few laying down their lives for the gospel's sake. As I have said, the *many* and the *few* is not my ratio, but the heart and mind (and the arithmetic) of GOD in the commands of sanctification and the acute sieving of the truth.

✳

For the time will come when they will not endure
sound doctrine; but after their own lusts shall they
heap to themselves teachers, having itching ears.
2 Tɪᴍ. 4:3

✳

There was a distinct and protracted season in which I had convinced myself of a form of hypothetical faith and a doctrine of all-forgiving, all-liberal whimsical grace with no accountability to the truth. And I was not alone. We circumvented Calvary and eschewed the austerity and self-denial of the cross. We fancied ourselves going directly to sitting together in heavenly places with Jesus Christ and peering with self-importance and imperious contempt below. We were the *"righteous right,"* the untouchables, the entertained and the secular (carnally) incestuous, anesthetized by pseudo-religious ceremony and a hybrid church service.

We were predominantly content with a theoretical Jesus, and an academic (abstract) speculative resurrection life, and a conceptual, postulate (presumptive) power. You understand. Surface Christianity. We were enthralled with the very real and pragmatic circumnavigation of having to die unto sin, mesmerized and enchanted, and ensnared, by the sensible and serviceable, uh, saving our lives for ourselves. Ah, to sit in heavenly places (and present superior and holier) without having to die. Mainstream Christian nirvana.

But, alas, such was the sorrowful and traumatized state of my own soul, that I could not be sustained with supposition and mainstream contemporary Christian conjecture or satisfied with a hypothetical holiness (if you will). Now, I am notably not a wise man, I am a country boy from up *coal hollow,* but even I realized that posturing as being born again without having first died to sin was a (pointedly) preposterous hypothesis.

There are those who seem to thrive on a postulated or inferred resurrection life and a one-dimensional cardboard Christianity, but I was such a blatant and illustrious (bare-assed) sinner that I could not be sustained with anything short of a miracle. I needed to be born again, and although I was not the sharpest knife in the drawer, I knew that would necessitate my first having to die.

When I first heard the LORD Jesus Christ say, *"Follow me,"* it was not an abstract or theoretical cursory instruction, but an absolute command. It was not a direction open to personally skewed (or favored) interpretation or a behest into which I could interject sparing and self-indulgent, evolving and unceasing conditions common to a generous connotation of an all-permissive grace. Uh, you know how we do it. You know how we spin it.

GOD purposed that I would become generally disaffected and discontented with mainstream denominational (divisive) religious politics and inane posturing. (The pretense made me sick.) I saw our multifarious forms of faith and innumerable religious enclaves as (frankly) symptomatic of our fundamental ignorance of GOD. The preponderance of us mechanically and indifferently followed dissociative religious routines with vague core values and beliefs that we could not even articulate.

Ye worship ye know not what.

re. JOHN 4:22

＊

My restless dissatisfaction and disenchantment with going through the motions of (what I began to call) (as you know) mainstream contemporary Christianity, began to progressively distress me. My friends and acquaintances (and the other parishioners) did not seem to share my disillusionment. They were fundamentally satisfied with a *"feel good about me"* (hybrid) worship service mingled with secular elements. You know, teaching and preaching of an attenuated Word of GOD: Bible principles mingled with a composite common-sense and self-help ideology and worldly counsel.

Most of my peers (in a very broad or general sense) seemed to be completely satisfied with a synthetic church service. They seemed to have found what they were looking for: a way to save their lives for themselves while appeasing their guilty consciences at the same time, contented with being able to consider themselves Christians. You know, convinced that they had worshipped well. Christian form.

Try as I might, I could not become better acquainted with the LORD Jesus Christ participating in a ceremony primarily designed to make me feel good about myself while seeking the honor of other posers just like myself. Frankly, we were a self-affirming, self-sustaining religious entity, and we did not want the austerity and self-denial of the gospel of Jesus Christ and him crucified to uh, suppress or demoralize our wonderful ceremony. Do we have to talk about sin and death and hell on such a beautiful day?

To be painstakingly (even brutally honest), I had intuitively apprehended (as by the Holy Spirit) that in order for me to have the resurrection life of the LORD Jesus Christ in a dynamic life-transforming (functional and serviceable) experience, that I was going to have to die to sin and self and my love of the world in the pride of my life. Concisely, I was emphatically not being born again, and it troubled me immensely.

On the outside, I looked as good as the average parishioner going through the religious motions of a predominantly superficial contemporary Christian ceremony. But on the inside, I still needed a miracle.

On paper, or one-dimensionally, I was as good a Christian as the next guy. Superior to some, if you counted service work and assorted religious duties performed. But internally, my core character had not been converted. That is, I was certainly not radically born-again, or truly a new creature.

Candidly, I confessed my misgivings and dissatisfaction to GOD, my doubts and my fears and my disenchantment with contemporary Christianity and cursory church ceremony. Over time, and with much prayer and fasting, GOD gave me an growing interest, and then an unquenchable love, for the gospel accounts of the life and death and resurrection of the LORD Jesus Christ. The gospel according to John became especially dear to me. The following is what most of you should know by now is what I call my first absolute: *"God is a Spirit"* (re. John 4:24).

I had much to learn, and GOD constrained me to go directly to the Source. Concisely, GOD is a Spirit, and he is a *Holy* Spirit. *He is a Holy Spirit of a Living dynamic Word.*

I earnestly and forthrightly still have much to learn, and I still single-mindedly and unwaveringly still go directly to the Source. And, as I say, The Word of GOD speaks best for GOD. Indeed, it is the Word of GOD that rightly divides the Word of GOD. Amazingly, he never misquotes himself or takes himself out of context.

The LORD Jesus Christ indisputably had an inner circle comprised of Peter, James, and John, of whom John was the dearest or most intimate, the Beloved. The comprehensive Word of GOD irrefutably establishes these facts.

The 13th through the 17th chapters of John are what is often referred to as the *Upper Room Discourse.* They are a rich and what is a (fundamentally) unparalleled body of theology and preeminent teaching (or doctrine) of the coming and infilling (and Baptism) of the Holy Spirit.

These chapters are the thoughts and Words of the LORD Jesus Christ immediately preceding his arrest, trial, and death by crucifixion. You see, Jesus Christ did not go directly to heaven. He first had to go through some things here on earth. It is we Christians who are predisposed to posture as if we were saved and then went directly to sitting together with the LORD in heavenly places. Moreover, it is amazing how quickly (and thoroughly) the preponderance of us transition from sinners into saints. You might think we had never sinned. It seems our manifest destiny was to sit high and holy and point pretentiously and judgmentally down below.

As our forerunner and as the firstborn among many brethren, and, as I am persuaded of the prophetic Word of GOD, everything that the LORD Jesus Christ experienced, and every Word he says, has a relevant eternal significance unto us. Humanity has spent multiple millennium perfecting ways to circumvent the austerity and self-denial of the gospel of Jesus Christ and him crucified. We covet and (posture for) the resurrection life and power and eschew and elude the suffering fellowship and explicit conformity to the death of his cross.

I am convinced that everything the LORD Jesus Christ confronted and endured is prophetically made mine (and every Christian's) by an acute suffering association. Jesus Christ irrepressibly intends that every Christian be radically transformed and progressively transitioned into ardent disciples and incendiary priests and kings in the earth.

This Holy Spirit of the resurrection life and power of the LORD Jesus Christ is the earnest of our redemption and the evidence and substance of our faith. It is the preeminent gift of GOD's love and the impetus and continuity of the gospel of Jesus Christ and him crucified. The Holy Spirit of the resurrection life and power of the LORD Jesus Christ is the effectual dynamic of every Christian's radical transformation in this divine phenomenon called being born again.

Christian, the life GOD gives is the same one he laid down. The same Spirit that raised Christ Jesus from the dead, quickens (gives life to) our mortal bodies even now (re. Rom. 8:11). This radical and militant and miraculous metamorphosis from death unto life is transpiring Now, and into eternity.

✳

Likewise reckon ye also yourselves to be dead indeed unto sin, but alive unto GOD through Jesus Christ our LORD.
Rom. 6:11

✳

Who would have thought that a discourse on resurrection life would focus so much upon death? The Holy Spirit is predominantly addressing mainstream contemporary Christianity and the erroneous notion that I can have the resurrection life and power of the LORD Jesus Christ without first dying unto sin and lust and my love of the world. The process cannot be emphasized enough. The need for my thorough transformation and radical conversion cannot be accentuated enough. The urgency and the imperative can bear the weight of its own redundancy.

Jesus Christ is the *Exemplar* of the selfless *(agape)* love of GOD. He taught us how to die. And he taught us how to love. Children, the LORD Jesus Christ laying down his life, began well before Calvary.

❋

Greater love hath no man than this, that a man lay down his life for his friends. Ye are my friends, if ye do whatsoever I command you.
JOHN 15:13-14

❋

(And) concisely, he is our archetype and model, our forerunner, into this preemptory gospel principle and compulsory process of *losing the life to find it.* Jesus Christ teaches us how to die so that he may give us this Holy Spirit of resurrection life and power.

This is the Spirit of an endless life. *"GOD is a Spirit"* (re. John 4:24), and this is *He.* GOD gives himself away in the resurrection life and power of the LORD Jesus Christ. This *Holy Spirit* is the *"One called alongside to help"* me in this inexorable process of losing the life to find it. He is the agent and the stimulus of my radical transformation.

This Holy Spirit gives me new horizons and new perspectives. New vision. New fire. Fresh breath. Three distinct times, the LORD Jesus Christ called him *"the Spirit of Truth"* (see John 14:17, 15:26, 16:13).

(In a quick aside, I share the following.) Out of the depths of my Bible study one morning, while intermittently praying and writing and meditating, I abruptly asked, *"Holy Spirit, is your name Jesus?"* Immediately, in that small still (precious) voice, mingled with just a suggestion of amusement, he answered, "Of *course it is."* Christian, such is the intimacy he shares with them who receive it.

From a *true* vista (that is, from the perspective of the Word of GOD), this unquenchable process of laying down my life in the expression and continuity of the love of GOD in Christ, is a commandment. We all should know that this commandment of love is the only commandment, and simultaneously, it is every commandment. As I like to say, this is commandment enough to keep each of us thoroughly occupied.

Children, it is the Word of GOD's unwavering objective to transform me into someone fit for heaven. Now, I know that the LORD Jesus Christ is my righteousness, and that I can in no way earn or merit the LORD's salvation. Trust me, I was sinner enough to realize that I am saved by grace through faith. But I also know that the grace of GOD does not leave me where he found me. The same grace that is powerful enough to save my soul from sin, is also completely capable to keep me from sin. We speak predominantly of willful, repetitive sin. It was a momentous and liberating day when I first apprehended the revelation that the grace of GOD, by the Holy Spirit, was eager to teach me how to live a godly life.

✳

For the grace of GOD that bringeth salvation hath appeared to all men. "Teaching" us that, denying ungodliness and worldly lusts, we should live soberly, righteously, and godly, in this present world.
Titus 2:11-12

✳

Let us make it plain. The true and uncompromising reality of GOD (that is, the perspective of him whose name is *HOLY*), is that, I will learn to live a life that honors GOD now (in this life), or I shall not be living with him eternally in the afterlife. Someone has to say it. Succinctly, some of us are living as if we can wait until we get to heaven to start living a righteous (and sanctified) lifestyle.

The grace of GOD taught me no such thing. The manifest overwhelming goodness of GOD taught me to love and to reverence God. The grace of GOD that brings salvation in its wake, also brings the comprehensive power and essence of the resurrected Christ to bear upon my unregenerate character. The goodness of GOD will not leave me where he found me.

With the grace of GOD comes the knowledge of GOD, and the understanding that his love is born out of the truth and holiness of his divine essence. It is his love which elicits my obedience to the commandment. I find that I cannot continue to willfully sin against such an immeasurable goodness, and truly, amazing grace.

All men (and women) have experienced this grace, the Word of GOD says so. This is the goodness of GOD that teaches me to die (unto what my natural man might rather do). GOD has made a way for me to meet the commandment, and to yield myself as an instrument in the perpetuation of this inexhaustible love of GOD.

This grace not only teaches me, but also empowers me, to deny ungodliness and worldly lusts. In plain English, it teaches me to say no to sin. This unrelenting process of my dying unto myself and unto sin and unto my love for the world, and progressively coming alive (or being born again unto Christ), begins the moment I first accept Jesus Christ as my LORD and Savior.

The process begins Now, *"in this present world"* (re. Titus 2:12). All things being made new, my being made a new creature in Christ Jesus, is a *"perpetual present tense."* This life, in this world, is my *"becoming"* a son of GOD. In this life, there is no ethereal Christian nirvana of sinless perfection. In short, there is no grace for the sin I continue to (impudently and obdurately) volitionally allow.

＊

For if we sin willfully after that we have received the knowledge of the truth, there remaineth no more sacrifice for sins.
Heb. 10:26

＊

This implacable and uncompromising Holy Spirit of resurrection life never ceases to progressively raise me up unto newness of life. Sin and death and the grave could not hold him. And that same omnipotent Spirit of the resurrection life and power of the LORD Jesus Christ will not leave me subsisting and enervated in sin either. And neither will he leave me anesthetized and apathetic, dozing listlessly in the corner of the pew. He never stops raising me up. And he never stops baptizing me with fire.

＊

Brethren, I count not myself to have apprehended.
re. Phil. 3:13

*

If I have another day to live, then I have another day to die unto sin, unto the love of the world, and unto the lust and the pride of this life.

In this present world, in the here and now, in this one moment of its immediate mercy, the grace of GOD that brings salvation teaches me and empowers me to deny ungodliness and worldly lusts. *Now* is when I begin to live soberly and righteously and godly, in *"this present world"* (re. Titus 2:12).

What are we waiting for, Christian? As much as possible, I try to personalize these manuscripts that arise out of my Bible study. But all of humanity must be included in the universal indictment of the insurrection of sin against GOD. We all have Adam's nature. We all are admonished not to love the world, or the things that are in the world. It is necessary that I cite (what I call) John the Beloved's short list (from GOD).

*

Love not the world, neither the things that are in the world. If any man love the world, the love of the Father is not in him.

For all that is in the world, the lust of the flesh, and the lust of the eyes, and the pride of life, is not of the Father, but is of the world.
1 JOHN 2:15-16

*

Concisely, the evil spirit that precipitated Adam and Eve to sin is still very much in the world. Of course, this is Satan. The Apostle Paul calls him *"the god of this world"* who has blind-ed the minds of them that do not believe the gospel (see 2

Cor. 4:4). He also calls him *"the prince of the power of the air,"* the *"spirit"* that is now working in the children of disobedience (see Eph. 2:2).

For this teaching to be so fundamental, the evidence (or lack thereof) predominantly suggests that many of us need to review these elementary and foundational truths. Children, Satan is alive and well, and obviously more impassioned to wreak havoc and sow evil than we (Christians) have been to advance the love of GOD in Christ Jesus by our vocal and behavioral testimony and witness. Just saying. There is nothing complacent or lukewarm about evil.

Satan (and his minions) are the evil spirit(s) that still govern and motivate this world system. It is the same evil that colluded with the spiritual wickedness in high (religious) places, namely, the leaders and chief priests of Judaism, to coerce and incite the Romans (and the Jews) to crucify Jesus Christ over 2,000 years ago. We do not want to admit it (and accept) it, and we do everything within our power to circumvent it, but this is the Word of GOD's perspective concerning the spirit which still governs this world system (whose ass we kiss to keep the goods and services flowing uninterrupted). May GOD forgive or mitigate the expletive, but it is the very same evil that conspired with the Pharisees and Jews to provoke the Romans into crucifying GOD's only begotten Son, Jesus Christ.

Therefore James, the brother of the LORD, writes that anyone who would be a friend of the world, is the enemy of GOD (see James 4:4). He concisely and unapologetically calls such friendship adultery. Children, the Holy Spirit of GOD inspired these men to scribe the thoughts and feelings of GOD, as well as the wrath to come.

And either I am inspired by the Holy Spirit to declare the thoughts and feelings of GOD, or you are wasting your time reading this book. GOD sees our surreptitious (and often-times overt) love of the world, and our pandering and kow-towing to the powers that be, (and our keeping silent about the LORD Jesus Christ), to fit in, and not draw undo atten-tion to ourselves. He sees our covetousness and our clutch-ing and our striving to have what the world has, its electronic toys, questionable amusements, and sordid entertainments.

GOD hears our silence where the witness of Jesus Christ ought to be. He sees our love for the world contending and supplanting where our love for Jesus Christ should be. He smells and tastes our perfunctory church ceremony and self-serving, self-congratulatory religious services.

The world commands our silence about Jesus Christ or they can/and will make our life circumstances difficult for us. These are the same evil spirits which compelled men to deny and spit upon Jesus Christ, that beat him and crucified him over 2,000 years ago. This world system still denies and spits upon him and despises him. And if I have allowed the world to push me into a corner and command my silence, then I am denying him also.

John the Beloved establishes what I call God's dynamic *con-tinuum*, a sometimes fluctuating and interdependent balance between the love of the world, and the love of the Father. Concisely, the love of the Father is his Son, Jesus Christ. Yes, Christian, GOD loves you, but he loves you in Christ Jesus, his

Son. I must be hidden (as it were) in Christ Jesus. I must have him, and he must have me. The Father will find me in Jesus Christ, his Son, or I am as lost as I ever was. I must lie down in Christ and rise up in Christ. To be alive in Christ, I must be dead to my own life, and dead to the lust of the flesh, and dead to the love of this world, and dead and dying to the pride of this life.

GOD is not going to collaborate or cohabitate with the same spirit that denied and crucified his Son. Our alliance, and even our friendship or wanton fraternization with the world, is enmity (or *mutual hostility*) with GOD (see James 4:4). We are spiritual beings, and GOD sees our partnership with the world as spiritual adultery. This is GOD's reality, and the only one that eternally matters.

The Word of GOD is the Reality of GOD, the comprehensive essence, and the absolute of GOD. If I am a friend of the world, I am an enemy of GOD (re. James 4:4). If I love the world, the love of the Father is not in me (re. 1 John 2:15). That is correct. This is the absolute unequivocal reality of the Word of GOD that I must face and accept. If I love the world, Jesus Christ (the love of the Father) is not in me.

It behooves each of us to submit ourselves to the Holy Spirit of the living Word of GOD, and beseech him to distinctly show us where we are spiritually on this *"continuum"* of the love of the world, and the love of the Father (Jesus Christ). In other words, how much are we *in the world* but *not of the world?*

Our natural tendency is to resist this revelation, this explicit reality of GOD. Concisely, it is severe. But from GOD's perspective, how should he react to the spirit that denied and spit upon his Son?

In another volume, I wrote, *"How much (natural) life I have left to lose, is the measure of Jesus Christ that I have left to gain."* While I have breath, this implacable, inescapable process, this miraculous phenomenon of me *"becoming"* a son of GOD, continues to occur. It is enough to make me marvel, just as it evidently astonished the man, Nicodemus.

✳

Marvel not that I said unto thee, Ye must be born again.
JOHN 3:7

✳

It has been my experience, that while I have breath, the nature of Adam, and the exceeding sinfulness of sin, is not totally dead or eradicated.

✳

But he that shall endure unto the end, the same shall be saved.
MATT. 24:13

✳

It has been my experience, that, the lust of the flesh, the love of the world, and the pride of life, are formidable foes. Concisely, this is my cross, what I sometimes call *"the season of my humanity."* The propensity and predilections of my flesh to compromise with lust were once notorious and daunting. Often, I have said that the lust of the flesh seems to be the last frontier for many men, if you follow. David and Solomon and Samson, to name a few. (And myself.)

Hence the exhortation of the Word of GOD to deny myself, and to take up my cross daily (see Luke 9:23). While I have breath, I comprehend and apprehend the gospel revelation of the sustenance and increase of a genuine faith as being a fight every time. However, for the preponderance of us, {and I include myself because this was my static (and stagnant) spiritual state for decades}, our radical transformation ceased as soon as we became comfortable in the corner of the pew.

The preponderance of us take our rest in spontaneous and immediate sainthood, or not long after we first make a profession of faith in Jesus Christ. We are not so much converted into the image of Christ, as we are confirmed (coerced and indoctrinated) into the religious ideology of our denominational brand. And then I (or we) go through the motions. The religious ceremony (yes, the church service), and perhaps a little altruistic volunteer service work, becomes the evidence of my Christianity. Remarkably, the only change our neighbor sees is our superficial religious affect.

The only thing that I have effectively *"died"* to are a couple of overt aberrant behaviors, or sometimes they are simply transformed into "covert" aberrant behaviors. My Christianity in short order becomes my self-righteous cloak that the real me hides behind. Alas, I become a Christian without a cross, and tragically, without a (viable, dynamic, radical) Christ in the center of my Christianity. Well? Someone has to say something.

Remarkably, and disturbingly, my death unto sin precedes my resurrection unto newness of life. (I am trying to make a point.) The trend of a superficial Christianity and an all-permissive grace is so alarming and so pervasive that I must interject sarcasm into the conversation.

GOD looks beyond my ceasing a couple of aberrant behaviors to a radical transformation of the heart and mind and a revolutionary character conversion. It necessitates the austere unapologetic preaching of the cross of Jesus Christ and him (and I) crucified.

❉

Knowing this, that our old man is crucified with
him, that the body of sin might be destroyed,
that henceforth we should not serve sin.
Rom. 6:6

❉

A genuine faith sees and accepts the necessity of the cross, progressively assimilates the austerity and self-denial, and then systematically apprehends the suffering association in the joyous anticipation of sharing the resurrection life and power of the LORD Jesus Christ.

The reality of the gospel makes the cross of Jesus Christ distinctly and inescapably mine. Contemporary mainstream Christianity, and all advocates and proponents of all-permissive grace, and all who vainly hope in the remission of sin (somehow) without the accountability of a genuine repentance of sin, need to read the fine print. Only dead men (and women) are raised to the newness of resurrection life.

The kingdom of GOD is formed within me in order to perpetuate the kingdom of GOD (through me) and out of me. It is my prayer and aspiration that the kingdom of GOD come, that his will be done in earth, as it is in heaven. My highest ambition and greatest objective is to be a gracious and effective host of GOD's presence, his Holy Spirit.

I have expressed this desire as wanting to be the edge upon his sword, to be on the front-line fighting, in the trenches. I want to be upon the cusp of the next revelation of GOD, to live by the violence of my faith upon (what I call) the edge of trespass. To push the envelope, we used to call it.

My greatest joy is to see the prophetic unfolding of the Word of GOD, to watch (and experience) the power of the resurrection life within the Word of GOD miraculously transform not only my own life, but the next person's life. To experience the miracle of the resurrection life of the LORD Jesus Christ, I must first be One with the sacrifice upon the altar by an astute suffering association, coalesced with Christ into his death.

Christian, ultimately (and resolutely) GOD wants to restore you to the place of fellowship and authority from which Adam fell. He wants to make you his king and priest in the earth. You are the earthen vessel of a heavenly treasure, a host and a custodian (if you will) of the excellency of his presence, and a facilitator of his power.

Christian, you and I, and every one of us, must submit (acquiesce, absolutely surrender) to the transformation, and totally yield ourselves to his surrogate death – a holy fire. We must take up our cross in the revelation and in the context, in the continuity and the outreach of the love of GOD for our neighbor's soul. This is how the kingdom of GOD is perpetuated: by our becoming One with the sacrifice, incorporated into the love of GOD. It is not our portion to sit silent and dumbfounded or complacent in the corner of the pew.

✳

But ye are a chosen generation, a royal priesthood,
an holy nation, a peculiar people; that ye should
shew forth the praises of him who hath called you
out of darkness into his marvelous light.
1 PET. 2:9

✳

This world commands (and expects) my silence about the LORD Jesus Christ. Under the guise of being intolerant, I am indicted and condemned for calling sin, sin. If so be, that the Word of GOD is in me, it (He) shall speak. And it shall not be otherwise. Moreover, my personal awe and wonder as the object of a radical transformation must be expressed. I must tell someone about my miracle.

The inimitable process of my character conversion ensues with my purposeful capitulation to the cross of Jesus Christ. I allow his death to have its way with me (if you will, or if I can put it like that), so that I can have (share) his resurrection life and glory.

✳

For if we have been planted together in the likeness of his
death, we shall be also in the likeness of his resurrection.
ROM. 6:5

✳

The Master taught us how to die to the lust of the flesh and the pride of this life, and he taught us how to live. He was manifestly the meek and lowly Son of man, but he was never a victim of circumstance or taken by surprise. And with his resurrection life and power residing in the temple of my spirit man, neither am I a casualty of circumstance or a helpless victim of sin.

Before we metaphorically follow the LORD Jesus Christ into the Garden of Gethsemane, the Holy Spirit wants us to place ourselves figuratively in the Upper Room, after the supper had ended. John makes a distinct point in his narrative that the LORD Jesus Christ was acutely aware of who he was in GOD (and as GOD), and ever conscious of what he had come to do.

✳

Jesus knowing that the Father had given all things
into his hands, and that he was come from GOD, and
went to GOD. He riseth from supper, and laid aside
his garments; and took a towel and girded himself.
JOHN 13:3-4

✳

The Master taught us how to die to the pride of this life that we might apprehend the enigmatic power that comes with a complete surrender to GOD's perfect will. Jesus Christ is our exemplar of obedience and sanctification and holiness unto GOD, our brother in affliction, the forerunner of our own acute suffering fellowship and conformity unto the death of his cross. He shows us how to live and die, as it were, (and if you follow).

The Word of GOD according to John says here *"that the Father had given all things into his hands"* (into Jesus' hands) (see John 13:3), yet he both literally and figuratively *"laid aside his garments"* (see vs. 4).

Just who was (and is) this foot-washer depicted by the Word of GOD in the thirteenth chapter of John? We must address the deity of the LORD Jesus Christ. John the Beloved, here in our present text, references or contrasts the LORD's deity with his profound humility and meekness of character.

The following is (relatively) a lengthy scripture quotation, but we may be better served if I go ahead and list it in its entirety. You know, just get it out there. The very nature of the text exacerbates its own enormity, if I may put it like that. Actually, and as we shall see, it is only six scriptures, yet it manifests as much, much larger.

The Apostle Paul is writing in general to the saints and the faithful everywhere, but to the Colossians specifically. In my opinion, only John 1:1 rivals the following scriptures for the most explicit expression of the deity and preeminence of the LORD Jesus Christ in the entire Word of GOD. Let us keep in mind that the Apostle Paul is describing whom he first met on the road to Damascus one appointed day.

❋

*In whom we have redemption through his
blood, even the forgiveness of sins.*

*Who is the image of the invisible GOD, the
firstborn of every creature.*

*For by him were all things created, that are in heaven,
and that are in earth, visible and invisible, whether
they be thrones, or dominions, or principalities, or
powers: all things were created by him, and for him.*

And he is before all things, and by him all things consist.

*And he is the head of the body, the church: who is
the beginning, the firstborn from the dead; that in
all things he might have the preeminence.*

For it pleased the Father that in him should all fullness dwell.
COL. 1:14-19

✳

This is comprehensive, exhaustive, absolute. This is the "GOD-man". This is Jesus, the Christ of GOD. This is Alpha and Omega, the Almighty GOD.

On the Road to Damascus, Saul of Tarsus was favored (and subjected) to see (what I call) a glimpse of the LORD Jesus Christ. Just a glimpse, and he did not see another thing with his physical eyes for three days. But every time I consider this radical conversion of Saul of Tarsus, I ponder what mysteries and wonders he may have seen with his spiritual eyes.

Saul of Tarsus glimpsed what I have called the *reality* of GOD. He received just a peek of the "real" person of the LORD Jesus Christ. He would later tell King Agrippa that he saw a light from heaven *"above the brightness of the sun"* (see Acts 26:13). Saul heard a voice speaking unto him in the Hebrew tongue, and in response he asked, *"Who art thou, Lord?"* And the LORD said, *"I AM Jesus, whom thou persecutest"* (see Acts 26:15).

It was the Son of man who the disciples saw and heard in the upper room, preparing to wash their feet; it was the Son of GOD whom Saul of Tarsus glimpsed on the Road to Damascus. Yet he is One and the same, the Almighty GOD. This is who laid aside the glory he shared with the Father before the world began and made himself of no reputation. He took upon himself the form of a servant and was found in fashion as a man. He humbled himself and became obedient unto death, even to the death of the cross (see Phil. 2:7-8).

Oh my. We get but a glimpse of this washer of fishermen's feet. This is the Almighty GOD, laying aside his garments, and girding himself with a towel. This is Alpha and Omega, the Creator of the heavens and the earth, becoming the volitional and obedient servant of humanity. Frankly, it is beyond finite comprehension. Through a glass darkly we glimpse this glory.

How to intellectually and operationally grasp the impossibility of GOD washing the same feet he created? While we Christians vie and contend for who is going to be the greatest in the kingdom of GOD, a most solemn and pivotal teaching moment predominantly passes us by.

✳

What I do thou knowest not now; but
thou shalt know hereafter.
re. JOHN 13:7

＊

How to accurately conceptualize that GOD has willingly laid aside his glory to become the servant of man, I cannot find. Notably, not even washing our feet is sufficient obeisance and love to make us understand that there is nothing GOD would not do to redeem man. He died to give us life, and still many of us will not receive it.

Many of us are much too wise and self-sufficient, too accomplished, too mature to receive the gift of life like a little child. We must find some way to finagle the commendation and praise for having pulled ourselves up by our proverbial bootstraps. We clutch and misappropriate GOD's grace as if it were our due. Many of us do not rightfully esteem the breath in our lungs.

＊

The wicked, through the pride of his countenance, will not seek after GOD: GOD is not in all his thoughts.
Ps. 10:4

＊

By him and *for* him (that is, the LORD Jesus Christ), were all things created (re. Col. 1:16), and many of us do not give him the time of day, as it were. The Potter deserves the honor of the clay; the creature ought to praise and worship the Creator. Too many of us call ourselves by the name of Christ, and so few of us abnegate (or relinquish) the throne to allow him to rule.

How to reconcile (and assimilate) that this washer of fisherman's feet is the Almighty GOD, the Creator of the universe?

Frankly, I must first confess my finite cognitive inadequacy and dearth. Uh, my ignorance. My mental retardation concerning things spiritual. (I am not trying to sound scholarly; I am trying to get honest.)

Are we hearing what this washer of fisherman's feet is saying by unprecedented illustration?

＊

For I have given you an example, that ye
should do as I have done to you.
JOHN 13:15

＊

First things first, as they say. Before the LORD Jesus Christ imparts his resurrection life unto us and teaches us how to apprehend and live the abundant life, he first teaches us to die unto pride and notoriety. Ah, the Master shows us how to acquiesce to humility, and how to mortify pride and reputation.

Jesus Christ redirects my love and worship of GOD back into the service of humanity and teaches me how to wash feet. Before he gives me life, he teaches me how to die.

＊

Marvel not that I said unto thee, Ye must be born again,
JOHN 3:7

＊

Christian, ought we not live this life in the acknowledgement and acute consciousness and honor of him whom has given us the breath of life? I mean, do we not call ourselves by his holy name?

The hands that washed these fisherman's feet took up an old rugged cross for the worst of humanity. They forever have nail prints in them. What more could he have done to demonstrate his love, than to wash my feet, and take my place upon that cross? Plainly, this is not enough for many to aspire to believe, but that recklessly and impudently persist living unto themselves.

✳

A son honoureth his father, and a servant his master:
if then I be a father, where is mine honour? and
if I be a master, where is my fear? saith the LORD of
hosts unto you, O priests, that despise my name. And
ye say, Wherein have we despised thy name?
MAL. 1:6

✳

The repentance must not be cursory or perfunctory, it must be genuine. The honor and the worship must not be a self-affirming, self-sustaining presentation, but it must be in Spirit and in truth. The life upon the altar as my offering unto GOD must not be a superficial religious form, but the living sacrifice of a dynamic faith.

Before I can functionally tap into the power of the resurrection life of the LORD Jesus Christ, as it were, or partake of such miraculous greater grace and divine favor, I must first be an obeisant and reverent metaphorical washer of feet. I must be dead to striving for superiority and position, spiritually insensate or indifferent to either the honor or the defamation of other men.

When I present before the LORD a worship (and a lifestyle) initiated or founded upon a surface or external religious observance, but my heart and soul are not engaged or espoused unto Christ, GOD calls it (by the prophet Malachi) *"offering polluted bread upon the altar"* (see Mal. 1:7).

GOD's grievance is first directed at the priests, and then at the assembly or congregants, for bringing less than their best as an offering unto him who gives us life and breath. The priests [*prophetically* – preachers] who should have been setting the example, were offering diseased or defective animals upon the altar. And then they were allowing the congregation of GOD's people to do the same.

※

And if ye offer the blind for sacrifice, is it not evil? and
if ye offer the lame and the sick, is it not evil? offer it
now unto thy governor, will he be pleased with thee,
or accept thy person? saith the LORD of hosts.
MAL. 1:8

※

Concisely, this prophetically corresponds to my essentially saving my life for myself, and just going through the motions of being a Christian. Someone has to say it. When my love for the world, and the things of the world, displaces or supersedes my fidelity to GOD, I subsequently and consequently end up offering him leftovers, a superficial religious ceremony from which my heart is disengaged, and the best of my consciousness elsewhere.

GOD knows when I skim off the top and deal off the bottom. He knows when I delegate a harried fifteen minutes for Bible study and a five-minute fleeting dispassionate prayer. The reality at the end of another fateful day is that I have fundamentally lived unto myself. If I earnestly seek after GOD, it most often is out of desperation, and as a last resort. If I have waited upon GOD, it is most often because he has sat me down and made me to wait. GOD knows that I have better, but that I have spent it upon myself.

✻

> *But cursed be the deceiver, which hath in his flock a male, and voweth, and sacrificeth unto the LORD a corrupt thing: for I am a great King, saith the LORD of hosts, and my name is dreadful among the heathen.*
> MAL. 1:14

✻

That which I covet and clutch and conserve exclusively for myself has a curse upon it. The life lived entirely for my own pleasure and gratification shall not ultimately prosper me. What I am not willing to give effectively owns me – I move from proprietor to prisoner.

The Word of GOD is not specifically referencing money here, but GOD knows exactly how much I have given, and I am most likely acutely and painfully aware of it, also. No matter how you divide its interpretation, the prophetic implications for contemporary worship and giving are the same:

GOD reckons my net worth in both time and money, and the breath in my lungs, as well.

How much it hurts and distresses me to give is a pretty accurate measure of how profoundly I am bound. How desperately that I cling to earthen treasure is a good indication of how little heavenly treasure that I have laid up. Frankly, it is dead or disassociated from the love and pleasures of the things of this world, and the demands of this temporal life, that I may best experience the resurrection life of the LORD Jesus Christ. GOD is trying to set me free. The Apostle Paul addresses the process.

✳

Set your affection on things above, not on things on the earth. For ye are dead, and your life is hid with Christ in GOD.
COL. 3:2-3

✳

Jesus Christ gave us the preeminent example of a life lived in obedience and reverence to GOD by spending (or giving) his life in the service of humanity. The pride of this life, and/or the covetousness and love of this world, cannot master me if I am figuratively girded with a towel, and busy washing the feet of humanity. Jesus teaches me how to die.

What I can give away without regret has no hold upon me; what I can give with joy, I am the master of. It becomes a matter of honor to express my love for GOD with the very best of my flock, as it were. Nothing (of my life) is exempt from the altar.

What Bible scholars refer to as the *Upper Room Discourse* begins in the thirteenth chapter of John with Jesus washing the disciple's feet and culminates with his high priestly (intercessory) prayer in the seventeenth chapter. And then the eighteenth chapter begins with him retiring to the Garden of Gethsemane to pray even more.

❋

When Jesus had spoken these words, he went forth
with his disciples over the brook Cedron, where was a
garden, into the which he entered, and his disciples.
JOHN 18:1

❋

If I will follow him, Jesus Christ will explicitly demonstrate this radical comprehensive gospel process of losing the life to find it. The LORD Jesus Christ did not go directly to heaven from the upper room. It is only as I follow him that I learn to die, so that I might also experience his resurrection life, and this marvel of being born again.

This has been my mandate to write, and the principle impetus of these books born out of my personal Bible study. And that is, (predominantly) contemporary Christianity's, and organized mainstream religion's, desperate tendency to circumvent this irrepressible process of a metaphorical (but no less real) death to the pride of our life. We figuratively and wistfully (and fantastically) go directly to sitting together with Jesus Christ in heavenly places, while fundamentally saving our natural lives for ourselves.

Frankly, bending and kneeling to wash the feet of an ungrateful and irascible humanity ruins the crease in our trousers. It causes our self-righteous cloak to slip and our spiritual and religious elitism to show. Uh, you know. Everything I have not died to must be cleverly concealed: my pride and ethnic prejudices, my feelings of societal and spiritual superiority. It all necessitates a complex religious form to emulate the forward momentum and radical transformation of a genuine faith. *Real* faith, you see, commands a real conversion. Uh, oh my, the marvel of being born again.

For decades, I was a patron (and effectively a prisoner) of outward religious observation. I reference these decades of religious stasis frequently. These were the years that my salvation and my structured Christianity were primarily founded upon (and dependent upon) an irregular church attendance and sporadic service work. You know, religious ceremony. If I may speak in the figurative (and the prophetic), I was indirectly and surreptitiously taught to cleverly (and cunningly) circumvent the suffering fellowship of Gethsemane, Pilate's Hall, and Calvary.

I started out just as sincere as the next Christian. You know, a babe in Christ. It was mainly older (and supposedly more mature) Christians who taught me the principles of Christianity. It was not until many years later that I realized that, primarily, what I was being taught was a religious form that imitated a genuine faith and avoided the suffering association of the cross of Jesus Christ and him crucified. Yes, Jesus died, but we (the righteous congregation) escaped with our carnal lives relatively intact.

We then perpetuate the species. Only in retrospect did I realize that sometimes it is from the preacher on down or starting with the head and spreading (relatively) throughout the body. Often, I have referred to us (you know, the solemn assembly) as the saints of the status quo, silently colluded on how much ceremony and service work will adequately sustain our, uh, external Christian affect. Formal contemporary mainstream Christianity: How to be saved and not have a cross or have to die.

There are, of course, variations of the general genre, uh, denominational (or familial) tweaking. You know, this is how we do it here. But for the most part, the congregation (or conglomeration) covertly concur (or collude) on how much formal ceremony will salve our corporate conscience and reputably sustain our Christianity.

Some of us still called it being born again, or at least occasionally referenced the phenomenon, but nobody was really dying. A sort of silent standard was set. Most bizarre observable behaviors were discontinued. What could not be stopped must be hidden. Any cynical exaggeration is interjected to emphasize a point.

The point is: there is a marked difference between gong to church or sustaining a ceremonial Christianity, and the radical character conversion of being born again. The difference is, frankly, one of life and death. The authentic resurrection life of the LORD Jesus Christ can be recognized by its radical evangelical outreach – the expression and continuity of the love of GOD as evidenced in the cross of Jesus Christ; Christians, progressively laying down their lives for their friend.

The resurrection life and power of the LORD Jesus Christ is the indubitable fruit of suffering fellowship and conformity to the death of his cross. The love of GOD in Jesus Christ is received and then disseminated and cannot be effectively emulated by religious form or ceremony. I must die to have it. Otherwise, I must vainly attempt to imitate it by religious exercise.

An indispensable element of this gospel process of losing the life to find it is my associative (confederate) Garden of Gethsemane experience (and encounter).

*

*Then cometh Jesus with them unto a place called
Gethsemane, and saith unto his disciples, Sit
ye here, while I go and pray yonder*
MATT. 26:36

*

To be painstakingly honest, I had been adhering to outward religious observation for decades. Going through the motions. Christianity was something I did, and not necessarily who I was. Although I had not relatively (and/or realistically) followed Jesus Christ very far, I still arrogantly (and self-righteously) presumed myself to sit together with him in heavenly places. This is what I had been taught. Until one day, I heard the Master specifically and personally say, *"Follow me."*

GOD began to open my understanding of the scriptures. I had begun to listen with godly intent and earnest, righteous purpose. *"And unto you that hear shall more be given"* (re. Mark 4:24). Frankly, I began to comprehend that this resurrection life of the LORD Jesus Christ was the life that few find, that it is, indeed, through a strait gate and upon a narrow way, just as the LORD said, (re. Matt. 7:13-14). Moreover, (I began to realize) that the wide gate which leads to destruction may well include religious ritual and complacency without a radical internal conversion.

The yearning and urgency of my soul was no longer appeased with the minimal and the nominal. I began to fall in love with the LORD Jesus Christ, and this radical, militant, selfless love was compelling me to become a disciple.

And then I began to look around me at the righteous congregation, at whom I would later (unapologetically) refer to as the *Holy Brethren* and the *Sisters of Sanctity*. We rehearsed the same old denominational tenets and vague religious principles that made us uniquely peculiar and singularly correct, and therefore (better than) all the other multifarious denominational flavors on the, uh, spiritual market, or rainbow.

Watching and listening to other mature Christians, you know, the best, primarily Sunday school teachers and preachers, and the deacons, I learned to effectively hide the aberrant behaviors and irascible personality characteristics that I should have (and would have) been empowered to mortify if I had continued following the LORD Jesus Christ. Frankly, none of us were going anywhere, literally or figuratively, and certainly not spiritually. We sat anesthetized and apathetic in the same pew and tonelessly and listlessly sang the same old songs, supposedly waiting for Jesus to come back and rapture us.

The general congregation that I envisage is a model comprised of bits and pieces of roughly six decades exposure to ordinary mainstream Christians. I reference the median assembly of the best and worst of us. We have (relatively) done no better than the proponents of Judaism who conspired with the Romans to crucify Jesus Christ. Though they were the custodians and the wardens of the Word of GOD, they had not given that Word of GOD uninhibited access to their hearts and minds to radically convert their characters. Much of our religion has not fundamentally changed us, either. Not to the extent we can accurately call ourselves *born again.* Please.

Had we continued in GOD's Word (and followed Jesus Christ far enough) we would have learned to die unto the pride of this life and the love of this world and the lust of our flesh. We would also be dead to the elitist religious opinions we (not so secretly) harbor of ourselves, the inflated estimation of our own righteousness. We would be dead unto sin and immune to the allure of the latest model smart phone, alive unto GOD in Christ. We would have a viable, prospering testimony of the resurrection life and power of the LORD Jesus Christ.

✳

If ye continue in my word, then are ye my disciples indeed. And ye shall know the truth, and the truth shall make you free.
re. JOHN 8:31-32

✳

My religious teachers and preachers insisted that I was born again, that I was a new creature in Christ Jesus, that old thing had passed away and that all things were made new. I thought there was something profoundly wrong with me. And so, this is how I was silently taught to cleverly conceal all the character eccentricities and bad attitudes (and not a little sin) that I had not effectively died to. Duh. For decades, I thought I was the only poser in the righteous congregation.

Ah, but if my death to sin and self and world-love was fundamentally illusory, then it was no wonder that I had to emulate and effect having the resurrection power of Jesus Christ over sin. My religious form and righteous posturing became a vicious self-sustaining, self-memorializing, religious ceremony, always propping the illusion up. This is how hypocrites are made. As I say, we perpetuate the species.

This cyclical religious form began to dissolve as the Holy Spirit incited me to desire becoming a genuine disciple of the LORD Jesus Christ. The turning point for me began with a forthright confession of my inability to love; my total ineptitude to love either my neighbor or myself. This had subsequently and consequently evolved from my not functionally knowing or loving GOD. Or, at least not with what I considered all my heart and soul and mind.

The Holy Spirit led me into (what I call) my correlative Garden of Gethsemane experience. The word *Gethsemane* is derived from the Aramaic, and essentially means *olive press.* I have written that this is where the oil of anointing for evangelical outreach is won, and that this is where a great King "takes" his oil. After the crushing, as it were.

Initially, I believe that all eleven original disciples entered the garden with Jesus, and perhaps many more, as was often the case. Jesus then took his inner circle further into the garden.

✳

*And he took with him Peter and the two sons of Zebedee,
and began to be sorrowful and very heavy. Then saith
he unto them, My soul is exceeding sorrowful, even
unto death: tarry ye here, and watch with me.*
re. Matt. 26:37-38

✳

Until I metaphorically entered into the suffering fellowship of the LORD Jesus Christ in the Garden of Gethsemane, I essentially had a theoretical salvation and a linear (one dimensional) religious ideology of GOD. That is, I had no practical or realistic concept of the gospel principle of losing the life to find it, or of being conformed to the death (of the cross) of Jesus Christ. Intercessory prayer was a foreign hypothesis to me, I could barely pray for myself.

Until, by an acute suffering association, I found myself kneeling (and then prostrate) in that lonely garden, I had a speculative, academic, abstract Jesus. Until I began to repeatedly resort there, disenchanted by the shallow allure of the world, cynical and discouraged by organized perfunctory religious ceremony and service, looking for something real – desperate for definitive change.

Until I began to tarry in that dismal garden with Jehovah's suffering servant, I did not effectually know Jesus Christ. It was a dreadful and pressing suffering association that made him mine.

It was in this melancholy and disconsolate garden that I first saw the Savior; and where I first saw the love of GOD wrestling with the wages of (my) sin. Here is where he first taught me to die to what I would rather do. Here I learned to keep my body and my desires subjected to the will of GOD. Here I first saw the life surrendered to find it, and the Savior of the world on his face.

✳

And he went a little farther, and fell on his face, and prayed saying, O my Father, if it be possible, let this cup pass from me: nevertheless not as I will, but as thou wilt.
MATT. 26:39

✳

It was in this dreadful garden, as I watched the Son of GOD accede to the death of the cross, that I first realized that his cross is my cross, as well. By sharing this acute suffering fellowship my own will is surrendered to the Father. Metaphorically (if you will), I found myself upon my face in the midnight of my soul, wrestling with the seemingly immortal inclinations of sin and my own obdurate will.

Jesus Christ was teaching me how to die. In a fateful and execrable hour, and in a figurative (and personally appointed) corresponding Garden of Gethsemane experience, I first functionally apprehended the command, *"Follow me."*

It was through my own sweat and tears that I first glimpsed the reality and intimacy of my own cross. Only by the acute suffering association of the cross of Jesus Christ can I apprehend the marvel (and the miracle) of being born again. Dying, I first saw it. Grieving for the loss of my life, I first glimpsed it by great grace and suffering fellowship.

This was not *"feel good about me, ain't I pretty"* mainstream contemporary Christianity; this was the down and dirty ardent fighting of devils in the trenches of being born again. This was (and is) the blood, sweat, and tears of a radical and irrepressible transformation. This is the reality and the phenomenon of losing the life to find it, that I must first die to apprehend and share the resurrection life and power of the LORD Jesus Christ.

My own propensity to ignore or evade this process is prophetically foreshadowed by the original disciples of Jesus Christ.

✳

And he cometh unto the disciples, and findeth them asleep, and saith unto Peter, What, could ye not watch with me one hour?
MATT. 26:40

✳

It was a momentous (and propitious) day, when the LORD Jesus Christ opened my understanding of the holy scriptures and their prophetic, living nature, and caused me to operatively grasp that the comprehensive Word of GOD applies to me. That is, every Word that proceeds out of the mouth of GOD is mine, as I make it mine. The Word of GOD is here, and it is *now,* applicable to the immediate context of my every circumstance.

The Word of GOD came to me as I was enmeshed and anesthetized in the morass and misdirection of ceremonial ritualistic religion, figuratively and prophetically asleep in the corner of the pew.

Jesus Christ died to his own will and acceded to bear the wages of my sin, and I was volitionally asleep to the prophetic commands and expectations of my own death to self and to sin, and to the pride of life and the love of the world.

It is amazing what lengths the righteous assembly will go to circumvent the suffering fellowship of the LORD Jesus Christ, and to skirt the pressing conformity to the death of his cross. We allow religious form to lull us into complacency. We put our trust in ceremony and service and check our righteousness in the cloudy reflection of one another.

We are the self-affirming assembly, confident in the honor one of another. We have fundamentally found a way (and a formula) to enable us to save our lives for ourselves, and be born again, too. Of course, we must feign to possess the resurrection life and power of the LORD Jesus Christ because we have not comprehensively died to have the reality.

The LORD's indictment of the apostles sleeping when they should have been praying is gravely and markedly and prophetically made mine. The Holy Spirit of the living Word of GOD found me impervious and inanimate (uh, lukewarm and apathetic) in the quagmire and dead end of denominational elitism and organized religious bigotry. The death of Jesus Christ set me free from religious form, and having followed him into death, he raised me to newness of life, and the reality of being born again.

Honestly? When the Word of GOD reached me and unsparingly shook me awake, I was spiritually immobilized, trusting primarily in church attendance to call myself a Christian with a minimally satisfied (or salved) formal religious conscience. Honestly? I was naturally alive and spiritually dead. My pious claims of resurrection life and power were repudiated and invalidated by my never having died to my own will and worldly pleasures in the first place.

In fact, it is scripturally incorrect (and impossible), and the height of arrogance and presumption, to posture and pontificate as possessing the resurrection life and power of the LORD Jesus Christ without having first emphatically died to my natural life and my love for the world.

Not being able to watch with the LORD one hour, or to pray for (at least) an hour, is the epitome and definition of a lukewarm spiritual state. It is the prophetic reality of my being asleep and insensate and immobilized in religious stasis in the corner of the pew. The peril of contemporary Christianity parallels my redundancy.

To speak comprehensively of the resurrection life of the LORD Jesus Christ, we must first logically address the death we are desperate and clamoring not to die, the cross we are frantic not to take up. It is out of the heart and mind of the LORD Jesus Christ, and as a friend of the Bridegroom (if you can receive it), that I have written extensively about our contemporary aberration of Christianity without a viable and qualifiable Christ in the center of our Christian testimony.

GOD is looking for the metamorphosis of a distinct character conversion which begins with a genuine repentance, and not ostentatious religious ceremony and pious posturing. Frankly, the Father is seeking someone to spend some significant quality time watching and praying, and living and dying, with the LORD Jesus Christ. The Father is seeking someone to get brutally honest about themselves and their abject spiritual poverty, and to draw nigh in spirit and in truth.

It has been my experience that this correlative Garden of Gethsemane encounter is interminable, my following is endless. The crushing is excruciatingly eternal, the being poured out unceasing. Children, the cup of suffering association is bottomless, endless dregs, the bitter dynamic of a perpetual death (and) the incessant mortification of pride.

＊

*Watch and pray, that ye enter not into temptation:
the spirit indeed is willing, but the flesh is weak.*
MATT. 26:41

＊

It was in this dreadful garden that Jesus Christ first tasted the imminent wages of my sin. (Let us make it personal.) Outside the constraints and commands of time, I tarry with him there, given place in the sovereign annals of Alpha and Omega.

In watching and in prayer, the lust of this life and the love of the world are mortified. What I would rather do is bound with cords to the horns of the altar, it is here my will is sanctified and assimilated into the LORD's own. It was in this figurative garden in the silence of suffering association that my will was subdued and coalesced with the cross of Jesus Christ, and the intimacy of his impending death was first made mine.

There is no audience here in the midnight terror of the truth of it, that GOD desires my (absolute) all. It is in this glorious garden that the greater graces are won, and the lust of the flesh confounded. Here, I accede to die.

Here, I am made a living sacrifice, here in the secret place of the Father, the covenant of death and life is made.

Here, in the shadow of Calvary, contemporary Christianity cunningly circumvents the crushing, and sleeps for sorrow. If I have not consented to the cross here, in my metaphorical Garden of Gethsemane experience, then in the forthcoming trial of public opinion, I will contend and dissimulate and desperately strive to save my life for myself.

It is in the secret place of the Father that I accede to die, and here I am strengthened to conquer the temptation to come. All things are made mine in Christ: betrayal, spittle, thorns, wounding, piercing crucifixion.

It is in the watching and the praying that the drama of the life lost to find it is played out, and the death of it decidedly not pretty. In the crushing death throes of a covenant transaction, I learn to pray, and to take up a cup and a cross.

※

And being in an agony he prayed more earnestly: and his sweat was as it were great drops of blood falling down to the ground.
LUKE 22:44

※

This is no casual undertaking; these are the commands of covenant love. This is not the perfunctory prayer of posers and religious pretenders; this is an appointed place for a priest and a king.

The true disciples of Jesus Christ come here with a single eye and sanctified purpose. There is no keeping of time here in the secret place of the Ancient of Days.

This is an appointed place of critical, urgent preparation; a place of pouring out, of utter crushing and total emptiness. At the end of myself is my value to GOD. The Father is seeking such.

Some of us only thought that we wanted to learn how to pray, many of us give this Garden a great latitude. Here, a few of us are taught to host heavenly treasure.

He who hosts the resurrection life of the LORD Jesus Christ shall also share his sorrows. Suffering fellowship is an all-consuming Baptism of fire, and a cup of trembling besides. The loyal and vocal witness of the resurrection life of the LORD Jesus Christ has no individual will or personal aspiration. Out of the burning they rise, out of the crushing they come, the anointed of GOD.

It is a Holy Fire that transitions my faith into trust, and that graciously converts my irascible and imperious character to host an unimpeachable testimony. The Master fashions and tries his own tools. The GOD of anointed orchestrated circumstance hones the edge upon his own sword.

*

And the LORD said, Simon, Simon, behold, Satan hath
desired to have you, that he may sift you as wheat.
But I have prayed for thee, that thy faith fail not: and
when thou art converted, strengthen thy brethren.
LUKE 22:31-32

*

One might presume that the Apostle Peter was singled out for public infamy and disgrace, but his humiliation was ultimately revealed to be an usher and harbinger of honor.

✳

Humble yourselves therefore under the mighty hand of GOD, that he may exalt you in due time.
1 PET. 5:6

✳

The figurative death of pride and misdirected self-confidence occurs well before the literal loss of one's life. But both shall glorify GOD (see John 21:19). If we will search the scriptures (and read between the lines), we will see that our natural death to lust and pride is the direct result of the command, *"Follow me."*

Christian, I cannot speak for you, but it is given unto me by the acute agony of greater grace to follow the LORD Jesus Christ to Gethsemane, Pilate's Hall, and then Calvary. He who has ears to hear, let him hear. In the Spirit, I have been there many times. As often as the Spirit leads and the LORD deems necessary, I go there again and again in the season of my humanity, and in the perfecting of faith, even as often as love commands.

Each new day comes with its own certain dross and detritus, its own specific sediment and leavings; you know, scat. This world system is enterprising and innovative in its noxious methodology to cling to Christians. It is a holy flame that resourcefully and masterfully searches out my wood, hay, and stubble, seeking the pure gold of an undefiled faith.

Each new day, fellow pilgrim, we take up our cross afresh. Even as a few have learned, that without the suffering fellowship and conformity to the LORD's death, there will be no glory of resurrection life. Anything less than the whole animal for a living sacrifice, is religious form and self-veneration, vanity and presumption. Oh my.

Not many seem to require the absolute crushing that the Apostle Peter sustained, the infamy and humiliation of vocally denying the LORD Jesus three times in quick succession, and in a public forum. Indicted and convicted by a rooster, and a servant girl.

Indeed. The preponderance of mainstream contemporary Christianity's denial of Jesus Christ in the public arena is much more subtle and surreptitious, if you will. We avoid (and cleverly circumvent) direct confrontation of our faith. Very few of us take the initiative, or the deliberate offensive, of an overt, vocal public testimony. Alas, to have a viable witness of the resurrection life of the LORD Jesus Christ in my mouth, the witness must first be abiding in my heart. I must have first died. To be able to bear testimony of the resurrection life of Christ, I must have first personally experienced the dynamic of dying to self and to sin and to pride, and that of having been raised to newness of life.

If more of us comprehended how that this world system cunningly and methodically orchestrates adverse circumstances eliciting and coercing the Christian's covert denial of Jesus Christ, we would weep as bitterly at the revelation as did the Apostle Peter (see Luke 22:62). Most of us deny Christ by our silence. Our silence is a compromise, a token and a sign of our friendship, and our collusion with the same spirit of this world system that originally coerced the Jews and the Romans to crucify Jesus Christ.

Someone must say something. Our silence must be confronted and defined. A true Christian disciple of Jesus Christ has a genuine faith. A genuine faith is the dynamic of the LORD's salvation, and we may say that the LORD's grace is the catalyst, or impetus. A genuine faith is self-perpetuating. It is the dynamic force in the outreach and continuity of GOD's love for the world in Christ Jesus. It is the evidence and the substance of it. It is a vocal witness and a visible testimony of the love of GOD in Jesus Christ.

A genuine faith (and a genuine disciple) of the resurrection life of the LORD Jesus Christ has both a vocal and a (marked) behavioral witness of having been raised to newness of life. The very same Spirit that raised Jesus Christ from the dead has also raised them, and he will not be silent, and cannot be suppressed. Where the Spirit of the LORD is, there is liberty and power (re. 2 Cor. 3:17). The Spirit of resurrection and life within the genuine disciple of Jesus Christ is tactile and demonstrative in the neighborhood, and in the marketplace, and in the workplace.

*

Now if any man have not the Spirit of Christ, he is none of his.
re. ROM. 8:9

*

A candid (unbiased) daily self-assessment is an essential spiritual discipline. Frankly, the preacher should not have to repeatedly admonish and instruct me to live a sanctified, holy lifestyle. Distinctly, if the resurrection life of the LORD Jesus Christ is in me, he can no more be bound or suppressed than death, hell, and the grave could bind him. A genuine faith will not be silent in the face of testing or adversity in the public arena.

✴

Examine yourselves, whether ye be in the faith; *prove your own selves. Know ye not your own selves, how that Jesus Christ is in you, except ye be reprobates?*
2 Cor. 13:5

✴

Concisely, the catalytic, dynamic difference between the dreadful day when Peter denied he knew Jesus three times, and his powerful, electric preaching on the Day of Pentecost, is a direct consequence and outcome of his radical character conversion. The Apostle Peter passed through the bitter weeping of the midnight of the soul, the crushing of pride and self-confidence, and the excruciating loss of his natural life, to enter into the resurrection life and power of the LORD Jesus Christ. He would never be the same.

After the crushing press, and after being specifically targeted and sifted by Satan, he was personally restored to place by the LORD Jesus Christ. It was after his absolute (and dreadful) conversion that he was empowered to strengthen his brethren.

GOD revolutionarily and deliberately sharpens his own tools, purposely separates his Apostles and disciples from pride and misguided self-confidence. He severs his prophets and priests from dependence and allegiance to this world system, and oftentimes must deliver them from mainstream religious orthodoxy to make them intercessors. They pointedly do not preach all-permissive grace; they purpose to know no other gospel except Jesus Christ and him crucified.

It behooves (every believer) to evaluate our own dependency upon the goods and services (and the amusements and entertainments) of this world system, to assess our own allegiance to the LORD Jesus Christ, to measure the level of our own faith, and the degree of our personal sanctification.

✳

For if we would judge ourselves, we should not be judged.
But when we are judged, we are chastened of the LORD,
that we should not be condemned with the world.
1 COR. 11:31-32

✳

(I have found) that if I really want to know, then the Holy Spirit of the living Word of GOD will graciously, and as gently as my attitude will allow, show me everything I need to know. We have covered this. The same grace of GOD, the same goodness of GOD that leads me to repentance (re. Rom. 2:4), the same grace that saves my soul, also teaches me how to live *"soberly, righteously, and godly in this present world"* (see Titus 2:11-12).

When I read the Word of GOD with godly intent, it releases its revelatory power to enable me to apply its precepts to my thoughts and behaviors, and to ultimately and irrepressibly convert my character. If I will not resist the recommendations and ministrations of the Holy Spirit, he will graciously teach me how to assimilate them unto a practical spiritual application.

First, I must objectively and honestly accede to everything he shows me. (I have found) that it is natural (and acceptable) to ask questions, but what the Holy Spirit confirms in me is not open to debate or argument, or to denial. It is the Holy Spirit of the living Word of GOD who rightly divides the Word of GOD; it is by grace that I am along for the ride, as it were.

✳

And it is the Spirit that beareth witness,
because the Spirit is Truth.
re. 1 JOHN 5:6

✳

It is the Holy Spirit of GOD who corroborates my evaluation and interpretation of the Word of GOD. Likewise, that I have died to sin and self and the world is substantiated by the Spirit of resurrection life that is made mine in Christ Jesus. The Holy Spirit delineates and validates what is newness of life and genuine character conversion.

It is not so much that I judge myself, but that I allow the Holy Spirit uninhibited access to my heart and mind and soul. It is his affirmation that I seek, and the witness of his good pleasure that I am in the perfect will of GOD. I have nowhere to spend the honor or accolades of men.

I deliberately and methodically separate myself from the spirit of this godless world system that coerces and demands my silence about the saving grace of the LORD Jesus Christ. It is the power of his resurrection life that I bring to bear upon the natural propensities and lusts of the flesh, and upon the pride of this life. It is all of grace and mercy, and of the same Spirit of resurrection life that raised Jesus Christ from the dead. It is as I die, that I am taught (and empowered) to live.

❋

But GOD forbid that I should glory, save in the cross of our LORD Jesus Christ, by whom the world is crucified unto me, and I unto the world.
GAL. 6:14

❋

It is the resurrection life and power of the LORD Jesus Christ which presses to the front of my physical life, after having mortified and eclipsed my natural desires and worldly lusts. This is the power of GOD that radically transforms my carnal covetousness and self-interests and pride of life into an humble and obedient servant of the love interests of Jesus Christ for my neighbor's soul. I am converted from the conceit and vanity of self-realization unto GOD-realization, and unto what I often call Christ-consciousness.

I am transformed by the renewing of my mind (re. Rom. 12:2), and the underlying catalyst for this radical evolution and comprehensive character conversion is the glory and power of the resurrection life of the LORD Jesus Christ. It is the Spirit and glory and power of an endless life, and it is only found in the cross of Jesus Christ, or on its other side, if you will. It is the same cross that I take up daily, the same cross I am integrated and assimilated into as a living sacrifice. The same cross that Jesus Christ bore.

That it necessitates, and even commands, the loss of our natural life, is what has inherently made the preaching of the cross unpopular among much of Christianity. It is tolerable or acceptable that the LORD Jesus Christ had to die, but it is insufferable and unconscionable for many Christians that we must die to pride and self-interests and our love of the world. This is relatively and predominantly why I am mandated to write: We will die unto sin and self and pride now, and be born again into GOD's interests, and live unto Jesus Christ now, or we will not be living with him eternally when he returns.

The spirit that drives this world system, whom the Apostle Paul calls *"the god of this world"* (see 2 Cor. 4:4), exploits or subjugates those who covet (or lust) after its goods and services, and its amusements and distractions and carnal entertainments. Again, *"GOD is a Spirit"* (re. John 4:24), the LORD Jesus Christ says so. And he is a *"Holy"* Spirit. The spirit of this world is the antithesis of the Spirit of GOD.

✻

> *Little children, it is the last time, and as ye have heard that antichrist shall come, even now are there many antichrists; whereby we know that it is the last time.*
> 1 JOHN 2:18

✻

When Bibles are being burned on the nightly, national news, especially in America, it is the spirit of antichrist in the world expressing his malevolence and hatred for all that is holy, for all things (and persons) pertaining to Jesus Christ. The love of the world, and the love of the Father, are extreme (polar) opposites, if you will. Just as Jesus Christ had to overcome the hostility and cruelty of men driven by evil, we must overcome it also.

The world wants to sell itself into our minds with glamorous advertising and subliminal suggestion. The packaging can be very attractive, and the promised commodity or service pleasant to the eyes, and desirous to make one wise. Everybody has one. But there is a price to pay for my indulgence, and for allowing the prince of this world (Satan) to rent space in my head and spread corruption throughout my heart. When I allow my lust to be conceived, or when I impulsively exercise or gratify my desire, it brings forth sin, and when sin is finished, it brings forth death (see James 1:15).This is the sin of self-realization and of placing my desires first, or before GOD's Word, the idolatry of serving myself, of being my own god (little "g").

The spirit of this world system contends for supremacy, demands my allegiance. And then once it has drawn me in, it extorts my silence about the LORD Jesus Christ. Children, this is the same spirit that induced and coerced evil men to crucify Jesus Christ, and he (Satan) is still in the world.

*

These things I have spoken unto you, that in me ye
might have peace. In the world ye shall have tribulation:
but be of good cheer; I have overcome the world.
JOHN 16:33

*

This world is not our home, and it is not our friend. The world is essentially (and relatively) an appointed place and time of my testing and temptation, and tribulation, in what I call the *season of my humanity.* As I have alluded to, the corruption of this world (and the wages of sin) is cleverly disguised within elaborate marketing schemes and hypnotic advertising.

To my detriment, I reach for that fruit. Alas, I must first convince myself that the spot I see is not a wormhole. Cunningly concealed at the core is the noxious corruption that commands my continued servitude. To have what the world has (with a minimally clear conscience), I must volitionally suppress and deny my knowledge of the wormhole, if you will. There is a plethora of poisons and a literal (and virtual) cornucopia of evil and corruption readily available, cleverly represented as not only harmless, but advanced as even wholesome. Besides, everyone else already seems to have one.

This world sucks us in: seduces and beguiles the best of us into a methodical compromise, an incremental collusion, a systematic but eventually total apostasy. Well? How many of us are sufficiently dead in a natural sense, that we might be markedly (significantly and accurately) described as born again? I am not alluding to the predominant compromise and carnal collusion of contemporary Christianity, but (by the Spirit of the living GOD, and as a friend of the Bridegroom), I am attesting to it, and witnessing against it.

If you think that I am reaching, then I challenge you to research how many of the seven churches in the first three chapters of the Book of Revelation are commanded to repent. Indeed, how many of the seven (which is relatively One Church), how many are called *"the synagogue of Satan,"* comprised of *"them that say they are Jews, and are not"* (see Rev. 2:9 and 3:9)? This is prophetically (and realistically) the contemporary equivalent of saying "them that say they are Christians, and are not."

(Broadly), contemporary Christianity in America does not view the world as something that specifically must be overcome, even while Bibles are being burned in our streets. Sanctification has always been a difficult subject to both conceptualize and realize. Concisely, it fundamentally means the separation of our affections and allegiance from this world system unto GOD. Sanctification is the process by which our character is miraculously transformed from self-veneration and self-realization to GOD-realization.

Satan cleverly manipulates events and circumstances so that this world appears to be our source. Of course, this has a certain logic in a natural sense. That is, for those of us who primarily consider ourselves a natural being. However (and the source of much of our difficulty), is that we Christians (ideally) are supposed to first consider ourselves as spiritual beings. This is telling, or illuminating, because it takes faith for me to conceptualize and realize (apprehend) that I am a spiritual being.

This inherently makes prayer and Bible study difficult, because they are not natural disciplines; they are spiritual disciplines to which my natural man must submit. It takes faith to pray, and to study and meditate upon the scriptures.

This world system is carefully and cunningly designed to hide from me the fact that I am (first of all) not only a spiritual being or entity, but an eternal one. This is the truth about life:

that my natural life is a drop in the bucket, as it were. The true essence of life is that it is eternal. This is the reality of life, GOD's reality, and the only one that matters.

(According to our faith) we understand and apprehend, that when the god of this world system incites society's denizens to burn Bibles in the street, that it is trying to deny, suppress and eradicate Jesus Christ from the earth. It is a premeditated evil and a telling diabolical act. Correlative to the faith I have, I see its significance, if you follow. I glimpse its spiritual significance, that the agents and perpetrators of this burning of GOD's Word have yielded themselves as instruments of evil, and are enemies of Jesus Christ – that is, antichrists.

The god of this world system is desperate to conceal from me the reality of life, that I am an eternal being. I have covered this extensively in other writing, that is, the truth of how I "spend" my time (and my life) is the manifest offering up of spiritual sacrifices. The season of my humanity will one day be revealed as having been a season of getting ready. Was I able to overcome? Was I able to live my life (or spend my life) in the worship and service of Jesus Christ in an environment that was determined to deny him? Was I able to walk and live by faith, and not by sight?

✳

For whatsoever is born of GOD overcometh the world: and this is the victory that overcometh the world, even our faith.
1 JOHN 5:4

✳

Christian, we are born again by the Holy Spirit of the Living Word of GOD. One momentous day, I boldly asked, "Holy Spirit, is your name Jesus?" I could almost hear the LORD's amusement and pleasure bundled within the precise inflection of his direct and simple reply, "Of course it is."

✳

Neither is there salvation in any other: for
there is none other name under heaven given
among men, whereby we must be saved.
ACTS 4:12

✳

The Holy Spirit of resurrection life by which we are born again is both the Spirit of the Father and the Spirit of the Son, who is One LORD. I never tire of receiving a fresh perspective of this phenomenal and perpetual (living and enduring) revelation.

✳

Hear, O Israel: The LORD our GOD is One LORD.
DEUT. 6:4

✳

The LORD Jesus Christ unambiguously says that *"GOD is a Spirit"* (re. John 4:24). He assumes the bodily form that pleases him: whether a pillar of fire or a pillar of a cloud, or one hundred and twenty cloven tongues like as of fire. But neither the earth nor the heavens, nor the heavens of heavens, can contain him.

For emphasis, I repeat a statement I scribed by the Holy Ghost just a couple of paragraphs ago. Christian, we are born again by the Holy Spirit of the Living Word of GOD.

＊

Being born again, not of corruptible seed, but of incorruptible, by the Word of GOD, which liveth and abideth forever.
1 Pet. 1:23

＊

The gift of GOD is the Spirit of an irrepressible Living Word. The Holy Ghost is (what I call) the regenerative, glorified breath of GOD. He is the Spirit of the eternal life of GOD. He is the indomitable Spirit of Resurrection Life who never ceases raising me from the dead to newness of life. Ah, you would have had to have been there. Saint, I do not know about you, but I am markedly not a finished product.

＊

Beloved, now we are the sons of GOD, and it doth not yet appear what we shall be: but we know that, when he shall appear, we shall be like him; for we shall see him as he is.
1 John 3:2

＊

(This morning, the LORD awakened me even earlier than usual.) The first point the Holy Spirit makes this morning is that John the Beloved elder is writing here to Christians who have transitioned into disciples, yet whom are still being radically transformed by a *"faith which worketh by love."* Concisely, I continue to be categorically and copiously converted. Pointedly, I have not arrived at some conjectural sinless perfection or ethereal Christian nirvana of flawlessness, and of resting upon my laurels, as they say.

"It doth not yet appear what we shall be" (we have not arrived) and there is the grace of opportunity available today to be do better than I did yesterday. Faith is the dynamic of the LORD's salvation, and the catalyst for my continuing conversion. *"Believest thou this?"* (re. John 11:26)

My faith is not incidental or purposeless. Faith in GOD is the effectual dynamic of my soul's salvation, and the impetus and driving force of my perpetual transformation. Genuine faith is never, ever static.

The stimulus of my conversion is the continuing revelation of Jesus Christ as GOD, *"line upon line, precept upon precept"* (see Is. 28:10). Pointedly, I am not finished seeing him. The pertinent question, is if I am still building upon the foundation of Jesus Christ as the Word of Life, or do I have a theoretical, one-dimensional, uh, "doctrinal" Jesus Christ as LORD?

(I mean) is Jesus Christ still showing me the Father, or did I arrive some time ago? Do I have GOD figured out, kind of like Saul of Tarsus on the Road to Damascus, you know, before his encounter? Some of us posture as if we had exhausted heaven: too holy to pray, too holy to tarry, and certainly too holy to serve.

GOD has always been hidden in Christ. Resurrection Life and the Word of Life are interchangeable terms for the same GOD. Kind of like, *"I and my Father are One"* (John 10:30).

GOD is forever in what he has said. It is eternally being said (present tense). Behold the profundity and the simplicity of Christ. *"So then faith cometh by hearing, and hearing by the Word of GOD"* (Rom. 10:17).

Christian, GOD is under no obligation to show the indifferent anything. One of my favorite scriptures is actually just a phrase, but it continues to contribute exponentially to my grace, and to my perpetual awe and wonder. It is transforming me in the perpetual here and now. *"And unto you that hear shall more be given"* (see Mark 4:24).

There were decades that I had a facile or narrow understanding of the word *"hear."* When God uses the word *hear,* he presupposes (and actually commands) my adherence and application, my obedience to, and my performance of, the Word. *"But be ye doers of the Word, and not hearers only, deceiving your own selves"* (James 1:22).

Hence, those of us who apply the Word of GOD shall be given more. The change (or repentance) the Word of GOD effects in me, is the evidence that I actually heard what GOD said.

When I read the Word of GOD with intent, I find that it is a living entity. His name is Jesus. When I read the Word of GOD with purpose, it is accompanied by a living Spirit who empowers me to apply its commands.

By faith, I encounter GOD (in the Word of GOD) and he augments my revelation by incremental, methodical grace and truth.

✳

*That which was from the beginning, which we have heard,
which we have seen with our eyes, which we have looked
upon, and our hands have handled of the Word of Life.
(For the Life was manifested, and we have seen it, and
bear witness, and shew unto you that eternal life, which
was with the Father, and was manifested unto us.)*

1 John 1:1-2

✳

John the Beloved is attesting to having seen the Author of Life in the flesh. The opening of this epistle parallels the opening of his gospel account. All (of) the eleven original disciples saw him in his glory, but not quite like Peter and James and John, the LORD's inner-circle. And none knew him as intimately as John. While it is true that GOD is no respecter of persons, it is also true what Pastor Alph Lukau of South Africa says: "There are levels and levels."

Christian, guard your inner circle zealously, if you indeed have one. And if not, wait upon the LORD. Guard diligently the grace of revelation afforded you. Conscientiously and zealously build upon what you already know to be true, and earnestly press up against the next revelation of the kingdom of GOD by faith.

We have quite enough text for our present exposition, but I must establish or clarify something. This I have from the Holy Ghost. The fundamental or principle glory of GOD is the brilliance and majesty of the eternal life which comprises or is integral to (and indivisible from) his essence. Briefly, for now, this is the glory that Martha saw. But please keep in mind that finite language will never be sufficient to describe the infinite glory of endless life.

✳

Jesus saith unto her, Said I not unto thee, that, if thou wouldest believe, thou shouldest see the glory of GOD?
JOHN 11:40

✳

To raise someone from the dead naturally entails the power to reverse corruption, and most markedly in the case of Lazarus. He had been dead for four days.

It is Jesus Christ who calls this resurrection event the "*glory of GOD.*" It is a divine, sovereign, *autonomous* Act of GOD. Nothing documents or authenticates the deity of the LORD Jesus Christ more so than forgiving sin (and before Calvary), healing all manner of sickness and disease and infirmity, and reversing the natural processes of human decomposition and raising the dead back to life.

Alas, what more can be said to aid those who still doubt the deity of the LORD Jesus Christ, and the veracity of GOD's Word? To doubt what GOD has said is to literally affront and insult the integrity of his holy character. The Bible calls it "*an evil heart of unbelief*" (re. Heb. 3:12).

John and company are documenting their witness of the resurrection life of the LORD Jesus Christ for posterity. For you and me, Christian. He attests that they have heard, seen, and touched the Word of Life. The Spirit of resurrection life is the self-perpetuating witness of GOD. His name is Jesus.

The Holy Spirit is the self-sustaining, immortal, abiding witness of both the Father and the Son. He is the *"we"* and the *"our"* of John 14:23, who come to make their abode within the body and the spirit man or spirit woman of the sanctified and obedient disciples of Jesus Christ.

This is who I call the Christ of GOD. This is the One LORD of Deuteronomy 6:4, who is the Spirt of both the Father and the Son coalesced into the One Spirit of GOD, *"which is Christ in you, the hope of glory"* (re. Col. 1:27).

Concisely, (if I may), Jesus is essentially saying, *"If you believe that I AM the Resurrection and the Life, you may share my glory."* This is the inherent, radiant and stately glory of an endless life, the very essence of GOD.

Dear reader, in the season of my humanity, by the violence of my faith, I press up against the kingdom of GOD to make the reality of the revelation mine. Remember, I call the glimpse of the LORD Jesus Christ that Saul of Tarsus was allowed to see on the Road to Damascus the *reality* of Jesus Christ, the glory of whose radiance and brilliance was brighter than the noonday sun.

The Apostle Paul would know. I believe his personal revelation of Jesus Christ rivaled John's, and Peter's. Pointedly, each of these three men's conversions were unique and radical. Christian, I wonder what it is that you and I most urgently need to die to, whether wealth or position or pride, what engrained character traits have we that most desperately need to be converted into the image of Christ?

(Here I must interject something.) Dear reader, if you have been patiently waiting for our narrative or exposition to finally focus on the raising of Lazarus from the dead, frankly, so have I. The Holy Spirit keeps on leading me and redirecting the emphasis or thread of this notebook (chapter) back onto the theme of death. I am beginning to get the point. Contemporary Christianity is much too naturally (and carnally) alive to experience significant signs and wonders of the LORD Jesus Christ's resurrection life and power – to either see or share his glory.

Contemplating the extraordinary conversions of Peter and Paul and John, the Holy Spirit suddenly reminds me of a distinct season in my own young Christian development. This was a protracted time of tribulation and testing in my struggle to become a definitive disciple of the LORD Jesus Christ, a seemingly interminable time of dying unto lust and pride, and to an intemperate love or affiliation (friendship) with the world.

Every time I think of Saul of Tarsus' three days of blindness, I ponder anew what things he not only experienced physically, but what he may have seen and heard spiritually. I refuse to believe he spent three drawn-out tortuous days doing nothing but lying in bed and staring at the wall with unseeing eyes. Bluntly, I think GOD took him to school. Personally, I believe the marvels and the mysteries and the revelations that the LORD Jesus Christ showed him (in the Spirit) were limitless and extraordinary and dreadful. I imagine him seeing both the miraculous and the unthinkable.

Bear with me, please. This is leading up to something that is going to help someone (besides myself) or the LORD would not have brought us this way. From acute and agonizing personal experience (and as poignantly revealed by the Holy

Ghost), I predicate that Saul of Tarsus had much to die to: much pride and bias and hatred, and much bad theology; you know, a whole lot of religious presumption and ego, spiritual elitism and personal prejudices.

It is my testimony that Saul of Tarsus experienced the same correlative agony of greater grace as I, (as I am wont to call it). Of course, not everyone has to die such an acute (or drastic) metaphorical death. Lest you presume that I am boasting, I trust my explanation to clarify things. None would volitionally choose to suffer such great things for his (Jesus Christ's) name's sake. I cannot speak for Saul, but I can still taste my own corresponding experience. If you can receive it, *"I am* (as it were) *the man that hath seen affliction by the rod of his wrath"* (Lam. 3:1).

(I do not attest to such things lightly.) You do not want my mantle upon your shoulders, or my portion across your back. That statement, I qualify with another. The Christian who is finished with dying has not begun to live.

After an arduous and painstaking (both exhaustive and exhausting) season of seeking and beseeching the LORD Jesus Christ to reveal to me some way or methodology by which I might experience and apprehend his glory and his power, to show me what I was doing wrong, and to show me what further discipline or sacrifice he desired of me, he led me to the following Word of GOD. This was spoken to certain of the scribes and Pharisees who were also seeking sings and wonders to complement their religious regimen and spiritual persona. They had asked, *"Master, we would see a sign from thee"* (re. Matt. 12:38).

✳

But he answered and said unto them, An evil and adulterous generation seeketh after a sign; and there shall no sign be given to it, but the sign of the prophet Jonas. For as Jonas was three days and three nights in the whale's belly; so shall the Son of man be three days and three nights in the heart of the earth.
MATT. 12 39-40

✳

It should not be necessary to say that I am still gleaning progressive (and perpetual) revelation from this living Word of GOD. Concisely, some days, what I would rather do must be crucified afresh.

Some days, the tendency of my natural man is to still flee from the presence of the LORD and his calling (and anointing) upon my life. Frankly, the difficulty is that self-will and pride and lust must be crucified with Christ to abide in the presence of the Holy One.

GOD had to definitively and acutely show me that I was essentially seeking signs and wonders and religious novelties and amusements to detract and supplant the astute commands of the cross of Jesus Christ, and the perpetual suffering association and continual death of my natural man. I needed signs and wonders (and a miracle) *"outside"* myself, so that I could cunningly circumvent the miracle GOD was commanding *within* myself.

My natural man lusts for, and surrounds himself with, religious curiosities and ornamentation and ceremony, distractions and folderol to keep the next fellow from examining my form of faith too closely; you know, impedimenta and misdirection. My true (unconverted) character must be cleverly concealed beneath an elaborate (and hopefully convincing) convoluted religious cloak.

I need a miracle outside myself, uh, so that I don't have to *be the miracle* within myself. The love I have for my neighbor today, who I would have robbed or defrauded thirty years ago, is the sign and wonder and the miracle. That today, I genuinely love people with a different color skin than my own, is simply miraculous.

My seeking external signs and wonders was revealed to be a shrewd and artful circumvention of the internal character change (conversion) that the gospel of Jesus Christ commands. Anything to get the focus off myself. Succinctly, I was saving (what I thought was) the best of my life for myself.

The corresponding sign of the prophet Jonas (Jonah) is concisely the cross of Jesus Christ, and my natural man crucified there. Seeking signs and wonders outside myself is revealed to be the covetousness and greed and idolatry of saving my life for myself. The Word of GOD (Jesus Christ) concisely and unapologetically calls it not only adultery, but evil, proceeding from the heart.

Contemporary mainstream Christianity, specifically in America, including current Pentecostal Christianity, is that evil and adulterous generation. Someone must say so. The kingdom of GOD is (broadly) being rent from us and given unto nations bringing forth the fruits thereof (see. Matt. 21:43). This is my mandate, and thus I cry aloud. It is my hope that this prophetic Word of GOD even now being fulfilled, will shake the House of Jacob in America to its foundations.

An evil and an adulteress generation is a comprehensive people who have a lover other than GOD. The word *cheater* represents the worldly appellation or euphemism for the unfaithful.

The best of us seek signs and wonders before we will sell-out to Christ, or capitulate to dismiss our surreptitious, uh, auxiliary lovers. You know, those second-string stand-ins or substitutes just in case things do not work out.

The preponderance of us attend church primarily so that we can refer to ourselves as Christians with a minimally acceptable salved conscience, but then still live as if this world is our source. We do not want our worldly goods and services threatened. Therefore, we mustn't alienate or anger the powers that be with a vocal testimony of Jesus Christ.

Concisely (and personally), the Holy Spirit is still making the sign of the prophet Jonas intimately mine. There was a distinct season in my young Christian development when I was feverishly seeking ritualistic or ceremonial religious thrills, dancing and shouting and theatrics. Now, religious zeal is admirable, and we should all be impassioned about the LORD's salvation, but I am especially referencing a concerted human emotional effort in helping the Holy Spirit express himself, as it were. Pumped-up histrionics specifically designed to inflate one's personal religious persona. You know, to make one appear more spiritual – so that we can be a Bigger Christian than the next fellow.

Notably, when the scribes and Pharisees had (pretty much) *demanded* a sign from the LORD Jesus Christ (re. Matt. 12:38), by that time he had already healed sickness and disease and cast devils out with his Word. The deaf could hear, the blind received their sight, and the lame could walk. And he had already amazingly raised Jairus' daughter from the dead (re. Matt. 9:24-26).

The LORD Jesus Christ consistently taught that seeking sings and wonders is indicative of unbelief. (In myself) it was a startling, piercing, progressive revelation of my deep-rooted mistrust of GOD, and an acute glimpse of my true ineradicable carnal nature and the exceeding sinfulness of sin.

Three days and three nights in the grave *"is"* the sign. Jesus said it is the *only sign* that will be given a sinful and adulterous generation. In the case of Jonah, he definitively needed to die to the self-will and obdurate attitude that was manifested by his brazenly fleeing from the presence of the LORD and impudently ignoring his instructions.

As we read Jonah's continuing story, or all that is made available to us, we also see how that Jonah had arrogantly presumed to know how GOD was going to respond to Nineveh all along. He used these suppositions to justify his having fled from GOD in the first place (see Jonah 4:1-3). Frankly, even after three days and three nights in the fish's belly, Jonah is found still struggling with anger and self-pity and self-justification, and we might even say, an evil spirit of suicide.

GOD uses the depth of Jonah's obdurate attitude, and his pertinacious determination to mitigate or justify his behavior and residual anger, to reveal the labyrinthine tenacity of mankind's carnal nature to rule, to complain. GOD specifically used this revelation to deliver me from the evil of self-pity and helped me to see how that murmuring and complaining displeases GOD.

GOD was also showing me that the precursor and methodology of all sings and wonders is the persistent crucifixion of my carnal nature, and the body of sin prostrate in the grave by the power of GOD in Christ. My profound change of character is the sign. The resurrection life of the LORD Jesus Christ will manifest without any assistance from me. It is as I yield that the miracle of my character conversion is progressively revealed.

Many of us are not sufficiently dead to manifest any marked resurrection life (if I may bluntly put it like that). Personally, when I refer to this specific season of the Holy Spirit's intense application of this Word of GOD to my Christian development, I am referencing the core, or initial teaching. And I further qualify that by saying that I am in continuing education. However (if I may), I press by the violence of my faith to apprehend him who first apprehended me.

Christian, the sign you seek is the miracle within yourself.

✳

The kingdom of GOD cometh not with observation.
Neither shall they say, Lo here or, lo there! for,
behold, the kingdom of GOD is within you.
re. Luke 17:20-21

✳

The kingdom of GOD (cometh) with the complete and unconditional capitulation of my carnal nature. As I abide in the Word of GOD and as the Word of GOD abides in me, the miracle will resolutely manifest in the mirror. Disciples of Christ, the signs and wonders of our miraculous transformation will manifest in the workplace and in the marketplace for the whole world to see.

Let us not (necessarily) covet signs and wonders outside ourselves. As I have written before: GOD comes with the changes I allow him to make.

Be the miracle.

I mean, is it not all about being born again? In my juvenile or undeveloped Christian reasoning, I concluded that if the sign of the prophet Jonas was going to be the *Only* sign given me, then it warrants a meticulous examination. Reminiscing on the convoluted and bewildering course of events orchestrated by the sovereignty of GOD to ultimately render me upon my knees, it occurred to me that I had spent quite a few episodic three days and three nights in the belly of various figurative whales, if you follow. Just to name a few: the *Kanawha County Criminal Justice System, Huntington State Hospital, the South Central Regional Correctional Facility, The Leestown Road Substance Abuse Treatment Program.* Well, you get the idea. I'm just being true (brutally honest) to my testimony of the grace and mercy of Jesus Christ. (Ha! And as the kids are fond of saying, There's no shame in my game.)

My progress as a developing Christian disciple was agonizingly slow. By prayer and fasting, I sought the LORD, beseeching him to show me what I was doing wrong. If you can receive the metaphor or the allegory, the Holy Spirit showed me that I was trying to live in the power of the LORD's resurrection life before I had adequately died.

I cannot speak for anyone else's experience, but the Holy Spirit revealed to me that I had been a player and a shaker (a professional sinner) for so long, that I was going to have to get brutally and unsparingly honest – first with myself. The best I can probably express it is that the Holy Spirit showed me the *reality* of repentance from GOD's perspective. I had to step into the light of the revelation – of the *real* me in the presence of a Holy GOD.

The pride of life and the love of the world clung tenaciously to me. At times, I imagined or envisioned myself from GOD's perspective, or in the acute biblical context of the sign of the prophet Jonas. I was (essentially and metaphorically) trying to get up before the third day.

Figuratively, I was (periodically) presenting before GOD, trying to apprehend the resurrection life and power of the LORD Jesus Christ before I had completely died to sin and self and the world. But (representatively), I was one or two-days dead, as it were. Later, I would term this phenomenon (or religious anomaly) a hybrid-Christian.

Here is another portion of the Word of GOD that was instrumental, or actually, indispensable, in my radical and comprehensive transformation. If the sign of the prophet Jonas was the *only* sign that I was going to be given, I resolved to make it mine. With that determination, this Word of GOD was released:

✳

*Come, and let us return unto the LORD: for he hath torn,
and he will heal us; he hath smitten, and he will bind us up.*

*After two days he will revive us: in the third day he
will raise us up, and we shall live in his sight.*

*Then shall we know, if we follow on to know the LORD: his
going forth is prepared as the morning; and he shall come unto
us as the rain, as the latter and formal rain unto the earth.*
Hosea 6:1-3

✳

For a seemingly interminable season, I endured a perpetual correction and chastening. The Holy Spirit mightily used this Word of GOD to give me a visual, if you will. GOD showed me that I was presenting before him as *revived* externally, or looking pretty good one-dimensionally, appearing to be alive. But, if you can receive it, I was fundamentally two-days alive but still one-day dead. I may have looked acceptable externally, but I still had some residual (internal) corruption.

I had forthrightly asked the LORD what the difference was between being *revived* on the second day and *living in his sight* on the third day. By the violence of my faith (from a certain perspective), I commanded the Word of GOD to give me an answer. (Yes, we have that authority in Christ.) Concisely, GOD showed me that, externally, I can be polished to a high sheen or a perfunctory religious luster, and yet inside still be full of wickedness or corruption. And as I say, the Word of GOD speaks best for GOD.

✳

Woe unto you, scribes and Pharisees, hypocrites!
for ye are like unto whited sepulchres, which indeed
appear beautiful outward, but are within full of
dead men's bones, and of all uncleanness.
MATT. 23:27

✳

I still glean and gather sheaves from the sign of the prophet Jonas. With everything Jonah experienced (the storm, the sea, the whale) he still emerged with residual anger and a marked propensity for self-justification and self-pity. Ah, nothing will do for the body of sin and the pride of life except to be crucified with Christ. This (to me) is the sign of the prophet Jonas, that the death of the natural man must have its full season.

Frankly, we have too many hybrid Christians. We have not taken the time to die. We have not taken the time to tarry for the LORD, or the time to tarry with him. No one is going to give us time, we must *take it.* We must take authority over our time and command the natural man to submit to the cross of Jesus Christ. Here I deliberately reverse two phrases from Hosea 6:3 to make a point for gospel cause and effect, as it were. *"If* we follow on to know the LORD, *then* shall we know."

It is only as we enter into the intimacies of the suffering fellowship and death of the LORD Jesus Christ, that we are raised up to live in his sight, and to share the glory and power of his resurrection life. To share his resurrection glory, I must not only share his cross and his death, but also his grave. I must allow the death of my natural man (and the body of sin) to have the fullness of its season.

Christian, too many of us are one-day and two-day dead; or one third and two thirds worldly. Not enough of us have followed on to know the LORD in the acute and unabbreviated austerity and intimacy of his cross, that the world might see and experience the witness of the resurrection power of the LORD Jesus Christ to radically transform and raise to newness of life.

Frankly, as I have said, we have too many hybrid Christians, and too many walking dead. Too many whited walls.

Children, it is the *following* which makes the difference: denying ourselves, taking up our cross, and following the LORD Jesus Christ not only to Calvary, but *through* Calvary. The resurrection life of the LORD Jesus Christ can only be presented to the world in and through Christians who have died to pride and self-realization, and to their love of the world.

Them who have followed on to know the LORD have also fellowshipped with his sufferings and shared his death. He has raised them up, and they live in his sight (re. Hos. 6:3). They know and understand that *"his going forth is prepared as the morning"* and they live accordingly. They can be seen living the life more abundant. That is, the essence and virtues of Jesus Christ can be seen living in them and being perfected in them. The world sees and marvels at the boldness and power and percipient wisdom of these (*unusual*) Christians, and takes knowledge of them, as it were, that they have been with Jesus (as inspired by Acts 4:13).

That is correct. From my general comprehensive casual everyday observation, these are *unusual* Christians. Just saying (as they say).

Christian disciples who have followed on to know the LORD can be identified as them that have had both the former and the latter rain of the season upon their testimony. You can see the refreshing of the Holy Ghost manifested upon them. They encounter and experience the same adversity and opposition as everyone else, but they live in victory by the resurrection life and power of the LORD Jesus Christ. They are not victims of fear and unbelief, or seasonal contrary circumstance.

*

If ye then be risen with Christ, seek those things which are above, where Christ sitteth on the right hand of GOD.

*

Set your affections on things above, not on things on the earth.
Col. 3:1-2

*

Them living the abundant victorious (resurrection) life in the LORD Jesus Christ are not victim to fluctuating societal circumstance or morals, interest rates, or the stock market. Their affections and investments are elsewhere. Dear children, it is an astute reflection of genuine faith. Many will be disappointed, but *real* estate is not house(s) and land. It is spiritual, for *"GOD is a Spirit"* (re. John 4:24). Children, the heart and mind of GOD's perspective is the true reality.

These *unusual* Christians not only reckon themselves dead, but also risen. If we could apprehend the reality of where we are truly (spiritually) seated, we would move mountains, indeed. Alas, I first mourn my own shortfall.

The longer I am alive, the more fully I comprehend grace. Each new breath ought to be a continuing (flowing) revelation, and the impetus of my living sacrifice. I touch the face of GOD in the service of my fellow man. It is kings and priests who sit in Christ upon the throne, where justice and mercy meet.

Christ Jesus sits on the right hand of GOD indivisible. In the process of perpetual consummate perfection (in the season of my humanity), I sit with him there complete. Unto him who is Alpha and Omega, my redemption is *now.* Finite reasoning, and religious and theological arguments, will not alter the reality of GOD.

By virtue of his blood upon the mercy seat, and in the love of Christ's intercessions for my neighbor, I sit with him there, where grace and truth in righteousness rule.

※

Resurrection Life is the Holy Spirit of the regenerative breath of GOD in Jesus Christ gathering all things into One.

This is He who delivers me from the body of this death, and by whom I get a taste of heaven, and wonders to come. Yet, in this, the season of my humanity, the dying and the living are indivisible, the sorrow and the joy are One.

Is not Christ first a priest, and then a King? Even so, by suffering association and conformity to his death, *the glory of Resurrection Life* is made mine. Selah.

6

I AM the Way, the Truth, and the Life

"I AM the Way, the Truth, and the Life: no man cometh unto the Father, but by me."

–John 14:6

THE SCRIPTURE from which this chapter takes its title is a Word that the LORD Jesus Christ spoke to Thomas, who is also called Didymus. Christianity has traditionally dubbed him *doubting* Thomas, but let us rather commend him for his boldness, and for being interested enough (and invested enough) in the things of GOD to ask questions. John later records that he (Thomas) unabashedly admitted his unbelief when the other disciples told him that they had seen the LORD. There are multiple scripture references which establish that when unbelief is honestly confessed, it is promptly given strength and consolation.

※

LORD, I believe, help thou mine unbelief
re. MARK 9:24

※

In the case of Thomas, and the occasion that resulted in his receiving the unflattering sobriquet of *doubting Thomas,* we know that the LORD Jesus Christ appeared to him eight days later and addressed his unbelief directly and personally. Indeed, and moreover, he addressed it intimately and comprehensively. Children, the LORD Jesus Christ can be trusted with our fear and unbelief. He already knows we have them, so let us list them and add them to our every care and lay them daily at his feet.

※

Now unto him that is able to do exceeding
abundantly above all that we ask or think,
according to the power that worketh in us.
EPH. 3:20

✳

Christian, GOD wants to have a personal (in depth) encounter and interaction with every one of us, specifically a conversation. GOD is a Holy Spirit of a Living Word. This is his character and essence. This is how it pleases him to manifest.

As I like to say, introductions happen, but relationships develop. Pointedly, there is nothing indifferent or lukewarm about the nature of GOD. It is faith which dictates the level of my asking, seeking, and knocking. And my revelation is corresponding.

Children, we must develop (what I call) *Christ-consciousness.* I believe this is what the Apostle Paul meant when he said, *"continuing instant in prayer"* (re. Rom. 12:12). Keep a running dialog with Christ, maintain an uninterrupted conversation with him. Our difficulty is that this life we are living in the flesh presents itself as the reality. But the reality of life is that we are a spiritual, eternal being. Growing spiritually, and laying up heavenly (eternal) treasure, ought to be our priority.

✳

It is the Spirit that quickeneth (gives life); the
flesh profiteth nothing: the Words that I speak
unto you, they are Spirit, and they are Life.
JOHN 6:63

✳

Hence, *"God is a Spirit"* (re. John 4:24), as the LORD Jesus Christ told the Samaritan woman at Jacob's well, and he is the Holy Spirit of a Living Word. Not to be deliberately obtuse or antagonistic, but GOD is emphatically not three persons with three different offices and/or duties and with three distinct personalities. I am not trying to debunk anyone's doctrine or any particular theological (man-made) religious reasoning and logic or the traditions of our forefathers. The revelation of the Living prophetic Word of GOD creates its own chasm.

✳

Hear, O Israel: The LORD our GOD is One LORD.
DEUT. 6:4

✳

Beyond what man has said, *deep calleth unto deep* (re. Ps. 42:7). The revelation creates its own chasm, which the relevance and imperative of can also bear its own redundancy. *And unto you that hear shall more be given* (re. Mark 4:24).

How far (that) I am willing to reach alters my perspective, enlarges my horizons. Before we focus primarily upon our main text of John 14:6, the LORD wants me to share something that continues to help me immensely concerning his conversation with Thomas in John 20:24-29.

As we mentioned, the LORD had already appeared to the disciples eight days earlier, and Thomas was not with them when Jesus came.

✳

The other disciples therefore said unto him, We have seen the LORD. But he said unto them, Except I shall see in his hands the print of the nails, and put my finger into the print of the nails, and thrust my hand into his side, I will not believe.
JOHN 20:25

✳

As we discussed in the last chapter, every Christian should have a testimony of the resurrection life and power of the LORD Jesus Christ. That is, as many of us who have been radically and miraculously born again. My personally having been forgiven my trespasses and sins, and having been raised to newness of life, makes me an eyewitness. That is, if I have genuinely died to sin and self and pride, and the love of the world. My character should have been so supernaturally converted, that anyone spending just a little time in my company, would have to conclude that I have been with Jesus (*re. Acts 4:13*). Frankly, if I want to make it into the kingdom of GOD to spend eternity with the LORD Jesus Christ, then there better be nothing lukewarm about my Christianity. It needs to be said.

I believe that Thomas (must have) intuitively discerned that the other disciples had truly seen the LORD, and that his own disappointment at having missed this visitation, manifested in his vocal expression of unbelief. Thomas may well have been upset or disheartened at his own dereliction of duty. He may well have been disgruntled and frustrated at his own obdurate attitude and negligence.

(Personally) I believe that it would have been markedly obvious that the other disciples had been with the LORD. The

Resurrected Christ, with all power in heaven and in earth given unto him, had breathed upon them, and they had received the Holy Ghost. I will not speculate on how the Holy Ghost manifested in them and through them, except to say that it must have been evident, even pronounced, remarkable.

The Church (and the first Revival) would have already begun. Frankly, this is a notable demonstration of the sovereignty and deity of the LORD Jesus Christ. For those of us who would constrain him to a doctrinal or denominational box, here is the Almighty GOD bestowing the gift of the Holy Ghost, and before the Day of Pentecost.

Notwithstanding, whether it was truly his unbelief, or his disappointment and anger at himself (or a combination of the two), Thomas refreshingly and candidly confessed it as unbelief. By way of contrast, as a young Christian, I was surreptitiously and subtly taught to suppress my unbelief and confess a faith I did not really possess. As a result, I became such an expert at religious dissimulation and misdirection, that the Holy Spirit would later be forced to orchestrate circumstances which repeatedly compelled me into the light and commanded my honesty.

There is no remedy for what I insist upon hiding, (using myself as an example). We know that the Word of GOD defines condemnation as the fact that light has come, but that I still prefer the darkness because my deeds are evil, (re. John 3:19).

(By the Holy Ghost), I attest, that from GOD's perspective, Thomas' bold, spontaneous, explicit confession of unbelief is an unparalleled utterance of pure honesty for our example and admonition. He immediately dismisses any thought of pretense, and without shame lifts the veil to expose his true self.

From a certain perspective, Thomas' naked declaration of unbelief is the barefaced challenge of a raw or unrefined faith. (If I may), I care, but I don't care, what you have seen. I must see him for myself.

Behold the prophetic implications of just getting honest. Thomas' spontaneous declaration is what I have termed *a faith nigh unto trespass.* None but the most intimate friends of GOD utter such marvelous impudence. Why, Thomas' impromptu statement is the unadorned declaration of a little child! But behold its reward.

Here we get a privileged glimpse of just how gracious the LORD Jesus Christ is toward our candid confessions of frailty. He not only personally appears to Thomas, but explicitly addresses his challenge. Children, this is a singular encouragement for us to be unreservedly transparent with GOD, especially about our shortcomings.

※

Then saith he to Thomas, Reach hither thy finger, and behold my hands; and reach hither thy hand, and thrust it into my side: and be not faithless, but believing.
John 20:27

※

The LORD's response to Thomas' blatant honesty is remarkable; both by what he said, and what he did not say. By contrast, the religious environment and regimen of my youth discouraged questions, especially expressions of unbelief.

Overt or confessed weaknesses were disparaged. By example, by allusion and aspersion, and sometimes by intimidation, I was taught to conceal both my shortcomings and my questions. Frankly, I was taught to suppress my childish zeal and secrete my adult sin. I was indoctrinated to external religious etiquette and righteous deportment, and my innermost character was left fundamentally unconverted.

Well? We perpetuate the species. Please do not ask for anything that the Holy Brethren and the Sisters of Sanctity have not pre-assessed and preapproved. Please refer to your handbook, to your copied list of the church and denominational tenets and do not ask the elders any embarrassing questions. Sit up straight and say *Amen* occasionally. Tithe regularly (or you will be going straight to hell when you die).

In his gospel narrative, John takes great care to record the extraordinary visitation and conversation of the LORD with Thomas, much like he does in the next chapter to portray the singular nature of the LORD Jesus Christ pointedly restoring the Apostle Peter to his grace. Christian, you and I are hereby encouraged to seek such intimacy, and to be satisfied with nothing less. Some will say that this is a bold statement, and without a basis for substantiation – and by their limiting of my faith, obliquely reveal their actual limitations imposed upon the LORD Jesus Christ.

It is the dynamic of a healthy faith never to be wholly satisfied with the status quo. Robert Browning is quoted as saying, *"Ah, but a man's reach should exceed his grasp, or what's a heaven for"?* To me, this sounds like an explicit expression of a virulent (proliferating) faith.

Within the scope of my faith, even confined to a finite (physical) nature, the prophetic living Word of GOD speaks to me. If I may express it like this, I reach to experience what Thomas encountered. But I better clarify something. I boast of no physical (or visible) angelic visitations or corporeal (bodily) appearances of the LORD Jesus Christ. But until I meet him in the clouds, I nurture a lively hope.

Jesus distinctly tells Thomas twice to *"Reach,"* (re. John 20:27). Children let us reach beyond this (physical) life to GOD's Reality.

❄

If in this life only we have hope in Christ, we
are of all men most miserable.
1 Cor. 15:19

❄

To qualify, I frequently see brief images (or visions) of Jesus Christ before my face. If you can receive it, what I experience (in the Spirit) may be closer to what David expresses, except I most often see the LORD (for some reason) just left of center, and just two or three times (ever) centrally before my face. Here is the scripture I referenced concerning David. This is the Apostle Peter on the Day of Pentecost, quoting David.

❄

For David speaketh concerning him, I foresaw
the LORD always before my face, for he is on my
right hand, that I should not be moved.
Acts 2:25

＊

Christian, prophetically, I heard the LORD Jesus Christ say (or ask rather), *"How far into me do you want to reach?"* Well, needless to say, I have been reaching ever since. I still glean and gather and reap from this living Word of GOD. Indeed, GOD still speaks, or he never spoke at all.

Thomas' brazen spontaneous utterance, unabashedly confessing his unbelief, is one of the most honest expressions I have ever heard. This helped me immensely to come out from behind my self-righteous cloak and put a stop to the religious posturing and pious affectation and commenced to set me free from the bondage of hiding my doubt and unbelief. Amazingly, my faith increased exponentially.

GOD honors honesty. In this startling account of Thomas, we are encouraged to resist timidity, and shake off all restraint and religious pretense, to confess before GOD and man the abundance of the heart and mind. Children, *the Omniscient One* is already apprised of my unbelief and misgivings, I might just as well go ahead and confess them with my sins. The quicker confessed and repented of, the quicker resolved and delivered from.

GOD is not impressed with my posturing and religious signifying, as it were; and the men I am trying to impress cannot help me, as such. It is profitable to remember, however, that when GOD answers, he answers explicitly and comprehensively. Jesus answers Thomas' complaint and confession almost verbatim. This teaches me to assess myself and put words to my fears and unbelief, to confess every spot and wrinkle in my Christian persona, to forsake religious posturing and one-upmanship.

It is not only okay to reach beyond things seen, but also encouraged by the Word of GOD. By the Holy Spirit, I attest that Thomas's spontaneous outburst of unbelief was mingled with the challenge and the press and the expectation of faith.

For those of us who can receive it, here (eight days later) we witness, as it were, the circumcision of Thomas' hardness of heart. And, I must add, his revelation of Jesus Christ as not only Savior and LORD, but also as Creator and Almighty GOD, granted him a broader and deeper vista and a greater perspective.

※

And Thomas answered and said unto
him, My LORD and my GOD.
JOHN 20:28

※

For those who will reach beyond things seen, and past the religious status quo of our forefathers, beyond what others may have seen, GOD is still hid in Christ.

In these passages, it is significant that, two times *"the doors were shut,"* two times Jesus *"stood in the midst,"* two times Jesus said *"Peace be unto you,"* and two times the LORD Jesus told Thomas to *"Reach."* Let us think upon these things.

We need not, and we must not, settle for one serving. We must not be satisfied with the one-dimensional and the linear, complaisant to the constraints of this natural life and things seen. We must not presume that GOD cannot and will not do a new thing. Moreover, a double portion is not unprecedented. Indeed, let us press up against things seen, and reach beyond the testimony of the next fellow, to feel after a fresh touch from the Living GOD for ourselves.

Returning to our main text, it must be noted that Thomas was not the only disciple with misgivings or questions. Within the fourteenth chapter, John also records Philip and Judas (not Iscariot) as asking pertinent, life-transforming questions, and the LORD Jesus Christ personally addressing each of them. Frankly, a disciple without questions is going no further. Someone needs to confront us just like that.

In the primary text from which our chapter derives its title, the LORD Jesus Christ says, *"I AM the Way"* (re. John 14:6). It is relatively easy to first believe on the LORD Jesus Christ. After all, he suffered and died and rose from the dead to make our *Way* available, and he did all the work, as it were.

But to first believe, and then to follow by faith *in the Way*, is an altogether different endeavor, or not as easy as it first appears. Indeed, this is also an inherent *Truth* of the gospel of Jesus Christ and him crucified – the *Way* is narrow. Moreover, its critical imperative for my Christianity can bear its own redundancy.

✳

Enter ye in at the strait gate: for wide is the gate, and broad is the way, that leadeth to destruction, and many there be which go in thereat. Because strait is the gate, and narrow is the Way, which leadeth unto life, and few there be that find it.
MATT. 7:13-14

✳

As I frequently mention, the *many* and the *few* are what I call GOD's mathematics; or the ratio of GOD's *reality*, and the only one that matters. The revelation is (indeed) intense, and unsparing. The remedy, or the elixir, if you will, is necessarily bitter, or melancholy. It is the way of self-denial and sanctification, and the way of an old rugged cross. We mostly mourn for them upon the broad way to destruction.

It is the Word of GOD (Jesus Christ) who says he is the *Way*. It is the Word of GOD (Jesus Christ) who says the way is narrow, and it is the Word of GOD (Jesus Christ) who says, *"and few there be that find it"* (see Matt. 7:14).

To *find it* presupposes that I have been searching. That the gate is *"strait"* and the way is *"narrow"* necessitates that I have been searching diligently. Jesus also exhorts us to *"strive"* (see Luke 13:24). Ah, even thus, I have found it to be so, that the indifferent and the undecided are swept along with the irrepressible tide of the many upon the broad way to destruction.

"Many of the many" if you will, are so anesthetized and mesmerized, and the Deceiver is so adept at disguise and misdirection, that they do not even feel the systematic loss of their soul. It must be emphasized (and prioritized), however, that "many of the many" on the broad way include those of superficial religious ceremony and church attendance as evidence that they are saved. Children, the narrow *Way* which leads unto life is for the radically born again, and for them that have presented and surrendered their character to be converted, and few there be that find it.

We must (each of us) purpose in our heart to be one of the few. The gate is strait, and the way is narrow, for various reasons.

To name a few: (death to) sin, self-denial, the gospel principle (and process) of "the life lost to find it," (death to) world-love and pride, sanctification, holiness. The *Way* which leads unto life is a composite of all these variables or factors, and it is walking and living by faith, and walking and living in the Spirit. And of course, the *Way* is an intimate relationship with a person. His name is Jesus.

It must be noted, that when Luke records the LORD's teaching (doctrine) of this strait gate and narrow way in his gospel account, it is from a slightly different perspective, yet just as portentous. The teaching is pointedly prefaced with an ominous and urgently relative question. Although it is not asked much today in our era of all-permissive grace, its prophetic imperative has not paled from God's perspective.

✳

Then said one unto him, LORD, are there few that be saved?
re. LUKE 13:23

✳

The manner in which the LORD answers this question is (what I will call) obliquely. He does not address the *few* directly, he markedly references the *many.*

✳

Strive to enter in at the strait gate: for "many" I say unto you, will seek to enter in, and shall not be able.
LUKE 13:24

✳

The LORD Jesus Christ never understated or misrepresented the arduous and challenging nature of *the Way.* Incidentally, this is what Christianity was sometimes called in its early development in the Acts of the Apostles. Following Jesus Christ by faith is a "way of life." This is an integral, inseparable component of the comprehensive gospel.

✳

And he that taketh not his cross and followeth after me,
is not worthy of me. He that findeth his life shall lose
it: and he that loseth his life for my sake shall find it.
MATTHEW 10:38-39

✳

Persecution and hardship are intrinsic and indispensable to the promise. The Word of GOD does not circumvent, minimize, or apologize for the austerity of the *Way.* The Word of GOD repeatedly cautions us that the world will hate us. This world system and its evil is an opponent to be overcome.

It is the *"many"* who the LORD Jesus Christ references that would mitigate or diminish the inherent tribulation of this way of life. We have become expert and ingenious at circumventing the hardship and self-denial of the cross. We have become quite proficient at ceremonial form and sleight of hand. You know, adept (even cunning) at saving our lives for ourselves.

A strait gate and a narrow way will necessitate striving, the LORD said so (re. Luke 13:24). Uh, but fundamentally, we neither strive nor break a sweat. Concisely, mainstream contemporary Christianity is the *many.* I defy you to say they are not. Bluntly, they are the *many* who *"will seek to enter in, and shall not be able"* (see Luke 13:24).

We perpetuate the species. We withhold our best from the flames like we hide our secret character flaws. We have too much baggage for a strait gate and a narrow way. Only the radically born again and the comprehensively converted can squeeze through the strictures and specifications of the commandment of One Love. His name is Jesus.

Young Christians emulate older ones. We obliquely and silently teach them to hide their true selves. We never lost our lives – so that we could learn how to love, and we do not expect them to, either. The fire has not fell in decades because there has been no sacrifice, and no freewill offering, upon the altar. We do not wait upon GOD; we wait upon ourselves. We are out of the *Way.*

It was in the crushing press of personal sanctification that I first learned that my forefathers had done me a grave disservice. For literal decades I languished (and sometimes luxuriated) in ceremonial religious form, and it never occurred to me that I had to be literally born again. Just saying. What I needed was a Baptism of fire.

The *"few and the many,"* the *"strait gate and the wide gate,"* and the *"narrow way and the broad way"* are the gospel perspective and astute reality of a Holy GOD.

Children, the *"few and the many"* is GOD's acute ratio of eternal sanctification. You know, the doctrine (teaching) which we predominantly and summarily dismiss. This is the reality which engenders my fear and sense of urgency for mainstream Christianity. As a friend of the Bridegroom, this is the reality (and the commands of holiness) which cause me to tremble for the LORD's betrothed. (And I must have this as well, to see the LORD.)

Notwithstanding how confrontational the question may be, or how uncomfortable it makes us (or others), the Word of GOD establishes its precedent and relevance. It is a living, prophetic, aggressive question. *LORD, are there few that be saved?* (see Luke 13:23)

The Word of GOD is deliberate in recording this question for prophetic posterity, you might say. The anonymous inquisitor who asked this question was following the LORD Jesus Christ toward Jerusalem. We can only hope that he was one of the few who followed Jesus past the Garden of Gethsemane unto Pilate's Hall, and then on to Calvary, and the empty tomb. The Holy Spirit inspired Luke to purposefully record this piercing (prophetically pertinent) question that the preponderance of mainstream Christianity is not only remiss to ask, but terrified to ask. We would rather languish in denial and procrastination than stand that close to the flame. *"LORD, are there few that be saved?"* (re. Luke 13:24)

This question challenges us not only to assess our own salvation but illuminates our glaring lack of a viable witness of the saving grace of Jesus Christ to our loved ones. Where am I on the eternal continuum of walking and living by faith? How far along am I? Am I pressing into the strait gate and narrow way of a godly lifestyle, or am I amused and entertained and anesthetized by the allure of the world, self-celebratory and mesmerized on the broad way to hell?

Christian, why are we not asking this question of one another, or asking it of the solemn assembly and the righteous congregation? Do we realize that the LORD Jesus Christ teaches and preaches that the *"many"* who presume themselves to be the children of the kingdom shall be told, *"I tell you, I know ye not whence ye are"* (re. Luke 13:27)?

Child, before you align yourself with that multitude, ribald and celebratory, misappropriating the LORD's grace upon the broad way of worldly alliance and questionable confederations, take an exacting inventory of your Christian testimony. Get alone with the LORD and ask him some pertinent personal questions of your own. Objectively review the course your Christian sojourn is taking. Submit your way, and expose your heart and mind, to the omniscient eye of him whose name is *HOLY.*

✳

There is a way *which seemeth right unto a man,*
but the end thereof are the ways of death.
Pro. 14:12

✳

(Bluntly), am I following a man, or am I following every Word that proceeds out of the mouth of GOD? Beware of hybridizations attenuating the austerity of the Word of GOD, taking what is Holy and making it common.

Under the guise of tolerance, and to increase our numbers, we adulterate and abbreviate grace. Jesus Christ died to deliver me from the power of sin, not placate and excuse me in it. Concisely, it is Satan who aids and abets and excuses sin.

He is a master at subterfuge and misconception, a specialist in spouting vain philosophy and common sense. He is always available and eager to assist us in reasoning things out and helping us get our way.

Genuine love, a pure love of light and truth and holiness, seeks my highest good. This is, concisely, why GOD has established it, that man is not to live by bread alone, but by the Word of GOD. The patriarch Job expresses it well.

✻

I have esteemed the words of his mouth
more than my necessary food.
re. JOB 23:12

✻

Moreover, a life lived by faith is lived in the light of GOD's presence, beneath the auspices and explicit assessment of the *HOLY*, in the express freedom and unequaled liberty of absolutely nothing hidden.

✻

But he knoweth the Way that I take: when he
hath tried me, I shall come forth as gold.
JOB 23:10

✻

Ah, how refreshing the perpetual living revelation, that my *Way* is grace through faith. Indeed, his name is Jesus. Children, all that is not consumed by fire becomes One with the fire. Irresistible grace; pure gold.

The reality of my life is hidden with GOD in Christ. This physical body, and (what I call) the elusive season of my humanity, vies for dominion and superiority, but (praise GOD!), by grace through faith my spiritual nature is in the ascendancy.

Systematically (and inevitably) this physical existence, which strives against the nature of GOD in me, is incrementally headed for the grave. This existence that I am desperate to preserve inexorably fades day to day. It is Christ in me who is reaching unto immortality, and by greater grace I glimpse the faith of it – as in awe and wonder, I perpetually worship him.

Such is the eventual fatigue and decay of the physical body, the inescapable effects of age, and the wages of sin. Until the LORD comes, no one here gets out alive. When King David's days drew nigh that he should die, and he realized that his time was short, he expressed this phenomenon of physical limitations to his son Solomon like this: *"I go the way of all the earth: be thou strong therefore, and shew thyself a man"*, (re. 1 Kings 2:1-2).

We obsessively exercise and medicate and indulge this physical body as if it were the true reality of life. We spend decades meticulously preparing for retirement, laying up treasure here on earth, giving this physical existence the preeminence over the acute reality of eternity.

Children, we are, first, eternal (spiritual) beings temporarily housed within a physical body. I have written at some length of this in other works. *GOD is a Spirit*, (re. John 4:24), and mankind is made in the image, and after the likeness of GOD, (see Gen. 1:26). Our physical body is made of earth, and some water; or perhaps some (convenient) spittle, while GOD was kneeling there upon the earth shaping humanity out of a mudhole. Our *Godlikeness* is spiritual, as GOD is Spirit.

This is the reality of GOD. I repeat, this is the Reality of GOD: The breath of GOD that he breathed into mankind's nostrils to make him a living soul, is an eternal entity.

This Adamic nature, this physical existence which I go to astronomical lengths to amuse and entertain and indulge, is a corrupted (fallen) nature, which left to its own designs and reasoning, is determined to drag me into hell. For eternity. Children, this Adamic nature (as David expressed it) is *"the way of all the earth"* (re. 1 Kings 2:2).

How I *spend* my life (my physical, natural life) is reckoned of GOD a spiritual investment unto eternity. This is the *Way* of God: that I offer up my life one day at a time unto GOD. The Apostle Paul, the apostle to us Gentiles, expresses it concisely.

❋

I beseech you therefore, brethren, by the mercies of GOD, that ye present your bodies a living sacrifice, holy, acceptable unto GOD, which is your reasonable service.
Rom. 12:1

❋

If I pass away before the LORD returns, I go *"the way of all the earth"* (re. 1 Kings 2:2). And if I have lived it unto myself, and *"spent"* my life abandoned to my physical senses and desires, busy being my own god (little "g"), then hell will await me at the end of it all. Simply put, how I *"spend"* my physical life shall determine my eternal destination.

Self-realization and GOD-realization are not on the same page. Indeed, they are not even in the same book, if you will. And by GOD-realization, I mean a life lived by faith unto the honor of GOD. *"By grace through faith"* is the dynamic of the LORD's salvation (re. Eph. 2:8). It behooves me to get on the same page as GOD (if I may put it like that), to align myself unerringly with GOD's reality.

✳

*Trust in the LORD with all thine heart; and lean
not unto thine own understanding. In all thy "ways"
acknowledge him, and he shall direct thy paths.*
Pro. 3:5-6

✳

It was human reasoning which concluded that the fruit in the Garden of Eden would be good for food. Adam concurred with his wife. This is an illustration of man(kind) getting his *"way"* with the help of an ostensibly wise counselor, contradicting the Word (and the *Way*) of GOD.

When my will is aligned with GOD's will, I can be said to be in *the Way of Life Everlasting.* It is in Christ Jesus that I am reconciled to GOD's will and GOD's reality, and my true destiny in the *Way* of my life bringing GOD honor and glory. When the desires of my heart merge and coalesce into the LORD's desires, it can be said that I am in *the Way* of the perfect will of GOD. It is all in Jesus.

✳

*Commit thy "Way" unto the LORD; trust also
in him; and he shall bring it to pass.*
Ps. 37:5

✳

A godly commitment is an absolute adherence and worshipful allegiance to the comprehensive Word of GOD. My *Way* is a grave and covenant undertaking with GOD in Christ. This is the *Way* of a single purpose and undivided loyalty.

✳

*The light of the body is the eye: if therefore thine eye
be single, thy whole body shall be full of light.*
MATT. 6:22

✳

To trust the LORD is an astute expression of a settled intimacy and mature apprehension of the enterprising *Ways* of faith. Do not let the language intimidate you. Read it again. *Trust* transcends faith in what GOD has said to lay holy hands upon his character. After the crushing press of repetitive failure, and on the other side of the fires of a genuine faith, I may touch the face of GOD by trust, and by greater grace. The *few* know what I am referring to.

The Holy Spirit seizes this opportunity to attest to the unequivocal deity of the LORD Jesus Christ. There is unlimited potential (and predominantly untapped) power, within the progressive dynamic revelation of the deity of the LORD Jesus Christ.

✳

Hear, O Israel: The LORD our GOD is One LORD.
DEUT. 6:4

✳

This is not conjecture or supposition, but the revelation of GOD by the doctrine (or teaching) of the LORD Jesus Christ, (the Word of GOD).

Jesus Christ is LORD, to whom all the patriarchs and prophets bear an inerrant witness.

We mustn't compartmentalize Jesus the Christ of GOD. We mustn't disassociate Jesus Christ from Father GOD. He told us plainly that he is indivisible from the Father, but I wonder how many of us heard him.

✳

I and my Father are One.
JOHN 10:30

✳

Do we really know who Jesus is? The LORD Jesus Christ spoke the following sentence to the Apostle Thomas, but he might just have well have prophetically spoken it unto you and me.

✳

If ye had known me, ye should have known my Father also.
see JOHN 14:7

✳

There is a continuous finite argument transpiring within my natural mind which refutes the deity of the LORD Jesus

Christ, (and it must be taken authority over). It is aided and abetted by the counsel and reasoning of this world system to deny Jesus Christ in the earth. It is the deliberate methodology of Satan to portray Jesus Christ as less than GOD. This earthly logic attempts to mask the eternal reality of my own existence, as well as deny the deity of the LORD Jesus Christ. This is what the warfare is about. And it is expedient that we take the time and space to address the concerted evil assault which would diminish the divinity of Jesus Christ.

*

For though we walk in the flesh, we do not war after the flesh. (For the weapons of our warfare are not carnal, but mighty through GOD to the pulling down of strong holds.) Casting down imaginations, and every high thing that exalteth itself against the knowledge of God, and bringing into captivity every thought to the obedience of Christ.
2 Cor. 10:3-5

*

Hear, O Christianity: The LORD our GOD is One LORD, and Jesus Christ is *"He"* (as inspired by Deuteronomy 6:4).

Christian, this is the precise revelation that Satan is desperate you never fully apprehend. Jesus Christ is the veil we look behind (and beyond) to behold the *reality* of GOD. This is the astute revelation of light and truth and holiness that casts Satan out.

The dynamic potential of my progressive revelation of the LORD Jesus Christ is as infinite as GOD. Jesus Christ has always been (existed). Moreover, he has always existed *with*

GOD, and he has always *been* GOD. John the Beloved could not have expressed it more eloquently or concisely.

✳

In the beginning was the Word, and the Word was with GOD, and the Word was GOD.
JOHN 1:1

✳

Every suggestion, or oblique (cloudy) finite rationale, that dares intimate that Jesus Christ is less than GOD (or 1/3 of a trinity of Gods), must be perpetually quenched. My faith must abide in the unseen territory which connects and abridges the finite with the infinite. Faith is the vibrant, dynamic *Pioneer* in the progressive revelation of GOD in Christ. The intimate acquaintances of Jesus Christ live upon the horizon there.

In the context of our chapter, Jesus Christ is the *Way,* or the *course* unto God, because he "*is*" GOD (emphasis mine). He is the Way "*to*" GOD, the Truth "*about*" GOD, and the Life "*of* "*GOD*. And no man (or woman) comes unto the Father except "*by*" him. Hence, in everything I write (I am hoping to express) that it takes GOD to *show* me GOD and to *give* me GOD.

The LORD moves me to make a point, and hopefully without offense, since I am no longer exasperated (and angry) at what I perceived as not only an impediment to my spiritual growth, but a potentially lethal illusion or deception. The religious orthodoxy that predominantly shaped and indoctrinated my young Christian mind, indirectly taught me that Jesus Christ did not fundamentally exist before he was born in Bethlehem of Judaea. This was primarily perpetrated by presumption, omission, and misdirection. By tradition, and by garden-variety ignorance and indifference, we perpetuate the species of superficial or titular Christian.

When souls are at stake, it is more complicated (and critical) than being an issue of mismanagement or negligence. I cannot speak for others, but I was a full grown (industrial strength) sinner, and I needed an Almighty Savior. The revelation that was withheld from me was not a deliberate oversight or a calculated intent to harm by my teachers (and/or preachers). They taught what they had first learned. And, of course, my level of comprehension (or specifically the lack thereof) was an issue.

But, speaking and reflecting from 20/20 hindsight, the specific revelation of the deity of the LORD Jesus Christ proved to be the catalyst of my victory over sin. My radical transformation from sinner to saint is dependent upon my realization of the deity and power of my Savior, Jesus Christ, his absolute Omniscience and Omnipresence and Omnipotence.

The LORD Jesus Christ spoke it, but I was not specifically taught it.

✳

If ye had known me, ye should have known my Father also.
see JOHN 14:7

✳

The progressive (and perpetual or constant, unceasing, dynamic) revelation of the deity of the LORD Jesus Christ is the key to the kingdom. It is Christ in me (coupled with my realization of Christ in me) who has power over sin and power to impart resurrection (eternal) life. Concisely, Jesus Christ is Savior and LORD and Baptizer with the Holy Ghost because he is GOD.

Children, Bethlehem of Judaea was not the beginning. Hear, O Christianity, the LORD our GOD is One LORD, and his name is Jesus.

✳

I AM Alpha and Omega, the beginning and the ending, saith the LORD, which is, and which was, and which is to come, the Almighty.
REV. 1:8

✳

The progressive revelation of the deity of the LORD Jesus Christ is the effectual removal of a veil from my heart and my mind and my understanding. The finite theology and human logic which would limit the LORD Jesus Christ must be cast down. Doctrinal strongholds that would restrict or reduce the deity of the LORD Jesus Christ by two thirds (2/3) must be cast down. He who has ears to hear, let him hear.

To label the presence of the LORD Jesus Christ in the Old Testament as *preincarnate visitations* is patently and deleteriously erroneous, noxiously false. The whole earth (and the universe besides) is eternally filled with his glory and majesty.

Jesus Christ is LORD. Jesus Christ is the *Way*, and no man comes to the Father but by him (re. John 14:6) because he is GOD. We must go to the Source.

At some critical theological juncture, some very wise men decided to help the rest of us by relegating the identity and nature of GOD into three distinct entities, if you will. And there are indeed, three that bear record in heaven, the Father, the Word, and the Holy Ghost, *but these three are One* (see 1 John 5:7). And there are three in earth that bear witness, the Spirit, and the water, and the blood, *but these three agree in One* (see 1 John 5:8).

These (unnamed) theological wise men and witch doctors compartmentalized GOD into three distinct persons. This may have been their first degree of error (if I may phrase it like that), because GOD is emphatically not a person. *"GOD is a Spirit"* (re. John 4:24). It is the LORD Jesus Christ (*the Word of GOD*) who says so. And (I attest) it is more than a matter of semantics when the soul of humanity is at stake.

The designation of "person" to define or classify him who is *Infinite* is woefully insufficient. Moreover, it is subtly (or cleverly and cunningly), automatically denigrating or diminishing of the omnipotence and autonomy of GOD. And (I attest) the methodology is an intentional spiritual wickedness in high (religious) places deliberately designed to undermine or deny the deity of the LORD Jesus Christ.

GOD is unceremoniously compartmentalized into three persons with three "offices" or duties. The subliminal suggestion of the doctrine (teaching) conveys that, at any given time, I have one third (1/3) of God available or present with me.

Let us hope, and even presume, that this diminishing of the omnipotence of GOD and deity of the LORD Jesus Christ is unintentional on our teacher's (and preacher's) part. However,

(I attest by the Holy Spirit) that this ideology or teaching is designed and driven by spiritual wickedness to subvert and impede the Christian's authority in Jesus Christ.

This teaching (doctrine) was a stronghold in my young Christian mind. This teaching was an impediment and a disparaging of my developing comprehension of GOD. This teaching rendered my conceptualization of GOD within finite parameters. Under the guise of helping me assimilate the identity and nature of GOD, this teaching limited him who is *Infinite* to finite constraints.

Frankly, this teaching exalted itself against the knowledge and truth of GOD's identity and character as expressed by the Word of GOD. This teaching covertly (and cunningly) reduced the omnipotence and sovereignty of GOD by two thirds. He who has ears to hear has even now heard.

Jesus Christ consistently taught that he was One with the Father, that the Father was always with him, that the Father never left him alone. The LORD our GOD is One LORD who is both Father and Son by the Holy Spirit. This is what the comprehensive Word of GOD teaches.

Please, I am not splitting hairs or pontificating to hear the sound of my own voice, I was a prisoner of a one-dimensional ideology and religious misinterpretation of the omnipotent nature of GOD in Christ. And I have proof. The revelation (and realization) of Jesus Christ as GOD was the impetus and sustaining catalyst of my victory over sin and self and the love of the world in the reckless pride of my life. My converted character is the evidence of things not seen. Concisely, I am a new creature.

Jesus Christ is the *Way* to GOD, well, because he *is* GOD. We cannot finitely describe or even imagine the heights and the depths of his preeminence or the glory of his nature. We possess the understanding we have of him by grace. And, I add, through faith and due diligence.

Frankly, I forage and scavenge and scour the Word of GOD to find the evidence and substance of the HOLY, and by greater grace elicit an encounter with him. By faith, I rummage and pillage and pursue him whom my soul loves.

Christian, you may have to turn your television off, and perhaps your telephone and your laptop, and straightforwardly offer the LORD that time. GOD wants my uninhibited unbroken consciousness.

GOD favors the insatiable heart and the inquisitive mind, and that soul on fire for another encounter. GOD favors them unafraid to stand by the flame and walk through the fire. Those who will offer up the wood, hay, and stubble of their irascible and petulant personality upon the altar of GOD's love for the world. It is even as I have said before: GOD favors the godly.

Indeed, I find that he has been present with me all along; that is, as I realize the kingdom of GOD within me. *For in him we live, and move, and have our being* (re. Acts 17:28).

Christian, if so be, that you are in Christ, even as you call yourself by his great name, then you are *holiness unto the LORD* (re. Jer. 2:3), a sanctified vessel in the sovereign pleasure of GOD.

In the chrysalis of Christ Jesus my soul is found in the *becoming*. I am not trying to be mystical or deliberately abstract; I am seeking to express the miraculous evolution and transformation, and the radical conversion of my innermost character, the development and burgeoning of the kingdom of GOD within me.

※

And of the increase of his government
and peace there shall be no end
re. Is. 9:7

※

Here, I must interject something, and thank you in advance for your indulgence. The following short text in italics, I sent my pastor, the Senior Pastor at Man O' War Church of GOD in Lexington, Kentucky, Pastor Mitchell Tolle, Sr. my "first-reader" and the exemplification of the LORD's grace: *We are being made One with the dynamic. I can literally feel the transformation. I don't even know who this guy is anymore. Praise GOD!*

Christian, the *Way* that you take is Christ. He is (the course and the manner) of living a deliberately sanctified existence in the presence of a Holy GOD by grace through faith. He is the Holy Spirit of the Father and the Son, Jesus Christ, and he is One LORD. He is the Christ of GOD, and the Holy Spirit of a Living Word. He still speaks.

※

And thine ears shall hear a Word behind thee,
saying, This is the Way; walk ye in it, when ye turn
to the right hand, and when ye turn to the left.
Is. 30:21

✳

There is no circumstance or crisis common to living that the Word of GOD does not (and cannot) address or confront or alter in a child of GOD's favor. Hear me. Correlative to my intent to apply them and live by them, the Word(s) of GOD come with a living, dynamic, circumstance-imploding power. Concisely, his name is Jesus.

As I hear him and learn from him, as I cognitively and internally assimilate the revelation of his deity, he directs and commands my every circumstance into the perfect will of GOD. By faith, the revelation assumes its place of practical application. Moreover, the prophetic unfolding of this exhilarating revelation (of the deity of the LORD Jesus Christ) can sustain its own redundancy.

✳

If ye had known me, ye should have known my Father also
re. JOHN 14:7

✳

My love for him (and my awe and wonder of him) burgeons exponentially with the revelation. My worship and prayer rise to new levels. Obedience and sanctification naturally and progressively evolve, and love overshadows the commandment. He is the *Way* that I take, even as I am made One with the revelation.

As I realize that Jesus Christ washed the same feet he created, I enter into the narrow way of life. When I let this mind be in me, which was also in Christ Jesus (re. Phil. 2:5), I am in the way of everlasting life. When I become the bond servant of Jesus Christ in GOD's love for the worst of humanity, I am entered into that narrow way: when I can be broken and disseminated in the sacrifice of Christ for my neighbor's soul and poured out for the insatiable thirst of mankind.

When I realize that the *Way* of GOD is to be his king and priest in the earth, and that it entails a cross, I will feel the straitness of the gate, and the agony and stricture of this narrow way – when I am made One with the sacrifice.

The gospel of Jesus Christ is by *Way* of an Old Rugged Cross. It is the *Way* of suffering fellowship and conformity unto death, and then, I may know him and the power of his resurrection (see Phil. 3:10). It is a narrow way, to be poured out like water, and pulled and twisted and broken in the grubby, thankless hands of a greedy horde of godless humanity, and perhaps not the prestigious and celebrated place that I (and you) had presumed.

Christian, if you are impugned and exploited and trampled by the ninety and nine so that Jesus Christ can get a Word of hope and exhortation to the one, perforce you are in the narrow way of the gospel of GOD's unquenchable love. You are spent in GOD's endeavors and irrepressible love for your neighbor's soul. *This is the Way; walk ye in it* (re. Is. 30:21).

In the pressing crush of a multitude's hatred, and having our name cast out as evil for Jesus' sake, we narrowly realize the life lost to find it (if you can feel me). Oftentimes the narrow way of life is a trail of tears. The crown of life, and to share the glory of Jesus Christ, is for them who overcome.

The way of an acute suffering association with the cross of Jesus Christ, and an explicit uncompromising sanctification from the love of this world, is not a popular (or palatable) doctrine (teaching).

Have you not known, son or daughter of GOD, that to be accepted in the Beloved is to be despised and rejected of this present (perverse) society and corrupt world system?

✳

*Wherefore Jesus also, that he might sanctify the people
with his own blood, suffered without (or outside)
the gate. Let us go forth therefore unto him without
(or outside) the camp, bearing his reproach.*
HEB. 13:12-13

✳

An integral (imperative) provision of a Baptism of fire is a comprehensive purification. Only after the sifting and the crushing and the burning, only after an explicit character conversion, have I somewhat with which to strengthen the brethren (see Luke 22:32). It is only as I am made One with the revelation, that Jesus Christ speaks out of me. And as I am made One with the sacrifice upon the altar, even so, I inherit eternal life.

The Way of the gospel of Jesus Christ is the way of an Old Rugged Cross. It is the acute substance and evidence of no greater love than this: that of the life laid down for its friend, and love in the service of all humanity. I am resolutely and progressively made One with this love, or I must deny it and disparage it, and ultimately be revealed to have hated it.

This is the *Way* of the love of GOD in the eternal interests of my neighbor's soul. I must align myself with the sacrifice of GOD's love in the service of (even) the worst of humanity, or eventually be revealed as a religious pretender playing a part. The narrow way of love is to freely extend the same grace and mercy that was extended unto me, or hide behind some empty religious form, saving my life for myself.

This is the narrow *Way* of genuine love which infuriates the hypocrite hiding behind ceremonial religious forms of faith. This is the love of GOD that must be eradicated (and crucified) by the religious pretender unable and unwilling to meet its commands. This dreadful revelation of the love of GOD is the astute narrow way of the cross of Jesus Christ, and few there be that find it; that is, few that take it up.

Uh, concisely, this is the strait gate and the narrow way that those upon the broad way of ceremonial form and all-permissive grace must speak disparagingly of.

※

For the mouth of the wicked and the mouth of the deceitful are opened against me: they have spoken against me with a lying tongue. They compassed me about also with words of hatred; and fought against me without a cause. For my love they are my adversaries: but I give myself unto prayer. And they have rewarded me evil for good, and hatred for my love.
Ps. 109:2-5

※

The *Way* of the love of GOD in Christ Jesus for (even) the worst of humanity, runs deeper than surface Christianity. The *Way(s)* of selfless love are higher, much finer than Religion.

The mysteries and intimacies of GOD in Christ are not taken lightly or dismissed or impugned without remuneration. It is the strictures and the commands of the love of GOD in Christ which religious posers and prostitutes separate from their company. It is, concisely, Christ *within* the disciple, which intuitively (and omnisciently) discerns the animosity and rejection of the multitude of pretenders on the broad way of all-permissive grace and love without the accountability of truth.

We (contemporary Christianity) have enough difficulty fellowshipping with, and, uh, loving those of like-minded denominational persuasion, much less persons of a different ethnic origin or color of skin, or those that dare to disagree with our opinion (or doctrine). Moreover, if we cannot love our fellow-saints and immediate peers adequately, how are we going to love sinners until they realize the LORD's saving grace?

*

For if ye love them which love you, what reward
have ye? do not even the publicans the same?
MATT. 5:46

*

Children, the *Way* of the love of GOD in Jesus Christ runs deeper than the shallow reciprocal fellowship of formal religion and is higher than seeking the temperamental honor one of another. When I investigate the Word of GOD, the Word of GOD investigates me. GOD intends that the revelatory epiphany of the Word of GOD is the unsparing correlative disclosure of the real me.

GOD wants the Christian intimately involved with the redemption of humanity. Every Christian is intended to be a virulent, infectious disciple of the gospel of the love of GOD in Jesus Christ. Every genuine Christian is resolutely and progressively transformed into an incendiary catalyst in the continuity of the gospel of Jesus Christ and him crucified. I am to be a contagious (communicable) carrier of the good news of GOD's love.

Part of my education in Christ is coming to terms with my inability to love like that. Speaking personally (and excruciatingly), some of us are damaged goods. How to love my neighbor when I despise myself? Waking up with a man I could no longer live with was the effectual catalyst which drove me to Jesus Christ in the first place, if you follow.

The love of GOD in Jesus Christ is a supernatural love. It had to be sent into this world. (I believe) it was somewhere within this very manuscript that I wrote: The love of GOD is not a natural species. It is the Holy Spirit of GOD who makes Christians.

We must stop teaching and preaching the love of GOD as a noble but (realistically) unreachable ideal. We teach and preach it peripherally, with the unstated undertones or suggestion that it is essentially unattainable for us earth-bound creatures. Children, the Holy Spirit of GOD can radically and irrepressibly (resolutely and progressively) transform me into someone that not only can miraculously love my neighbor as myself, but also into a Christian who can revolutionarily love my enemy as well. Indeed, my first effectual overture in procuring such a supernatural love is to confess and own my absolute ineptitude, and step into the light and truth of my deepest depravity.

Love for our neighbor, and even love for our enemies, is attainable for all in Christ Jesus who volitionally submit to the rigors of its strait gate and narrow ways. Moreover, none of us are too old, too mature, or too wise to bask in complacency or avoidance. The love of GOD in Christ Jesus has infinite, expanding, inclusionary horizons. And it is the only *Way* that the world is going to see the kingdom of the LORD Jesus Christ revealed in earth as it is in heaven.

✷

> *BY THIS shall all men know that ye are my*
> *disciples, if ye have love one to another.*
> JOHN 13:35

✷

Children, here is a personal observation. GOD's love is such upon me, and his mercy and grace are so freely and lavishly bestowed upon me, that loving my enemies in no way diminishes me. Rather, I can well afford to bless them that curse me, do good to the that hate me, and pray for them which despitefully use me, and persecute me (re. Matt. 5:44). For I am my Father's child. Notwithstanding that I am but precariously balanced upon the cusp of the revelation, nonetheless, in the LORD Jesus Christ, I am my Father's child.

Notably, being a Bigger Christian no longer (intemperately) appeals to me. By greater grace and gradients of incendiary faith, I walk and live upon volatile horizons. *And yet shew I unto you a more excellent Way* (re. 1 Cor. 12:31).

It has been my experience, and my progressive and dynamic breakthrough, that being intrepid enough to risk sincerely and comprehensively confessing my utter despair and inability to love my neighbor as commanded, has ultimately proven to be my passageway to empowerment. It is not an instantaneous phenomenon, as believing and confessing Jesus Christ as my LORD and Savior may be described. But when I have first sincerely confessed my absolute powerlessness to love as commanded, I have begun the process.

I can be said to be in the *Way* of eternal life, an active participant in my own *becoming* a son of GOD. My conscious, perpetual abiding in the LORD Jesus Christ by the Holy Spirit, even as he abides in the Father, is an unceasing miraculous sojourn. I am continually being transformed and matured while I am in the *Way,* (if you follow). Many of us, unfortunately, cannot sustain the rigors and discipline and the self-denial of this narrow *Way* which leads unto life. It is even as the LORD Jesus Christ says, *"Few there be that find it"* (re. Matt. 7:14).

I was not instantaneously transformed from a sinner into a saint, but the moment I confessed Jesus Christ as my LORD and Savior, I immediately entered *"the becoming"* a son of God. By faith, I enter into the narrow *Way* of eternal life, and by faith I take each subsequent step in the *Way.* The Word of GOD is a daily bread.

The Apostle Paul pointedly concludes chapter twelve of 1 Corinthians referencing love as the preeminence (and culmination) of all spiritual gifts. In fact, he goes on to say in 1 Corinthians 13:1-3, that without love (or charity) all other spiritual gifts profit us nothing. This is my point. To be so utterly indispensable, we teach and preach an idealistic standard that is a noble aspiration, but not one that is really within our reach. In fact, we usually cannot get done with our discussion of loving our neighbor and/or our enemies quickly enough.

To be such an integral imperative of the entire gospel message, and ostensible means of identifying genuine Christians, we predominantly do not deliberately address our difficulty in apprehending the gospel necessity and command of love. That is, we broadly and markedly do not talk about or confront our inability to love. We change the subject.

This leaves many of us on the broad way of church attendance and ceremony to qualify and designate our Christianity. Or, we are in the wayside, what I often refer to as listless and anesthetized in the corner of the pew. The preponderance of us are stuck in the status quo of a vain form of faith to emulate the forward momentum of a genuine repentance and radical character metamorphosis.

The Word of GOD found me subsisting there. The Holy Spirit unsparingly showed me that being commanded not only to love the brethren, but also my neighbor as myself, and my enemy also, yet not submitting to the power of GOD's Word that would enable me to, (for me), was sin. How readest thou, saint?

Enough faith to move mountains, without love (or charity), is utterly immobilized (see 1 Cor. 13:2). None of my elitist Christian appurtenances and special gifts will work without it. For love to be so indispensable to faith, we have relatively and predominantly been negligent.

Like any shortcoming or sin, a forthright confession is the catalyst of its radical conversion. There is no remedy for what I continue to hide or ignore. My emotional (and personality) dysfunction which rendered me unable to love or trust was the Biggest giant in the promised land.

We, as a people (Christianity), must address the incongruity of our testimony, and the dissonant, contradictory example which we present to the world. Concisely (bluntly), the world is well apprised of our inability to love not only them, but also among ourselves. We are barely cordial to those of our own denominational brand.

(This is not a new message the LORD lays upon my heart and mind and consciousness.) Bluntly, when the world looks at us, they do not see the love of GOD in Jesus Christ, they essentially see a disparate, disillusioned, disoriented reflection of themselves. Except we think we are better than them. Someone has to say it. For love to be the preeminent identifying virtue that purportedly designates Christianity, we have grossly missed the mark. We are out of the *Way*.

But there is hope. I must use myself as an example. Frankly, Satan had me convinced that I could never (not in a million years) love like that. So, there was no use talking about it. Granted, it was a lofty ideal and a noble notion, but an abstract, ethereal, uh, vacillating, dissipating, unattainable Christian nirvana. You understand. Thus, I learned how to effectively conceal my covert, seething, unfavorable feelings toward my neighbor, and my raving, volatile hatred for my enemies. I could, of course, be civil toward the Holy Brethren and the Sisters of Sanctity, uh, provided they had first been cordial to me.

The Word of GOD found me there procrastinating and disseminating, a self-appointed master of misdirection and religious deception, an unadorned garden-variety hypocrite. Every time I uttered some empty platitude referring to love, the Holy Spirit would convict me.

I pondered these things. If God would command me to do something that I was utterly unable to perform, such as to love my neighbor as myself, then my religion was not a real living entity, it was an obscure metaphysical ideology. I was theoretically (or hypothetically) commanded to love. GOD did not really expect it of me, right? Did he?

Yes, he did, or he would have never spoken it. My inane conclusion that I would never be able to love my neighbor as myself is a prominent example of human reasoning undermining and limiting the Holy One of Israel.

God has higher aspirations for me than I have for myself. It is by faith that I rise to meet them. Faith to faith, I effectually follow Jesus Christ into the righteousness (and perfect will) of GOD.

In retrospect, and in honesty, my inability to love was not the only variable or righteous virtue in which I limited GOD's power to effect change in me, for all he commands and expects of me. Frankly, I expected Jesus Christ to do all the work, you know, all the digging and the heavy lifting. The LORD wanted me to partner with himself. This is essentially the nature of walking and living by faith: encounter and engagement, mutual pursuit. Both hands full, next foot forward.

We know that the first (and great) commandment is to love GOD with all our heart, mind, and soul. And that the second commandment is to love our neighbor as ourselves. We know that these two commandments comprise all the law and the prophets (see Matt. 22:37-40). In my experience (and over time), I could not realize loving my neighbor, and could not even conceptualize loving my enemies, until I first fully apprehended the love of GOD. I speak of GOD's love for me as a personal possession (a perpetual living revelation), and of my aptitude and ability to return that love (an intense incessant dynamic process).

To be painstakingly honest, I did not know the first thing about love. The only thing that I knew well, and was really good at, was sin. Just saying. I did not even know how to love *the Brethren.* Uh, hell, I did not even like the majority of them. And they did not like me. Well? Someone must make a beginning; getting honest, that is.

(Basically), correlative to my practical apprehension of his mercy and grace lavished upon me, I progressively realized the love of GOD extended unto me in Christ Jesus. I had mercy and grace coming out my ears, as it were. I am still astounded. The love of GOD extended toward humanity is a living perpetual revelation of awe and wonder.

It is Christ within the genuine Christian who loves. Jesus Christ is the continuity and outreach of the love of GOD. It is an evangelical love, an incendiary fire. Because GOD loves them, it does not diminish (or cost) the genuine Christian anything to love them. There is not cost to count. The LORD Jesus Christ has already paid it. The love of GOD in Jesus Christ is an overflowing, overwhelming inestimable flood. Because the mature (obedient and sanctified) Christian perpetually realizes and abides in the love of GOD, they cannot help but extend and perpetuate that love.

Frankly, the love I have for my enemies is an accurate measure of my Christian maturity. Concisely, how much Christ do I have in me? That is, how deeply and profoundly do I abide in the (comprehensive) Word of GOD, and how pervasively and assiduously does the Word of GOD abide in me? (Like leaven works the lump.)

Children, Jesus Christ is the *Way* of this supernatural love of GOD. This is the Way that the world is going to see (and feel) Jesus, and subsequently be saved. This is the miracle. And we (predominantly) do not talk about it. Oh, we talk about how much GOD loves *us*, and how much we love him, but we uncomfortably breeze over the love we are supposed to have for our neighbor. And concerning loving our enemies, well, it feels like we have silently colluded that this is such an unreasonable and impossible spiritual fantasy that it need not be confronted at all.

The love of GOD in Christ Jesus for both my neighbor and my enemy is extravagantly available. It miraculously emerges and manifests as I abide in Christ. Out of the heart of a genuine mature disciple of Jesus Christ, the love of GOD for their neighbor and enemy cannot help but palpably materialize. The love of GOD is inherent or intrinsic with the presence of Jesus Christ by the Holy Spirit. It cannot be otherwise.

I refer to the genuine article; that is, the Holy Spirit abiding and given unbridled access to my character, and sedulously allowed to have his Way – to transform, to convert, to set ablaze. (Distinctly and deliberately) I am not referring to fraudulent religious smiling faces and Sunday morning supercilious (and superficial, and artificial) smarm.

The genuine love of GOD in Christ Jesus transcends all human and earthly definition of love. It is, indeed, a supernatural, miraculous love, a heavenly love. As we have said, it had to be sent into this world. The love of GOD in Jesus Christ eclipses all earthly love, like the heavenly overshadows the earthly.

*

For as the heavens are higher than the earth, so are my ways higher than your ways, and my thoughts than your thoughts.
Is. 55:9

*

The love of GOD in Jesus Christ is explicitly a *Holy* love; much like *GOD is a Spirit* (re. John 4:24), and he is a *Holy* Spirit. The character of GOD cannot be considered outside the constraints and (the) commands of his holiness. Only by the pure blood of Jesus Christ may I meet with, and commune with, a *Holy* GOD who dwells above the mercy seat, between the cherubim (see Ex. 25:22).

It is by faith in the blood of Jesus Christ that we may receive such boldness of access to the throne of all grace and comfort (re. Heb. 4:16). The LORD Jesus Christ is the *Way* of this access into the holiness and purity of the all-encompassing sovereign love of GOD.

*

Having therefore, brethren, boldness to enter into the holiest by the blood of Jesus. By a new and living Way, *which he hath consecrated for us, through the veil, that is to say, his flesh.*
HEB. 10:19-20

✳

This is not Religion. This new and living *Way* of the expression of GOD's love is the gospel of Jesus Christ and him crucified. This is not the dead way of ceremonial tradition and mindless preservation of the status quo, an elaborate external religious presentation leaving me fundamentally unchanged internally. This is the new and living (and radical) *Way* of sinners miraculously being born again.

The love of GOD is accountable to the shed blood and torn flesh of his only begotten Son, Jesus Christ. He is the *Way* into the inner sanctum of GOD's holy presence. We will come the same *Way,* or we will not enter in. The gospel of the cross of Jesus Christ is the miracle of my becoming One with the sacrifice (and the atonement) upon the altar. This is not the way of *"feel good about me, ain't I cute"* Christianity.

This is not Religion by title only, this is the dynamic *Way* of a living sacrifice, and the Christian disciple's life laid down in the love of GOD for the next sinner's soul. This is not the way of self-indulgence and listless indifference in the corner of the pew, this is the living *Way* of entering into, and aligning myself with, GOD's evangelical love in the earth. This is not formal religion and gold-star Sunday school attendance, this is the living *Way* of spiritual warfare in the relentless arena for souls, and the down and dirty of casting devils out.

Children, this is not the way of red carpet and accolades and the applause of men, this is the *Way* of the world hating you and I because we have identified ourselves with the love of GOD in Jesus Christ for our neighbor's soul. The LORD Jesus Christ has the authority to proclaim himself as the *Way* because he took my cross, and he took my sin. Frankly, I was busy going the other way.

All we like sheep have gone astray; we have turned every one to his own way; *and the LORD hath laid on him the iniquity of us all.*
Is. 53:6

Christian, the correlative *Way* of resurrection power and life is the *Way* of suffering fellowship and conformity to the death of his cross in the continuity of the gospel. By faith, the disciples of Jesus Christ enter into this *Way* of progressive sanctification and holiness to the LORD. Again:

And thine ears shall hear a Word behind thee, saying, This is the Way, *walk ye in it, when ye turn to the right hand, and when ye turn to the left.*
Is. 30:21

It has been my experience, that oftentimes I have heard some instruction from the Holy Spirit, that I had just as soon not heard, if you follow. That is, at the time. It is as the Word of

GOD became dear, that I hastened to develop the ear of the learned, or, as the prophet expressed it:

※

He wakeneth mine ear to hear as the learned. The LORD GOD hath opened mine ear, and I was not rebellious, neither turned away back.
see Is. 50:4-5

※

Concisely, Jesus Christ is the *Way* of total surrender and absolute consecration unto GOD. Moreover, consistent obedience begets progressive revelation. This is my favorite mantra from another perspective: *"And unto you that hear shall more be given"* (re. Mark 4:24). It is even as we have been saying. This is the *Way: "So then faith cometh by hearing, and hearing by the Word of God"* (Rom. 10:17).

The Word of GOD is the *Way* of radical character transformation, the revolutionary conversion of my soul, the metamorphosis of my life goals from self-realization to God-realization. The Word of GOD is the dynamic vehicle of my evolution from the physical to the spiritual, and from the temporal into the eternal. This is the *Way,* walk ye in it, (re. Is. 30:21).

GOD does not speak to hear the sound of his own voice. The Word of GOD is the explicit expression of his creative genius and the transforming power of the very thoughts of GOD into Word. When the earth was without form and void, and darkness was upon the face of the deep (re. Gen. 1:2), the same Word that spoke light into the darkness, and ordered calm into the chaos, is the same Word that miraculously transforms my soul. His name is Jesus.

The Word of GOD is the effectual catalyst and impetus of my progressive character modification, the precipitate or primary cause of my perpetual (active) conversion. The Word of GOD is not a one-dimensional text or arcane history book of Judaism and Christianity, but it is a living organism. Frankly, it is more alive than you and me, because it is *Infinite*, and we are bound by physical and finite constraints.

The Word of GOD, when read with godly purpose and the intent of applying it to my life circumstances and character by faith, is accompanied by the Sword of the Spirit and the resurrection power and life of the LORD Jesus Christ. When I read the Word of GOD with faith and resolution to obey its precepts and commands, the Spirit of GOD (of *both* the Father and the Son) take up residence in the temple of my body and my spirit man. According to the Word of the LORD Jesus Christ, it is so.

✳

*If a man love me, he will keep my Words: and
my Father will love him, and We will come unto
him, and make Our abode with him.*
JOHN 14:23

✳

Children, this is the Holy Spirit (the Holy Ghost) of GOD that makes me a Christian from the inside-out. This is the *Way* of love and obedience unto a progressive sanctification. And this sanctification, purposefully leads me into (what the

Word of GOD refers to as) *"perfecting holiness in the fear (or reverence) of GOD"* (primary reference 2 Cor. 7:1).

Sanctification refers predominantly to the process of my being purposefully separated from sin and from self and from this world system, unto GOD. Holiness (with sanctification) more specifically refers to the progression of my usefulness to GOD. Through the separation and the cleansing of my body and spirit man as a result of sanctification, and by the effectual power of the Holy Spirit and the Living Word of GOD, I am progressively made holy as he is Holy.

Holiness is the process of our taking our appointed place in the perfect will of GOD as his intercessory priests and kings in the earth. We have been converted and made fit and empowered to strengthen the brethren.

By obedience to the Word of GOD, and separation (sanctification) from this world system, my earthen vessel is progressively made conducive to house (or host) the heavenly treasure of the Spirit of GOD, a Spirit who is a *Holy* Spirit. It is GOD's desire to not only live among his people, but to also dwell *within* his people.

❋

> *For ye are the temple of the living GOD; as GOD hath*
> *said, I will dwell in them, and walk in them; and I will*
> *be their GOD, and they shall be my people.*
> re. 2 Cor. 6:16

❋

GOD desires his people to separate themselves from this corrupt world system because (bluntly) a *Holy* Spirit is not going to dwell in a defiled or unholy temple. The prince of the power of the air (re. Eph. 2:2), and the god of this world, Satan (2 Cor. 4:4), is the same spirit force of this world system that colluded with the Pharisees and the Jews and the chief priests, to coerce the Romans to crucify Jesus Christ over 2,000 years ago. Concisely, the Holy Spirit of GOD is not going to cohabitate in a vessel (or person) who loves, is controlled by, or partnered with, the same evil spirit that crucified Christ.

✳

Wherefore come out from among them, and be ye separate (sanctified), saith the LORD, and touch not the unclean thing; and I will receive you.
2 COR. 6:17

✳

Children, this *Way* of sanctification is an extension of the essence and character and holiness of the LORD Jesus Christ. *"This is the Way, walk ye in it"* (re. Is. 30:21). This is not Religion. This is not legalism, this is relational. *True* Christianity is to walk uprightly by faith according to the Holy Spirit of the Resurrected Christ Jesus who walks in you. He is the *Way*.

This doctrine (teaching) of sanctification unto holiness is not a popular subject, but it has always been the explicit desire (and command) of GOD that his people be distinctly separate from the other peoples and nations around them. Our definitive separation from the love and dictates of this world system has always been one of the primary means by which the children of GOD are differentiated from the children of the world. In the following scripture, Moses expresses it eloquently and concisely.

✳

For wherein shall it be known here that I and thy people have found grace in thy sight? is it not in that thou goest with us? so shall we be separated, I and thy people, from all the people that are upon the face of the earth.
Ex. 33:16

✳

Christian, the temporal and the eternal, the spiritual and the physical (the Spirit and the flesh), *"are contrary one to the other"* (see Gal. 5:17). The pleasures and comforts and demands of this temporal life strive for ascendancy and preeminence over the spiritual. But we are (in particular) and primarily, an eternal spiritual entity created in the image and after the likeness of GOD (see Gen. 1:26). This is GOD's reality.

How we *spend* our lives, that is, how we spend our time and attentions and affections, is reckoned of GOD as a spiritual sacrifice. This is primarily because *"GOD is a Spirit"* (re. John 4:24), and we are his spiritual heritage, his children.

In GOD's estimation, our pandering and fellowshipping and partnering with worldly and carnal elements has covenant implications. It is as we receive the revelation and understanding that the Word of GOD is living and eternally, prophetically pertinent, that we realize these things as *Truth*.

Succinctly, what was intended for the children of Israel in their specific wilderness is also intended for us (contemporary

Christianity) in ours. Unapologetically, this was GOD's reality then, and this is GOD's reality now.

＊

Take heed to thyself, lest thou make a covenant with the inhabitants of the land whither thou goest, lest it be for a snare in the midst of thee. Lest thou make a covenant with the inhabitants of the land, and they go a whoring after their gods, and do sacrifice unto their gods, and one call thee, and thou eat of his sacrifice.
Ex. 34:12, 15

＊

Children of GOD, we are not to be confederate in affection with the carnal elements that govern and drive the children of this world system. We are to markedly come out from among them and be distinctly separate (re. 2 Cor. 6:17). Not better, but different. The *unclean thing* that we are commanded not to touch is the modus operandi and underlying spiritual methodology of this world system which commands our silence about Jesus Christ in exchange for its acceptance and camaraderie.

Our submission to the coercion and suppression of our Christian witness is a complicity with covenant-like implications. This evil world system targets vocal evangelical Christians for tribulation and persecution, and pointedly withholds its affirmation or acceptance. In short, this world makes life as difficult as possible for those who will not remain silent about the light and truth (and holiness) of the LORD Jesus Christ.

To touch the *unclean thing* is to be complicit (and/or silent) about this world's subliminal evil disguised as innocuous amusements and entertainments. Frankly, to partake of sin and evil is to endorse sin and evil. There is no oblique human reasoning or argument to mitigate or excuse my participation and preoccupation (and bondage) to sordid television, uh, reality shows, sexually perverse advertising or pornographic internet sites, or the multifarious covert evil influences contained within the ostensibly benign apps of my (duh), *smart* phone.

To be swept along in the relentless tide of this world's lust and covetousness for the newest shiny thing is to partner with an *unclean thing.* Frankly, the Word of GOD unapologetically (and accurately) defines this as spiritual fornication and adultery. Children, this is the wide gate and the broad Way that leads to destruction (see Matt. 7:13-14).

Once more, the comprehensive gospel of Jesus Christ (the Word of GOD) is the strait gate and narrow *Way* of sanctification unto holiness. To have the manifest presence of the LORD Jesus Christ walking and laboring together with us, his presence and power living and abiding within us, and his anointing and mantle of authority upon us, we must markedly separate ourselves from this corrupt world system, pursuing and perfecting holiness in the reverent fear of GOD (re. 2 Cor. 7:1). This is the Way.

✳

> *And a highway shall be there, and a Way, and it*
> *shall be called The Way of Holiness; the unclean*

shall not pass over it; but it shall be for those: the wayfaring men, though fools, shall not err therein.
Is. 35:8

✳

Concisely, the way of holiness is the Way of an acute accountability and exacting remuneration of the blood and life sacrifice of Jesus Christ. It is GOD's *filter*, to use a currently popular buzz word. It is the Way of (the) absolute unsparing exposure of the light and truth of GOD's living Word, the LORD Jesus Christ.

Christ in me (and in you) is the narrow Way of self-assessment at the mercy seat of GOD. This is not a morbid self-consciousness. It is the perpetual liberty of living in the exact moment and the immediate presence of that holy place where the blood of Jesus Christ is applied. Here at the mercy seat in the holy place of perpetual communion with GOD, is the narrow Way which leads unto life. Truly, even as Jesus Christ says, *"And few there be that find it"* (see Matt. 7:14).

Grace answers to Truth in the Most Holy Place, at the mercy seat of GOD, between the cherubim which are upon the ark of the testimony (re. Ex. 25:22). This is the inner sanctum of GOD's residence in the Christian's soul. This, dear child, is the holy place where GOD desires to dwell.

Distinctly, this is behind the veil of all type and shadow and religious ceremony. This is the holy place of a radical character conversion, and the reality of GOD in Christ. (To paraphrase), Many are *called*, says Oswald Chambers, but few press their Way into this place to prove themselves *chosen.*

Conspicuously, this is beyond the outer courts, primarily meaning deeper than religious tradition and surface Christianity. This is the holy place of a militant character transformation. This is beyond the outer courts of religious observation. This is the acute realization of the kingdom of GOD within me.

✳

And let them make me a sanctuary;
that I may dwell among them.
Ex. 25:8

✳

This is pointedly not the wide gate of all-permissive grace or the broad way of worldly affiliations and carnal collusion. This is the narrow way of self-assessment in the immediate presence of the blood of Jesus Christ, the mercy seat, and the holy place of GOD. Indeed, this is the narrow way of a genuine Christian's soul and the marvel of being born again; the mystery and the wonder of Christ in me, and in you, the hope of glory.

Children let us ponder the peace and the potential of this holy place of GOD's manifest presence. This is the holy place of all intercessory prayer. This is the source and the cradle, the origin and anointing, of all evangelical endeavor.

Jesus Christ is the Way of sanctification and holiness unto GOD, and he has not changed. It is still the Way of self-denial and the austerity and commands of an old-rugged cross. The Way is still a definitive and resounding, *"Follow me."*

Children, this is the Way, and the realization of me preparing the King of Glory a place of habitation, and of his presence, in turn, making me an amenable and steadfast host of him who is *Holy* in all his ways. This is the miraculous process and apprehension of the kingdom of GOD within me; his kingdom come, on earth as it is in heaven. This is life more abundant *now*, the Way of life everlasting *now*.

We must definitively separate (sanctify) ourselves from this corrupted world system to be unmistakably and intimately identified with the LORD Jesus Christ, and in order to be an effective and constant host of a Spirit who is a *Holy* Spirit.

✳

As obedient children, not fashioning yourselves according to the former lusts in your ignorance. But as he which hath called you is holy, so be ye holy in all manner of conversation. Because it is written, Be ye holy, for I am holy.
1 PET. 1:14-16

✳

Jesus Christ is LORD. He is One LORD who is both the Father and the Son (the Word) by the Holy Spirit. This *Holy* Spirit is the *we* and the *our* who takes up residence within the obedient and sanctified disciples of Jesus Christ as delineated in John 14:23. He is *both* the Spirit of the Father and the Spirit of the Son. This is how *both* the Father and the Son may be said to send and/or give this Holy Spirit. For review, here are the primary scripture references that designate and support this doctrinal truth. This is the LORD Jesus Christ, teaching on the coming of the Holy Spirit, speaking in both scriptures.

✻

*But the Comforter, which is the Holy Ghost, "whom
the Father will send" in my name, he shall teach
you all things, and bring all things to your
remembrance, whatsoever I have said unto you.*
JOHN 14:26

✻

*But when the Comforter is come, "whom I will send unto
you" from the Father, even the Spirit of Truth, which
proceedeth from the Father, he shall testify of me.*
JOHN 15:26

✻

"GOD is a Spirit" (re. John 4:24), and he is One Spirit who is *both* the Spirit of the Father and the Spirit of the Son. It is even as the LORD Jesus Christ taught it, and attested unto it, *"I and my Father are One"* (John 10:30). The emphasis (and apparent redundancy) is warranted in every chapter.

It is even as John was favored to witness and transcribe GOD's record (of himself) in heaven. *"For there are three who bear record in heaven, the Father, the Word, and the Holy Ghost: and these three are One"* (1 John 5:7).

This is more than semantics, this is the revelation of Jesus Christ as One LORD, the stone that the builders of men's religions have rejected. This is the revelation of Jesus Christ as GOD; and not the revelation of GOD as three persons.

This is the Old Testament and New Testament precursor and preamble, and prerequisite, to every Word (and commandment) that proceeds out of the mouth of GOD.

✴

Hear, O Israel; The LORD our GOD is One LORD.
DEUT. 6:4 AND MARK 12:29

✴

Concisely, we were to *hear* this before we heard any other thing. It is the relentless theme of One LORD, and Jesus Christ as I AM THAT I AM resounding throughout the Word of GOD as inspired by the Holy Ghost. This is the gospel of Jesus Christ as One LORD.

This is Jesus the Christ of GOD and the One LORD of Christianity. Hear ye him. This is the acute (and continuing) revelation of our comprehensive manuscript, *I AM (Jesus),* and the unmistakable, irrepressible Voice of GOD.

✴

*I AM the Way, the Truth, and the Life: no man
cometh unto the Father, but by me.*
JOHN 14:6

✴

This is a fitting place to shift our main text somewhat from Jesus Christ as the *Way,* to Jesus Christ as the *Truth.* This revelation, this Truth of Jesus Christ as One LORD, is what the Holy Spirit severed me from formal denominational religion to show me. Concisely, Jesus Christ and the Father are indivisible.

Only the intrepid, and the teachable, proceed from here. The revelation of Jesus Christ as One LORD is specifically what John the Beloved calls *the Doctrine of Christ,* and it must be kept unpolluted from, and undiluted by, the teaching (or doctrine) of religious men (with or without a theology degree).

It is the Holy Spirit who takes this time and place in the interests of mainstream Christianity's soul. Moreover, this is the name that GOD, Yahweh, or Jehovah, sovereignly designated for me to have. Jesus Christ is LORD.

✳

Neither is there salvation in any other: for
there is [none other name] under heaven given
among men, whereby we must be saved.
Acts 4:12

✳

The potential consequences of my obstinacy and reluctance to abnegate or release the traditional teaching of religious men which had kept me spiritually bound and motionless for decades were dire. John the Beloved expresses it concisely and unapologetically.

✳

Whosoever transgresseth, and abideth not in the Doctrine
of Christ, hath not GOD. He that abideth in the Doctrine
of Christ, he hath both the Father and the Son.
2 John 1:9

✳

Jesus Christ is the *Truth* of GOD. He pointedly teaches that he and the Father are One. Once more, he says it as directly and concisely as possible.

✳

I and my Father are One.
JOHN 10:30

✳

May the Holy Spirit qualify my redundancy. When specifically asked, what is the first (and great) commandment, the LORD Jesus Christ prefaces his answer with what can only be called a cautionary prerequisite that he purposefully admonishes us to *hear.*

✳

And Jesus answered him, The first of all commandments is, Hear, O Israel; The LORD our GOD is One LORD.
MARK 12:29

✳

Some of you may not see it from there (or hear it), but the LORD Jesus Christ is alerting and exhorting us all, that before we enter into considering even the first commandment, he has an imperative instruction that precedes it. In fact, it is an integral (indivisible) component of the first commandment, as inseparable as the Father and the Son.

We then, without meditation (or mediation), immediately reduce the Almighty GOD by two thirds. This we do with human reasoning to help GOD explain himself. Even worse, we reduce him to one *person* of a trinity or (a three *person*) God. The unspoken subliminal suggestion of this spiritual wickedness in high religious places, is that I can only have one third of God with me, or ministering to me, at any given time.

No, I am not nit-picking or splitting hairs or merely arguing semantics. Where, and when, there is a soul's eternal (destination) and salvation at stake, to refer to GOD as a *person* (at any time and in any context) is totally and abysmally inadequate. Jesus Christ could not have told us more emphatically that we need to *hear* this.

The nucleus of the eternal argument is the deity of the LORD Jesus Christ. Even the most subtle suggestion that he is less than the absolute of GOD is suspect; and will eventually be exposed as an insinuation of the cunningness of the powers of darkness desperately seeking to diminish the light.

In the context of our chapter, it is appropriate that this is our first *Truth* in the *Way* of our understanding and apprehending the identity of GOD. (If I may), *"I AM the Truth about GOD"* says Jesus.

*

Sanctify them through thy Truth: thy Word is Truth.
JOHN 17:17

*

Full circle. Complete in Christ, (re. Col. 2:10). Behold the indispensable, indivisible nature of One LORD, the head of all principality and power.

Jesus Christ is the *Truth* who is the antithesis of the modus operandi of this world system. It behooves me to make significant note here and now, that during the LORD Jesus Christ's specific teaching (doctrine) on the *Comforter (the Holy Ghost)* as recorded by John, that three distinct times he calls the Holy Spirit, the Spirit of *Truth.* I list them now consecutively.

✳

Even the Spirit of Truth; *whom the world cannot receive, because it seeth him not, neither knoweth him: but ye know him; for he dwelleth with you, and shall be in you.*
JOHN 14:17

But when the Comforter is come, whom I will send unto you from the Father, even the Spirit of Truth, *which proceedeth from the Father, he shall testify of me.*
JOHN 15:26

Howbeit when he, the Spirit of Truth, *is come, he will guide you into all truth: for he shall not speak of himself; but whatsoever he shall hear, that shall he speak: and he will shew you things to come.*
JOHN 16:13

✳

"GOD is a Spirit" (re. John 4:24), is a quote which I often call my first fundamental, or an absolute of GOD. Concisely, GOD is a *Holy* Spirit of Truth like GOD is *Holy* Light and like GOD is *Holy* Love. These are inalienable, indivisible attributes of GOD's character. Emphatically, GOD is not a person; GOD is a Holy Spirit.

The ideology or methodology of this world system is predicated upon what I call *"The Big Lie."* It is Satan's initial assault upon the veracity of GOD's Word and the integrity (or Truth) of his very character. If you are alive and are a denizen of this all-encompassing contemporary environment (this world), then you have heard its evil mantra. *"Ye shall not surely die"* (see Gen. 3:4).

Of course, the other half of the equation (if I may put it like that), is GOD's instruction to Adam concerning the tree of the knowledge of good and evil. *"For in the day that thou eatest thereof thou shalt surely die"* (see Gen. 2:17).

The rudimentary ideology of this world system, as driven and governed by the god of this world, Satan, is to refute or discredit the Truth of GOD's Word. The prince of the power of the air (again, Satan), would have us believe that there are many alternatives other than offering the gift and substance of our life back unto GOD who gave them. The devil wants to aid and abet and persuade every person that he can, that they (we) can save our lives for our own enjoyment and indulgence rather than live for GOD's glory and honor.

Satan concurs with and reinforces our carnal counsel and helps refine our human reasoning and self-realization. His cunning design is to cloudy the reality of our eternal essence and present the temporal and the immediate as the substance or importance of life. He does not want me to think about eternity. He is a master of dissimulation and illusion, of distraction and misrepresentation, of veiling the Truth about eternal life: that our choice is really one of twain.

※

For the wages of sin is death, but the gift of GOD
is eternal life through Jesus Christ our LORD.
Rom. 6:23

※

"GOD is a Spirit" (re. John 4:24), and as I have mentioned, it is significant that when teaching about the Holy Ghost that

was to come and dwell among us, and within us, that Jesus referred to him three distinct times as *"the Spirit of Truth."* Jesus Christ could have accurately said that GOD is a Holy Spirit of *Love* or of *Light,* or of *Joy* or of *Peace,* but he specifically chose to call the Holy Ghost (or the Comforter), *the Spirit of Truth.*

Jesus Christ said, *"Thy Word is Truth"* (re. John 17:17). Moreover, the LORD Jesus Christ said, *"I AM the Truth"* (re. John 14:6). Children, we see the revelation of One LORD full circle, as it were. All things coalesce in Christ: for so it pleased GOD to present himself.

A lie is the antithesis of the Truth, and the deity of Jesus Christ is the front line and nucleus of the fighting. When Satan cannot convince me to accept a lie, he then offers me supposition and shadow, and the doctrines and postulations of wise men and witch doctors of shade tree theology.

Truth is an absolute. Jesus Christ did not say "I will teach you the truth." He said, *"I AM the Truth"* (see John 14:6).

Truth is an absolute: a whole number, as it were. Truth is an *"integer,"* an independent entity, complete in itself and by itself.

The LORD Jesus Christ is the Truth of GOD. And he is not one-third of God, he is One LORD; or three-thirds of GOD, if you must.

Once upon a time, I said that the Father was the substance of GOD, Jesus Christ was the Word of GOD, and the Holy Spirit was the Voice of GOD. I also pondered: *thought – Word – illumination.* Now, these meditations are not necessarily incorrect, they are just not complete. Finite words fall short ever time. Frankly, *"the wind bloweth where it listeth"* (re. John 3:8).

And, as such, we must conclude that it has a mind and a will. In awe and wonder, I run my metaphorical fingers through the mysteries and grace of GOD.

Jesus Christ is One LORD who is both the Father and the Son by the Holy Spirit. He is the Spirit of GOD who leads me into all Truth, as only Truth can (*re. John 16:13*).

The kingdom of GOD is the manifestation and realization of Jesus Christ in me, and me in Jesus Christ. In me, through me, and out of me.

Faith is the dynamic. I am always whole, yet always increasing. Christians are progressively (and perpetually) coalesced and assimilated into Christ by the One Spirit of GOD.

Truth, being the antithesis of the lie which this world system is predicated upon and governed by, naturally distances me (separates me) from worldly influence and domination. Jesus Christ is so much Truth that this world system was compelled to crucify him, thus exposing its evil and deception for what it was. Jesus Christ viewed (and taught) that this world system was something to resist and overcome, not something to be partnered with and subjugated by.

✻

In the world ye shall have tribulation, but be of
good cheer; I have overcome the world.
re. JOHN 16:33

✻

Jesus Christ is the Truth, *the reality*, which separates me from the illusion. Truth is the integral and indivisible essence of

Jesus Christ's character, as inseparable as the Father and the Son. *"Thy Word IS Truth"* (re. John 17:17). And we know that Jesus Christ is the Word made flesh, *"who is the image of the invisible GOD"* (re. Col. 1:15).

As I receive the Truth (which is inseparable and interchangeable with the essence of Jesus Christ, the Word of GOD), it intuitively and resolutely separates me from this corrupt world system. This is Jesus Christ's (high-priestly) prayer. This is what he came to do.

❋

Sanctify them through thy Truth: thy Word is Truth.
JOHN 17:17

❋

Jesus Christ sets me free from deception. He exposes the corruption behind the illusion. The LORD's salvation is an active, perpetual enterprise. By grace through faith, I apprehend progressive striations of the Truth of GOD, (if you follow). He who has ears to hear, let him hear. The Word of GOD puts a distinct difference between a fundamental belief, and that of a resolute following by faith.

❋

Then said Jesus to those Jews which believed on him, If ye continue in my Word, then are ye my disciples indeed. And ye shall know the Truth, and the Truth shall make you free.
JOHN 8:31-32

❋

Only as I pass through the world, only as I press into that strait gate, and only as I navigate that narrow way shall I know. Only as I walk in the light as he is in the light, (re. 1 John 1:7). Only as I reject the darkness. Faith is not a dormant listless waiting unto complacency and apathy, it is the dynamic violence of making the Word of GOD manifest, and the salvation of GOD in motion.

Concisely, I must stay within the sound of his Voice. Truth is a living organism in perpetual transition (at least from a finite perspective). Frankly, I follow, or I am left behind.

Passively and inertly waiting for a theoretical rapture is not realizing the kingdom of GOD, it is the sweeping evidence of my unbelief. There are giants occupying the promised land, and a militant opposition to the apprehension and realization of the kingdom of GOD within me. I am an active combatant now, and a soldier in Jesus Christ. I shall fight for the promises of GOD, for each progressive striation of grace and truth, or I shall not have them.

Such is the austerity and the strictures of being radically born again, the truth about a Baptism of Fire that contemporary mainstream minimalist Christianity does not teach. This is not your Grandma's Sunday school, but the bitter Truth in the reality of Jesus Christ and him crucified.

Such is the malevolence of this current world system's animosity toward Jesus Christ that we must keep moving or risk being swept away. Faith in GOD is a perpetual forward momentum toward an eternal destination. But such is this world system's focus and emphasis upon the temporal and the immediate satisfaction of our carnal senses, that it structures and presents the physical and the temporary as the reality of life. It is designed to distract and anesthetize me from the comprehension and realization that I am an eternal being housed in a temporary vessel.

This corrupt world system still loathes and hates Jesus Christ and his followers today just as much as when they crucified Christ over two thousand years ago. And GOD still despises the evil spirits that coerced wicked men to crucify his only begotten Son, Jesus Christ. James concisely describes this mutual hostility.

※

Ye adulterers and adulteresses, know ye not that the friendship of the world is enmity with GOD? whosoever therefore will be a friend of the world is the enemy of GOD.
JAMES 4:4

※

Children, GOD has an eternal, spiritual perspective, concisely because *"GOD is a Spirit"* (re. John 4:24). Jesus said so.

Satan convinced Adam and Eve to satisfy their temporal hunger and lust, and to satisfy their immediate physical senses to the neglect of their eternal (spiritual) well-being. They chose to believe a lie so they could have what they wanted. Satan convinced Eve that she could satisfy her temporal lust without endangering her eternal welfare, in direct opposition to what GOD had already said.

As I endeavor to write out of the heart and mind of Christ, an exposition of Truth inherently presses itself upon the page and pervades each manuscript I produce. It cannot be otherwise. The nature and modus operandi of this world system is in direct opposition to the character of Jesus Christ. Nevertheless, Truth prevails.

Jesus Christ is the living Word of the Grace and Truth of GOD that progressively and specifically separates (sanctifies) the Christian from the illusion and deception which drives and enslaves the denizens of this evil fallen world. The Truth naturally, spontaneously, miraculously, unmistakably sanctifies.

✳

Sanctify (separate) *them through thy Truth: thy Word is Truth.*
John 17:17

✳

GOD is a Spirit so Holy and True that he will not partner or cohabitate with any person controlled or subjugated, or even friendly with, this corrupt and false world system. Jesus Christ distinctly teaches that the Holy Ghost, the Comforter, is the Spirit of Truth *"whom the world cannot receive, because it seeth him not, neither knoweth him"* (re. John 14:17)

The premise (or presumption, rather), upon which this world's operative philosophy is founded is that the temporal, physical life is the primary reality (or truth) of life. But Jesus Christ says, *"I AM the Truth"* (re. John 14:6). Jesus Christ is the Way to GOD, the Truth about GOD, and the Life of GOD.

Concisely, GOD gives himself away in Christ Jesus. He is, succinctly, the Gift of GOD. He is the Gift of GOD of himself, all of GOD, the comprehensive GOD. Jesus Christ is One LORD who is both Father and Son by the Holy Spirit.

Jesus Christ is the Grace and Truth of the glorious Gospel of GOD that fulfills the Law of GOD. It is fitting (appropriate) that only GOD can satisfy the Law of GOD. This is the Truth about the Grace of GOD that fulfills and satisfies the Law of GOD – his name is Jesus, the Christ of GOD.

This world system, mercilessly driven rabid by the god of this world, goes to elaborate lengths to present this physical existence (and our natural senses) as the reality or truth about life. Through smoke and mirrors and labyrinthine machinations and deception, and through a plethora of distractions, sordid amusements and outrageous entertainments, the devil blinds our consciousness to the *true* reality of life, and the gospel of Jesus Christ. He lures us and enlists us (and enslaves us) with shiny things and an elusive (and illusory) social acceptance, and we then aid and abet in our own deception.

❋

But if our gospel be hid, it is hid to them that are lost. In whom the god of this world hath blinded the minds of them which believe not, lest the light of the glorious gospel of Christ, who is the image of GOD, should shine unto them.
2 Cor. 4:3-4

❋

Out of the heart of GOD, I cry; out of the acute abiding consciousness of the LORD Jesus Christ, I am allowed (and mandated) to write. The preponderance of mainstream Christianity is volitionally deluded, convinced that they are (whom I often call) the *righteous right.* And the doctrine of the trinity is the last bastion and the preeminent stronghold of spiritual wickedness and human wisdom ensconced (sheltered and entrenched) within *"high"* religious places.

I do not say these things lightly. Rather, I am constrained to say what I have been markedly reluctant to say. It is true that GOD is triune in nature and essence. It is true that there are three in heaven that bear record of One LORD, and that these three also bear witness of this truth in (the) earth (see 1 John 5:7-8). But they are decidedly not three persons. Rather, as the LORD Jesus Christ says, *"Hear, O Israel (or, O Christianity); The LORD our GOD is One LORD (see Mark 12:29 and Deut. 6:4).*

We cannot address and comprehend Truth without encountering these awesome and terrible mysteries of GOD in Christ. Once again, we come full circle, as it were.

✳

And it is the Spirit that beareth witness,
because the Spirit is Truth.
see 1 JOHN 5:6

✳

Please pardon my redundancy, but these are what I call *absolutes* of GOD, simple (but profound) utterances of the LORD Jesus Christ, the eternal, inerrant, infallible Word of GOD.

GOD is a Spirit

see JOHN 4:24

I and my Father are One

JOHN 10:30

The LORD our GOD is One LORD

re. MARK 12:29, DEUT. 6:4

Succinctly, Jesus Christ is all GOD, and pointedly (and unapologetically) *"not"* three persons. This is the Truth of GOD. His name is Jesus.

Jesus Christ is (and has always been) One LORD who is both the Father and the Son by the Holy Spirit. Moreover, *"Jesus Christ the same yesterday, and today, and forever"* (Heb. 13:8).

*

We think we know the Truth. We posture and pontificate as if we were the exclusive proprietors of the Truth. But there are aspects or perspectives of Truth that we have been hesitant to draw too closely to, if you follow. And there are aspects (and strongholds) of our personality and innermost character which preclude our apprehending the next striation or gradient of Grace and Truth. As Pastor Alph Lukau of Alleluia Ministries International in Johannesburg, South Africa is fond of saying, *"There are levels and levels."*

Now, as I was saying, concerning the world's blindness, as well as much of contemporary Christianity's, I referred to our blindness as volitional, meaning we are willfully deceived or self-deluded, surreptitiously partnered with the devil. There are truths about each of us which we would rather not know. Oh, such as personal biases and prejudices and our true feelings about not only our neighbor, but about our brothers and sisters in Christ, as well.

Frankly, there are greater levels of Truth than what we have apprehended. Concisely, there are deeper intimacies with

GOD in Christ than we have pursued. Bluntly, we have settled. You have heard me call it surface Christianity. Now, please do not be angry with me. Someone has to say something.

The progressive revelation of the Truth about myself that I deny or eschew, gets in the way of my perpetual (and more intimate) revelation of the LORD Jesus Christ. Duh. It becomes an excruciating issue of how much light (and illumination) (and exposure) I can stand or endure, and then sustain. Not just a glimpse by grace, but can I walk and live by faith in the light of the revelation? Can I endure (what I call) the agony of my grace, that is, the unembellished Truth of the Word of GOD radically transforming the character and nucleus of my inner man? Can I sustain the change (repentance), that the next level and intimacy of Truth commands? Can I continue to conform (and convert) to Christ?

Children, this Holy Ghost whom the LORD Jesus Christ emphatically taught must come is the very Spirit whom GOD is. He is as much GOD as the Father and the Son because he is the Spirit of the Father *"and"* the Spirit of the Son coalesced or united into One Spirit. This is the One Spirit of GOD whom the LORD Jesus Christ referenced five distinct times within just three verses of his *high priestly prayer* in the seventeenth chapter of the gospel according to John (see John 17:21-23).

Once more, this is the Spirit of Truth *"whom the world cannot receive"* primarily because they are allegiant and blinded (and enslaved) by a system that is predicated upon a lie and governed by deception. Jesus said of the world, relative to the Holy Spirit of Truth, *"it seeth him not, neither knoweth him"* (see John 14:17).

The world does not recognize or honor the presence of Jesus Christ by the Holy Spirit, his authority or his deity. Many who refer to themselves as Christians live a lifestyle that totally refutes their testimony and dishonors the name and character of the LORD Jesus Christ.

GOD is a *Holy* Spirit, and we must live a sanctified (separate) and holy lifestyle to honor him. In order to possess or host a Spirit who is *Holy*, we must disassociate ourselves from the sin and evil and corruption of the world through lust and covetousness and immorality.

As a young believer, it should not have come as a surprise to me, that in order to possess and host a Spirit who Jesus specifically and repeatedly called the Sprit of *Truth*, that I would first have to get painstakingly honest. The difficulty I experienced may have suggested otherwise. I cannot speak for anyone else, but my natural man did not want to die to self and to pride, or to the love of the world. As always (it seems), I took the long way around. Living in the Spirit, in the light and truth of GOD's living Word, is only as difficult as separating oneself from the darkness and deception which mercilessly drives the denizens and prisoners of this world system.

As we have discussed, it is the Truth that makes me free (re. John 8:32). His name is Jesus. It is the Truth of GOD's Word that sanctifies (re. John 17:17). His name is Jesus, the comprehensive GOD.

This is the revelation of Truth that makes men mad, in every sense of the word. This world system is so pervaded and surfeited with lies and orchestrated (organized) falsehood, that its innate antipathy and hatred of Truth cannot be overemphasized. Christian, a friend of GOD is an enemy of the world, like a friend of the world is an enemy of GOD (see James 4:4). It is that definitive. It must be said. Indeed, it must be cried aloud: There are no hybrid Christians in the kingdom of GOD.

The acute revelation of the deity of the LORD Jesus Christ makes worldly men (and women) desperate to deny and discredit him, and to silence him. It provokes posers and pretenders and religious prostitutes to malevolence and re-sentment, and to clandestine evil.

The Truth infuriates the Deceiver, and them that are de-ceived. Jesus Christ is the Truth that exposes the patholog-ical deception of mankind's reckless and obsessive (insane) lust for self-realization and instant gratification. The Truth is a threat to reveal that the world does not revolve around me: the startling offensive revelation that all things do not exist to primarily bring me pleasure.

The Truth commands my ego (and my appetite) into proper perspective. It is a light and a mirror into the reality of GOD, and the excruciating revelation into the depths and deprav-ity of my soul. The Truth inherently and aggressively sancti-fies (separates) from deception, it is the revelatory light and nature of the LORD Jesus Christ's character, his essence, his innate holiness.

The Truth explicitly and unapologetically clarifies, i.e. *Light has come, but men* (still) *prefer the darkness* (re. John 3:19).

(If I may). It is as I continue in the Word (Jesus Christ), that I shall know the Truth (Jesus Christ), and the Truth (Jesus Christ) shall make me free. Children, the criteria and measure of my salvation is do I know Jesus Christ, and what is the level of *Our* intimacy and fellowship?

Have I taken the time to get to know Jesus Christ as Savior and LORD? Have I turned my telephone off long enough to have a relevant (life-changing) conversation with him? Or turned my television and computer off long enough to have significant (character converting) fellowship with him? Have I allowed the Word of GOD to radically transform my heart and mind and soul so that I might accommodate and host a Spirit who is a *Holy* Spirit? Or have I gotten brutally honest enough to house a Spirit who Jesus Christ repeatedly calls a Spirit of Truth?

Knowing Jesus Christ as LORD and Savior goes beyond surface Christianity and religious form. The essence and character of Jesus Christ is inseparable from the Grace and Truth of the Living Word of GOD. Mainstream Christianity fundamentally presumes upon the Grace of the LORD Jesus Christ without submitting to the austerity and rigors of the self-denial (and sanctification) that the Truth of the Word of GOD commands.

Concisely, we resist the Truth of GOD which commands a behavioral modification and a character transformation. Grace saves my soul, but it is Truth that sanctifies (severs) me from the subservience and subjugation that my allegiance to the world, and my love for her, commands of me. The absolute transfer of my affections and devotions from the world to the Grace and Truth of Jesus Christ's character and essence requires a radically being born again. This is no casual acquaintance; this is an eternal covenant of infinite love.

The progressive knowledge and intimacy of a burgeoning relationship with the Truth of the Word of GOD (Jesus Christ), irrepressibly separates (sanctifies) me from my obligations and homage to this world system. The LORD Jesus Christ radically transforms me into an obedient and loyal citizen of the kingdom of GOD. My separation may (at times) be incremental, and even faltering or hesitant, but no less quantifiable. The Spirit of Truth confirms and establishes his own witness (re. 1 John 5:6); that is, it is the Holy Spirit of GOD who corroborates his own presence and power within the temple of my body and my spirit man.

To be enmeshed in worldly affairs, or inordinately attracted to carnal amusements and entertainments, and/or worldly goods and services and pleasures, is suspect for a person who calls themselves a Christian. It is James (the half brother of the LORD Jesus) who says that even a friend of the world is an enemy of GOD (see James 4:4). Frankly, this is (indeed) a militant statement. Ah, but such is the nature, or such should be the nature, of being born again of another Spirit – a *Holy* Spirit.

The comprehensive gospel of Jesus Christ and him crucified is a radically distinctive gospel, and its adherents and disciples are to be explicitly known by love, holiness, and sanctification from the world system. That "Christians" predominantly are not, does not change the Truth of it.

*

Sanctify (separate) yourselves therefore, and be
ye holy: for I AM the LORD your GOD.
Lev. 20:7

*And ye shall be holy unto me: for I the LORD
am holy, and have severed you (separated you)
from other people, that ye should be mine.*
LEV. 20:26

❋

Frankly, we predominantly live as if this sanctification should not have to be resolutely occurring now, (in the present). We (broadly) live as if we could wait until we get to heaven to finally tear ourselves away from our love for the world and the things of the world. Honestly, we live as if we have heard very little of what the Word of GOD says.

This may mitigate my redundancy, but it will not diminish my urgency in Christ. I have earnestly sought the heart and mind of the LORD Jesus Christ, and this is what he has given me: our knowledge and intimacy of the LORD Jesus Christ neither parallels nor warrants the presumption of (the majority of us) calling ourselves by his great name – for his name is *Holy*, and we are not.

Children, someone must call us out just that definitively and unapologetically, lest when this corrupt world system is judged of a Holy GOD, we are condemned right along with it. We have not rightly esteemed the significance of Jesus Christ's high priestly prayer unto the Father, that we (Christians) be sanctified through the Truth of GOD's Word (re. John 17:17). Frankly, we have either predominantly ignored GOD's desire that we be distinctly different (and separate) from the peoples of the world, or grossly underestimated the degree or importance of this command of GOD.

We are much too casual about the sanctification GOD desires (actually commands) for his people. The degree of our separation is infinitesimal. Notably, the verb *"have severed"* in Leviticus 20:26 is the same verb that is used in Genesis 1:4 to describe GOD having *"divided"* the light from the darkness. The Word of GOD is quite deliberate about it.

✳

I AM the LORD your GOD, which have
separated you from other people.
Lev. 20:24

✳

GOD's perspective is explicit, and uncompromising. This is the Truth of GOD's holiness, the character of his Word, the nature of his essence. This is the unequivocal Truth about the sanctification and holiness that GOD desires, but that we (contemporary mainstream Christianity) do not broadly teach or preach. We must be called out just like that. These things persist so that we, as Christians, can have unfettered access to the things of the world with a relatively clear conscience.

This is revelatory Truth, the unassailable expression of the holy character of GOD. His name is Jesus (the Word of GOD). He exposes our perfidy and mendacity. We make Christianity common.

Children, the difference GOD puts between light and darkness cannot be adequately described. The separation defies any (and all) discussion of degree. Christian disciple, the darkness must flee your coming in Christ Jesus. The *light* that is in you inherently displaces darkness, the Spirit of *Truth* within you exposes error and deception, and acutely identifies the liar (Satan).

Jesus Christ says, *"I AM the Truth"* (see John 14:6). This is the absolute of GOD. Truth is the essence of the Spirit who GOD is. Just as he is *Light,* and he is *Love,* and he is *Holy.*

When we reject or refuse the Truth, we are among them that deny Jesus Christ. From GOD's perspective, we have preferred a liar in his place. The following is mostly taught in an end-time prophetic context, but I attest to its present dynamic in the perpetual (ceaseless) sanctification of GOD's people.

*

Because they received not the love of the Truth, that they might be saved. And for this cause GOD shall send them strong delusion, that they should believe a lie. That they all might be damned who believed not the Truth, but had pleasure in unrighteousness.
re. 2 THESS. 2:10-12

*

A Christian who does not love their Bible (the Word of GOD, Jesus Christ) is an oxymoron, a nominal religious oddity, and an imposter. Concisely, there is no such animal in the kingdom of GOD. I speak the Truth in the Love interests of GOD for the incongruous disseminating soul of mainstream Christianity. It is not my desire to offend, but to awaken. We have had platitudes and a pass and empty religious palaver and are no closer to having an intimate relationship with the LORD Jesus Christ. This only, defines a Christian.

A Christian is someone who has progressively fallen in love with the LORD Jesus Christ. Receiving a love of the Truth is as simple (and as complex) as incrementally and irrepressibly getting to know the LORD Jesus Christ, for to know him is to love him. Of course, as in any relationship, there are levels and levels (once more, thank you Pastor Alph Lukau).

As the Apostle Paul wrote the Thessalonians, receiving a love for the Truth is how we are saved. It is synonymous with receiving Jesus Christ as our LORD and Savior. And as I often say, introductions happen, but relationships develop.

Concisely, Jesus Christ came by Grace and Truth to fulfill the Law. As inspired by the Holy Spirit, John wrote that Jesus Christ was *"full of grace and truth"* (see John 1:14). Moreover, this is how we receive him.

*

And of his fullness have all we received, and grace for grace.
JOHN 1:16

*

Let me try to speak for myself, out of my own experience. Frankly, I am a sinner saved by grace. And I was not instantaneously made a saint upon first making the acquaintance of Jesus Christ, or upon receiving him into my heart and mind and soul by faith. Yes, all my sins were forgiven instantaneously, and I remember that I immediately resolved to stop what were obvious (even glaring) external offensive behaviors, but my inner character (at first) remained fundamentally unchanged.

There are (what I call) striations of Truth, just as there are depths or levels of intimacy in my getting to know Jesus Christ. GOD intends that I grow in the grace and knowledge and revelation of Jesus Christ. Children grow.

(It has been my experience) that GOD lavishly releases his grace (his favor and good will) upon me to enable me to accept and acclimate the truth he shows me, not only about Jesus Christ, but also the truth about myself. Indeed, I will need grace to submit to the revelation of truth that the Holy Spirit shows me, and I will need grace to implement the changes (or repentance) that GOD requires. Praise GOD, it is all in Jesus Christ, and grace for grace.

What an awesome and wonderful and mysterious odyssey is this getting to know Jesus Christ as my LORD and Savior. But, alas, (woe is me) for each new striation of the Truth of GOD (the LORD Jesus Christ), is the simultaneous revelation (or exposure) of me. The Holy Spirit of the living Word of GOD (the LORD Jesus Christ) is ardently and purposefully and progressively transforming my irascible attitudes and converting my innermost character.

Truth is synonymous with the LORD
Jesus Christ, the Word of GOD.

Sanctify them through thy Truth: thy Word is Truth.

JOHN 17:17

✳

Moreover, it is only as I *continue* in the Word of GOD that I will know the Truth, and the Truth shall make me free (see John 8:31-32). My external behaviors are only a symptom of my true pathology. It is my engrained bad attitudes, childhood and developmental prejudices, biases and hatred, and my innermost character flaws that have me bound. It is only as I continue to know Jesus Christ in a progressive intimacy that he converts my character from the inside out. This only makes me a Christian. Indeed, this only makes me free. His name is Jesus.

Children, to present as a Christian (for decades), I was forced to emulate and affect the true repentance (change) that a viable and burgeoning relationship with Jesus Christ would have naturally and resolutely brought forth. Not only did I remain a prisoner of my unregenerate (unchanged) character, but I also became a prisoner to the religious form and activities that helped me to front as if I had changed. Granted, I had ceased a few glaring external behaviors, but there remained large tracts of uncultivated, recalcitrant, impenitent areas of my inner man and core personality that remained unchanged.

Getting to know Jesus Christ as friend and confidant, and as Savior and LORD, is the enigmatic process of navigating these truths of his holy character in the light and progressive revelation of my unholy (or unregenerate) character at the same time. Thus, the critical necessity of grace for grace. And then, more grace.

The grace and truth of the LORD Jesus Christ does not leave me as he found me. He is determined to present me before the Father radically transformed and definitively converted to his own character.

GOD has always been hidden in Christ from the cursory inquiry and the casual penitent. GOD is (according to his own wisdom, sovereignty, and pleasure) hidden within the striations of the Grace and Truth of the LORD Jesus Christ. (It has been my experience) that, grace for grace my pilgrimage in getting to know Jesus Christ is truth upon truth. As I successfully acclimate to this present truth in getting to know GOD (as I get to know myself), GOD faithfully releases the next bolus of grace (if you will) to prepare me for the encounter (and the confrontation) of the next level of truth. Or so I have found it, even as by the Spirit of the Living Word of GOD.

(I have, through much affliction and trial and error found) that I shall accede to this present revelation, and walk by faith in the light and truth of what the Spirit of GOD is showing me today, if I am to have grace for my journey tomorrow, (if you follow). Obedience begets unbroken continuity of fellowship, and the grace of the next revelation. This walking and living by faith commands fresh vision.

The *reality* of GOD, and the mystery and wisdom of the kingdom of heaven, is found in the LORD Jesus Christ. It is just as he said.

✳

I AM the Way, the Truth, and the Life: no man
cometh unto the Father, but by me.
see JOHN 14:6

✳

It is all in Jesus. This is the absolute reality of GOD, the progressive, irrepressible revelation of the Father in Jesus Christ, the Son, by the Holy Ghost. Again, it is even as he says.

✳

*If ye had known me, ye should have known my Father also:
and from henceforth ye know him, and have seen him.*
JOHN 14:7

✳

Had we looked beyond a superficial religious ceremony and formal dissociative church service we should have seen him. That is, had we plumbed the depths and the heights of GOD's Word beyond a surface Christianity, we would not only have seen the Father revealed there in the Son, but we would have begun to understand and apprehend him as One LORD as well.

The LORD Jesus Christ effectively says, *"If you had known me (well enough), you would have known the Father, also, because we are One."*

GOD is hidden in Christ (the Word) deeper than the apathetic and the casual care to go, dwells beyond the perimeter the perfunctory have set for the limits of their investment, beyond where the lukewarm care to live.

Before I can adequately apprehend the Truth of GOD, the truth about myself must be repented of. There are levels and levels.

I will go no further than my submission and obedience, and sanctification, allows. My innermost secret is the impediment, my deepest, most intimate character flaw will be revealed to have been my greatest obstruction. GOD wants it all: my greatest treasure, my nethermost lust and corruption, my innermost peculiar (particular, most private) pathology.

Unfettered fellowship in the light and truth of GOD's Living Word is a revelatory free fall, as limitless as GOD. He promised to lead us into *"ALL Truth"* (see John 16:13). My own dissimulation and duplicity (as aided and abetted by Satan) is the barrier.

Jesus pointedly told Thomas, *"from henceforth ye know him [meaning the Father]"* (see John 14:7), and a moment later emphatically told Philip, *"he that hath seen me hath seen the Father"* (see John 14:9).

The LORD Jesus Christ is the image of the invisible GOD (re. Col. 1:15). Jesus Christ is everything that GOD wanted you and I to see of him, nothing lacking. *Until that day we see him as he is,* (re. 1 John 3:2). Moreover, the LORD Jesus Christ is every Word that GOD has ever said, and he still speaks.

Thomas and Philip had spent three and one-half years following the LORD Jesus Christ, and (I advance) that they spent (relatively) every waking moment in his presence and acquiescent to his doctrine (teaching). As I told the men at Harbor House Christian Center in Henderson, Kentucky, just yesterday: Introductions happen, relationships develop. It is relatively easy for a willing heart and mind and soul to be introduced to the lovely Jesus, but it is quite a different dynamic altogether to *"know"* him. This enigmatic miracle and wonder of a man or woman being born again belongs unto GOD, yet by the violence of our faith, and by his grace, we press up against these intricate kingdom mysteries.

(If I may), after three and one-half years of intimate association, Thomas and Philip were upon the precipice (if I may put it like that), of pressing their way into the perimeter of the divine revelation of the Father and the Son (Jesus Christ) as One LORD.

It is with a passing angst and great regret that I must pronounce that it was the doctrine of the trinity which (for years) occluded my realization and apprehension of such amazing revelatory (and empowering) Truth.

✳

And ye shall know the Truth, and the Truth shall make you free.
JOHN 8:32

✳

Christian, if we will review the eighth chapter of the gospel of Jesus Christ according to John, the LORD is notably addressing people that believed on him. John emphasizes this remarkable fact by repeating it twice in short order, (see verses 30 and 31).

The scribes and Pharisees and Jews who Jesus was addressing took great pride in their spiritual heritage. They were direct descendants of Abraham and the prophets, GOD's special people, and they were quick to tell you so.

These were very religious people. The Pharisees prided themselves as the interpreters and custodians of the Word of GOD, and administrators of the Law. Their entire existence (one might say) evolved around their religion, customs, ceremony and traditions. Yet, despite their religious pedigree and qualifications, they were not free. Alas, it can be said that too much religion was part of their problem. Yet, despite their impressive religious pedigree and qualifications, they were not free.

There may be no servitude so tenacious or so comprehensive as religious bondage. I suspect there is more hope for an ordinary sinner. He who has ears to hear, let him hear.

✳

*If therefore the light that is in thee be
darkness, how great is that darkness!*
see MATT. 6:23

✳

They (the self-righteous, the religious bigot, the hypocrite), were occluding the portal to the kingdom of heaven then, and they obstruct it now. Sometimes, everything that I (think) I know, is the impediment. If I am not vigilant, my expertise begets arrogance, disdain, a closed mind.

Some men jealously covet the position of telling others how to get to GOD. Their doctrine (teaching) has a decidedly denominational slant, and all other denominations are in gross error, of course. The LORD Jesus Christ is the Way, the Truth, and the Life of GOD. If I direct your attention and affections anywhere else, I am the same as a thief and a robber.

GOD wants me to see the Father in Christ by the Holy Spirit. This is the Doctrine of Christ, that he and the Father are One. The Father is not aloof or as abstract as the doctrine of the trinity suggests (subliminally and otherwise). GOD is found in his Word (Jesus Christ), and nowhere else.

This speaks to personal relationship. How well do I know the LORD Jesus Christ? Jesus effectively says, *"If you had known me well enough, you would have known the Father, also"* (see John 14:7).

Only the LORD Jesus Christ can take me there. The heights and depths of the Father are revealed in the progressive intimacy of my personal relationship with Jesus Christ the LORD. Introductions happen, relationships develop. It is by repentance, by denying myself and renouncing the world, that I make room for the magnificent (dynamic, ever-developing) revelation of GOD in Christ.

Thomas and Philip were pressed up against the glass darkly in the fourteenth chapter of John.

I am not trying to be mystical; I am trying to make a point. After three and one-half years of intensive discipleship, of hearing the words of Jesus Christ and witnessing his miraculous works, they were on the cusp of a magnificent breakthrough. It is significant (to me) that they were still markedly struggling with the marvel and phenomenon of the Father and the Son (Jesus Christ) as being One LORD.

The Spirit of GOD corroborates my place in Christ, comforts me in my difficulties in assimilating the infinite revelation of the Father and the Son (Jesus Christ) as One LORD. Pressing up against the horizon of *greater works than these,* I look into Christ for the grace which facilitates the next revelatory truth in my getting to know the Father.

Only by the revelatory gradients of the grace and truth that are in the LORD Jesus Christ can I get there. The Father is wrapped in the glorious depths of the intimacies of Christ. Wise men (and witch doctors) and would-be proprietors of the Word of GOD, cloudy the waters with their presumptuous doctrines and denominational constraints. Frankly, the LORD Jesus Christ wants to tutor his own disciples.

✳

*Come unto me, all ye that labor and are heavy laden, and I will
give you rest. Take my yoke upon you, and* learn *of me;
for I am meek and lowly in heart: and ye shall find rest unto
our souls. For my yoke is easy, and my burden is light.*
MATT. 11:28-30

✳

Jesus Christ is the Way to GOD, the Truth about GOD, and the Life of GOD. It pleased the Father that his only begotten Son, Jesus Christ, should be the veil and the avenue and the source of all revelation, and that *"in him"* should all the fullness of GOD dwell (see Col. 1:19).

GOD dwells in Christ. We have seen that only by continuing in GOD's Word (Jesus Christ) can I know the Truth, and the Truth will subsequently make me free (see John 8:31-32). This is relational. It is revelatory. It is only as I get to know Jesus the Christ of GOD that I can know the Father. Being made One with GOD in Christ is the most intimate relationship in the universe. It only seems to be impossible (and out of reach) because it is *infinite*. It takes faith to vein the depths of Christ.

Jesus Christ's exhortation *"Follow me"* is not a figure of speech or something profoundly religious to say: it is the narrow Way and the revelatory Truth that leads unto the everlasting Life of GOD in his Christ. It is the way of obedience unto sanctification and the perfecting of holiness in the fear (and reverence) of GOD.

Have you not known, Christian, that Jesus Christ was pierced so that you and I could reach into eternity? Reaching into

Jesus Christ is both literal and figurative, just ask Thomas (Didymus).

"Follow me" is the revelatory command of the prophetic nature of the Living Word of GOD. It is the key to the kingdom of GOD progressively formed (and revealed) within me. It is the restoration of order, of peace and joy and love, and (what I call) the regenerative Breath of GOD. I exhale my humanity, and inhale eternity.

Jesus says, *"Come unto me."* He has already told us that no man (or woman) can come to the Father except by him. The innate difficulty with the simplicity (and profundity) of "*Come unto me"* is as I have said: When I look into the Word of GOD, the Word of GOD looks into me.

Consider this. Sometimes it is easier to volunteer for more service work than take an objective and purposeful look at what Jesus Christ wants to show me about myself. I speak from experience. It is easier to cut the Church's grass than it is to change (repent). It is easier to pass out tracts or volunteer at the food pantry. It is easier to tithe. It is even easier to attend Church all year without missing a service than to submit and accede to the change (the conversion) that the Word of GOD wants to effect in me.

To purposefully step out into the light and truth of GOD's Word day-in and day-out (as it were) is the most difficult thing (encounter and revelation and challenge) that I have ever done. *[Until what I had to do transitioned into what I love to do.]* Until I understood that GOD commanding me to live by every Word that proceeds out of his mouth is his divine and perfect love seeking and establishing my highest good.

Coming unto Jesus is frankly the strait gate and narrow way which leads unto life, *"and few there be that find it"* re. Matt. 7:14). Jesus also said, *"Many will seek to enter in, and shall not be able"* (re. Luke 13:24). May the urgency and severity of our situation mitigate my redundancy. The *few* and the *many* are the ratio of the Word of GOD.

Coming unto Jesus may accurately be likened to *"dead men walking."* Truly, coming unto Jesus is the death sentence of my natural man. Children, in his presence is a holy place. We meet the Father in Christ above the mercy seat where the blood of Jesus Christ is applied, and where willful sin ceases. GOD assesses my intent and facilitates my coming. When I am earnest and obedient, he sends me a *"Helper."*

It occurs to me that much of the reason that I was so heavily laden was due to the lengths I went in circumventing the loss of my life. As I was saying, it is easier to go to revival seven nights in a row than to acquiesce to the brutal honesty that the Word of GOD commands of me.

Religious form and ceremony, service work and a precise church attendance, are palatable alternatives to the bitter cup of an acute character conversion, or so I have found it. Alas, it is easier to be a religious poser than submit to a *Baptism of Fire*. Many of us have too much wood, hay, and stubble, to stand too close to the flame. It is easier to sing a little louder and smile a little broader than to align my lifestyle with a Spirit whose first name is Holy.

Only by yoking myself with Jesus Christ can I realize the Father. The grace and truth of GOD's Word (Jesus Christ) found me there subsisting, heavy laden, burdened with the religious form and ceremony and spotless church attendance that I submitted to establish and qualify myself as an exemplary Christian. It became so tedious tweaking my religiosity that I could not smile brightly enough.

Saving one's natural life for oneself is exhausting. Running from the truth about myself was interminable. Hiding the secret treasure of my innermost character was an unsustainable burden. Jesus Christ wanted to set me free from the religious partitions the real me hid behind.

To be symbolic or metaphorical, the yoke that Jesus is talking about is real. In fact, it is the yoke of a blood covenant. Jesus can say that the yoke is easy for you and me because it is his blood that is shed. Yet this yoke entails and commands an accountability of me. (I have found) that the burden becomes progressively lighter, and the joy and peace expressly fuller, the further I come.

It is as I learn of Jesus that the Father is revealed to have been in Christ since (before) the beginning of time. It is the revelatory Truth about the deity of the LORD Jesus Christ which makes me explicitly free from not only sin, but free from religious prevarication and dissimulation and all forms of pretense and posturing, as well.

✻

If the Son therefore shall make you free, ye shall be free indeed.
JOHN 8:36

✻

In the depths of Christ is where the Father dwells. Beneath enigmatic exhilarating layers and gradients of Grace and

Truth, the Father is hidden in Jesus Christ, the Living Word of GOD. Jesus says, *"Learn of me,"* and I will take you there. Christian, can you see the Father from there? wrapped in the swaddling clothes of Christ?

It is within the meek and lowly heart of Jesus Christ that the express deity of the Father dwells, safe from the pride and pretense of wise men and contemporary Pharisees and religious front men.

There is rest for the humble, and joy unspeakable for the children in the kingdom of their Father. Conversely, doctrinal and denominational envy and one-upmanship is an immortal weight and an odious burden.

The Father dwells in the bowels of Christ, in the secret places of the Son of man, with the unaffected and the unassuming, and with then not too proud to beg: with sinners and tax collectors and lepers, with the merciful and the upright, and with the meek.

※

The meek will he guide in judgment: and
the meek will he teach his Way.
Ps. 25:8

※

The yoke of the LORD Jesus Christ is a covenant transaction, a holy compliance, an absolute intimate mediation: (the merging) and the coalescing of the Christian into One. Under the grace and auspices of covenant love, reverential fear transitions into the worship of GOD in Spirit and in Truth, and in the beauty of his holiness.

The yoke of the LORD Jesus Christ is the progressive alignment and perfecting of my will with GOD's love for the world, and the revolutionary conversion of my innermost character. The yoke is easy, and the burden is light, just as the LORD says (re. Matt. 11:30), but my accountability is no less real. Notably, a chafed neck indicates my pulling in the wrong direction.

The yoke of the LORD Jesus Christ is my resolute walking in the way of GOD's love in Christ for my neighbor's soul. My interests and my will, and the desires of my heart, are coalesced into Christ.

Within the intricate recesses of Christ, the Father is progressively revealed. Father GOD is wrapped within the mysteries and wisdom of his Word. This is what pleases him.

Yoked to Jesus Christ, the acquiescent and the intrepid, the meek and the sanctified, are taken to where the Father dwells. Above the mercy seat, upon the ark of the covenant of his own testimony, GOD awaits his children. This is the secret place of GOD in his Christ, and where Christians are made perfect in One (see John 17:23).

"Learn of me," says Jesus. *"Follow me,"* says the LORD. *"Take my yoke upon you"* (re. Matt. 11:29). Children, this is (metaphorically) meeting the Father behind the veil, and where his mercies are everlasting. Markedly, neither the pride of life nor the lust of the flesh, nor the will of man enter in here. Only by covenant love is the Law fulfilled.

It is yoked to the LORD Jesus Christ that I learn to walk uprightly and enter into the holy place. Only within the veil will I see the Father, to finally apprehend that he has been sheathed in the mysteries and wisdom of Christ since (before) the world began. Christian, these great and terrible things behind the veil are the revelations that the prophets and the patriarchs and the angels of GOD have desired to look into – the revelation of the deity of the LORD Jesus Christ that makes devils and pietists mad.

*

The secret of the LORD is with them that fear (reverence and obey) *him; and he will shew them his covenant.*
Psalm 25:14

He that dwelleth in the secret place of the most High shall abide under the shadow of the Almighty.
Psalm 91:1

And there I will meet with thee, and I will commune with thee from above the mercy seat, from between the two cherubims, which are upon the ark of the testimony, of all things which I will give thee in commandment unto the children of Israel.
Exodus 25:22

*

The deeper into Christ that we go, the more meticulously this Living Word refines and transforms the innermost attitudes, values, and beliefs of our character.

Living Word definitively transforms the innermost attitudes, values, and beliefs of our character. It is within the secret catacombs of Christ, and where Christ likewise dwells within the convoluted chambers and corridors of my innermost character, that I am changed (converted), and the eyes of my enlightenment are opened. (Personally), the deity of the

LORD Jesus Christ continues to be the key of the progressive, irrepressible revelation of the kingdom of GOD within me.

In Spirit and in Truth, trusting the efficacy and deity of the LORD Jesus Christ, I enter into the realization of my Father, the regeneration of my spirit man, the redemptive revelation and assimilation of an eternal reconciliation. When the spirit of my life is the sacrifice upon the altar, that is, my 24/7/365 capitulation to the Lordship of Jesus Christ, it is then that I fellowship (commune) with the Father at the mercy seat. When there is nothing between my soul and the revelation (and reconciliation) with the Father except the blood of Jesus Christ.

In a place of full disclosure, in a holy place of unabbreviated light and unmitigated truth, the blood of Jesus Christ meets the mercy of the Father. Here only, in the place and consummation of covenant love, my character is radically converted, and my soul is seamlessly integrated into the beloved.

Deep calleth unto deep at the mercy seat of GOD, at the covenant place of the intimacies of the LORD Jesus Christ, and the revelation of his deity.

Christian, someone must ask us some terrible, penetrating things. How well can I see the Father from my (current) place on the dynamic continuum of the covenant love of GOD in Christ? Have I followed on to know the LORD Jesus Christ far enough (and intimately enough) to see the Father plainly?

✳

These things have I spoken unto you in proverbs; but the time cometh, when I shall no more speak to you in proverbs, but I shall shew you plainly of the Father.
re. JOHN 16:25

✳

How comprehensively have I allowed the Word of GOD to convert my innermost character? Indeed, have I allowed the LORD unfettered access to the secret chambers and covert corridors of my forbidden personality? And have I delved into the mysteries and wisdom of the Father hidden in Christ, or by the violence of my faith plumbed the furthest depths of the Word of GOD?

Sheathed in progressive gradients of amazing grace and revelatory truth, the Father eagerly awaits the children of faith.

The LORD's command *"Follow me,"* is a living prophetic directive, as pertinent today as yesterday; the explicit (eternal) utterance of him who is Alpha and Omega, and the Ancient of Days.

✳

I thank thee, O Father, LORD of heaven and earth, because thou hast hid these things from the wise and prudent, and hast revealed them unto babes. Even so, Father: for so it seemed good in thy sight. All things are delivered unto me of my Father: and no man knoweth the Son, but the Father; neither knoweth any man the Father, save (or except) the Son, and he to whomsoever the Son will reveal him.
re. MATT. 11:25-27

✳

Notably, these enigmatic scriptures above were spoken in the immediate context of the LORD Jesus Christ exhorting all those who labor and are heaven laden, to come unto him. He counsels us to take his yoke upon us, and to *"learn of me"* says Jesus, *"and ye shall find rest unto your souls"* (see Matt. 11:28-30).

Moreover, he promises us rest two distinct times as a direct result of partnering with him and learning of him (or getting to know him). It is in the nethermost recesses and intimacies of the character and essence of the LORD Jesus Christ that the intrepid and the faithful find the Father.

GOD has been forced for millennium to hide himself from the asinine assumptions and self-serving conclusions of wise men, and especially *religious* wise men. The very first designation of a *Father* (as it were), is his children. And we want to impress him (and one another) with our acumen and sagacity.

Nevertheless, there is always hope for them that remain teachable, to go deeper into Christ. Markedly, even in the physical presence of Jesus Christ, as recorded in the fourteenth chapter of John, Thomas and Philip were still struggling to assimilate the revelation of the Father and the Son as One LORD. (Even after three and one-half years of intense discipleship and the daily doctrine (teaching) of the LORD Jesus Christ.)

It is beneath progressive, interdependent (and interactive) layers of amazing grace, and in the wrestling, in the acute agonies of midnight truths, faith to faith the righteousness of GOD is revealed in the gospel of Jesus Christ (re. Rom. 1:17). My acquiescence to the present truth (at my place in the continuum of GOD's grace), is the prerequisite and precursor of the next revelation of Father GOD residing in his Christ. As I can receive it.

There is rest for the children, and most often a chafed and stiff neck for the wise and prudent. As I frequently say, "It takes GOD to show me GOD, and to give me GOD." Only in partnership with Jesus Christ will I learn the intricacies and intimacies of covenant love. Children, our reconciliation with the Father is on the dynamic continuum of getting to know Jesus Christ (the Word of GOD).

The acuity of my vision is dependent upon what the Word of GOD calls a single eye, meaning primarily a sincere and honest purpose (re. Matt. 6:22). The sanctity of GOD's purpose lies in the evangelization of the whole world, extending to the very worst of humanity, one sinner at a time.

What am I looking for when I look into the Word of GOD? Notably, the first words spoken by the LORD Jesus Christ as recorded in the gospel according to John is *"What seek ye?"* (see John 1:38).

Am I really looking for GOD, or am I looking for more of myself? Let us get brutally honest, beginning with me. There were literal decades that I was looking for corroboration of what I had already decided to believe. Frankly, I was wanting the Word of GOD to sign off on my carnal compromise and religious pandering: you know, my surreptitious self-realization.

To be yoked with Jesus Christ is to be completely aligned with the evangelical purposes of GOD in the earth, to love sinners until they come to a saving knowledge and faith in the LORD Jesus Christ. (Or not.) But to love then anyway. To love them where and how I find them, at the same place that saving grace found me – distinctly unlovable.

To be yoked together with Jesus Christ is to be completely surrendered and abandoned to his purposes, to have no hidden agenda of my own. Some of us primarily look into the Word of GOD because we have a doctrinal argument to win, and we want to get all our ducks in a row, as they say. To defend our doctrinal or denominational slant, to prop up our religious form, even to be a Bigger Christian than the next fellow. It distresses me to be so coarse, but Jesus Christ is not going to help me pull that load of manure.

The meek and lowly Son of man will not be yoked to those with a religious bias, with those that harbor a sense of spiritual superiority in the pride of their life. Only yoked to Jehovah's suffering servant shall I see GOD. Only learning the ways of the Son shall I realize the Father. Only when my purpose is pure.

✳

Blessed are the pure in heart: for they shall see GOD.
MATT. 5:8

✳

We must plumb the depths of Christ to realize the Father, as well as traverse the abyss of our own innermost character. The glory of the Father is only revealed in the resurrection life of the Son, the LORD Jesus Christ.

✳

For GOD, who commanded the light to shine out of darkness, hath shined in our hearts, to give the light of the knowledge of the glory of GOD in the face of Jesus Christ.
2 COR. 4:6

✳

Only the Spirit of GOD can open my understanding of the scriptures, and he is a *"Holy"* Spirit. When I have no self-interests, I will see the Father most clearly. The Word of GOD declares that *"One thing is needful"* (see Luke 10:38-42), and it is, of course, sitting at the feet of Jesus to hear his Word.

We should know this passage of scripture well. This is some of the most imperative teaching (doctrine) of the LORD Jesus Christ. He says that Mary has made a conscious choice to give the Word of GOD the preeminence, and it (her choice) shall not be taken from her. The LORD's affirmation of Mary's choice is so sweeping that she does not have to say a word in her own defense. *"One thing is needful"* is the concise ad startling utterance of the comprehensive Christ of GOD.

The Father and the Son are One LORD by the Holy Spirit. They are explicitly indivisible. You cannot realize the Son without apprehending the Father; nor can you know the Father except by fully assimilating (integrating) the Son. Once more, the Father and the Son are One LORD by the Holy Ghost, no matter how hard we try to make then three persons to fit our doctrinal and denominational strictures and parameters.

It pleased the Father that *"all fullness"* should dwell in the Son (see Col. 1:19). That is, the comprehensive identity and essence of GOD, the absolute infinite GOD. It cannot be adequately expressed in finite terms. Jesus Christ says, *"ALL things that the Father hath are mine"* (re. John 16:15).

Such is the Father's good pleasure in the finished work of the Son in the earth, that he has glorified Jesus Christ with his own essence and omnipotence. This is the prelude and rallying cry of all evangelical outreach and endeavor in the earth. This is the living cistern where the disciples and missionaries of Jesus Christ get their faith.

*

All power is given unto me in heaven
and in earth. Go ye therefore...
see MATT. 28:18-20

*

Hear, O Christianity, the LORD our GOD is One LORD, and he is *both* the Father and the Son by the Holy Ghost (my personal extrapolation as inspired by Deut. 6:4, John 10:30, and 1 John 5:7).

This is, concisely, more of the comprehensive *Doctrine of Christ*, and, uh, the infinite enigmatic collaboration of the Father and the Son (Jesus Christ) as One LORD. The LORD knew there would be gainsayers and naysayers defending their own one-dimensional, flat-lined doctrinal and denominational position and exclusivity.

*

*Murmur not among yourselves. No man can come
to me, except the Father which hath sent me draw
him: and I will raise him up at the last day.*

*It is written in the prophets; And they shall be all
taught of GOD. Every man therefore that hath heard,
and hath learned of the Father, cometh unto me.*
re. JOHN 6:43-45

＊

Ah, more proof this, that the Father and the Son are indivisible in works, and in Word. These (that are taught of GOD) are the sons and daughters of GOD who progress through asking and receiving and knocking – and refusing to be denied. These, by greater grace and by the violence of their faith, have irrepressibly transitioned, and been transformed, from servants to stewards to sons and daughters of GOD.

There is (of a necessity) only One LORD who can attest to being *"both"* the Father and the Son; *"each"* of whom can be said to send the Holy Ghost. To know and to apprehend these things, to assimilate and internalize these great and terrible things, is to be *"taught of GOD"* (re. John 6:45). These great things are discovered in the unfathomable depths of Father GOD, and within the living waters and the dayspring of Jesus Christ, the Son of GOD.

May the sweeping fullness of the Holy Ghost surfeit your soul, open the eyes of your enlightenment, and take you to school in Christ.

＊

But the Comforter, which is the Holy Ghost, WHOM THE FATHER WILL SEND IN MY NAME, he shall teach you all things, and bring all things to your remembrance, whatsoever I have said unto you.
John 14:26

✳

May the Holy Ghost (himself) justify what is his own redundancy. He who has ears to hear, let him hear. Dear children, may you by greater grace overtake this fullness of joy in the fellowship of the Father and the Son.

✳

But when the Comforter is come, WHOM I WILL SEND UNTO YOU FROM THE FATHER, even the Spirit of Truth, which proceedeth from the Father, he shall testify of me.
John 15:26

✳

"GOD is a Spirit" (re. John 4:24), and this is He. The Holy Spirit whom GOD is, (is) *both* the Spirit of the Father and the Spirit of the Son (Jesus Christ) indivisibly coalesced into One unified glorified Spirit of GOD. This is, concisely, the Holy Ghost. This is the kingdom of GOD come: in earth as it is in heaven.

As many as reach far enough and earnest enough into the pierced side of the resurrected Christ have realized and internalized this revelation, to find the Father resting and waiting in the bosom of Christ for the intrepid. Even as Jesus Christ the Son is found in the bosom of the Father.

This is the gift of the Holy Ghost according to the measure of my faith in the favor and auspices of the *greater grace* of GOD. For those who follow far enough this is face-to-face fellowship, even as a man speaks unto his friend (re. Ex. 33:11).

This is the holy place of full disclosure, unabbreviated light, and the place of both the marvel and the terror of authoritative incontrovertible truth. This is the whole animal bound to the horns of the altar.

Children, the acute revelation of the Father is only found in Christ. It is just as he said, *"No man cometh unto the Father but by me"* (re. John 14:6).

The Father waits behind the veil. The holy place of GOD's redemptive mercy has not changed. Again, and again, the Holy Spirit leads us into the same unchangeable theme.

✳

> *And there I will meet with thee, and I will commune*
> *with thee from above the mercy seat, from between*
> *the two cherubims which are upon the ark of the*
> *testimony, of all things which I will give thee in*
> *commandment unto the children of Israel.*
> Ex. 25:22

✳

Christian, how is it that we did not know? That it is only in the holy place, where the Father and the Son (Jesus Christ) are One LORD, that we see GOD? This is the doctrine (teaching) of Christ, and the holy place where humanity may be made One with Jesus Christ. Dear Christian, this is where you are made a priest and a king, and an intercessor in the love of GOD for your neighbor's soul.

This is the work and the irrepressible prayer of Jesus Christ, that we progressively be made *"perfect in One"* (see John 17:23). The wise and the prudent, and those bound by religious ceremony and tradition, say *"How can these things be"* (re. John 3:9)? And the children say, "Show me more." Indeed. He who has ears to hear, let him hear. *"Then are the children free"* (see Matt. 17:26).

GOD meets the children of men at the revelation of One LORD. At the holy place where the Father and the Son are One LORD by the Holy Ghost; it is there, that we are made One with them. May the GOD of all Grace increase our measure of revelatory Truth as we meet him at the mercy seat. For those who intuit and esteem what time it is, let us tarry for his return right there.

✳

That in the dispensation of the fullness of times he might
gather together in One all things in Christ, both which
are in heaven, and which are on earth; even in him.
Eph. 1:10

✳

As we saw in Chapter 3, many go as far as the *Door,* but they will not enter in. We might say metaphorically that many tentatively approach the well but have developed no taste for *living water.*

I repeat and reemphasize (and I somberly attest), that the gospel ratio of the *"many"* and the *"few"* is not mine. It belongs to

Christ. *Many* come hesitantly and provisionally to the cross of Jesus Christ, *many* acknowledge its necessity and even consider and admire its efficacy. But *few* enter in. I must enter into Christ, the Door. I must meet GOD inside the veil, at the mercy seat where the Father and the Son are One LORD.

Many of us stop and have ceremony at the very place our natural man and his love for the world in the pride of his life is required of us by the gospel of Jesus Christ and him crucified. That is correct, this is the place where religious forms are established to emulate the forward momentum of a genuine faith. Yes, here we have our superficial church service and self-celebratory, self-affirming ceremony. Because (I know) that behind that dreadful veil of the LORD Jesus Christ, my natural life and its lust of the flesh and love of the world is unceremoniously and unapologetically commanded of me.

Frankly, few Christians press into the cross and out its other side, as it were (and if I may put it like that). Behind the veil is where the business of GOD takes place. In Christ. It is where dead men are raised to newness of life. That is, as I enter into the suffering fellowship, the intimacies and conformity of his death, in Christ, to be made One with the Father.

"No man knows the Father except the Son, and he to whomsoever the Son will reveal him" (re. Matt. 11:27). This is another gospel expression and astute witness of our current text; that is, the LORD Jesus Christ saying, *"No man cometh unto the Father, but by me"* (re. John 14:4).

It must be asked: How clearly can I see the Father from my place in Christ? How far have I followed? Where am I on the infinite continuity of becoming intimate with the LORD Jesus

Christ by suffering fellowship and conformity to his death (see Phil. 3:10)? Do I really know him in the acute realization and apprehension of his resurrection power? That is, am I radically born again? You know, a new creature. Or am I the same old irascible, disgruntled character and close-minded bigot that I have always been, but hiding behind vague religious ceremony and convoluted worldly counsel and misdirection? You know, Sunday morning smoke and mirrors and smiling faces.

(*Many* of us want to be saved altogether at someone else's expense; *few* of us have taken up our crosses to follow very far.)

It is in the depths of the mysteries of the Grace and Truth of Jesus Christ that the Father is revealed. It is within the infinite wisdom and knowledge of the Father that the Son is found by *Grace through Faith*. Can I see the revelation of the Father and the Son as One LORD from where I am in the Word of GOD?

The Father and the Son (Jesus Christ) exist in the unbroken fellowship of One Spirit. *"GOD is a Spirit"* (re. John 4:24), and this is *He.* It is Jesus Christ's prayer that we (Christians) be made One, even as the Father and the Son are One (see John 17:21-23). Where am I along (or upon) the progressive scale of this revelatory Grace and Truth?

Am I being made One with the Word of GOD, or am I essentially disconnected from GOD's reality, still fundamentally living my own life, pandering and kowtowing to the flesh, yielding to worldly lusts and covetousness and pride? Children, the *reality* of this season of our humanity will be revealed by the answer to this question. Am I living my life connected and acquiescent to the Word of GOD, or am I principally living in the midst (and maelstrom) of the reckless acquisition of wealth and material things, and in the self-realization of my ego and my libido as a volitional prisoner of the lust and the pride of my life?

The preponderance of contemporary mainstream Christianity appears to be the *many* on the broad way of a casual acquaintance with Jesus Christ. Many of us prop up and/or facilitate the religious form that emulates the forward momentum of a genuine faith. You know, the practical *following* of the prophetic command, *"Follow me."*

Relatively (or correlatively) *few* of us have followed the LORD Jesus Christ as far as Calvary. Oh, we capitulated to *his* having a cross, all right, but have conveniently concluded the idea of us having one as theoretical. The abstract, you see, has no expectations of me.

Frankly, to traverse the Grace and Truth of the character of the LORD Jesus Christ equates to becoming agonizingly familiar with the raw truth of my own. Few of us look that deeply and earnestly into the depraved reality of our personal unregenerate nature to expose ourselves to the radical conversion and regeneration of the Spirit of GOD.

Few of us know our own abject penury (sufficiently) to present as honest and humble penitents.

Children, rest unto our souls is a calm reservoir and pool of living waters waiting for the thirsty in the intimacies of Christ. The life more abundant is found on the dynamic continuum of a virulent faith; freedom, and freedom indeed, await the intrepid. For the diligent and the fearless, the Father awaits within the inner sanctum of Jesus Christ, within the veil at the mercy seat. The *Holy Place* of GOD is a place of sinners saved by grace.

Pointedly, no man (or woman) comes to the Father except by Jesus Christ (re. John 14:4). Now, there is no distinction, and no degree of separation, between the Word of GOD and the essence and character of the LORD Jesus Christ. Moreover, the Father and the Son are indivisible. They are One LORD (see John 1030, Mark 12:29, Deut. 6:4). This is one of the absolutes of GOD.

"GOD is a Spirit" (re. John 4:24). Moreover, GOD is a Spirit of a Living Word. His name is Jesus. In this life, that is, in this the season of my humanity, I have but One name for GOD.

✳

Neither is there salvation in any other: for
there is none other name under heaven given
among men, whereby we must be saved.
ACTS 4:12

✳

Behold the simplicity that is in Christ: that GOD is found in the Word of GOD, and nowhere else. Only in the extremities and intimacies of Jesus Christ is the Father found, where deep calleth unto deep. Behold the simplicity and the profundity of Christ, that GOD hides from the casual and the indifferent, secreted within the intricacies of Christ for the invested and the purposeful to find.

None come to the Father except by Jesus Christ (the Word of GOD), and sadly (and broadly), we grudgingly and carelessly read or study our Bibles. This alarming situation indicates that the gate is indeed strait, and the way is indeed narrow which leads unto life (eternal), and *"few"* there be that find it (see Matt. 7:14). Just as the LORD Jesus Christ says. *"Says"*, present tense.

The resurrection life and power of the LORD Jesus Christ is the nucleus or the marrow of his essence, the core of his character. The diligent and the intrepid find the Father and the Son (Jesus Christ) indivisibly existing and ruling as One LORD by the Holy Ghost. (Once again) this is the Doctrine (teaching) of Christ.

(No disrespect intended, but) frankly, as a young Christian, the doctrine of the trinity left me disassociated and distant from the nuclei and dynamic of the Father and the Son as One LORD in the unity of One Spirit. The doctrine of all-permissive grace without the accountability of Truth (common to contemporary Christianity), left me markedly incomplete. Notwithstanding (at the time), though I was too young to articulate what was missing, it left me painfully hungry and thirsty for genuine righteousness. That is correct, playing church could not make me whole.

Fresh vision is painstakingly veined within the intimacies of Jesus Christ. The Word of GOD still speaks. Cutting edge revelation is the meat and potatoes of importunity upon the perimeter of trespass, for that faith which will not be denied.

The asceticism and austerity and suffering association of the cross of Jesus Christ is the strait gate and narrow way through the veil to the holy place. This is where the sons and daughters of men have transitioned into the kings and priests of

GOD. This is the holy place of communion, of ultimate identification, of being made One. This is where I ask what I will in the sanction of Christ to manifest the fruit of my abiding – and by the violence of my faith it is given. Ah, even as I *take* it.

Within the depths and intimacies of the knowledge of Jesus Christ, his disciples are resolutely being made One with their LORD. It is the Son who takes me into the revelatory Grace and Truth of the Father, into the knowledge and wisdom of the Ancient of Days.

What I call the dissociative theology of my youth, and the traditions and rituals of my forefathers, kept me segregated from the hidden wisdom of Jesus Christ, detached by doctrine, isolated from my heavenly Father. According to the religion of my youth, the Father was in heaven, Jesus was at his right hand, and I was stuck here on earth with never more than one-third of God, as it were, fighting all these devils.

It is by the Word of GOD (Jesus Christ), that the kingdom of heaven is realized on earth as it is in heaven. Within the mysteries and wisdom of Jesus Christ, the Father awaits the children of men with open arms.

When I look into the depths of the Word of GOD (the LORD Jesus Christ), the Word of GOD looks into the depths of me. Jesus Christ (the Word of GOD) is committed and ardent to covert my unregenerate character, and progressively make me One with the Father. Sadly, it is at the very portal, if you will, of the revelatory deity of the LORD Jesus Christ, that the preponderance of contemporary Christianity pauses to have *church*. We intuitively know, that to look too deeply (and honestly) into the character of Jesus Christ, is going to cost us our natural life in its love for the world, and uh, ahem, ex-cuse me, but we are saving them for ourselves.

This is precisely where the portal to the kingdom of GOD is occluded with posers and pretenders and worldly prostitutes. Even our preachers and teachers pander and dissemble to save their positions of honor within our formal religious hierar-chy and forms of faith, promoting and upholding the stasis of an one-dimensional ceremony which supplants the wisdom and righteousness of a progressive relationship with GOD.

❋

But woe unto you scribes and Pharisees, hypocrites! for ye shut up the kingdom of heaven against men: for ye neither go in yourselves, neither ye suffer them that are entering to go in.
MATT. 23:13

❋

The LORD Jesus Christ is the strait gate and narrow "Way" unto reconciliation with GOD. The LORD Jesus Christ is the *"Truth"* (the Reality) of GOD. The LORD Jesus Christ is the Resurrection *"Life"* (eternal Life) and power of GOD.

It is within the Word of GOD (Jesus Christ) that the fullness of the love and joy and peace in the fellowship of the Father is found.

❋

*That which we have seen and heard declare we unto you,
that ye also may have fellowship with us: and truly our
fellowship is with the Father, and with his Son Jesus Christ.*

And these things write we unto you, that your joy may be full.

1 John 1:3-4)

✳

This is what each of these chapters by the Spirit of the Living Word of GOD progressively reveal.

There is a distinct difference between organized religious observation and the intimacies of GOD in Christ by Grace and Truth. There is a religious *form* of self-preservation and self-veneration, and that of saving the innermost life for oneself. And then there is the purposeful abandon of living by a dynamic faith which works by the love of GOD.

Notably, the preponderance of Christianity has not functionally apprehended the fullness of joy (or the abundant life) that Jesus Christ promises his followers. This fullness is only found in the acute fellowship of the Father and the Son as One LORD by the Holy Ghost. Bluntly, we have no effectual cross. We have an ideological Jesus whom we (*presume to*) placate with the theoretical offering up of our life and the hypothetical loving of our neighbor.

We are reduced to emulating the power of resurrection life because we have eschewed the suffering fellowship of the LORD Jesus Christ and eluded the conformity to the death of his cross.

As much as I would like to end this chapter with a more palatable subject, the Holy Spirit reminds (us) of the LORD's grave caution concerning organized religion without a relationship inspired and governed by the love of GOD in Christ.

The Father is sheathed within the secret places and intimacies of Jesus Christ. Sadly, many practitioners of religious observation and ceremony will be exposed as enemies of the intimacies of Jesus Christ. They would not give their life (and their love of the world) to know him.

✳

These things have I spoken unto you, that
ye should not be offended.

They shall put you out of the synagogues: yea,
the time cometh, that whosoever killeth you
will think that he doeth GOD service.

And these things will they do unto you, because
they have not known the Father, nor me.

7

I AM the Vine

"I Am the Vine, ye are the branches: He that abideth in me, and I in him, the same bringeth forth much fruit: for without me ye can do nothing."

–John 15:5

THERE IS NO LIFE outside of Jesus Christ, only the illusion that this world system espouses and advances as the reality. The lust of the flesh and the pride of this natural life has a rapacious and insatiable appetite to be fed and pampered, aided and abetted in gluttony and covetousness, given the preeminence always.

If we are not vigilant to live by every Word that proceeds out of the mouth of GOD, our religion has a propensity to transmogrify into a form that emulates the forward momentum of living by faith. The religions of men have a tendency to extemporaneously spawn priorities other than GOD's.

In this, the season of my humanity, the natural (or physical) never stops striving for ascendancy, for comfort and considerations, for some escape from the austerity that the gospel (and the cross) of Jesus Christ commands. (Let us keep this in the first-person possessive tense, if possible.) I never stop seeking some mediation from the weight of it all, some byway or rest area upon this narrow way, some technicality or loophole, some exemption or exculpatory excuse to put my cross down.

GOD has no hybrid Christians, no composite children, no incestuous progeny. GOD has no compartmentalized Christians.

Christian is not to be something I do; it is to be who I am.

Once upon a time, I had an established minimally acceptable criteria of religious activities and service which (I assumed and Presumed) qualified me calling myself a Christian. And the rest belonged exclusively to me. You know how we do it. Until a perfunctory church attendance (and precise, or parsimonious tithe) salves our parsimonious Christian conscience.

What is an honest and realistic self-assessment? Well? From where does my core essence extract (or extort) its sense of fulfillment? Where am I rooted and grounded? What brings me joy? Who is my Source?

From GOD's perspective, how I spend my time (my life) is the offering up of a perpetual spiritual sacrifice. Upon whom or what I spend my time and energy and affections, I am giving homage, or worship. Frankly, I am either living for GOD, or I am living for myself as aided and abetted by the god of this world, Satan.

Just because I have made a tentative confession of faith which I presume justifies me calling myself a Christian, that does not mean that GOD's primary objective has shifted to accommodate my every capricious whim. Jesus Christ did not die to join himself to the purposes of my self-realization. He died so that I could align myself with the singular purposes of his love in the redemption of humanity.

This teaching (doctrine) of the LORD Jesus Christ as recorded in the fifteenth chapter of John naturally culminates in the commandment of love, and as we shall see, it is the commandment of *One* Love. To be a branch in the Vine is to have yoked myself to the LORD Jesus Christ by faith. The salvation of GOD is a living entity, the evidence of his will being done in earth as it is in heaven. The developing Christian is, concisely, not only a branch in the Vine, but is ultimately intended to bear kingdom fruit *"whose seed is in itself"* (re. Gen. 1:11).

This doctrine (teaching) of the LORD Jesus Christ using the analogy of agricultural endeavors to represent the kingdom of GOD was not new to the disciples. We should all be familiar with the LORD's teaching on the parable of the sower, as well as the LORD's exposition of it when the disciples asked for an explanation. It is the LORD Jesus Christ's beginning statement in this explanation that is the concise clarification (and the key) to apprehending all kingdom principles.

✳

Now the parable is this: The seed is the Word of GOD.
LUKE 8:11

✳

The redemption of mankind is the collaborative phenomenon of the Father and the Son (the Word) moving and working as One LORD by the effectual power of the Holy Spirit. *All* of GOD effects the salvation of man (and woman). The comprehensive gospel affirms this elementary, foundational Truth. (Until we get it, I will cry it aloud.)

✳

The first of all the commandments is, Hear, O Israel; The LORD our GOD is One LORD.
re. MARK 12:29

✳

Of course, this is what I call the *preamble* (and the *prerequisite*) to the first commandment. It is no accident that the LORD Jesus Christ recites it in conjunction with the first commandment of our loving GOD. Moreover, the LORD deliberately uses this occasion to irrefutably and indivisibly unite the second commandment with the first. Here is his complete answer, immediately following the preamble above.

✳

*And thou shalt love the LORD thy GOD with all thy heart,
and with all thy soul, and with all thy mind, and with all
thy strength: this is the first commandment. And the second
is like, namely, this, Thou shalt love thy neighbor as thyself.
There is none other commandments greater than these.*
MARK 12:30-31

✳

In a quick aside, I must qualify something. The redundancy within these notebooks attesting to the revelation of the LORD our GOD as One LORD, originates and arises out of the heart and mind of Christ. The repetition parallels the magnitude and urgency of the revelation, and sadly, our hardness of heart.

The Father and the Son (Jesus Christ) think and feel and act as One by the Holy Ghost. Concisely, this is the record in heaven that John saw and attests to.

✳

*For there are three that bear record in heaven, the Father,
the Word, and the Holy Ghost: and these three are One.*
1 JOHN 5:7

✳

Now, John the Beloved revelator, as he is known in some quarters, is certainly faithful to record all that the Spirit of the LORD instructs him to. To be accurate, he is not the revelator, per se, but the revelation of Jesus Christ is entrusted unto him. (Uh, which makes him [technically] the *"revelatee"*).

It is the Word of GOD who says he is Three, and it is the Word of GOD who says he is One. Or, precisely, *"these three are One"* (re. 1 John 5:7). It is the Word of GOD (Jesus Christ) who says it. It is GOD's record, or what GOD has to say about himself; and nothing else will do.

We ponder the properties, and parameters, of infinite phenomenon and divine wonders. We presume upon the identity of GOD with finite strictures and unsanctified hearts. Frankly, we are quicker to settle for what wise men and contemporary Pharisees have to say about GOD, rather than enter into the Word of GOD with all our heart and all our mind to worship him in Spirit and in truth. Well might the LORD Jesus Christ say of us, *"Ye worship ye know not what"* (re. John 4:22).

The LORD Jesus Christ did not come to earth to accommodate and confirm us in the reckless pursuit of indiscriminate appetites and mindless rabid acquisition of things in the panicked self-realization of the pride of our life. He came to save us from the tyranny of ourselves and to coalesce us into the love of GOD.

✺

That in the dispensation of the fullness of times he might gather together in One all things in Christ, both which are in heaven, and which are on earth, even in him.
Eph. 1:10

✺

In another brief aside, I must interject something here. And this I have of the LORD. This chapter may prove to be the most controversial of this manuscript. The revelation I have

633

of the LORD Jesus Christ evinces that the comprehensive (mostly subliminal) argument of this world system's counsel, as well as much religious deception in high places, is the raging denial and disallowance of the deity of the LORD Jesus Christ. Concisely, this is the revelation that makes men free; but it is also the revelation that makes men mad, in every sense of the word.

As I tried to express in our last chapter, it is within the depths (within the wisdom and knowledge) of the LORD Jesus Christ that the Father is found. Or, as the Word of GOD (the LORD Jesus Christ) says, *"No man cometh unto the Father, but by me"* (re. John 14:6).

The treasures (of the secret wisdom) of GOD are found only in the pursuit of GOD. Again, if you follow.

(Bluntly), the Word of GOD is the revelatory gauntlet to the wisdom and knowledge of (and reconciliation with) the Father. The Word of GOD is the irrepressible (omnipotent, omniscient, omnipresent) system of checks and balances, and the living dynamic (*n.*) which radically converts my character and leads me into the comprehensive revelatory Truth of the Father. The LORD Jesus Christ (the Word of GOD) introduces me to, and progressively makes me One with, the Father.

The LORD Jesus Christ is the (Grace and Truth) of GOD who satisfies the Law of GOD. For he is indubitably both. Frankly, this is more manifest evidence of his deity. None can fully satisfy the Law of GOD except the same GOD who wrote the Law. Behold, then, the finger of GOD.

Welcome to my Bible study. It is my desire to stir up your hunger and thirst for the revelatory Grace and Truth of GOD hidden in the mysteries and wisdom of his Christ. Beyond the tentative (daring) preincarnate visitations of the LORD Jesus Christ in the Old Testament, which the orthodoxy of the wisest religious minds allowed me, I progressively see the Christ of GOD in the beginning, and in the ending. Even as *Alpha and Omega*.

Hidden in the type and figure of dark and hard sayings, the reality (Truth) of GOD is found. Within revelatory layers, beyond the illusion, as it were, the reality of GOD awaits the intrepid, and them dissatisfied with the status quo of forms of faith. Beyond the stasis (and stagnation) of religious presumption and positional complacency, the Father awaits children with Living Water.

Christian, I ask you, who but a devil would deny me the deity of the LORD Jesus Christ, and forbid me the revelation of GOD in the beginning? Children, the Word (Jesus Christ) was not only *"with"* GOD in the beginning, but the Word (Jesus Christ) *"was"* GOD in the beginning, (re. John 1:1).

Jesus Christ was GOD when the earth was without form, and void, and darkness was upon the face of the deep (see Gen. 1:2). Jesus Christ was GOD when the Spirit of GOD moved upon the face of the waters.

Jesus Christ was the Voice and Word of GOD unto Moses out of the midst of the burning bush. Jesus Christ was GOD upon Mount Sinai with Moses, and GOD upon Mount Horeb with Elijah; just as he was God when Moses and Elijah came to him on the Mount of Transfiguration. Indeed, Moses knew him as One LORD (see Deut. 6:4). And Elijah knew him as a consuming fire (re. 1 Kings 18:38), and as a still small Voice (re. 1 Kings 19:12).

Jesus Christ was Savior and LORD in the portal at Passover. And he was a pillar of a cloud by day during the Exodus in the wilderness, and a pillar of fire by night. Jesus Christ is forever GOD before the Son of man came. And before there was a babe wrapped in swaddling clothes and laid in a manger in Bethlehem of Judaea, Jesus Christ is LORD.

※

Moreover, brethren, I would not that ye should be ignorant (uninformed), how that all our fathers were under the cloud, and all passed through the sea.

And were all baptized unto Moses in the cloud and in the sea.

And did all eat the same spiritual meat.

And did all drink the same spiritual drink: for they drank of that spiritual Rock that followed them: and that Rock was Christ.
1 Cor. 10:1-4

※

Within intricate glimpses of greater grace, the Father is secreted in Christ, where time is enfolded into eternity, and where Alpha and Omega reigns. The Apostle Paul says (if I may paraphrase), that he would not have us ignorant (and unarmed or unempowered) of the omnipotent and omniscient and omnipresent nature and essence and character of the LORD Jesus Christ. Eons before there was a Christmas story, Jesus Christ is GOD (and the tense of it cannot be changed).

The Apostle Paul, by the Holy Ghost, tells us two distinct times here in the tenth chapter of 1 Corinthians, that the things or circumstances which befell the children of Israel are written for our definitive example and admonition (see 1 Cor. 10:6,11). Like much of contemporary Christianity, the LORD Jesus Christ was with his people in the wilderness, but his people were not necessarily with him. Hear me. *"That which hath been is now"* (re. Eccl. 3:15).

It is Christ who sustained the children of Israel in the wilderness, and it is Christ who sustains Christianity today. What has already been is prophetically transpiring now (as inspired by Eccl. 3:15). He who has ears to hear, let him hear. It was George Santayana who said, *"Those who cannot remember the past are condemned to repeat it."*

Many of us (contemporary Christians) presume to partake of Christ while pursuing self-interests. (I speak of excess.) Like the children of Israel in the wilderness, with *"many"* of us GOD is not well pleased (see 1 Cor. 10:1-14). This portion of scripture concisely defines (especially single-minded) self-realization and self-indulgence as idolatry, the worship of something (or someone) other than the One True GOD. Concisely, I either live a sanctified life perfecting holiness in the reverence of the LORD, or I live a vain existence of wanton self-realization in the lust and pride of my own life.

Children, this is idolatry, the dynamic of the original sin of insurrection, and my insistence upon being my own god.

How I spend the substance of my life, primarily my time and my affections, is reckoned of GOD as a spiritual sacrifice. Jesus Christ holds the breath of my life and the beat of my heart in his nail-pierced hands. I am to justly aspire to honor him who saved me and sustains me.

These Christians portrayed here in the tenth chapter of 1 Corinthians are representative of hybrid (and/or) part-time Christians everywhere, and in every age. We casually and presumptuously take the name of Christ unto ourselves, and then arrogantly and impudently expect him to aid and abet and uphold us in a reckless self-realization. Children, whom GOD delivers with a strong hand and sustains with unwavering grace, he expects to reflect that goodness by righteous living.

In our current text of the tenth chapter of 1 Corinthians, the Apostle Paul is saying that he would not have us (Christians) ignorant or uninformed that our Savior and LORD of the New Testament, is also the Almighty GOD of the Old Testament. Jesus Christ was the Rock of our salvation long before Calvary. He is (concisely) the Lamb that was slain from the foundation of the world (see Rev. 13:8).

Moreover, the LORD Jesus Christ was at Calvary before the world began, and this makes him Alpha and Omega, the Almighty GOD with the times and the seasons in his hands. Jesus Christ was LORD long before he was a babe wrapped in swaddling clothes and laid in a manger. He was not a victim of evil men and untoward circumstance. His life was not taken, it was given.

The Apostle Paul would not have us (Christians) ignorant of the acute revelation of Jesus Christ as GOD. He would not have the Church of GOD at Corinth, or the Church of GOD in our individual city or province, uninformed of the dynamic revelation that empowers us to live a sanctified and godly lifestyle, free from sin and free from pride, and free from religious posturing and one-upmanship.

GOD has always had a chosen people and a definitive purpose. Christian, the Old Testament shadow and type is our contemporary reality. If we truly believed in the prophetic (*living*) nature of the Word of GOD, we would know this is so. If we genuinely believed that GOD once spoke, we would also truly believe that he still speaks, and we would know that every Word that proceeds out of his mouth is relevant admonition for the people of GOD.

✳

Thou hast brought a vine out of Egypt: thou hast cast out the heathen, and planted it. Thou preparedst room before it, and didst cause it to take deep root, and it filled the land.
Ps. 80:8-9

✳

Unlike our primary text from which our chapter takes its title, and the LORD Jesus Christ saying, *"I AM the Vine"* (re. John 15:5), here we have GOD's people depicted as the Vine. (Speaking broadly) we might say that the presence of GOD was *with* his people as he brought them out of Egypt, whereas (ideally) his presence (or Holy Spirit) lives and abides *within* his people today. Notwithstanding times and seasons and dispensations, it is GOD who sustains the life of his elect people.

If we (contemporary Christians) can accept the prophetic revelation, (ideally) GOD has brought us out of the cruel servitude and bondage of sin, just like he brought the children of Israel out of the captivity and slavery of Egypt.

It is GOD's desire not only to deliver his people from the captivity and slavery of sin and idolatry, but he also wants to lead us into a land flowing with milk and honey. He wants to lead us through the flood and through the fire and establish us in the life more abundant.

＊

But the GOD of all grace, who hath called us unto his eternal glory by Christ Jesus, after that ye have suffered a while, make you perfect, stablish, strengthen, settle you.
(1 PET. 5:10

＊

Children, there are giants in the promised land in every dispensation. In this, the season of our humanity, faith is a fight in every circumstance. While it is true that GOD fights my battles, there is also battle enough for me. I must take possession of what is promised. Faith and obedience are the dynamic which unleashes the phenomenal power of Almighty GOD, and the promises of his Word into my every contrary circumstance.

＊

But if thou shalt indeed obey his Voice, and do all that I speak; then I will be an enemy unto thine enemies, and an adversary unto thine adversaries.
Ex. 23:22

＊

It is the Christ of GOD who goes before his people in every dispensation, and it is Christ who follows behind. As you can receive it, this I have of the Holy Ghost, and have written many times: that the Christ of GOD is both the Father and the Son by the Holy Ghost, and the One LORD who is the GOD of Israel in every era.

As I have written, (whom I call) the *older generation* of the children of Israel, believed the evil report from ten of the twelve spies that were sent out to search the land of Canaan on a reconnaissance mission. When we refuse to trust in what GOD has said, and to take possession of what GOD has already promised, then we are justly relegated to the wilderness of our own unbelief.

Walking and living by faith and obedience is the perpetual unfolding and fulfilling of the prophetic living Word of GOD in every era or dispensation. *"That which hath been is Now"* (re. Eccl. 3:15). Between the pages of the sovereign annals and wisdom of Alpha and Omega, I walk and live by faith in what GOD says to me Now. Concisely, this is covenant faith. *"Hear, and your soul shall live"* (see Is. 55:3).

By the violence of my faith (nigh unto trespass as necessary), I provoke the Word of GOD to manifest within the parameters of my present circumstance. I remind GOD of what he has already said. Often, this is faith bordering on impudence: my importunity pressing into what GOD has said. By the virulent, genuine, incendiary faith of the disciples of Jesus Christ, the kingdom of GOD comes . . . on earth as it is in heaven.

By faith, I clear the clutter and contrary circumstance which occludes the portal to the kingdom of GOD. Life does not happen to me here; I happen to life. I am not a victim of circumstance. By faith in Christ, contrary circumstance is beneath my feet.

(It must be clarified.) I no longer have a compartmentalized Christ. The wise men and witch doctors of contemporary theology would diminish the omnipotence, omniscience, and omnipresence of GOD by two-thirds in any given circumstance. My forefathers erroneously taught me that GOD had three personalities, two of which were disassociated from my plight at any given moment. He who has ears to hear, let him hear.

✳

The first of all the commandments is, Hear, O
Israel; The LORD our GOD is One LORD.
see MARK 12:29

✳

Everything GOD does and says is the collaborative, concerted, comprehensive sovereign decree of One LORD who is both Father and Son by the Holy Ghost. GOD is in the One unified mind of One indivisible personality. Even though the word *personality* is finitely insufficient.

Children, the Word of GOD speaks best for GOD. The following two statements, one initially spoken to Thomas, and the other to Philip, help me apprehend and assimilate the infinite Truth of the essence of GOD.

✳

"If ye had known me, ye should have known my Father also"
see JOHN 14:7

"He that hath seen me hath seen the Father"
see JOHN 14:9

✳

Dear reader, thank you for your indulgence and patience as I trouble the waters and share the ruminations of my Bible study in preparation for our main text. *"I AM the true Vine, and my Father is the husbandman"* (John 15:1).

It is in the marrow of Jesus Christ that I meet with the Father; Jesus at the center of it all. This is the holy place of reconciliation, the revelation (and the realization) of the Father and the Son as One LORD by the Holy Ghost. We have spoken of this holy place of revelation and convergence.

✳

And there I will meet with thee, and I will commune with thee from above the mercy seat, from between the two cherubims which are upon the ark of the testimony, of all things which I will give thee in commandment unto the children of Israel.
Ex. 25:22

✳

This is where the covenant is ratified: in the roots of Jesus Christ, in the acute revelation of the Father and the Son as One LORD. Only in the depths of the Word of GOD will I realize the Father, in the hidden corridors of the heart and mind of Jesus Christ. The revelation of Jesus Christ as LORD is the

Most Holy place of GOD, where the Father and the Son are One at the mercy seat.

This is the high priestly prayer of the Son (Jesus Christ) and this is the will of the Father, that we be made One with the Father in Christ; even perfect in One (see John 17:21-23). This fellowship by faith, this divine communion and perfect reconciliation with the Father, is consummated at the mercy seat.

In the shadow of the revelation of the Father and the Son as One LORD by the effectual working of the Holy Ghost, I am made whole. Here is where the kingdom of GOD is being realized within me by sanctification and obedience.

✸

If a man love me, he will keep my words: and
my Father will love him, and "we" will come
unto him, and make "our" abode with him.
re. JOHN 14:23

✸

Beyond initial introductions and formal religious ceremony, within the intimacies and suffering association of Jesus Christ, the mysteries and wisdom of the Father is found. It is even as the LORD says, *"If ye had known me, ye should have known my Father also"* (re. John 14:7).

(If I may put it like this), the revelation of the Father is enshrouded in the deity of Jesus Christ. From personal experience, it became a matter of how far into Jesus Christ that I had looked with resolve and godly purpose. (Or not.) It is even as the LORD says, *"He that hath seen me hath seen the Father"* (re. John 14:9).

Frankly, there were decades in which I had not looked any further than a cursory introduction to Jesus Christ. I knew about the cross, but I had not entered into the reality of the cross from GOD's perspective. In GOD's reality, he fully intended to make the austerity and self-denial, and the death of that cross, personally mine. To be figurative, the death throes of the body of sin and the crucifixion of the natural man, the mortification of the pride of life and love of the world, are excruciatingly real.

These were the decades I embraced a religious form to emulate the forward momentum (and the radical character conversion) that is indicative of a genuine faith. Uh, so that I could escape the gospel of the cross with my natural life intact, and my love of the world unthreatened. Well? Someone must get honest about our religious dissimulation. Every time I looked deeper into the LORD Jesus Christ; the LORD Jesus Christ looked deeper into me.

The casual and the indifferent summarily (and swiftly) dismiss the deity of the LORD Jesus Christ. Bluntly? Because this is the revelation that is going to cost me my life as I know it. The religions of my childhood (and early to mid-adulthood) stopped on the periphery of this acute revelation and had church. That is correct. On this side of the kingdom portal which commanded the death of my natural life, and the love of GOD for my neighbor. Well? We cannot say that Jesus did not forewarn us.

*

Marvel not that I said unto thee, Ye must be born again.
JOHN 3:7

＊

It is the will of GOD that this revelation be the place of my abiding. That is, the place of my apprehension that the Father and the Son are One LORD by the Holy Ghost. If I have looked into Jesus Christ earnestly and deeply enough, and if I know him intimately enough, I have seen the Father in Christ. The Holy Spirit belabors the point introductory to our primary text.

＊

I AM the true *Vine, and my Father is the husbandman.*
JOHN 15:1

＊

The ideal place of my abiding is in the depths of the doctrine (teaching) of the LORD Jesus Christ, where the Holy Ghost leads me into all Truth (re. John 16:13). This guidance and teaching is the effectual working of the Father and the Son as One LORD by the Holy Ghost. Here is where GOD reveals himself to me and integrates me into his purposes. In this place, I see all that the Father has and is, and his *all* that he has given the Son (Jesus Christ).

＊

"All" things that the Father hath are mine: therefore said
I, that he shall take of mine, and shall shew it unto you.
JOHN 16:15

＊

The revelation of the Father is woven into the doctrine of Christ. In fact, we might say that the revelation of the Father is the correlative revelation of the deity of the LORD Jesus Christ. Not to intentional confuse anyone, but we are trying to get a glimpse of an infinite being. I used to say, "I cannot wait for GOD full of myself." Indeed, I will not perceive him with my natural eye, nor will I know him or see him from a natural or worldly perspective.

＊

Blessed are the pure in heart: for they shall see GOD.
MATT. 5:8

＊

Looking at our (current) primary text of John 15:1, it is presented in two distinct parts. 1) For the LORD Jesus Christ to say he is the *"true"* Vine, presupposes or indicates that there are also *"false"* ones. 2) The Father knows if I am *"in"* Christ, or if I am an imposter; for the Father abides at the revelatory juncture where the Father and the Son are seamlessly unified and coalesced as One LORD.

As the LORD Jesus Christ boldly declared in our last chapter, *"I AM the Truth"* (see John 14:6), hence he is also the only *"true"* Vine, and the only *"true"* Source of eternal Life.

Jesus Christ as *"Truth"* is also interpreted as *"Reality."* The reality that ought to concern every man, woman, and child most, is the reality or the truth about life, both temporal and eternal life.

That I am fundamentally an eternal being housed in a temporary, earthen vessel, is the reality about my life that the Word of GOD (Jesus Christ) came to declare the grace and truth of. Ah, but we know that the physical, temporal life never ceases to impinge upon the preeminence of our spiritual, eternal (life) essence. Whichever is in the ascendancy, or whichever consumes the majority of my time and affections and considerations, is an accurate reflection of the state of my soul.

Of course, this may be simplistic, but it begs the question, "Where am I laying up treasure," or "Who and what am I living for?" (The Holy Spirit has repeatedly showed me) that in GOD's reality, how that I spend my life, primarily my time and energy and wealth, is reckoned of GOD as the offering up of spiritual sacrifices.

Nothing is wasted, meaning unaccounted for, of the Gift of Life. It is GOD's breath that makes me a living soul (see Gen. 2:7). Every minute (even every second) of our life has value to GOD. Every moment is being taken precisely into account. As I have said, "The Holy One balances his own books" (see Rev. 20:11-15). If we truly believed this concise, mysterious and terrible revelation, that GOD has books, then we would take more care with how we "spend" our lives.

The aches and pains (and the appetites and accommodations) of this natural life conspire to usurp or wrest the preeminence from my spirit man. This is congenital to the human condition, we might say. The lusts (desires) of the flesh and of the eyes, and of an unregenerate mind, never cease to lay siege upon my consciousness demanding excessive (even constant) considerations.

✳

Hell and destruction are never full; so the
eyes of man are never satisfied.
Pro. 27:20

✳

Moreover, the pride of this natural life is a noisome, virulent, rapacious contender for preeminence and mastery. (Such acerbic adjectives arise out of an acute, protracted, personal experience and a brutal spiritual warfare.)

There is (what I call) a dynamic continuum or measure in the Word of GOD which delineates my degree of sanctification. I also call these scriptures John the Beloved's short list of the enemies of our soul.

✳

Love not the world, neither the things that are in the world. If any man love the world, the love of the Father is not in him. For all that is in the world, the lust of the flesh, and the lust of the eyes, and the pride of life, is not of the Father, but is of the world.
1 John 2:15-16

✳

GOD has showed me that there is a concise spiritual continuum within these scriptures, where at any given moment, my soul may be found. And it will be precisely identified on the Word of GOD's fastidious scale of sanctification between *"the love of the world"* and *"the love of the Father."*

As I have written, the (*first*) love of the Father is his Son, Jesus Christ. It is, therefore, my soul's grave and dreadful imperative to be identified as having Christ in me, and me in Christ. In simplistic terms, how well do I know Jesus Christ as LORD? That is, what is the degree of our intimacy?

My growth in the grace and truth (and in the knowledge and personal intimacy) of my relationship with Jesus Christ, will be an accurate reflection of the degree of my soul's (and my life's) separation from the love of the world unto GOD. It is the Word of GOD (Jesus Christ) who separates me from my allegiance and subjugation to this world system.

※

They are not of the world, even as I am not of the world.

Sanctify (separate) *them through thy*
Truth: Thy Word is Truth.
JOHN 17:16-17

※

It is (what we call) the LORD's *high priestly* prayer, and the Father's irrepressible desire, that the disciples of Jesus Christ be definitively separated from the loyalty and confederation (and the love and addiction) of this world system. From the Father's perspective, the spiritual powers and principalities who govern and drive this world system (and enslave its denizens) has not changed.

(Bluntly), the god of this world system, who deludes and deceives its denizens, has not changed. It is the very same spiritual wickedness in high governmental (and even religious) places which conspired with the Jews (to coerce the Romans) into crucifying Jesus Christ.

It is GOD's sovereign design as One LORD, who is *both* the Father and the Son by the Holy Ghost, to separate me from my allegiance and love of this world system (through the lust of the flesh, and the lust of the eyes, and the pride of life), unto Christ.

Although it is not popular teaching or preaching, GOD has always earnestly desired (and commanded) a distinct (unmistakable) degree of sanctification between his people, and the peoples of the world around them.

Well, some might say (as I was taught in my youth and young adulthood), "Either you're saved, or you ain't." (Please pardon the grammatical or punctual license.) As some of you know I was raised in the hollows of West Virginia.

While that statement above is true in principal, not all saved persons are separated from the love and attraction (and deception) of this world system to the same degree. As we shall (hopefully) see later, this will be reflected in the Christian disciple's ability to produce fruit for the kingdom of GOD: whether 30, 60, or 100-fold. And, as we shall see in the LORD's teaching of the Vine in the fifteenth chapter of John: as fruit, more fruit, and much fruit.

All variables belong unto GOD: the sun and the soil and the rain, the seed and the field and the laborer, the times and the seasons, the health of the Vine and the glory of a prodigious harvest. Undeniably, in the recorded annals of my abiding in the Vine, there have been varying degrees of depth, if I may put it like that. In retrospect, and as you can receive it, my growth in the grace and knowledge of the LORD Jesus Christ has fundamentally paralleled my degree of separation from this world system.

Sadly (but honestly) there were distinct seasons of my novitiate or apprenticeship as a disciple of Christ that my degree of separation from my love of, and alliance to, this world system, was infinitesimal. And, naturally, my production of fruit was negligible (or nonexistent).

I had not learned, and productively assimilated, that the depth of my abiding in Jesus Christ, and the depth of his abiding in me, depended upon the degree of my separation (sanctification) from my love and dependence upon this world system. This is the intrinsic and resolute theme of the Holy Spirit's mandate upon me to write, and to cry aloud, as it were.

Frankly, the doctrine (or teaching and preaching) of an acute sanctification of the disciples of Jesus Christ from the love (and the lust) of this world system, and its many corrupted amusements and entertainments (and things), is an imperative non-negotiable gospel principle. Concisely, a Spirit who is a "*Holy*" Spirit is not going to cohabitate with the unclean spirits associated with much of our polluted, aberrant, moral and social standards.

The spirit of this world system is predicated upon what I call *The Big Lie*, or as Satan told Eve, *"Ye shall not surely die"* (re. Gen 3:4). The necessity and urgency for a distinct sanctification (separation) of contemporary Christians from this world evil substantiates my redundancy. It is the Word of GOD that delivers me and separates me, that saves me and radically transforms me, from the illusion and indoctrination (and bondage) of this world system.

✳

Sanctify (separate) them through thy Truth: thy Word is Truth.
JOHN 17:17

✳

Concisely, *"GOD is a Spirit"* (re. John 4:24), and he is a Holy Spirit of a Living Word. He is One LORD who is *"both"* the Father and the Son by the Holy Spirit. The revelation is so startling, and so imperative, that it bears repeating from every possible perspective.

✳

I and my Father are One.
JOHN 10:30

✳

This is the *Doctrine of Christ.* As the LORD Jesus Christ was teaching on the coming Comforter, the Holy Ghost, who is to take up his abode within the obedient and sanctified disciples of Jesus Christ, he explicitly says that it is *"both"* he and the Father who will take up their abode.

✳

If a man love me, he will keep my Words: and
my Father will love him, and "we" will come
unto him, and make "our" abode with him.
see JOHN 14:23

✳

As simply as I can state it, this Spirit who is *"both"* the Spirit of the Father, and the Spirit of the Son, is the Holy Spirit (or the Holy Ghost) whom GOD is. Notably, three distinct times, while teaching on the Holy Spirit (Holy Ghost) that was to come, the LORD Jesus Christ explicitly called him *"the Spirit of Truth"* (please see John 14:17 / 15:26 / and 16:13).

Here is the first instance for your review. The Spirit of Truth (whom GOD is) is the antithesis of the god of this world, the father of lies (Satan), who presents this temporal life as the reality, and this world system as its source. Markedly, those persons in subjugation and allegiance to this world system cannot receive the Spirit of GOD (the Spirit of Truth).

✳

Even the Spirit of Truth; "whom the world cannot receive,"
because it seeth him not, neither knoweth him: but ye
know him; for he dwelleth with you, and shall be in you.
JOHN 14:17

✳

We might say, to bring this into our chapter's context, that this revelation and teaching is the very place (the precise juncture) of our abiding in the Vine. Although I have written it many times, I want to make it plain, and leave no misunderstanding. This is the doctrine (teaching) of Christ, and it is precisely that the Father and the Son are One LORD by the Holy Spirit.

This doctrine (of a necessity) is repeatedly reaffirmed throughout the chapters of this manuscript. The mandate of the Spirit of GOD is laid heavy upon my soul. And the following is what I call the indispensable preamble and prerequisite of all commandments.

✳

The first of all commandments is, Hear, O Israel (and/
or Christianity); *The LORD our GOD is One LORD.*
see MARK 12:29

✻

This statement immediately precedes the LORD Jesus Christ making it plain that loving GOD, and loving my neighbor, is seamlessly coalesced into the one (great) commandment of love.

This is the *Doctrine of Christ*. There is no distinction which can be drawn: this is the *Doctrine of GOD*. This is the doctrine that delivers me from what some man has said. The LORD Jesus Christ explicitly and deliberately emphasizes that the LORD our GOD is One LORD, just like the comprehensive commandment is One Love. Loving GOD, and loving my neighbor as myself, is as indivisible as the Father and the Son (Jesus Christ) being One LORD by the Holy Spirit.

Jesus Christ emphasizes the importance that we *"Hear"* that GOD is One LORD in the immediate context of his commandment of One Love. To *"hear"* is to apprehend and internally assimilate the revelation. John the Beloved affirms and reinforces the LORD's urgency that we realize the utter importance of this revelation (doctrine).

✻

Whosoever transgresseth, and "abideth" not in the doctrine of Christ, hath not GOD. He that "abideth" in the doctrine of Christ, he hath "both" the Father and the Son.
2 John 1:9

✻

Once more, we look behind the veil to the mercy seat where the covenant is consummated. Moreover, it is in the light and revelatory truth of One LORD that the commandment is met, and the Law is satisfied. In the presence of angels, (even between the cherubim), mercy and faithfulness are kept.

This is the precise juncture of the healthy branches' (the disciples of Jesus Christ) abiding in the Vine. *"Ideally"* this is where I am to abide, essentially meaning where I am to live – in the Word of GOD.

This is the Most Holy place: where the Father meets the Son at the mercy seat. This is precisely where the Christian is made One with the Father in Jesus Christ, the Son, by the effectual working of the Holy Ghost.

This is where the blood of Jesus Christ satisfies the Law and ratifies the covenant of One Love. This is, also, (relatively and ideally) the preeminent place of the progressive revelation of the Father and the Son (Jesus Christ) as One LORD.

Frankly, this is the dispensation of the fullness of times, and all things in heaven and in earth being gathered together in One; that is, in Jesus Christ (see Eph. 1:10).

Notably, the Holy Spirit repeatedly turns the emphasis of this manuscript to the expedient and incomparable place of the Christian disciple's abiding. Here, relatively and analogously, is the precise place where the branch meets (and is made One with) the Vine.

It is here that I truly realize the Father and the Son as One LORD by the Holy Spirit. The place of my redemption, and my reconciliation with the Father, is One and the same.

This Most Holy place is the correlative place of the Christian disciple's abiding in the Vine, and the place of our progressively being made perfect in One.

Thank you, dear reader, for your forbearance. Frankly, my redundancy reflects the protracted warfare which raged to withhold this revelation from me, as well as a reflection of its urgency and imperative for all believers and disciples of the LORD Jesus Christ. Only as we abide in the Vine, in the doctrine (teaching) of the LORD Jesus Christ, can we advance as disciples (and grow as branches), to produce kingdom fruit.

Only in the Word of GOD (is) the place of my productivity. To further emphasize this place (this Most Holy place), I deliberately jump ahead a few scriptures in our primary text to accentuate the indispensable necessity of our abiding in Jesus Christ (the Word of GOD).

※

I AM the Vine, ye are the branches: He that abideth in me, and I in him, the same bringeth forth much fruit: for without me ye can do nothing.
JOHN 15:5

※

Christian, it cannot be overemphasized; this is the preeminent place of revelation and fellowship. Here, I grow in the grace and knowledge of GOD, even as he sustains me.

(By the Holy Spirit) I attest to drawing no distinction, and seeing no discrepancy, between abiding in the *person* (essence and nature) of the LORD Jesus Christ and abiding in the doctrine (or teaching) of Christ. They are effectually One and the same. The Word of GOD is the Vine of GOD. *"GOD is a Spirit* (re. John 4:24), and he is a *"Holy"* Spirit of a Living Word. His name is Jesus.

We mustn't compartmentalize Christ. It must be noted, that much of the doctrine (teaching) and traditions of my forefathers unintentionally disassociated me from the fullness of GOD in Christ. By innuendo and by implication, and by presumption and misdirection, I was taught that Jesus dwelt in my heart and soul, but that the Father primarily stayed (isolated and largely out of touch) in heaven.

This doctrine was (hopefully) inadvertent and unconscious on my teacher's (and preacher's) part. Still, it gravely diminished the deity of the LORD Jesus Christ. And, as such, it must be concluded that its initial catalyst was spiritual wickedness in high places (even religious ones), determined to disassociate (distance and/or separate) believers from the omniscience, omnipresence, and omnipotence of GOD in the redemptive affairs of the sons and daughters of men.

Frankly, as regarding my prayer life alone, the damage of this erroneous doctrine (teaching) was inestimable. Come to find out (as we say up the hollow), it is much easier to get a prayer through than what I had been taught to believe. Children, if I am One with the Father in Christ by the Holy Spirit (abiding in the Vine), well, he hears my every prayer, my every inhalation and exhalation, and my every heartbeat, as well.

GOD is closer than my own right hand. The Word of GOD by John the Beloved, explicitly states that if I abide in the doctrine of Christ, I definitely have *"both"* the Father and the Son (see 2 John 1:9). And here, once more, is the exemplification (and clarification) of the doctrine (teaching) of Christ, as concisely spoken by the LORD Jesus Christ.

※

*If a man love me, he will keep my Words: and
my Father will love him, and "we" will come
unto him, and make "our" abode with him.*
see JOHN 14:23

✳

GOD is closer than my next (or present) heartbeat, my next breath, my next thought. This will ultimately be proven to be the only relationship that really matters, in that, my every other relationship should have its foundation laid upon my living by this faith. The revelation of One LORD is the Reality of GOD.

This juncture, where the branch is joined to the Vine, is the umbilicus of (spiritual) life. Is this not, in effect, the womb where the fetus of my spirit man is first born again by grace through faith? Precisely, this holy juncture is the portal to the kingdom of GOD manifesting and being realized within me.

Frankly (even dreadfully and alarmingly) this is indubitably holy ground. This juncture of my abiding in the Vine as a branch is the epicenter of life, the very axis and confluence of the finite and the infinite, the nexus of revelation.

Remarkably (and oftentimes disturbingly) this is ground zero. Miraculously and wonderfully, this juncture is the quintessence of life, the mystery and wisdom of GOD, the secret to the fullness of joy.

This is a holy place of transition (and covenant transaction). The blood (and life) of the LORD Jesus Christ is the coin of exchange in this hallowed place. Here, I abandon my self-interests, and step down from pride. Here I abnegate self-will.

This is the place of my face-to-face with GOD, even as a man speaks to his friend. This is the abandon of faith, and the place of a holy fire. Here, the kingdom of GOD is given and taken. This is a holy place of prayer and worship, and the temple of GOD.

※

What? know ye not that your body is the temple of the Holy Ghost which is in you, which ye have of GOD, and ye are not your own? For ye are bought with a price: therefore glorify GOD in your body, and in your spirit, which are GOD's.
1 Cor. 6:19-20

※

Children, this is where the transaction is made, and where the union of life is made sure, even as the kingdom of GOD is realized within me. A temple is where prayer is wont to be made, and where worship in spirit and in truth are offered up. It is a clean and holy place, free from distraction, sanctified for one purpose. Behold, the celebration and the thanksgiving are an informal, internal phenomenon, a most intimate association.

I speak finitely of an infinite phenomenon, figuratively of the reality of GOD, and the enigmatic manifestation of eternal life. This is the womb of life, wonderfully and mysteriously secreted within my soul. This is where the sacrifice is bled out by faith before the altar of GOD, and where eternal life is given and taken.

I cannot help but speak in the same figurative or metaphorical as our primary text. This theoretical place where the branch is joined to the Vine is the reality of GOD transforming my character by the Holy Spirit of a Living Word. It is here that I am fearfully and wonderfully made, and where my (spiritual) members are wrought (re. Ps. 139:14-15).

Frankly, this holy juncture is the incomprehensible acreage of a fastidious husbandman. Jesus said so. *"I AM the true Vine, and my Father is the husbandman"* (John 15:1).

The *true* Vine is the LORD Jesus Christ, and then there are religious forms and facsimiles. If I appear to be hypercritical, it is a reflection of the decades my soul subsisted in peril of hell by virtue of erroneous teaching and preaching. The preponderance of the teaching and preaching of contemporary Christianity is a clever (and cunning) subterfuge and spiritual delusion which aids and abets me in the clandestine saving of my life for myself. Thankfully, there are exceptions: pockets of resistance to an all-permissive grace, oases of sanctification and holiness preaching.

The truth about my union in the Vine (Jesus Christ), is that, where the branch meets the Vine is the holy place of an indispensable gospel principle. It is where my life is lost to find it. Concisely, it is where my absolute all is unconditionally surrendered to the health and prosperity and the glory and honor of the Vine.

As I have written, anything less than the whole animal is a token sacrifice. The LORD Jesus Christ did not teach us how to save our lives for ourselves; the gospel of Jesus Christ teaches us how to die, so that we might be born again.

Children, I do not want teaching and preaching that will assist me to ingeniously and resourcefully save my life for myself, but at the expense (and eventual loss) of my soul. You know, some conscience-salving religious form or the imposter of an all-permissive grace. Ultimately, I am responsible for the counsel I receive. The only *true* Vine is the Word of GOD (the LORD Jesus Christ).

※

Every plant, which my heavenly Father hath not planted, shall be rooted up. Let them alone: they be blind leaders of the blind. And if the blind lead the blind, both shall fall into the ditch.
re. MATT. 15:13-14

※

We know that the Pharisees were one of the preeminent religious groups of their time. They were the custodians and administrators of the Word of GOD. They took great pride in this position. They were the religious elite in possession of the books of Moses and the Words of the prophets and the psalms.

Duh. We can have the Word of GOD, as it were, and the Word of GOD still not have us. We can presume upon both possession and religious position, and later find that GOD did not place us there. Uh, we came up some other way, the same as a thief and a robber (see John 10:1).

The LORD Jesus Christ taught us that the Father is seeking *"true"* worshippers, to worship him in spirit and in truth (see John 4:23-24). The spirit of my life is the whole man sanctified – the whole man as a living sacrifice. The spirit of my life is who I *truly* am 24/7 – 365, and not necessarily the imposter I perfunctory present before the righteous congregation (and the preacher) on Sunday. That guy may not actually exist, if you know what I mean.

By implication and innuendo (and by example), as a young Christian, I was taught to suppress what I really felt, and to hide my *true* self. (We wouldn't want to shock anyone.) What the solemn assembly was really hiding was the surreptitious saving of our lives for ourselves. However, the observation of external religious ceremony has its appointed place in pleasing GOD only as it arises out of a genuine (unfeigned) faith.

✳

Behold, thou desirest truth in the inward parts: and in the hidden part thou shalt make me to know wisdom.
Ps. 51:6

✳

Walking and living by a genuine faith commands truth in response to the grace of GOD: accountability. I knew how to hide, and how to dissimulate. Frankly, what I needed above all else was to confess my true self. I was already proficient at sleight of hand and misdirection, saying one thing and meaning another, transacting shady business. What I needed was to step into the light.

The point has been made. We can have the Word of GOD, and the Word of GOD still not have us. We must enter into the Word of GOD (Jesus Christ) to be saved. See Chapter 3.

✳

I AM the Door: by me if any man enter in, he shall be saved, and shall go in and out, and find pasture.
JOHN 10:9

✳

Concisely, this entire manuscript is about entering into Jesus Christ, and about being made One with the Father, in him, by the Holy Spirit. Bluntly, this teaching on the *"true"* Vine is about abiding. Not about visiting occasionally, or just passing through, but about living and remaining there. Children, this is not about religious exercise or ritual ceremony, or even about religious or spiritual discipline; this is about being born again.

Being in the Church does not always equate to being in Christ Jesus. Joining myself to a specific denomination does not necessarily parallel or equal (to) my abiding in the Vine. Being a Christian is living a radically transformed life. Joining a Church does not make me a Christian, rather, individual Christians joined together make a Church.

Abiding in the Vine is about walking and living by grace through faith according to every Word that proceeds out of the mouth of GOD. We have said that the primary difficulty (especially initially) is that, when I look into the Word of GOD, the Word of GOD looks into me.

Frankly, the Word of GOD is an astringent and an antiseptic, a detergent, a fumigant and a purgative. Being a Christian is not about playing Church, it's about radical transformation. Let us stop misleading Christian novitiates and neophytes (newborns) and initiating them into our particular denominational brand of religious bigotry and dissimulation. Let us stop perpetuating the species. GOD is looking for new creatures, not denominational proselytes.

✳

Woe unto you, scribes and Pharisees, hypocrites! for ye compass sea and land to make one proselyte, and when he is made, ye make him twofold more the child of hell than yourselves.
MATT. 23:15

✳

First thing first, as they say, and the Word of GOD will do his own work. About this *"abiding"* and this fruit bearing, the Holy Spirit makes preliminary and integral points. It has been my experience and learning by the Word of GOD, that what can be called the *initial* fruit, are the profound changes the Word of GOD effects in me. This is pertinent to our primary text.

✳

Bring forth therefore "fruits" meet for repentance.
MATT. 3:8

✳

It must be noted here that John the Baptist is addressing the Sadducees and the Pharisees, the two predominant religious groups of the time (see Matt. 3:7). Many of them were coming to his baptism. These two groups were the ruling religious elite during the ministry of John the Baptist and the LORD Jesus Christ. (Without naming names), I wonder what two contemporary Christian groups (or denominations) might be represented by this prophetic (eternally pertinent) Word of GOD?

The Word of GOD makes his own point. The religious elite, the best Church folk of the time, were needing fruit meet (or representative) of repentance. Obviously, they were not demonstrating any, or, at least, not *edible* fruit.

These Sadducees and Pharisees might accurately be said to be a vine other than the One *"true"* Vine. (And) by the Holy Ghost, I am compelled to say, *"That which hath been is Now"* (see Ecclesiastes 3:15). The Church is still infested with inedible, oftentimes ostentatious fruit, and infested with aberrant pernicious growth.

Concisely, fruit meet (or representative) of repentance would be distinct signs or evidence of personal reformation. Has the Word of GOD changed me? In the case of the Sadducees and the Pharisees, has the Word of GOD that I attest to being the custodian and administrator of, changed me after a godly sort? Or has my proprietary presumption of ownership simply made me proud and judgmental; arrogant, intolerant, unbearable? You know how we do it.

Before there can be fruit representative of the essence and character (and loveliness) of the LORD Jesus Christ, there must be demonstrable and qualifiable fruit of my repentance. As they say, I cannot give away what I do not have. Sadly, we can presume upon position and it make us proud and closed minded, and blind to our own need. The Pharisees presumed themselves righteous, proprietors of the Word of GOD. John the Baptist said they had need of repentance.

They had missed the preliminaries (and prerequisites) of repentance and went on forwardly and presumptuously establishing formal religious ceremony and tradition. John the Baptist recognized (and addressed) their religious growth, that the Pharisees and the Sadducees were indeed manifesting growth, or foliage and fruit, but it was not the proliferation that GOD was looking for.

*

And now also the axe is laid unto the "root" of the trees: therefore every tree which bringeth not forth good fruit is hewn down, and cast into the fire.
MATT. 3:10

*

The Pharisees were the preeminent example in John the Baptist's and Jesus Christ's era of producing the wrong kind of fruit. (I shouldn't have to say) that we have religious groups in our own era who parallel this prophetic Word of GOD. Indeed. I never tire of reflecting on the living perpetual prophetic nature of the Word of GOD. *"That which hath been is Now"* (see Eccl. 3:15).

The time has come, proclaims John the Baptist, that GOD is going to get to the heart of the matter. (And) moreover, by the Holy Ghost, I say, the LORD whom you profess to seek, even the messenger of the covenant, is suddenly come to his temple (see Mal. 3:1).

The emphasis and the redundancy are warranted. The prophetic implications must be taken to heart. The message must be internalized and assimilated into the foundational structure of our religion. We must build only upon the initial message, and notably, John the Baptist and the LORD Jesus Christ came out of their respective wildernesses preaching the identical message.

✳

Repent ye: for the kingdom of heaven is at hand.
see MATT. 3:2 AND 4:17

✳

The fruits meet (or representative) of repentance are a demonstrable change of heart and mind. This will naturally and inevitably manifest as profound behavior and attitude modification. Character conversion, a new creature. A radical spiritual phenomenon known as being born again. You get the idea.

In GOD's reality, formal religious ceremony and service cannot supplant a genuine repentance. The Pharisees were the religious elite of their era, but the comprehensive New Testament exposes them as proud and arrogant, contemptuous of whom they considered their spiritual inferiors, and ultimately revealed to be haters and suppressors of the Truth.

They had established a religion based upon the tradition of their being GOD's chosen people, ostensibly a good place to start. However, John the Baptist (and the LORD Jesus Christ) confront them with the fact that they have persisted fundamentally unchanged in heart. Frankly, if I boast of loving GOD, but have nothing but contempt for my neighbor, and antagonism toward my brother, there is something terribly wrong with my testimony.

GOD (himself) will see to the integrity and verity of the place of my juncture with Jesus Christ, the *true* Vine. Frankly (bluntly), GOD is still fastidious for fruit *meet* (or representative) of repentance.

It is the pinnacle of presumption for me to speculate or surmise that I am going to functionally join myself to the LORD Jesus Christ while my heart is still glutted with strife, envy, lust, pride, hate, et. al. Indeed, I can look the religious part outwardly, and still be a rotten apple at the core. In fact, I became quite adept at camouflaging worm holes, masking blight, and masquerading as a good apple.

In GOD's reality, *first-fruits* are those meet (or representative of and/or demonstrative of) a genuine repentance. It cannot be said any plainer.

GOD is looking for a profound, even radical change of heart and mind, and then progressively and ultimately, a converted character.

When we receive the power to become a son or daughter of GOD, this power (the Holy Spirit who GOD is) immediately begins this irrepressible process. This demise of my natural man, and the new birth of my spiritual man, is a spontaneous reaction to the power (and presence) of the Holy Spirit of GOD. However, oftentimes in a desperate attempt to save our natural man (and our love for the world, and the lust of our flesh), and to spare ourselves the austerity and self-denial which a genuine faith commands, we enter into forms of godliness that help us emulate the forward momentum and radical character change (repentance) which the power of GOD wants to effect in our heart and mind. The Apostle

Paul warns his protégé, Timothy, about these religious forms without an accompanying character conversion.

✳

Having a form of godliness, but denying the
power thereof: from such turn away.
2 Tim. 3:5

✳

Using myself as an example once again, as a young Christian, I was expected by my teachers and elders to exhibit or produce demonstrable religious growth, and foliage, as it were. I was obliquely or indirectly taught to emulate (whom I call) the Holy Brethren in dress and speech and deportment. Concisely, I was taught external Christian etiquette, to sit up straight, to sing when expected, to say *Amen* occasionally, and not to sleep so soundly in the pew that you snored.

It is not humorous, and of course I somewhat exaggerate to make a point. But these things must be addressed. That is, false growth or erroneous religious exercise or activities which produce the fake fruit of a form of godliness, rather than the genuine fruit of abiding in the One *true* Vine, Jesus Christ. That is correct, like the fruit Grandma kept on the dining room table that we grandchildren were forbidden to joke about or pretend to eat. Plastic fruit.

In a relevant contemporary context, multifarious religious and denominational vines exist and propagate, that are not congenital or hereditary to the One *true* Vine, Jesus Christ. That is, imitations and imposters proliferate, Oh, bad apples abound. Notably, John the Baptist and the LORD Jesus Christ concur as concerns trees and vines that bear bad (or ungodly) fruit, unproductive branches – they are cast into the fire (see Matt. 3:10 and John 15:6).

Jesus Christ characterizes the Father as a meticulous husbandman. Truly, staying with the same analogy, the greatest yield per acre originated with (and is dependent upon) the health and productivity of the individual branch as it taps into the life of the Vine. GOD takes great care with the individual Christian.

The Father knows the depth (or the level) of my abiding in Jesus Christ (the Word of GOD), as only One LORD can. We mustn't imagine that the Father is disassociated from the Vine in any particular. In every perspective, and from every possible revelatory vista, *"The LORD our GOD is One LORD"* (see Deut. 6:4 and Mark 12:29). Each chapter of this manuscript bears this out. This is the perpetual (abiding) revelation that puts the power and authority of the resurrected Christ in the middle of my Christianity.

The indispensable point that the Holy Spirit emphasizes is that first fruits are those of an initial (but profound) change of heart and mind, a demonstrable *"turning"* away from (what I call) self-realization to GOD-realization. Turning away from sin and from self and from the love of the world and turning unto the One *true* God (Jesus Christ).

(Ideally) my steadfast abiding in the One *true* Vine, the Word of GOD, will be progressively reflected in my Christian testimony, and produce the essence and nature of the LORD Jesus

Christ within me – to bear his witness outside of me, and to advance the kingdom of GOD in the earth.

Unapologetically, GOD is expecting and seeking fruit from his disciples (followers). And the Holy Spirit further clarifies and qualifies that statement by saying that every *believer* in Jesus Christ is empowered to become, and fully expected to progressively transition into, avid followers and ardent disciples of the LORD Jesus Christ. Otherwise, the prognosis (we might say) is poor.

※

Every branch in me that beareth not fruit
he (the Father) taketh away.
JOHN 15:2

※

Now, not to be facetious, or deliberately intolerant, but it is the Word of GOD that is stringent and uncompromising here. Succinctly, this is how the LORD Jesus Christ goes on to address the man (or woman) who does not stay connected to himself, or who does not live in (or abide in) the Word of GOD.

※

If a man (or woman) abide not in me, he is cast forth
as a branch, and is withered; and men gather them,
and cast them into the fire, and they are burned.
JOHN 15:6

※

To be *"withered"* (we might say) indicates an advanced state of corruption and decay. Indeed, *"and sin when it is finished, bringeth forth death"* (see James 1:15). Christian, it must be irrevocably settled in our heart and mind, there is no life outside Jesus Christ (the Word of GOD).

Concisely, the comprehensive gospel teaches that there will be definitive evidence of the Christian disciple abiding in Jesus Christ, the Word of GOD. There will be fruit (corroborating evidence), and as we have said, first there will be a marked change in my thoughts and behaviors, a quantifiable change of direction in the *Way* that I take. And second, the nature and characteristics of Jesus Christ will begin to show forth in my radical transformation. There will be an observable progression to the dynamic miracle of my *being* born again.

GOD is looking for kingdom fruit to manifest in my lifestyle and in my character. In fact, he intends that my growth or proliferation (if you will) shall eventually overtake my neighbor. The phenomenon of the love of GOD in the earth, as evidenced in the gospel of Jesus Christ and him crucified, is a purposeful irrepressible evangelical endeavor. His Truth is marching on. I will join myself to the love of the Truth, or there shall be no life in me.

(Bluntly), unproductive trees are hewn down, and fruitless branches are removed and cast forth to be withered, and eventually gathered together and cast into the fire (Mall. 3:10, John 15:6). We can hope (I suppose) that the Word of GOD means something other than literal hell fire, but (to me) everything indicates that unproductive (or unchanged) Christians are going to be cast into the lake of fire to have their part with the devil and his angels, to experience what the Word of GOD calls *the second death.*

Our avoidance must be addressed. Our volitional ignorance does not change the reality of the Word of GOD. Frankly, we know the indubitable and ineradicable message is there, we just do not teach it or preach it. And, as we shall see (as our chapter progresses) the standard is *holy love.*

✳

Behold, these three years I come seeking fruit on this fig tree, and find none: cut it down; why cumbereth it the ground?
see LUKE 13:6-9

✳

It has been my experience, that what I give away, I am graced to keep. This is my portion. (I will not speculate on yours.) Indeed, I shall perpetuate the kingdom of GOD, or I shall have no part therein.

The Word of GOD teaches that the Father is the husbandman who precisely knows the state (or the depth) of my progression (advance) in Christ Jesus. I sometimes call this infinite awareness the Omniscient eye of the HOLY.

The Father perpetually reveals the Son, and the Son continually reveals the Father, and (ideally) my life is made One in the exchange.

✳

All things are delivered unto me of my Father: and no man knoweth the Son, but the Father; neither knoweth any man the Father, save (or except) the Son, and he to whomsoever the Son will reveal him.
MATT. 11:27

※

This revelation washes over me grace for grace, even as faith to faith the righteousness of GOD is revealed (re. Rom. 1:17). My life is lost in the transition, assimilated into GOD. I am not trying to be mystical; but reference the manifestation of the sons of GOD and the marvel of my being born again. This glory of GOD, and my adject penury, are precisely balanced upon a divine and sovereign correlative of GOD by faith. I see him most clearly from the perspective of my absolute poverty.

The Life is in the Vine. As I have written, it belongs to me about like the dew belongs to the grass. Or like the wind belongs to the turbine, or the kite, or the sparrow.

It is Christ who perpetuates the kingdom, and the Christian disciple is, as it were, along for the ride. It is by grace that we travel together with a mighty terrible One. By grace in the greatness of his strength and the sovereignty of his will, *"so is every one that is born of the Spirit"* (see John 3:8).

To *abide* in the Word of GOD, in Christ Jesus, the *true* Vine, we should understand, is to principally live by every Word that proceeds out of the mouth of GOD. Moreover, GOD shows me, that to personally *abide* in the Word of GOD is to willingly submit to its (his) perpetual assessment. Children, this *truth* remains elementary because we have not (predominantly) realized and internalized its significance. It is because of our hardness of heart (and our hearing impairment) that GOD must repeat himself.

※

For the Word of GOD is quick (alive) (to exist in an absolute sense and without end, *Strong's Greek*

Dictionary), and powerful, and sharper than any two-edged sword, piercing even to the dividing asunder of soul and spirit, and of the joints and marrow, and is a discerner of the thoughts and intents of the heart.
HEB. 4:12

*

GOD, in essence and character, is a Holy Spirit of a Living Word. It is in this perpetual, progressive revelation that I write. If you follow. As I say, I write on the edge of revelation, and in the evolution of faith. Today is intended to be a fresh encounter.

We communicate with GOD by the Holy Spirit of his Living Word.

The Word of GOD is the living definitive expression of his heart and mind, his feelings and thoughts and his expectations. Dear, dear children, this Word with whom we communicate is the same infinite mind and creative genius who spoke this world into existence. His name is Jesus.

Know you not, dear children, that this Spirit of a Living Word is the ethereal Grace and Truth of GOD seeking embodiment? Alas, we must take the time and space for another critical Truth not much taught.

*

Know ye not that ye are the temple of GOD, and that the Spirit of GOD dwelleth in you? If any man (or woman) defile the temple of GOD, him shall GOD destroy; for the temple of GOD is holy, which temple ye are.
1 COR. 3:16-17

*

(I must also take the time and space to clarify something.) There is no convenient place to interject it but here and now. Just yesterday (as I discern and interpret the nuance and implications and innuendo common to religious men), I was obliquely or indirectly indicted with (uh, perhaps) being too verbose, or having a vocabulary that was inordinate or deliberately disproportionate to my audience. You know, as if I were putting on grammatical airs, if you will.

First, I am not trying to impress with intelligence or vocabulary. (If anything), I am seeking to alleviate myself of a clinging, profound, personal ignorance. The revelatory Grace and Truth of GOD, hidden and layered within the mysteries and wisdom of Jesus Christ is such, that I am not only attempting to express something totally new and perpetually fresh to me, but that which is infinite and omnipotent in scope.

I attempt to express the inexpressible, the infinitely perpetually evolving and constantly speaking spontaneously fulfilling prophetic inexhaustible essence of the marvel of Almighty GOD. It is my understanding that is evolving.

Frankly, I exhausted my own vocabulary many years ago. It is my aspiration, each of my remaining days, to progressively abandon my volitional ignorance and wanton self-seeking in the single-minded realization of the kingdom of GOD within me. I indulge myself in GOD now.

Second, there is nothing wrong (primarily meaning pretentious) about a constantly evolving vocabulary. The suggestion that pretentiousness is the primary catalyst of learning new words is indicative of the very ignorance that has . . . well, that has kept us ignorant for so long. Perhaps it is not the vocabulary that is so unpalatable, but that it is the austerity of the message that is indigestible.

Third, *"words"* are the medium that GOD chose to reveal and express himself. When my intent is pure and my eye is single, the Word of GOD is accompanied by a quickening (life-giving) Spirit. It is GOD, and only GOD, who rightly divides the Word of GOD.

The Holy Spirit of this Living Word of GOD, when he manifested as flesh, was the image of the invisible GOD. His name is Jesus, GOD Incarnate. His name is still Jesus. By his own mouth he attests to being both Alpha and Omega, the beginning and the ending (see Rev. 1:8).

He told John, *"What thou seest, write in a book"* (see Re. 1:11). Dearest children, by the same Spirit, I vouchsafe to do the same; nothing more, and nothing less. He who has ears to hear, let him hear.

The Holy Spirit of the Living Word of GOD (Jesus Christ) is everywhere present and nowhere absent, except, of course, the heart and soul of the impenitent and the unclean. We still speak primarily about *abiding*, and that the initial evidence of my abiding in the Vine, Jesus Christ, the Word of GOD, is fruit representative of repentance (change, transformation, reformation, conversion). Concisely, *"Ye shall know them by their fruit"* (see Matt. 7:16).

Once again, the teaching (doctrine) of Jesus Christ parallels and corroborates the teaching and preaching of John the Baptist.

✺

*Every tree that bringeth not forth good fruit
is hewn down, and cast into the fire.*
compare MATT. 3:10 AND MATT. 7:19

✺

I can claim ignorance of the metaphorical or prophetic context of the Word of GOD, but it is not going to alter its message and irrepressible outcome.

The Holy Spirit of the Living Word of GOD is One LORD who is both the Father and the Son everywhere present and nowhere absent, restlessly and purposefully seeking reconciliation with men. The LORD Jesus Christ making the statement, *"But the Son of man hath not where to lay his head"* (re. Luke 9:58), is an evangelical appeal and tender overture unto intimacy and fellowship, cohabitation, mutual *abiding.*

"Where is the place of my rest?" (re. Is. 66:1), is the ardent cry of a loving Father in fervent search for a wayward child. Christian, GOD is seeking a tabernacle to entrust with housing his *Testimony.* The fiery inextinguishable *One* is seeking a faithful reservoir. The incendiary *Witness* of the Living Word of GOD is urgently seeking a home.

The blood of Jesus Christ is seeking a holy place of mercy upon which to ratify the love covenant of the Father, reuniting him with his child.

GOD is seeking a temple, a sanctified (oftentimes secret) place of prayer and worship, a holy place of unseen sacrifice, a platform from which the Word of GOD is spoken. A heart to house the expression of holy love.

About this cohabitation and mutual (amenable) *abiding*, it is he whose name is *HOLY* that makes the vessel holy. Let us be concise. *"Every branch that beareth fruit, he purgeth it, that it may bring forth more fruit"* (re. John 15:2).

A good husbandman envisions a bountiful harvest. *"Every"* branch is cleaned and pruned (cut back) to engender and maximize productivity. Staying with the Word of GOD's own agricultural analogy, the branch is expected to bear fruit *"after his kind"* and *"whose seed is in itself"* (see Gen. 1:11).

This is GOD's perspective and GOD's reality. Concisely, heaven is his throne, and earth is his footstool (re. Is. 66:1). The Word of GOD speaks for GOD.

※

Now the parable is this: The seed is the Word of GOD.
LUKE 8:11

※

This Word is, principally, the key to the kingdom of heaven developing within me and manifesting out of me. I am eventually expected to produce fruit (disseminate seed) of the same Word of GOD which first quickened me. My conversation is to be imbued with the same Word of GOD which first gave me life. There is a precise gospel term for this dynamic phenomenon, but it is in danger of becoming extinct. It is called *"Witness."*

One of the prevailing difficulties that the righteous congregation experiences in assimilating this kingdom principle is that (it) the agricultural analogy unceremoniously reduces all our religion to dirt. That is correct, the piercing unsparing revelation of garden-variety soil, common earth, plain old dirt.

Oh my. This reduces me to presenting without pretext or dissimulation. (Why, suddenly I am naked beneath a threadbare religious garment.)

The seed is the Word of GOD, and I am the soil. *"That no flesh should glory in his presence"* (1 Cor. 1:29).

The revelation is that *raw*, it (the reality of all that I am not) kind of makes me want to rend my garments like the Pharisees must have done. It (GOD's perspective, and holiness) makes me want to repent in sackcloth and ashes. Uh, (if I may), *"When I see you"* says Job, *"I abhor myself."* (re. Job 42:6)

Indeed, in the sudden and acute remembrances of my origins, I am finally silent. Suddenly, the aspirations of an earthen vessel have always been pretentious, and presumptuous . . . and, uh, preposterous.

✳

The only place I have of consequence, my LORD, is the
portion you have appointed me in your Word by grace;
in your nail-prints, and in your pierced and opened
side. I am, my dear Savior and LORD, as it were, the
travail of your soul in which you are satisfied (re. Is.
53:11), and the man that hath seen affliction by the rod
of thy wrath (re. Lam. 3:1); an unprofitable servant
re. LUKE 17:10

✳

*It is the Spirit that quickeneth (gives Life); the
flesh profiteth nothing: the Word(s) that I speak
unto you, they are Spirit, and they are Life.*
JOHN 6:63

More critical, the teaching (or doctrine) of *abiding*, than that of fruit production or yield per acre, if you follow. He who has ears to hear, let him hear. Behold the spontaneity and natural process of fruit production in nature, in the physical. Even so (relatively) is the spiritual.

The seed (the Word of GOD) comes with a quickening (life-giving and life-sustaining) Spirit. *"GOD is a Spirit"* (re. John 4:24), and he is a *"Holy"* Spirit. The first pertinent question, therefore, is how conducive or amenable is my earthen vessel to the cohabitation of a Spirit who is first of all a *"Holy"* Spirit?

We know (in theory) that GOD does not dwell in temples made with hands (primary re. Acts 7:48. That is, we know this truth one-dimensionally (as I call our conditional, superficial grasp of some Truths). But this has not prevented us from continuing to build bigger ones. It could be argued that we did not hear this *Word of GOD* at all.

The temple, whether an elaborate, stain-glassed edifice of brink and mortar, or my own body and spirit, the temple adds nothing to GOD. Nevertheless (and as we have covered), the temple must be holy, for he is Holy (re. 1 Pet. 1:16).

(I wonder) how much or to what degree, the emphasis we place upon erecting a massive, ornate (often ostentatious) cathedral, is a subconscious contrivance to get the attention off (of) ourselves. You know, the decrepit and disgraceful condition of our clandestine and dissimulating innermost character – the temple of GOD according to GOD's reality, the Word of GOD.

(I mean) do we really need a bigger Church? (I suspect) that some consistent sanctification and holiness preaching would sufficiently thin out the self-righteous crowd of posers and prostitutes we currently have.

Much of this has been covered also. And if you think me severe and intolerant, I refer you to the LORD Jesus Christ's last written Word to the seven churches in the first three chapters of the Revelation to John the Beloved. Two of the seven he unsparingly and disconcertedly called *"the synagogue of Satan"* (see Rev. 2:9 and 3:9).

Even as a sinner, I knew there was something glaringly incongruous and suspicious about contemporary Christianity's (general) testimony. Children, GOD does not assess the state of the marble floors, the stain-glassed windows, or the whited walls; he astutely beholds the inner sanctum of the heart and mind of the parishioners.

We need bigger churches because we perpetuate the species. We need an expression and a memorial of all we will not give. We are, concisely, the self-celebratory hoarders of the honor one of another. If nothing changes, nothing changes. Or, as the Word of GOD says it, *"That which hath been is Now"* (see Eccl. 3:15).

If we are not vigilant, the ceremony will supplant the character conversion that GOD desires. He who has ears to hear, let him hear. I am not being hypercritical and legalistic; I scribe out of the urgency of the love of GOD in Christ, from out of the despite and indignation, and the agony of his grace, and in the tender overtures and outreach of his mercy.

✳

And if thy right eye offend thee, pluck it out, and cast it from thee: for it is profitable for thee that one of thy members should perish, and not that thy whole body should be cast into hell.
MATT. 5:30

✳

This is not my doctrine (teaching), this is the reality and absolute of the Word of GOD.

Frankly, to be holy is to be a single-minded reservoir of the Holy Spirit of GOD, a cistern and a fountain of living water, an un-occluded conduit of the love of GOD in Jesus Christ.

Before we get all proprietary and covetous (and idolatrous), the Life is not mine. It is mine (as I say) like the dew belongs to the grass. Once more, *"It is the Spirit that quickeneth"* (gives and sustains life), *the flesh profiteth nothing: the Word(s) that I speak unto you, they are Spirit, and they are Life.* (re. John 6:63).

It behooves us to take the time and space to review the teaching of the LORD Jesus Christ from which this scripture arises. We view it in the immediate context and priority of *abiding.* In lieu of the preeminence the Word of GOD places upon the consistent abiding of the branch in the Vine, or the Christian in Christ, it cannot be emphasized enough. *"For without me ye can do nothing"* (re. John 15:5).

Concisely, there is no life in the branch (the Christian) that it does not first receive from the Vine (the LORD Jesus Christ). The depth and consistency of my abiding from GOD's perspective transcends (and eclipses) the ceremony and the singing and the comprehensive imperious (and pretentious) church service. As I say, multiple adjectives are warranted in lieu of our one-dimensional grasp and casual (theoretical) consideration of the Word of GOD.

To be brutally honest, there were multiple decades that I subsisted on the Word of GOD that (I may have) heard the preacher read on Sunday to generally qualify calling myself a Christian. And I was not alone. Dear children, this is not *abiding*; this is church attendance.

[I speak (first) personally, and concisely, and without apology.] On a good week, my religion (my Christianity) consisted of about 3-4 hours of lackadaisical (lukewarm) church attendance and apathetic ceremony. Frankly, I carried my Bible around (on Sundays) with about the same honor one would give an antiquated history book, or with the same disconcerting self-consciousness as an overdue library book. My TV-Guide and Sports Illustrated received considerably more time and attention, and honor.

Well? Someone must say something. If this manuscript confronts someone's perfunctory Christianity other than my own, then my time has been well spent. May you receive the Holy Spirit's admonition without GOD turning up the index and weight of his hand. He who has ears to hear, let him hear. Personally, it was mercy and grace which orchestrated the contrary circumstances which initiated the sovereign intervention of GOD Almighty into my debilitated and indifferent Christianity.

GOD's Word is (by GOD's design) a daily Bread. In fact, the scripture in which the LORD Jesus Christ says, *"The Word(s) that I speak unto you, they are Sprit, and they are Life"* (re. John 6:63), are found in the immediate context of his declaration to be the *Bread of Life.* Indeed, this teaching (doctrine) of the Bread of Life encompasses the entire sixth chapter of John. Moreover, it is also fitting, and relative, that it was the nucleus of the first chapter of this manuscript, *"I AM the Bread of Life"* (see John 6:35).

In the context of this chapter (of Jesus Christ as the Vine) the imperative is the phenomenon or dynamic of the Christian's *abiding* in Jesus Christ, the Word of GOD. And by the Holy Spirit of the Living Word of GOD, we delve more deeply into this allegory of the branch abiding in the Vine.

Abiding in Christ is dramatically and exponentially more than religious ceremony or regular church attendance and service. Granted, many Christians excel at these activities. But without the Word of GOD given the preeminence, and the Spirit of this Living Word to give them life, they are reduced to works of the flesh.

✳

The flesh profiteth nothing.
re. JOHN 6:63

Without me ye can do nothing.
re. JOHN 15:5

✳

Concisely (and markedly), the doctrine (teaching) of the LORD Jesus Christ in the sixth chapter of John is that his flesh and his blood are the *"Eucharist"* or the consecrated elements of the New Covenant. We may also say that the LORD Jesus Christ teaches that his flesh and blood are the sacrament of our Holy Communion with GOD. They are the consecrated elements, or the bread and the wine of the Last Supper, of which we are commanded to partake in remembrance of the LORD.

It is when I look closely and purposefully into the Word of GOD that he reveals his expectations of me. The *friends* of the Bridegroom follow this far. In (what I call) gradients of greater Grace, and in the midnight terrors of intimate Truth, GOD reveals the level of commitment and allegiance he desires of me. It is at this precise juncture of explicit revelation, that many of the believers (and would-be disciples) of the LORD Jesus Christ (in every era), follow no more or fall away into *"forms of faith."* Here is how the LORD Jesus Christ (the Word of GOD) acutely expresses the level of intimacy he expects of his followers (disciples).

✳

> *Then said Jesus unto them, Verily, verily, I say unto you, Except ye eat the flesh of the Son of man, and drink his blood, ye have no life in you.*
> JOHN 6:53

✳

(We might say) this is for *"believers"* who aspire to be *"disciples."* (If I may), I am going to have to delve significantly deeper than surface Christianity and formal religious ceremony. Oh my.

Before we go any further, I want to put this in the immediate context and urgency of our *abiding* in the Vine from the Word of GOD's (the LORD Jesus Christ's) perspective.

*

*He that eateth my flesh, and drinketh my
blood, "dwelleth" in me, and I in him.*
JOHN 6:56

*

Frankly, this is a level of familiarity that the forms of faith of my forefathers did not reflect. This is not Grandma's Sunday school. Concisely, this is the suffering fellowship of the crucified Christ, and an intimacy attained only at an old-rugged cross. This is where the blood of the Lamb is both shed and applied, both given and received. This is a Most Holy place.

This cup of suffering association is shared at the foot of the cross. This is where the true disciples of Jesus Christ are made One with the sacrifice of GOD's love for the world – in the immediate context of the blood of Jesus Christ being perpetually applied. In the consciousness of the crucified Christ of GOD, I eternally *abide* in the Most Holy place of a perpetual atonement.

Relatively, I *abide* at the mercy seat of GOD, above the ark of his own *Testimony*, and in the immediate presence and acceptance of GOD. The glory of this diving dwelling place can bear the weight of my redundancy. This is where sinners are saved by grace, and where kings and priests take their *place*.

*

*And there I will meet with thee, and I will commune
with thee from above the mercy seat, from between
the two cherubims which are upon the ark of the
testimony, of all things which I will give thee in
commandment unto the children of Israel.*
Ex. 25:22

✳

Children, this is (as it were) the secret (*dwelling*) place of the
"*Most High,*" where the sons and daughters of GOD *abide* under the shadow of the Almighty (*see Psalm 91:1*). Concisely,
those made complete (perfect) in Christ *abide* in a perpetual
state of *Passover.* It is here, at the place of an eternal atonement, that the *true* disciples of Jesus Christ dwell.

In the perpetual awareness and immediate presence of the
torn flesh and shed blood of Jesus Christ, the disciples of Jesus
Christ *abide.* It is the place of the LORD's *Passover.*

From within the ark of the Testimony of GOD, the manna
represents the flesh of Jesus Christ, the Bread of Life. Upon
the ark of the Testimony rests the mercy seat, where the covenant is ratified by the blood of the Lamb. It is here that the
sons and daughters of GOD are made One with him in Christ.
"*And there*" (and only there), "*I will meet with thee*" (re. Ex. 25:22).

The consecrated elements which effectively activate and validate the Christian disciple's covenant with GOD are the flesh
and the blood of the LORD Jesus Christ, (mingled with faith,
of course). This holy meeting place occurs again and again
throughout this manuscript. This is no accident. This is the
sovereign expression of GOD's perspective reality of *abiding.*

This is no casual conditional (fair-weather) Christianity. This is the Christian disciple's becoming One with the sacrament of GOD's love in Jesus Christ for the next sinner's soul. This is the Most Holy place where kings and priests are made, and where the disciples of Jesus Christ yield themselves to be broken as bread and poured out as wine, assimilated into the sacrifice of Jesus Christ, and disseminated in the love of GOD for humanity.

This is where my Christianity becomes real, in this Most Holy place of being made One with the love of GOD for the world, at the juncture of the branch in the Vine. It is said that the saints of old looked ahead by faith with Abraham to the cross of Jesus Christ, and that the saints of today look back to the cross. (I could not find a reference to attribute credit for this saying), but it resonates with the perpetual prophetic revelation of the LORD Jesus Christ by the Holy Spirit of a Living Word.

✳

LORD, thou hast been our dwelling place in all generations.
PSALM 90:1

✳

Uh, this is (from one perspective), the Most Holy place of a perpetual LORD's Supper. This is the Most Holy place of perpetual remembrances, and a consciousness seared and consecrated unto the love of GOD in Christ. It is where I find grace for the next fellow. It is, as it were, the fruit of my *abiding*.

This is the Most Holy place where prayers are answered: the inner sanctum of the disciple's soul where the Son of GOD dwells. Here is where servants and stewards are transformed into sons and daughters, right where I enter into the fellowship of the Father and the Son by the Holy Ghost – here where all things are gathered together in One, even in Christ (see Eph. 1:10).

Children, the LORD Jesus Christ is the sacrament of GOD's love for the soul of the world. This is a great deep, an impenetrable immeasurable perpetual revelation. GOD takes me in and receives me in Christ. But where am I on the continuum of GOD's love in the revelation of an old-rugged cross? Where am I in the love of GOD's outreach for the next fellow's soul?

GOD's presence is inseparable from his purpose – as indivisible as the Father and the Son. Where am I on the perpetuity of the kingdom of GOD? How far have I reached into the side of Christ? Where am I in the miraculous enigmatic transformation of the servants and stewards of GOD into sons? Have I taken my place as a priest and an intercessor for the souls of the sons and daughters of men? Have I laid down my life for my friend, in exchange for stripes and spittle and a crown of thorns?

✳

Verily, verily, I say unto you, Except ye eat the flesh of the Son of man, and drink his blood, ye have no life in you.
re. JOHN 6:53

He that eateth my flesh, and drinketh my blood, "dwelleth" in me, and I in him.
JOHN 6:56

✳

These scriptures are expressive of the intimacy of *abiding* from the perspective of the LORD Jesus Christ. Am I integrated as a branch into the Vine like that?

By faith, I submit to the loss of my life to be made One with the love of GOD in Christ. For the resurrection life of Jesus Christ to be mine, I must share his death, as well. Is my life given, even as GOD gave his only begotten Son (see John 3:16)? Is my life (out there) like that, broken like bread?

There is no distinction between the life flowing in the Vine and the life flowing in the branch. The sacrifice is for the sustenance of the whole world. Christianity is the dissemination of the love of GOD in Jesus Christ. Am I One with the sacrifice, or has the gospel (effectively, relatively) stopped with me?

Once upon a time, I colluded with a self-celebratory congregation in the desperate and clandestine saving of our lives for ourselves. Surface Christianity. We loved who would love us first. We loved who looked conspicuously like ourselves. We loved within the four walls of our elitist religious enclave. We loved who would buy us lunch.

We wept at the acute realization that GOD expected us to love *"them"* like he had loved us. Christian, when was the last time you were *"torn"* for some sinner in the love of GOD?

The love of GOD is not an ethereal theoretical religious ideal, but an old-rugged cross and my life laid down for my friend. *"As the Father hath loved me, so have I loved you: continue ye in my love"* (John 15:9).

Duh. Love the next fellow and be radical about it: love him before adjudicating him worthy of it. Reach beneath the surface, step out of the comfort of religious form to embrace the practical (un)reality of GOD's incendiary love. Reach into your pocket, or rather, reach into your heart. Take the love of GOD out of the sanctuary where we cower from having to love our neighbor.

When I say that I cannot love like that, what I really mean is that I cannot die like that. I cannot be torn like that, broken, and disseminated, feasted upon by the unruly unholy masses of unregenerate society, pawed upon and picked over by the unclean and the impoverished, poured out in the love of GOD for the worst of humanity.

※

This is my commandment, That ye love
one another, as I have love you.
JOHN 15:12

※

Uh, and specifically (in my case) while I was yet unlovable. Concisely, to *"dwell"* in Christ (to abide in the Vine) is to become One with the sacrifice of the love (and the life) of GOD. The metaphorical meaning of eating the flesh of the Son of man, and drinking his blood, is the correlative reality of the disciples of Jesus Christ being made One with his cross. My life is GOD's to spend.

The juncture of the branch in the Vine is where I capitulate to the will of GOD and accede to the conditions of love: that loving GOD and loving my neighbor as myself are merged into One indivisible commandment. Jesus Christ made it so.

GOD's presence, and his omnipotence (his power), meet me at the apprehension of his purpose – concisely, the evangelization of the whole world in the love of GOD (the revelation of Jesus Christ).

GOD's essence (and personality, as it were), and the unction and endowment of his anointing, are revealed within the dynamic purposes of his love. Ideally, this is where the Christian disciple converges as a branch in the Vine, where he/or she is made One with the love of GOD in Jesus Christ for sinners. Well. Where grace and mercy abound and life is held forth, where forgiveness is freely found. Where grace meets truth, and mercy checks justice.

True Christianity is found in the conversion: the initial fruits of a genuine repentance, and the progressive fruits of the essence and character of Jesus Christ manifested within (and through) his disciples – the fruits of the Holy Spirit. A branch will bear the traits and characteristics of the life of the Vine.

✳

Verily, I say unto you, Except ye be converted, and become as little children, ye shall not enter into the kingdom of heaven.
re. MATT. 18:3

✳

Nothing can radically change me like being in the presence of Jesus, his touch, being connected to him by the Holy Spirit of a Living Word. The branch that is most completely yielded to the life of the Vine will bear the most fruit.

My relationship to the consecrated elements of my covenant with GOD is to be so intense and so intimate that the Word of GOD likens it to eating the flesh of Jesus Christ and drinking his blood (see John 6:53). This is the depth, and the degree, of GOD's expectation of my *"dwelling"* (or abiding). Again:

✳

*"He that eateth my flesh, and drinketh my
blood,* "dwelleth" *in me, and I in him"*
John 6:56

✳

At the juncture of the branch and the Vine, my own consecration to the purposes of GOD becomes One. My own life is sacrificed to the best interests of the Vine. I trust the Vine to provide my every necessity to fulfill his expectations of me as I become One with his purposes. That is, bearing kingdom fruit.

This teaching (doctrine) of the LORD Jesus Christ in the sixth chapter of John unsparingly exposes the preponderance of the religions of men as the shallow posture of self-representation and self-realization, uh, while seeking the honor and applause of prostitutes just like ourselves. The Father seeks spirit and truth, and we present someone that does not really exist; a religious effigy, a poor imposter of piety – plastic fruit.

The LORD Jesus Christ reckons the depth of my dwelling as symbolically eating his flesh and drinking his blood, or, becoming One with the sacrament (the sacrifice of love) – and the gospel of Jesus Christ and him crucified. In other words, get real. Remove your religious garments and gird yourself with a towel and become the servant of humanity. Prepare yourself to love the undeserving. And, for your love, you shall have stripes and spittle and your name cast out as evil.

In another manuscript, I called this teaching (doctrine) of the LORD Jesus Christ, the preeminent example of dark and hard sayings and things difficult to understand. In my hour of darkness and confrontation, as it were, I murmured along with the Jews in the sixth chapter of John. *"How can this man give us his flesh to eat?" "This is a hard saying, who can hear it?"* (see John 6:52, 60)

This doctrine commands me out of the cocoon of my self-interests and exclusivity. This doctrine commands spirit and truth of me; transparency, my secret treasure.

There are things (or elements) of my innermost character that even I am forbidden to look at. Or stir up. This doctrine finds me with unforgiveness and resentments that I am not prepared to forfeit.

Frankly, the spirit and truth of this commitment, the depth and intimacy of this *abiding* in Christ, commands a radical conversion of my character.

All my religion is filthy rags. My Christianity, in the acute exposure of this Word, is revealed as presumptuous superficial ceremony, external religious etiquette, vain supercilious table manners.

We boast of seeking GOD, of having a proprietary exclusive understanding of his character. We dress up and paint our faces to present pious and pretentious (and unchanged, uh, impenitent) before him in an ostentatious religious ceremony. Louis Evely says it well in his book, *Our Father. "He is not waiting for us on a pedestal, but on the level of the poorest of those whose feet we wash."*

Suddenly, it is not about religion anymore. It is about getting real, and about the cross of Jesus Christ overshadowing the great plans I had for myself. To *abide* in the Vine is the effectual correlative of the Christian disciple's deliberately aligning themselves with the evangelical purposes of GOD's love in the earth. To *dwell* in Christ is to become One with his sacrifice, his cross – to intentionally lay down my life in the love interests of GOD in the service of my neighbor's soul.

The love of GOD is not selective or denominationally or ethnically elitist, it is extended to the worst of humanity – bar none. This is how acute the Christian disciple's identification with their LORD and Savior, Jesus Christ, is to be manifested in the earth. That the world may see Jesus.

This gospel of giving oneself away in the love of GOD is not a popular doctrine (or teaching). But this is precisely how GOD loves, and how GOD gives: he gives himself away in the love-gift of Jesus Christ. Indeed, but the difficulty, you see, is that if I give myself away after the same manner, my own life is lost in the transaction. And I don't much care for these feelings of insignificance.

It becomes all about the love of GOD in Jesus Christ, and less and less about me. Suddenly, I am no longer the star of the religious production. You know, the spiritual prodigy of the elaborate supercilious ceremony. Suddenly, I am just another sinner saved by grace.

All dressed up, and nowhere to go (as they say). Suddenly it is less about me being seen and heard, and more about the next sinner getting saved. Ah, less and less about my righteousness, and more about mercy and grace. Indeed, in the acute revelation (and reality) of the love of GOD in the gospel of the cross of Jesus Christ, all my religious airs are exposed as vanity, and all my pompous pontifications as just another self-serving expression of pride.

In the service of GOD's love, my own life is invisible, and this is, well . . . this is intolerable. Why, it has taken me decades to design and produce and perfect this religious persona.

My *abiding* in the Vine is the (working, practical) reality of me becoming One with the sacrifice of GOD's love, broken and disseminated as bread, poured out as wine in the service of GOD's redemptive passion for the reconciliation of humanity. All else is (relatively) religious rags and the ineffectual notions of wise men and pretenders.

Flesh and blood cannot inherit the kingdom of GOD. The pride of my natural life cannot exist where the covenant is ratified. It is not about religion; it is the blood and guts (and the reality) of redemption. *"He that eateth my flesh, and drinketh my blood, "dwelleth" in me, and I in him.* (John 6:56).

It becomes insufferable to the poser and the prostitute, not to be permitted to play their religious part. The pride of man's life cannot abide anonymity.

*

*From that time many of his disciples went
back, and walked no more with him.*
JOHN 6:66

*

Rather double my tithe, than tell me I must get real. Rather give all my goods to the poor than abnegate my religious position. Rather burn me at the stake, than ask me to love the undeserving.

It is the love of GOD in Christ that challenges my surface Christianity and exposes my religious posturing as a self-serving, self-venerating ritualistic liturgy.

(I have written) that the love of GOD is not a native (or natural) species. It had to be sent into this world. Frankly, it most often finds us coveting and prostituting ourselves, posturing for the honor one of another, exposing our religious ceremony as self-salutatory ritualistic tradition.

That is correct, we serve and celebrate and deify ourselves. This is, by definition, idolatry. Well? *Someone* has to say something. Indeed. *"Ye worship ye know not what"* (see John 4:22).

A *true* disciple is a faithful follower of Jesus Christ through whom GOD keeps the miracle of redemption alive, by a vocal and behavioral testimony and an incendiary witness. They have aligned themselves with the love of GOD in Christ Jesus and their lives are lost in its outreach and continuity.

✳

If ye keep my commandments, ye shall "abide"
in my love; even as I have kept my Father's
commandments, and "abide" in his love.
JOHN 15:10

✳

It takes a convincing religious form to emulate a virulent radical faith which works by a genuine love. It takes an elaborate illusion to persuade the solemn assembly that they have worshipped well. Mainstream contemporary Christianity has evolved into just another common self-sustaining self-venerating religious entity, remarkably (and relatively) not unlike the Pharisees.

※

But I know you, that ye have not the love of GOD in you.
JOHN 5:42

※

We worship the religious ceremony (which we think) corroborates our Christianity, and which (we feel) confirms us as saved. We worship the idea that we have worshipped well. Frankly, we presume that GOD is just as pleased with us as we are pleased with one another.

We have a one-dimensional perspective of the LORD Jesus Christ having incorporated all the commandments into the One comprehensive commandment of the love of GOD in Christ. The preponderance of us have an ideological concept and a theoretical understanding of *"dwelling"* in Christ as taught by the LORD Jesus Christ in John 6:56. We have not plumbed the depths of the suffering association of the cross of Jesus Christ, or the excruciating intimacy of a *"flesh"* and *"blood"* fellowship. The preponderance of us have neither denied ourselves, nor taken up our cross.

Half of us do not care (fundamentally meaning *believe*) enough to delve into the deep and penetrating truths of the doctrine (teaching) of the LORD Jesus Christ. And the other half of us, as I have said, believe we have worshipped well. We presume upon a linear peripheral spiritual exercise usually called a church ceremony to substantiate our Christianity. Most of us, because we did not *hear* the first Word GOD said, subsequently did not hear, *"Follow me."*

(I wonder, ponder) what percentage of us (Christians) love outside the four walls of our structured, traditional church ceremony. (The tense of it cannot be changed.) The Christian sojourn or pilgrimage is intended to be a mysterious exhilarating process of walking and living by faith – as we are being gathered and assimilated into the One Love of One LORD.

If my worship does not originate or arise from a place of *abiding* in the love of GOD for the whole world, I have missed the point. I essentially sing to myself, and for myself. *"Ye worship ye know not what"* (see John 4:22).

The equivalent of my abiding in the Vine as a branch is my abiding in the love of GOD (the LORD Jesus Christ). It is my dwelling in both the essence and the character of Christ, as well as dwelling in the purposes of Christ. If I may use a finite term to reference him who is infinite, I abide both in the *person* of GOD, and in the purposes of GOD. Indeed, and I shall find they are One.

The love of GOD is the umbilicus of GOD extended to all of humanity. His name is Jesus. It is as we keep the commandments of Jesus Christ that we shall *"abide"* in his love; even as he kept the Father's commandments and abides in his love (see John 15:10). Notably, the LORD prefaced this verse with the word *"if." "IF" ye keep my commandments . . ."* (re. John 15:10).

GOD is aware of the depth of commitment of every Christian, and the level of intimacy of every branch in the Vine. We (every Christian) have a commandment to keep in order to *abide* in the love of Jesus Christ; even as he kept the Father's commandments and abides in his love. My redundancy parallels the imperative of the One commandment of love.

This place of *abiding* relative to the doctrine (teaching) of the LORD Jesus Christ here in the fifteenth chapter of John, is (what I call) the juncture of the branch in the Vine. This is the place of the Christian's (the branch's) complete and unconditional capitulation to both the life of the Vine (the LORD Jesus Christ), and the purpose (the redemptive evangelical love) of the LORD Jesus Christ.

This preeminent place of the branch in the Vine, or the *place of the Christian in Christ*, is both a place of eternal (or spiritual) life, and a *place* of natural (or physical) death. This juncture of the branch in the Vine is the allegorical expression of the gospel principle of *the life lost to find it.*

✳

For whosoever will save his life shall lose it; but whosoever shall lose his life for my sake and the gospel's, the same shall save it.
MARK 8:35

✳

My innate will and my natural life are surrendered to the LORD Jesus Christ to become One with his will (or purpose) and his life. What I am actually surrendering to is the *life more abundant* (see John 10:10). The exchange is inexpressible love and peace and joy (and much tribulation, also). Pointedly, overcoming adversity exacerbates the joy and peace.

Take heed, Christian, for the process and the exchange to be essentially metaphorical, the death throes and the suffering association are excruciatingly real. Indeed, it can accurately be said that the Christian's *place* in Christ is both given and taken. It is both a gift, and an intimacy of a suffering fellowship that must be won in the overcoming of opposition. It is the peace and love and joy of GOD in Christ beyond finite description.

The grace and truth which floods my soul unto surfeit is best submitted to as a little child, but I take my *place* as a soldier. Frankly, this is a most Holy place of life and death, and the reality of the gospel of Jesus Christ and him crucified. Definitively, this is not religion; and markedly, this transcends surface Christianity, and going through the motions of having church.

The inherent and/or collateral oppression and opposition which accompanies this gospel process are meant to be summarily and irrepressibly overcome. This is where the increase in my faith comes from – out of the fight. This is what exacerbates my joy and compliments my peace.

Christian, emphatically and undeniably (there are prophetically) giants in the promised land in every era or dispensation. Those who will not fight for what GOD has promised are rendered back into the wilderness of their unbelief. *"Behold therefore the goodness and severity of GOD"* (see Rom. 11:22).

Children, the refreshing aftermath and sweet sublime effect of victory totally overshadows the fight. To share Christ's death is to share his life; to partake of his victory is to taste his glory. The Vine and the branch share the same struggles, and the same overcoming Spirit of everlasting Life. This is *He* whom death could not hold.

At the heart of the conflict, at the juncture of the branch in the Vine, or the Christian in Christ, is the prophetic reality of giants possessing a land that GOD has already promised. Dear reader, people are fundamentally the same in every era or dispensation. Given for our explicit example and admonition are the children of Israel camped at the River Jordan. Here is their response when they learned that giants, specifically the sons of Anak, were occupying the land GOD had promised.

*

And all the congregation lifted up their voice, and cried; and the people wept that night.
Num. 14:1

*

Markedly, the children of Israel murmured against Moses and against Aaron (see Num. 14:2), and when Joshua and Caleb encouraged the people to go up and possess the land, the congregation *"bade"* (or recommended) stoning them (see Num. 14:10).

The correlative or equivalent of giants possessing the promised land are the comprehensive difficulties and opposition that I experience establishing an intimate relationship with the LORD Jesus Christ. This depth of intimacy can be likened to the juncture of the branch in the Vine (sharing the same *Life*). And, of course, the gospel reality is the cross of Jesus Christ, or sharing the same cross and the same death.

This intimacy of the cross is the allegorical eating the flesh and drinking the blood of Jesus Christ. This is the depth of intimacy and identification, and the level of commitment, that the reality of the gospel commands. (Regardless of what the purveyors of all-permissive grace have told you.)

This is the taking of my *"place."*

✳

*"He that eateth my flesh, and drinketh my
blood, "dwelleth" in me, and I in him.*
JOHN 6:56

✳

Dying to my will, and surrendering my life for the life of Christ, and to take my *place* as a branch in the Vine, is the gospel equivalent of crossing the Jordan River and fighting the giants in my personal promised land. To take and sustain (and defend) my *place* in Christ, there are many obstacles (giants) to overcome. Broadly, I include them all beneath the umbrella of (what I call) John the Beloved's short list of all that is in the world, and not of the Father: namely, the lust of the eyes and of the flesh, the love of the world, and the pride of life (see 1 John 2:15-17).

People being relatively the same in every era, many of us (contemporary Christians) still desperately try to circumvent the fighting of our personal giants: lust, pride, and love of the world. We all have them, and yes, they are huge. By comparison, they are, indeed, as the children of Anak, big enough to make the congregation cry.

By willfully and purposefully dying unto self and unto sin, and unto the love of the world and the pride of my life, I keep the LORD's commandments as he kept the Father's commandments (see John 15:10). This only is to *abide* in the love of Jesus Christ, even as the LORD Jesus Christ abides in the Father's love. This only is to take my *place*. Christian, graphically and prophetically, this is the reality of my taking up my cross and following the LORD Jesus Christ into the miraculous odyssey of my transformation from death unto life.

It is about my taking my *place* in the *"love"* of GOD that is in the LORD Jesus Christ, and that is extended to all of humanity. I either take my place as a branch in the Vine (the LORD Jesus Christ) or there is no life in me. No, not for myself; and certainly, no life to bear fruit.

We have become expert at circumventing this gospel process of *losing the life to find it.* Too often, the smoke and mirrors and misdirection we hide behind is our structured religious ceremony and superficial service work. We hope to be so busy about Christian things and religious oddities, that no one notices that there is fundamentally no effectual witness of the resurrection life of the LORD Jesus in us, or, reaching out of us.

Therefore, I write, and the mandate of the Spirit of GOD laid heavy and urgent upon my soul. This is what I mean, when I say that we (mainstream Christianity) are just another genre of perfunctory ritualistic part-time religious affectation and lifeless form of faith.

✳

But I know you, that ye have not the love of GOD in you.
JOHN 5:42

✳

Anyone can write a check to the missionary or feed the poor. But to be an effectual witness of the resurrection life of the LORD Jesus Christ, and to take my place in the dynamic evangelical love of GOD, I am going to have to first die unto sin and self and the world, and the pride of my own posturing religious persona. I am going to have to encounter and overcome the peculiar giants in my private promised land. To take my place in the love of GOD for my neighbor's soul, I am going to have to first take up my cross.

Without a faith which works by love, I am a superficial lifeless religious form; an aberrant growth bearing thorns and thistles and reproducing after my kind. Without love, I am as presumptuous sounding brass and a tinkling cymbal (see 1 Cor. 13:1), hot air, lifeless religious noise. Notably, the tragedy is not that my pretentious religious feelings must be confronted and disenfranchised (uh, hurt), but the necessity of the intervention.

For the world to see the love of GOD in Jesus Christ, they must see us (Christians) taking our place in the Vine. As we have said, to *"abide"* in the love of Jesus Christ, we are going to have to keep his commandments, as he kept the Father's commandments, and abides in his love (re. John 15:10). Again:

*

*This is my commandment, That ye love
one another, as I have loved you.*
John 15:12

*

My redundancy parallels our hardness of heart, as well as our profound hearing impairment and retardation. (Perchance the blatant offense will at least initiate a dialogue.)

The LORD Jesus Christ purposefully and indefatigably pressed into the place that the Father had appointed him. And it is the sovereign will of GOD that we follow him. The LORD Jesus Christ, knowing all that awaited him, and that his *place* in the love of GOD was an old-rugged cross, nevertheless unremittingly pressed into his appointed place.

*

*But that the world may know that I love the
Father, and as the Father gave me commandment,
even so I do. Arise, let us go hence.*
John 14:31

*

The LORD Jesus Christ's stated objective for keeping the Father's commandment of love is *"that the world may know."* Moreover, this is the objective and commandment of the LORD Jesus Christ imparted and entrusted to his every follower and disciple.

Christian, each of us are intended to be (what I call) the perpetuity and continuity of the love of GOD that is in the LORD

Jesus Christ. (As we can see it, and hear it), this last verse of the fourteenth chapter of John transitions us into the teaching (doctrine) of the *true* Vine in the fifteenth chapter. The Holy Spirit of this Living Word of GOD would not have me miss its exhortation and significance. *"Arise, let us go hence"* (see John 14:31).

(If I may), "Arise, let us be about the Father's business." The LORD Jesus Christ was always acutely conscious of his objective, and the Father's commandment of love; and of his appointed place in the purposes of GOD (and as GOD). The sin and death of Calvary loomed large as the obstacle to overcome. Moreover, every disciple of Jesus Christ is to be seamlessly incorporated into the gospel of that cross.

Children, our *place* is not to be just another generic lump in the pew; you know, a somewhat sentient body. We are intended to be contagious, incendiary witnesses of the resurrection life that is in the LORD Jesus Christ.

Children, the correlative (and equivalent) of the Father's commandment of love, is the austerity of the gospel of the cross of Jesus Christ – that his cross is my cross, and it is your cross. The enormity of the revelation can bear the weight of its own repetition. In the continuity and perpetuity of the love of GOD for a world still lost, the gospel of the cross of Jesus Christ and him crucified is mine, and it is yours.

✳

This is my commandment, That ye love one another,
as I have loved you. Greater love hath no man than

*this, that a man lay down his life for his friends. Ye are
my friends, if ye do whatsoever I command you.*
John 15:12-14

✳

The commandment is as seamless as the essence and character of Jesus Christ. He is, concisely, the Father and the Son indivisible by the Holy Spirit of GOD, the One LORD of Christianity (see Mark 12:29).

It should be no surprise that the commandments of GOD are coalesced into the character of GOD – that of Love. Children, the love by which we are commanded to love our neighbor was first exemplified at Calvary.

Concisely, we become One with this love as commanded, or there is no life in us. This is the brutal allegorical reality of the intimacy and suffering association of the disciples of Jesus Christ, and that of figuratively eating the flesh of the Son of man and drinking his blood. We will only realize the height and depth of the revelation by loving the distinctly unlovable and believing for the impossible.

Few of us (mainstream contemporary Christianity) have put our life out there like that. You know, to make ourselves available, so the undeserving and the unclean can take a bite out of our life. So that they can be sustained amid a miraculous transformation, to become a new creature in Christ Jesus, worthy of love, and capable to perpetuate that love.

Sometimes, all a sinner needs, is a friend. *"Ye are my friends, if ye do whatsoever I command you"* (John 15:14).

Well? What did we think the LORD Jesus Christ was referring to? His doctrine (teaching) is suffused with the revelation of his disciples being made One with the love of GOD in Christ. Did we really think he meant only for us to love the saints, and to honor one another in the prodigal celebration of ourselves? We usually call that *"church."*

The LORD Jesus Christ came out of the sanctuary and took up an old-rugged cross. He did it for love. By contrast, we (broadly) love who will buy us lunch. We love whom will tell us we are wonderful.

Analogous of the Christian being *"in"* Christ as the branch is in the Vine, it is the branch which bears up the fruit and conveys sustenance for its growth. (But) have we taken our *place* in the love of Jesus Christ? Do we bear up babes in Christ like that? or are we a self-sustaining self-celebratory elitist religious entity (and oddity) – plenty righteousness, but not much grace?

✳

> *Verily, verily, I say unto you, Except a corn of wheat*
> *fall into the ground and die, it "abideth" alone:*
> *but if it die, it bringeth forth much fruit.*
> JOHN 12:24

✳

The branch has its life in the service of the Vine to produce fruit. Behold (and ponder) the practical application of the gospel principle of the life lost to find it, and of the Christian in Christ.

By contrast, Christianity has broadly become the religious ceremony that corroborates its own existence.

The Father is found only in the depths of Jesus Christ, the Living Word of GOD. The deeper I delve into the depths of Christ, the greater my degree of abandonment of this natural life, worldly wisdom and counsel and *common* sense. Flesh and blood cannot taste, see, hear, feel, or smell after GOD, he must be revealed by his own Spirit.

To keep it simple, GOD and I transact all kingdom business in the one *place* that I am as he is – a living spirit. Upon the surface or periphery of the spark of life that GOD has already given, I fellowship with the Spirit of GOD – that is, in the one place (and the only place) that I am eternal, the only place where I am in his image and after his likeness.

At the place that the breath of GOD (*Ruach Elohim*) makes me a living soul, I seek and feel after GOD. In the stillness of his own *Breath of Life,* I wait upon GOD.

GOD favors me in the inquiry and in the seeking. At the one place that I converge with the purposes of GOD, I find my life in the abandonment of my own will and desires. With the letting go, I am taken into Christ.

There is an appointed place of rest for my soul, only yoked to the LORD Jesus Christ (see Matt. 11:29). Only as I partake of the sacrifice shall I share his glory.

(I have written), What is to be done for a hungry man today who ate his seed-corn yesterday? We all want a miracle without having to become the miracle. We want to keep our life and have the life of Christ, also. Only what I give away am I allowed to keep. When I hoard my life for myself, I have my reward; alone, sequestered with a fool.

Duh. I hoard and clutch and covet and fight to keep the very thing that has me bound.

Did we assume that Jesus Christ's high priestly prayer to the Father in the seventeenth chapter of John, that we (his disciples in every era) be made One with the Father in Christ, was just something profoundly religious to say? You know, a novel conceptual Christian nirvana, and greatly to be desired and pondered and meditated upon; but in reality, a theoretical abstract and ethereal (unattainable) ideal. Uh, a pipe dream. You know, a castle in the air.

Do we really believe that GOD intends to take (and receive) his abode within the spirit man or spirit woman of the ordinary transitory capricious Christian? Reading John 17:21-23, I hear the LORD Jesus Christ's earnest and fervent prayer to the Father that *ALL* his disciples be made One, even as the Father and Christ are One. And the Father always, always hears the prayers of the Son. The Word of GOD speaks best for GOD, and this is how the LORD Jesus Christ phrased it one appointed day praying at the tomb of his friend, Lazarus.

✳

Father, I thank thee that thou hast heard me. And I knew that thou hearest me always, but because of the people which stand by I said it, that they may believe that thou hast sent me.
see JOHN 11:41-42

✳

Unlike many wise men of every generation and contemporary Pharisees and religious front men, the LORD Jesus Christ does not pray (or preach) to hear the sound of his own voice; he prays to receive an answer. When GOD speaks, the invisible and the impossible conform to what he has said. *"And GOD said . . . and it was so"* (re. Gen. 1:9).

GOD intends that his every disciple be progressively made One with the miracle and the gift, and with the sacrifice and with the glory, of the LORD Jesus Christ. This is executed and realized (consummated) by the Holy Spirit of GOD. This is the gospel of the cross of Jesus Christ and him crucified, and me (and you), resolutely and irrepressibly made One with the perpetual sacrifice of the love of GOD.

Am I prepared to be delivered from my misconceptions of GOD? Not only to allow his humiliation, but to be identified and merged with his abasement and indignities? Can I share the metaphorical stripes and spittle (and wounds) of the LORD Jesus Christ in the love interests of GOD for my neighbor's soul?

We not only clutch and cling to our misconceptions of GOD (and what we will allow), but we have a gratuitous (excessive, inordinate) self-serving misunderstanding of what it means to be a Christian in GOD's Reality. We want to be born again and experience the love of GOD (for ourselves), but we abhor and eschew the reality of GOD's commandment that we be made One with that love – the reality of our becoming One with the sacrifice and with the death of the LORD Jesus Christ. He who has ears to hear, let him hear.

✳

If I wash thee not, thou hast no part with me.
re. JOHN 13:8

✴

I will join myself to the passion of GOD's evangelical campaign to express his love to the peoples of every nation and tribe, or I shall have no part with the LORD Jesus Christ.

Am I prepared to be a foot-washer in the service of the love of GOD for the dregs of humanity?

"But if it die, it bringeth forth much fruit" (re. John 12:24). Frankly, I either unmistakably align myself with the evangelical love of GOD in the LORD Jesus Christ, or there is no *Life* in me (and zero potential for fruit). *"For without me ye can do nothing"* (see John 15:5).

Now, there are demonstrable branches (Christians) adjoined to the *true* Vine (the LORD Jesus Christ), and then there are other, uh, obviously aberrant growths springing forth from the opinions and doctrines of wise men and religious entrepreneurs. Specifically, preachers of an all-permissive grace and a mutant prosperity gospel. You know, a sort of hybridization of gospel principles and worldly favor, affluence, and fellowship. Beyond our presumption that church attendance and ritual ceremony corroborates our Christianity, we also, sadly, too often posture as if we are doing GOD a favor by our (oftentimes) perfunctory indifferent presentation.

Well, someone must remind us that the Word of GOD is both the immediate and the eternal reality of GOD. Christian, if we are a branch in the *true* Vine, then it is for the prosperity and glory of the Vine. Even as much as GOD loves each individual Christian, our health and prosperity in sharing the life of the Vine is extraneous to the purposes of the Vine.

✳

Ye have not chosen me, but I have chosen you, and ordained you, that ye should go and bring forth fruit, and that your fruit should remain; that whatsoever ye shall ask of the father in my name, he may give it you.
JOHN 15:16

✳

(I wonder) just how far our religious presumption (and elitist opinions of ourselves) can be traced into the roots or principles of our proprietary Christianity, as if we did GOD a favor by our capitulating to be saved. What I am trying to say, is that it is amazing how quickly that we sinners transition into saints (whom by all appearances and arrogance) have never sinned.

✳

Or despisest thou the riches of his goodness and forbearance and longsuffering, not knowing that the goodness of GOD leadeth thee to repentance?
ROM. 2:4

✳

It was the grace and mercy and longsuffering love of GOD that precipitated and elicited my change of heart and mind from a reckless pursuit of self-realization to a resolute praise and service of the One True GOD. It was the LORD Jesus Christ that changed my mind, healed and transformed by heart, radically converted my innermost character, and who continues to regenerate and reanimate my spirit man by the Holy Ghost.

It is the LORD Jesus Christ who shows me who the Father is, and not my own percipient religious discernment or acumen. It is swept under the LORD's amazing grace that I encounter the terrible truths of GOD sheathed and layered within the intricacies of Christ. It is completely abandoned to the purposes of GOD that I best realize the essence and character of GOD. When I am made One with the gospel of Jesus Christ and him crucified.

❋

But if it die, it bringeth forth much fruit.
re. JOHN 12:24

❋

Startling (and humbling) the acute revelation, that I was not chosen for my impeccable religious persona or singular self-righteous affect. Concisely, I am chosen to die to the pride of my life and to the tyranny of my self-interests, and to find my eternal life in the service of Christ's sacrament of love for a world that is still lost and disillusioned. The life I have is the life I give as a branch in the service of the life of the Vine, *"for without me ye can do nothing"* (re. John 15:5).

Otherwise, *"it abideth alone"* (see John 12:24). *"It,"* meaning my life. And *"alone"* fundamentally meaning that I already have my reward in the religious posturing and seeking the honor of players and pretenders just like myself. I am relegated and assigned (and sentenced) to keep all I have not given away; stuck alone in the pew with a shameless self-promoter and shallow religious prostitute, going through the motions of another meaningless superficial religious service – having (in reality) given nothing, yet self-deluded into believing that I have worshipped well.

A church is not intended to be a closed elitist group of like minded individuals meeting periodically in a self-celebratory, self-sustaining ceremony – a Church is intended to be the *Eucharist* of Christ, broken bread and poured out wine in the service of GOD's love for my neighborhood. *"Except it die . . . it abideth alone"* re. John 12:24).

Rather, we have gotten fat on one another's praise, corpulent on self-affirmation, obese on an exclusive brotherly love – usually right in the midst of our communities' poverty. We have no witness of the love of GOD in Christ, and no edible fruit, because we eat our seed-corn (and save our lives) for ourselves.

Well? For whom is our fruit? For whom do we produce? Or are we, rather, ostentatious and proliferate with leaves and foliage and fraudulent forms of faith, but not one enervated fig or grape to be found. Well? GOD does not need (the noise of) our sounding brass and tinkling cymbals, and the poor of our neighborhood cannot eat it.

Well? I am not chosen to be a player in a self-sustaining, self-congratulatory religious ceremony; I am chosen to take my appointed place in the sacrifice of GOD's love in Jesus Christ for the soul of the world, my neighbor first. Concisely, Christian, you and I are chosen to take our place as a king and a priest (and an intercessor) in the gospel of Jesus Christ and him crucified.

Is my life (out there) like that? Am I available for the weak in faith, until their faith makes them strong? May the underserving regularly feed on my witness of the resurrection life that is in the LORD Jesus Christ? Am I periodically pummeled and pulled and torn by unwashed hands?

I am not talking about casting pearls; I am talking about breaking bread, and about being a friend of Jesus.

Can the world glimpse the grace and the love of GOD in Christ as my life is being systematically spent? Can my neighbor be sustained on the spiritual sacrifice of it? What does my life being spent smell like to GOD?

Well . . . what, and who, are the grapes for? They are for the wine that is the sacrament of the New covenant (the New Testament); they are the sacrifice of GOD's love for the soul of the world.

As a branch, I produce in the service of GOD's love for the worst of humanity; for the least of these, the LORD's brethren. As I experience the life of the Vine, the Vine experiences the life of the branch; even as One living entity. Children, this era in which we now live and produce in the Vine is the dispensation of the fullness of times, and the gathering together in One all things in Christ (see Eph. 1:10).

The reality is, that them chosen for life, were likewise chosen for death. To know Jesus Christ, and the power of his resurrection, I am also chosen for a distinct suffering fellowship and an acute conformity to his death (see Phil. 3:10-11).

It cannot be otherwise. The glory of harvest is found in my life being spent in the service of the Vine – in the production of the continuing Eucharist (sacrifice) of the New Covenant.

Concisely, I best experience the life (and the love) of GOD in its partnership and its perpetuation. Within the intricacies of Jesus Christ, within both the simplicity and profundity of the Word of GOD, I find the Father, and by grace realize that he has been with me all along. *And he that seeth me seeth him that sent me.* (John 12:45).

From the depths of Christ (as it were), the Father draws me in; even as deep calleth unto deep (re. Ps. 42:7). There is free-falling Grace for the intrepid seeker of Truth. Indeed, how great the Grace, not to settle for what some man has said. To realize that my hunger and thirst for righteousness is GOD's purview, and his own solemn (joyous) responsibility. I soar. *"So is every one that is born of the Spirit"* (re. John 3:8).

The Word of GOD (I find) is an exhilarating prophetic continuum of revelatory Grace and Truth. His name is Jesus. (On a personal note), I am blessed to be an inquisitor. I will not speak of cost, but of favor.

By the Holy Ghost, I anticipate an *addendum* to this manuscript. Indeed. And as it pleases GOD to sustain my portion. *"I suppose that even the world itself could not contain the books that should be written."* (re. John 21:25)

The revelatory Truth of the Father and the Son (Jesus Christ) as One LORD is its own perpetual reward – the empowerment, the endowment, the unction of GOD by the Holy Ghost. By faith, I press up against the revelation of the kingdom of

GOD within me, to take what is given. It is the invested and the abandoned (and the pure in heart) which see GOD.

(I attest) to there being no distinction between the Father and the Son (the LORD Jesus Christ) by work or by Word, by event or circumstance or presence. By Grace, I see the Truth of Jesus Christ, the Almighty GOD. The veil has been rent from my heart, and my eyes are opened to see the Christ of GOD.

On the constancy and perpetuity of the prophetic Word of GOD, the revelation is infinite in mystery and wisdom and substance. This manuscript is but a glimpse by grace of GOD, and the eternal utterance of *I AM*, the Word of GOD. *"And he that seeth me seeth him that sent me"* (John 12:45).

It ought to be no marvel that the Father is hidden in Christ Jesus, the Son, from the casual and the proprietary. It is the diligent and the purposeful (and them with no hidden agenda) which find revelatory favor.

The Father is eternally with the Son and hidden in the Son; even as the Son is eternally with the Father and hidden in the Father. What I am trying to say is precisely what GOD has progressively and repeatedly shown me as I penned this manuscript.

✳

> *In the beginning was the Word, and the Word*
> *was with GOD, and the Word was GOD.*
> JOHN 1:1

✳

Whom do I reckon by religious presumption and elitist doctrinal opinion was that Spirit of GOD who moved upon the face of the waters when the earth was yet without form, and void, and darkness was upon the face of the deep (re. Gen. 1:1-3)? Just who do I reckon said, *"Let there be Light?"* Where do I reckon Jesus was before the annual Christmas pageant or play at our Church?

Children, the Spirit of GOD that moved upon the face of the waters was the Almighty GOD: the Father and the Son by the Holy Ghost; the One LORD who is the GOD of Israel in the Old Testament (see Deut. 6:4), and the One LORD who is the GOD of Christianity in the New Testament (see Mark 12:29).

It is the LORD Jesus Christ who explicitly expresses the same Truth as follows: *"And he that seeth me seeth him that sent me"* (John 12:45). In other words, Christian, (if I may), *"How long am I going to be with you before you realize who I AM?"* (as inspired by John 14:9).

Where am I, then, on the revelatory continuum of the LORD Jesus Christ – in the realization of the Father (if you follow)? That is, can I see the Father from where I am in the Word of GOD (Jesus Christ)? How far along am I in the revelation of One LORD? Indeed. How close am I to being made One with the revelation?

How amenable, and how sanctified, and how effectual a host am I, of a Spirit who is above all things a *"Holy"* Spirit?

Am I an incendiary (and contagious) witness of the resurrection life and power that is in the LORD Jesus Christ? And do I know him well enough to introduce him into the life of my neighbor?

Do we really know who Jesus is? Who GOD is? How many tines must he tell us, *"I AM?"*

From here

In Christ,

I cry, Abba, Father.

How awesome the transition,

How exhilarating the odyssey. Selah.

❋

December 17, 2020

rdb